Gry

This *Companion* addresses the work of women playwrights in Britain throughout the twentieth century. The chapters explore the historical, political, and theatrical contexts in which women have written for the theatre and examine the work of individual playwrights

The volume brings together a transatlantic team of feminist theatre scholars and practitioners. A chronological section on playwriting from the 1920s to the 1970s is followed by chapters which raise issues of nationality and identity. Later sections question accepted notions of the canon and include chapters on non-mainstream writing, including black and lesbian performance. Each section is introduced by the editors, who provide a narrative overview of a century of women's drama and a thorough chronology of playwriting, set in political context.

The collection includes essays on the individual writers Caryl Churchill, Sarah Daniels, Pam Gems, and Timberlake Wertenbaker as well as extensive documentation of contemporary playwriting in Wales, Scotland, and Northern Ireland, including figures such as Liz Lochhead and Anne Devlin

ELAINE ASTON is Professor of Theatre Studies at Lancaster University. She is author of *Sarah Bernhardt: A French Actress on the English Stage* (1989), *An Introduction to Feminism and Theatre* (1995), *Caryl Churchill* (1997), and *Feminist Theatre Practice* (1999).

JANELLE REINELT is Professor of Theatre and Dance at the University of California, Davis. She has edited *Theatre Journal* and her books include *After Brecht: British Epic Theatre* (1994), *Critical Theory and Performance* (1992), co-edited with Joseph Roach, and the collection *Crucibles of Crisis: Performance and Social Change* (1996).

CAMBRIDGE COMPANIONS TO LITERATURE

CAMBRIDGE COMPANIONS TO LITERATURE

*The Cambridge Companion to Modern
German Culture*
edited by Eva Kolinsky and Wilfried van der
Will

*The Cambridge Companion to Modern
Spanish Culture*
edited by David T. Gies

*The Cambridge Companion to Modern
Russian Culture*
edited by Nicholas Rzhevsky

THE CAMBRIDGE
COMPANION TO

MODERN BRITISH
WOMEN PLAYWRIGHTS

EDITED BY
ELAINE ASTON AND JANELLE REINELT

CAMBRIDGE
UNIVERSITY PRESS

PUBLISHED BY THE PRESS SYNDICATE OF THE UNIVERSITY OF CAMBRIDGE
The Pitt Building, Trumpington Street, Cambridge, United Kingdom

CAMBRIDGE UNIVERSITY PRESS
The Edinburgh Building, Cambridge CB2 2RU, UK   www.cup.cam.ac.uk
40 West 20th Street, New York, NY 10011-4211, USA   www.cup.org
10 Stamford Road, Oakleigh, Melbourne 3166, Australia
Ruiz de Alarcón 13, 28014 Madrid, Spain

First published 2000

Printed in the United Kingdom at the University Press, Cambridge

Typeset in Monotype Sabon 10/13   *System* QuarkXpress®   [SE]

A catalogue record for this book is available from the British Library

Library of Congress Cataloguing in Publication data

The Cambridge companion to modern British women playwrights / [edited
by] Elaine Aston and Janelle Reinelt.
    p.   cm. – (Cambridge companions to literature)
ISBN 0 521 59422 7 (hardback) – ISBN 0 521 59533 9 (paperback)
    1. English drama – Women authors – Hisory and criticism.
    2. Feminism and literature – Great Britain – History – 20th century.
    3. Women and literature – Great Britain – History – 20th century.
    4. English drama – 20th century – History and criticism.   I. Aston,
        Elaine.   II. Reinelt, Janelle G.   III. Series
                    PR739.F45C36   2000
            822′.91099282 – dc21   99-36626 CIP

ISBN 0 521 59422 7 hardback
ISBN 0 521 59533 9 paperback

#41641348

CONTENTS

Contents

ILLUSTRATIONS

NOTES ON CONTRIBUTORS

ELAINE ASTON is Professor of Theatre Studies at Lancaster University, England. She is author of *Sarah Bernhardt: A French Actress on the English Stage* (Berg, 1989), *An Introduction to Feminism and Theatre* (Routledge, 1995), *Caryl Churchill* (Northcote, 1997), and *Feminist Theatre Practice* (Routledge, 1999).

SUSAN BASSNETT is Pro-Vice-Chancellor at the University of Warwick, England, and Professor in the Centre for British and Comparative Cultural Studies, which she founded in the 1980s. She is the author of over twenty books, and her *Translation Studies,* which first appeared in 1980, has become the most important textbook in the expanding field of translation studies. Her authored work also includes the internationally renowned *Comparative Literature: A Critical Introduction* (Blackwell, 1993), *Studying British Cultures: An Introduction* (Routledge, 1997), and *Constructing Cultures* (Multilingual Matters, 1998) written with André Lefevere. Besides her academic research, Susan Bassnett writes poetry and is a regular contributor to the 'View from Here' column in the *Independent*. She is currently completing a travel book.

SUSAN BENNETT is Professor of English and Associate Dean in the Faculty of Humanities, University of Calgary, Canada. She is author of *Performing Nostalgia* (Routledge, 1997) and *Theatre Audiences* (second edition, Routledge, 1997). She is also coeditor of *Theatre Journal*. Her current research concerns questions of gender, genre, and women's dramatic writing.

SUSAN CARLSON is Professor of English at Iowa State University where she teaches courses in drama, British and women's literature, and literary criticism. She has published two books, most recently *Women and Comedy: Revising the British Theatrical Tradition* (University of Michigan Press, 1991), and has published essays on Aphra Behn, the Omaha Magic Theatre, *The Taming of the Shrew*, and nineteenth-century women playwrights. She is currently working on a book entitled *Shakespeare and the Suffragettes,* a study of British suffrage theatre and its connections to Edwardian productions of Shakespeare.

SUE-ELLEN CASE is Department Chair of Theatre and Dance at the University of California, Davis. She is the author of *Feminism and Theatre* (Macmillan, 1988) and *The Domain- Matrix: Performing Lesbian at the End of Print Culture* (Indiana University Press, 1996), as well as being the editor of numerous anthologies of plays and critical essays, including *Performing Feminisms: Feminist Critical Theory and Theatre* (Johns Hopkins University Press, 1990) and *Split Britches: Lesbian Practice / Feminist Performance* (Routledge, 1996). She has published over thirty-five articles on feminism, theatre, and lesbian critical theory and is the editor of a book series for Indiana University Press entitled 'Unnatural Acts'.

MAGGIE B. GALE is Senior Lecturer in Drama and Theatre Arts at the University of Birmingham, England. Her research on mid-twentieth-century, commercial women playwrights is published in *West End Women: Women and the London Stage 1918–1962* (Routledge, 1996). She is currently co-editing a volume entitled *Interwar British Theatres 1918–1939* for Cambridge University Press, and is co-editor of the new 'Women, Theatre and Performance' series (Manchester University Press).

GABRIELE GRIFFIN is Professor of English at Kingston University in south London. She has published widely on women's cultural production. Her publications include *Gender Issues in Elder Abuse* (co-authored with Lynda Aitken, Sage, 1996) and *Straight Studies Modified: Lesbian Interventions in the Academy* (co-edited with S. Andermahr, Cassell, 1998). Together with Elaine Aston she has edited several volumes of plays by women, the most recent of which are *Pulp and Other Plays by Tasha Fairbanks* (Harwood, 1996) and a special issue of *Contemporary Theatre Review* on *Subversions: Playing with History in Women's Theatre* (vol. 6, pt 3, 1997).

CLAIRE MACDONALD is a writer and critic. As a performer and theatre-maker, she was co-founder of two influential visual theatre companies, Impact and Insomniac. Her theatre work includes *Dark Water Closing* (Theatre for the New City, New York, 1986), *An Imitation of Life* (Bush Theatre, London, 1986), *The Menaced Assassin* (Donmar Warehouse, 1989), *Storm from Paradise* (Bush Theatre, 1988), *The Fall of Lucas Fortune* (The Palace Theatre, 1991), and *Beulah Land* (ICA, London, 1994). She is co-editor of *Performance Research* and writes on performance and visual art. She has been Junior Judith Wilson Fellow at Cambridge University, Head of Theatre at Dartington College of Arts, Senior Lecturer and Research Fellow at De Montfort University, and a visiting professor at Mountholyoke College, Massachusetts. She lives in Washington DC, USA, and Cambridge, England.

MEENAKSHI PONNUSWAMI is Associate Professor of English at Bucknell University where she teaches dramatic literature and theatre history. She has written on Howard Brenton, Caryl Churchill, and other contemporary British playwrights. She recently completed a study of the uses of history in British socialist drama since the Second World War – *Performing Museums: Alternative History in Contemporary British Theatre, 1956–1989* – and is now editing a collection of new essays on post-war theatre and performance art, *Contemporary British Theatre: The New Left and After* (forthcoming from Garland Press). Her current research project concerns theatre and nationalism in Britain and its colonies between the World Wars.

JANELLE REINELT is Professor of Theatre and Dance at the University of California, Davis. She has served as editor of *Theatre Journal*, and her books include *After Brecht: British Epic Theatre* (1994), *Critical Theory and Performance* (1992), co-edited with

Joseph Roach, and the collection *Crucibles of Crisis: Performance and Social Change* (1996), all with the University of Michigan Press.

ADRIENNE SCULLION is lecturer in the Department of Theatre, Film and Television Studies at the University of Glasgow, Scotland. Her publications on Scottish cultural issues – and in particular on Scottish theatre and drama – include articles in the journals *Theatre Research International* and *Comparative Drama*, and essays in the collections *Gendering the Nation: Studies in Modern Scottish Literature* (Edinburgh University Press, 1995), *A History of Scottish Women's Writing* (Edinburgh University Press, 1997), *A History of Scottish Theatre* (Polygon, 1991) and *Contemporary Dramatists*. She also works on early women playwrights and is the editor of *Female Playwrights of the Nineteenth Century* (Everyman, 1996).

ANNA-MARIE TAYLOR has been a lecturer in Continuing Education at the University of Wales, Swansea, since 1995, where she is responsible for the Performing Arts and Writing programmes. Prior to this, she lectured for over a decade in Drama at the University of Wales, Aberystwyth. She has published widely on European drama, is editor of *Staging Wales* (University of Wales Press, 1997), and is currently working on a study of how biographies of self and place have been represented in drama.

MARY TROTTER is an Assistant Professor at Indiana University – Perdue University at Indianapolis. She earned a Ph.D. in the Interdisciplinary Program in Theatre and Drama at Northwestern University. She has published articles on theatre and performance practices during the Irish literary renaissance, as well as on contemporary Irish drama, in *Theatre Survey*, the *New Hibernia Review*, and *Crucibles of Crisis: Performing Social Change*, ed. Janelle Reinelt (University of Michigan Press, 1996). Her book, *Ireland's National Theatres: Dublin Political Performance and the Origins of the Irish Dramatic Movement* is forthcoming from Syracuse University Press.

MICHELENE WANDOR has a richly varied career as playwright, poet, critic, radio dramatist and presenter, and musicologist. Her dramatisation of *The Wandering Jew* was staged at the National Theatre in 1987, when her television adaptation of *The Belle of Amherst* was also winner of an International Emmy Award. Her poems appear in numerous anthologies and she has her own published collection, *Gardens of Eden* (Random, 1990). Major publications on feminist theatre include *Carry On, Understudies* (Routledge, 1986) and *Look Back in Gender* (Methuen, 1987). She was also editor of the first four volumes of *Plays By Women* (1982–5).

CHRONOLOGY

Date	Plays and theatre events	Politics
1900		Inauguration of the Labour Party.
1901		Death of Queen Victoria; accession of Edward VII.
1903		Founding of Women's Social and Political Union.
1907	*Votes for Women!*, Elizabeth Robins.	Women allowed to serve on Local Government Councils.
1908	Foundation of Actresses' Franchise League (AFL). *Diana of Dobson's*, Cicely Hamilton.	Foundation of Women's Freedom League.
1909	*How the Vote was Won* and *A Pageant of Famous Women*, Cicely Hamilton. *Chains*, Elizabeth Baker.	People's Budget introduced by Lloyd George. Women's suffrage movement turning militant.
1910	*The Homecoming*, Cicely Hamilton.	Death of Edward VII; accession of George V.
1911	Edy Craig establishes The Pioneer Players, which runs until early 1920s.	Industrial unrest amongst dockers, railwaymen and weavers.
1913	Women's Theatre season at the Coronet Theatre. *A Woman's Influence*, Gertrude Jennings.	First woman magistrate in Britain.
1914		Outbreak of First World War.
1917	*Billeted*, F. Tennyson-Jesse and H. M. Harwood.	

1918	*After the War*, Gertrude Jennings. *Miss Robinson*, Elizabeth Baker.	Cessation of War. Franchise Act gives women over thirty the vote.
1919		First woman MP, Lady Astor, takes her seat in the Commons. The Sex Disqualification (Removal) Act.
1920	*The Young Person in Pink*, Gertrude Jennings.	
1921	*Bill of Divorcement*, Clemence Dane. *Love Among the Paintpots*, Gertrude Jennings. *Will Shakespeare*, Clemence Dane. *The Child in Flanders*, Cicely Hamilton.	Foundation of The Six Point Group. First birth control clinic opened in London. Conditions of work for children under fourteen regulated by the Education Act.
1922	*Quarantine*, Fryn Tennyson-Jesse.	Carlton Club Meeting: Conservative revolt against coalition government.
1924	*The Pelican*, Fryn Tennyson-Jesse and Harold Harwood.	First British Labour government under Ramsay Macdonald, only to fall after 'Zinoviev Letter' Affair.
1925	*Bert's Girl*, Elizabeth Baker.	Pensions Act: provided Widows', Orphans' and Old Age Pensions.
1926	*The Constant Nymph*, Margaret Kennedy. *The Widow's Cruise*, Joan Temple. *Granite*, Clemence Dane.	General Strike, 1–12 May. Marriage of parents legitimised children born out of wedlock.
1928		Women given same voting rights as men.
1929	*The Matriarch*, G. B. Stern. *Her Shop*, Aimée and Philip Stuart.	Second Labour government under Ramsay Macdonald. First English woman Cabinet Minister.
1930	*Nine Till Six*, Aimée and Philip Stuart. *Charles and Mary*, Joan Temple. *Our Ostriches*, Marie Stopes.	Housing Act to deal with slum clearance.
1931	*The Man Who Pays the Piper*, G. B. Stern. *Autumn Crocus*, Dodie Smith.	Financial crisis in Britain; Labour government resigns. Sir Oswald Mosley leaves Labour Party; founds New Party.

Year	Work	Event
1932	*Service*, Dodie Smith.	Great hunger march of unemployed to London. British Union of Fascists founded by Mosley.
1933	*Escape Me Never*, Margaret Kennedy. *Wild Decembers*, Clemence Dane.	Hitler appointed Chancellor of Germany.
1934	*Family Affairs*, Gertrude Jennings. *Dark Horizon*, Lesley Storm. *Sixteen*, Aimée and Philip Stuart. *Moonlight is Silver*, Clemence Dane. *Touchwood*, Dodie Smith.	
1935	*Our Own Lives*, Gertrude Jennings. *Call it a Day*, Dodie Smith.	Ramsay Macdonald resigns as PM.
1936		Death of George V; accession of Edward VIII; abdication of Edward VIII; accession of George VI.
1937	*Autumn*, Margaret Kennedy and G. Ratoff.	Marriage of abdicated Edward VIII to Mrs Simpson, American divorcée. Divorce legalised for grounds other than adultery.
1938	*Dear Octopus*, Dodie Smith. *Quiet Wedding*, Esther McCracken.	Estimated that a third of British families lived below poverty line.
1939	*Tony Draws a Horse*, Lesley Storm.	Outbreak of Second World War.
1941	*Quiet Weekend*, Esther McCracken.	
1943	*Living Room*, Esther McCracken. *Lottie Dundass*, Enid Bagnold.	Beveridge Report lays foundation for post-war welfare state.
1944	*No Medals*, Esther McCracken.	Butler Education Act: secondary education for all children.
1945	*Great Day*, Lesley Storm.	Cessation of Second World War. Fall of war-time coalition government; Labour government elected under Clement Atlee. Family Allowance system introduced.
1946	*National Velvet*, Enid Bagnold. *No Room at the Inn*, Joan Temple.	

1948	*Cockpit*, Bridget Boland.	Mosley revives Fascist Party.
		National Health Service is introduced.
1949	*The Black Chiffon*, Lesley Storm.	
1950	*Lace on Her Petticoat*, Aimée Stuart.	General Election; Labour returned without overall majority.
		Anglo-Egyptian dispute over Sudan and Suez Canal begins.
1951	*The Day's Mischief*, Lesley Storm.	General Election: Conservative government returned under Churchill.
	Poor Judas, Enid Bagnold.	
1952	*The Mousetrap*, Agatha Christie (still running).	Death of King George VI; accession of Elizabeth II.
		Contraceptive pill is made for first time.
1953	Joan Littlewood moves Theatre Workshop into Theatre Royal, London, E15.	Coronation of Queen Elizabeth II.
1954	*The Prisoner*, Bridget Boland.	Civil Service introduced equal pay for women.
1955		General Election returns Conservative government under Eden.
1956	*The Chalk Garden*, Enid Bagnold.	Suez Crisis.
	The Long Echo, Lesley Storm.	
1957	*Roar Like a Dove*, Lesley Storm.	Eden resigns; Harold Macmillan PM.
		Wolfenden Report on Homosexuality and Prostitution.
		Suez Canal reopened.
1958	*A Taste of Honey*, Shelagh Delaney.	Race riots in Nottingham and Notting Hill.
	The Sport of My Mad Mother, Ann Jellicoe.	Matrimonial Causes (Property and Maintenance) Act.
1959	*Eighty in the Shade*, Clemence Dane.	General Election: Conservatives return to power under Macmillan.
1960	*The Last Joke*, Enid Bagnold.	
	The Lion in Love, Shelagh Delaney.	
1961	*The Knack*, Ann Jellicoe.	West Indian and Asian immigration into Britain.
	Time and Yellow Roses, Lesley Storm.	
1962	*The Ants* (radio), Caryl Churchill.	

1964	*The Chinese Prime Minister,* Enid Bagnold.	General election: Labour government under Wilson.
1965	*Shelley; or, The Idealist,* Ann Jellicoe.	Death of Churchill. Edward Heath becomes leader of Conservative Party.
1966	*Lovesick* (radio), Caryl Churchill.	General Election: Labour returned under Wilson.
1967		Abortion Act: allows termination of pregnancy with recommendation of two doctors. Sexual Offences Act: homosexual acts between consenting adults are no longer an offence.
1968	Abolition of theatre censorship. *Identical Twins* (radio), Caryl Churchill.	Welsh Language Society campaign and bombing by Home Rule group. Women machinists strike for equal pay at Ford's. Escalation of Civil Rights activism in Northern Ireland.
1969	*The Giveaway,* Ann Jellicoe.	Voting age lowered from 21 to 18. Divorce Reform Act: breakdown of marriage is sole ground for divorce. Bombs in Wales by Welsh National extremists. Increased activity of IRA.
1970		Equal Pay Act. Conservative government elected under Heath. Ruskin Women's History Conference. Shooting and bombing in Northern Ireland.
1971	*Look No Hands,* Lesley Storm. *Abortive and Not Not Not Not Not Enough Oxygen* (radio), Caryl Churchill.	
1972	*Sweetie Pie,* Bolton Octagon, Theatre in Education (TIE). *Owners,* Caryl Churchill.	Thirteen people killed in Londonderry 'Bloody Sunday'.
1973	Almost Free Theatre Women's Festival.	
1974	*Strike While the Iron is Hot,* Red Ladder's first women's play. Founding of Women's Theatre Group – *My Mother Says I Never Should.*	Labour government elected. Free family planning on NHS. IRA bombings on mainland.

1975	Founding of Monstrous Regiment.	
1976	*Dusa, Fish, Stas and Vi*, Pam Gems. *Light Shining & Vinegar Tom*, Caryl Churchill. Founding of Gay Sweatshop.	Women's peace movement. Asian women workers strike in Grunwick dispute.
1977	*Care and Control*, Michelene Wandor. *Queen Christina*, Pam Gems. Founding of Gay Sweatshop women's company.	
1978	*Piaf*, Pam Gems.	
1979	*Cloud 9*, Caryl Churchill. *The House that Jack Built*, Shelagh Delaney. Founding of Clean Break and Siren.	'Winter of Discontent'. Thatcher elected Prime Minister. Scotland and Wales vote against devolution.
1981	*Steaming*, Nell Dunn. *New Anatomies*, Timberlake Wertenbaker. *Ripen Our Darkness*, Sarah Daniels.	Major race riots in Brixton and other city areas.
1982	*Top Girls*, Caryl Churchill. *Blood and Ice*, Liz Lochhead. Founding of Theatre of Black Women.	Falklands War. Women's Peace Camp at Greenham Common.
1983	Founding of Charabanc. *Masterpieces*, Sarah Daniels. *Fen*, Caryl Churchill.	CND demonstrations.
1984	*Camille*, Pam Gems. *When I Was a Girl, I Used to Scream and Shout*, Sharman Macdonald. *Tea in a China Cup*, Christina Reid.	Miners' strike. Legislation passed to permit divorce after one year. Greenham Common cleared by police. IRA bomb members of Conservative government at Grand Hotel, Brighton.
1985	*8961: Caneuon Galar a Gobaith / Songs of Grief and Hope*, Lis Hugh Jones. *Ourselves Alone*, Anne Devlin. *The Grace of Mary Traverse*, Timberlake Wertenbaker.	Abolition of GLC. Anglo-Irish Agreement. Broadwater Farm estate, London, race riots.

	Clam & Pax, Deborah Levy. *The Glory of the Garden* (Arts Council).	
1986	First international festival of Magdalena Project, Cardiff, Wales. *Joyriders*, Christina Reid. *Chiaroscuro*, Jackie Kay. *Heresies*, Deborah Levy.	IRA bombings in England and Northern Ireland; strikes over Anglo-Irish Agreement and elections. Surge in unemployment figures of 14.4%.
1987	*The Wandering Jew*, Michelene Wandor. *Mary Queen of Scots Got Her Head Chopped Off*, Liz Lochhead. *Serious Money*, Caryl Churchill. *Drawing on a Mother's Experience*, Bobby Baker.	Conservatives re-elected for third term of government. 'Black Monday' as stock exchange falls; allegations of illegal share-dealing at Guinness.
1988	*Twice Over*, Jackie Kay. *Our Country's Good* & *The Love of the Nightingale*, Timberlake Wertenbaker. *Walks on Water*, Rose English.	Clause 28 discriminates against Gay community. AIDS crisis intensifies. David Alton attacks late-term abortion. NHS Review and move towards privatisation. Charter 88 Bill of Rights.
1989	Founding of Tamasha. *A Hero's Welcome*, Winsome Pinnock.	Collapse of Berlin Wall and removal of the Iron Curtain. Founding of Stonewall Group and ACT-UP.
1990	*Mad Forest*, Caryl Churchill.	Major replaces Thatcher as Prime Minister.
1991	*Bondagers*, Sue Glover. *The Kitchen Show*, Bobby Baker.	
1992	*Head-Rot Holiday*, Sarah Daniels. *The B-File*, Deborah Levy. Lois Weaver joins Gay Sweatshop (stays until 1996).	Unemployment at 2.6 million. Chwarae Teg (Fair Play) founded in Wales. Rise of Women's erotica: 'Feminists Against Censorship'.
1993	Closure of several women's theatre companies, including Monstrous Regiment. *Queer Bodies* series, Lois Weaver.	Conservative government attack on single mothers and welfare benefits.
1994	*The Skriker*, Caryl Churchill. *The Madness of Esme and Shaz*, Sarah Daniels.	Ceasefire in Northern Ireland.

Shiny Nylon, Deborah Levy.
It's Not Unusual, series, Lois
Weaver.
Essex Girls, Rebecca Prichard.

1995	*The Maiden Stone*, Rona Munro.	Green Party vs Labour on subject of ignoring environmental issues.
	The Break of Day, Timberlake Wertenbaker.	Closure of Tyneside shipyards.
	The Strip, Phyllis Nagy.	
	Blasted, Sarah Kane.	
1996	*Stanley, Marlene*, Pam Gems.	Charles, Prince of Wales, and Diana, Princess of Wales, divorce.
	Clowns, Christina Reid.	Attempt to outlaw Down's syndrome abortions after 24 weeks.
1997	*Hotel* & *Blue Heart*, Caryl Churchill.	Election of New Labour government under Blair.
		Scotland and Wales vote in devolved assemblies.
		Diana, Princess of Wales, killed in car crash.
1998	*Queen of Hearts*, Christine Watkins.	Good Friday peace agreement, Northern Ireland.
	Cleansed, Sarah Kane.	Bomb outrages in Omagh, Northern Ireland.
	Yard Gal, Rebecca Prichard.	
	Never Land, Phyllis Nagy.	

I

ELAINE ASTON AND JANELLE REINELT

A century in view: from suffrage to the 1990s

Early in 1998 both stages at the Royal Court, arguably England's most high-profile venue that supports new playwriting, were occupied by women playwrights: the late Sarah Kane's *Cleansed* played in the main house, Theatre Downstairs, while Rebecca Prichard's *Yard Gal* was premiered in the Theatre Upstairs studio. An outsider might be forgiven for thinking that the tables had finally turned: that women playwrights had at last achieved a significant presence at the close of the century. However, like several other 'stages' in our twentieth-century history of women's playwriting, the contemporary situation for women dramatists is far less propitious than one might at first suppose. Looking briefly at the 1998 productions of Kane and Prichard offers us a way into our *fin-de-siècle* moment of women's playwriting, and a way back to the different historical contexts of twentieth-century playwriting presented in this *Companion*.

*Kane and Prichard were contemporaries: both born in 1971; both from Essex; both university-educated (although Kane confessed that her experience of the Master's degree in playwriting at Birmingham University 'nearly destroyed her as a writer'),[1] and both were fortunate enough to launch writing careers through the Royal Court. There, however, the similarities end. Kane's playwriting career began in controversy over her first full-length play, *Blasted*, staged at the Court's studio venue in 1995, which outraged both the serious and the tabloid press for its scenes of horror – most particularly the cannibalism of a dead baby. Theatre critics were as enraged as they had been over Edward Bond's stoning-the-baby scene in *Saved* (Royal Court, 1965). Like *Saved*, *Cleansed* is also designed to re-awaken audience perception of our violent world through a theatrical style which 'shows', rather than 'tells' of, the persecution of a socially 'unacceptable' group of people whose bodies are variously injected with heroin, beaten, raped and hacked to pieces.

Unlike Kane, Prichard is more specific about the social class and gender of the communities in her plays. An apt description of Prichard's dramatic universe is one

---

* Regrettably, Kane committed suicide in February 1999, as our *Companion* was being prepared for production.

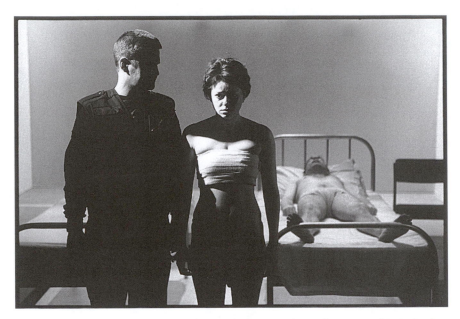

1 Stuart McQuarrie as Tinker, Suzan Sylvester as Grace, and Daniel Evans as Robin, in Sarah Kane's *Cleansed*

in which Caryl Churchill's prediction at the close of *Top Girls* – of a 'frightening' future for generations of young, underprivileged women – is seen to be coming true: *Essex Girls* (Royal Court, 1994) treats the issue of single, teenage mothers; *Fair Game*, an adaptation of Edna Mazya's *Games in the Backyard* (Royal Court, 1998), dramatises a teenage gang-rape; and *Yard Gal* tells of an all-female street gang from Hackney in London's East End. *Yard Gal* is narrated by two gang members, Boo who is black and Marie who is white, in the rhythms and slang of their East End, Caribbean street culture. Their lives are characterised by drugs, alcohol, prostitution, violence, and abuse. The girls look out for each other, band together to survive, but they live permanently on the edge of social acceptance and of survival.

Both Prichard's and Kane's theatrical landscapes are 'frightening', but in very different ways which it would be wrong to try and make 'fit' into some category of 'women's playwriting'. To a playwright like Kane, to be called a 'woman writer' was meaningless. She did not wish to be seen as a representative of a 'biological or social group'; gender, race or class issues were not her primary concern, rather she saw them as 'symptomatic of societies based on violence or the threat of violence' (*Rage & Reason*, pp. 133–5). Reviewing *Yard Gal* Benedict Nightingale observed that if such a play 'had been written 20, 15, even 10 years ago, it would have been very different', specifically, 'few dramatists of that era would have been able to resist making it abundantly evident that its two teenage characters were victims of society and society itself was in urgent need of institutional reform'.[2] While Nightingale reveals his own prejudices against feminism, stating that this would necessarily have been an 'inferior' kind of writing, his observation does, however, point towards the way that times have changed. In the late 1990s, women are not writing the issue-based theatre out of the feminist moment twenty years ago, nor are they working in the climate of anger from ten years ago, when playwrights, just before the 1989 collapse of socialism in Central Europe, were protesting against the reactionary policies of the right-wing British government (as evidenced for example in Caryl Churchill's *Serious Money* (1987), or Kay Adshead's *Thatcher's Women* (1987)). Similarly, our purpose in this Companion is neither to provide an exhaustive list of writers, nor to claim a 'fixed' identity for British women playwrights, but to examine the changing social, theatrical, and cultural contexts in which plays by women have been able to flourish – or not – this century.

The extent to which women dramatists find a 'place' in theatrical activity, or initiate their own 'alternative', counter-cultural, oppositional theatre 'spaces', is determined by the material, political, cultural, geographical, and theatrical circumstances of the historical moment. Writing on the 1970s birth of Sistren, the Jamaican Women's organisation, Honor Ford-Smith describes the conditions which made Sistren possible as a moment of 'democratic opening': 'a moment in history in which there was a possibility for those who are oppressed to intervene in history and transform their society'.[3] As we look back over different periods of British women's playwriting in this century, both in our introduction and in the volume overall, we shall see historical moments of 'democratic opening', moments when social transformation was deemed a possibility, but also decades where women's social and cultural status is so marginal as to make the possibility of change, of a more equal society, 'unthinkable'. This does not mean that women stop writing for theatre, but what they write about, in what form, and where, is subject to constraint as well as possibility. In the remainder of this introduction, we shall point out some of the major possibilities and constraints that shaped women's writing for the theatre in the central periods of the twentieth century.

Theatrical suffrage and suffrage theatre

In her chapter on 'The Vote' in her highly influential study *Hidden From History*, feminist historian Sheila Rowbotham sketches the campaigning activities of Emmeline Pankhurst and the suffrage organisation WSPU (Women's Social and Political Union) which she was instrumental in founding in 1903.[4] Rowbotham's account of the growing militancy of the Pankhursts' campaign later in the decade, as the Liberal government under the leadership of Prime Minister Asquith showed no signs of listening to their 'cause', draws on a theatrical vocabulary. She explains that the militant campaign relied on 'publicity', 'sensation' and 'ever more dramatic gestures' (pp. 88–9). Actresses working in theatre in this historical moment were well placed to assist with spectacular representations of the 'cause'.

The AFL (Actresses' Franchise League) was formed in 1908 for actresses to pledge their support to the campaign for women's suffrage. Upon its inception, the AFL declared it would support all suffrage organisations. The two main organisations at this time were the WSPU and the NUWSS (National Union of Women's Suffrage Societies), but they took very different stands over militancy. While militant action was characteristic of the WSPU, the NUWSS continued to campaign through the trade unions, insisting that working women needed the vote to improve their conditions of employment. The AFL had to consider its role in this more vigorous, direct style of campaigning which inevitably created tensions between those AFL members of a more peaceful persuasion and those many actresses attracted to the theatrical style of the WSPU which advocated 'deeds not words'.

Ultimately, it was neither reasoned debate nor direct action which was the most valuable contribution the League had to offer the campaign – rather it was the theatrical skills of its members. As women were largely unaccustomed to and unskilled at public speaking, actresses could use their training to help women with speaking at rallies. The skill of impersonation was particularly useful after the Prisoners' Temporary Discharge Act, more popularly known as the Cat and Mouse Act, which meant that militant women, imprisoned for their activities, might be temporarily discharged following hunger strikes, and then recalled to prison to continue their sentence. AFL members helped women with costumes and disguises to avoid recapture. Actresses could also help with the theatricality of demonstrations, staging political 'spectacles' in the hope of gaining public sympathy for the 'cause'. While the League had skills which it could offer the 'cause', the political climate of suffrage also encouraged women to learn a new skill – the skill of playwriting.

The masculinist managerial and organisational structures of Edwardian theatre offered little, if any, support to the woman playwright, but the demand for performances at suffrage events created a demand for writing. Consequently, the AFL set up a play department and appointed actress Inez Bensusan to run it.[5] While Bensusan's repertoire included suffrage pieces by men and women, it was particularly significant that this venture created the opportunity for women to write and to see their work performed.

The style and content of this suffrage drama was largely determined by the occasion of the political event. Plays commissioned as entertainment for a rally or demonstration needed to suit different suffrage factions, rather than to please one organisation at the expense of another. The message needed to be clear and immediately accessible, politically instructive, and entertaining, which promoted a style of agitprop comic-realism. The practicalities of 'touring' to different parts of the country meant that pieces tended to be monologues or duologues requiring one or two actresses and minimal props, rather than plays with large casts demanding full-scale productions.

The political demands of writing agitprop suffrage drama, however, had its limitations, as is illustrated in Bensusan's Women's Theatre season at the Coronet Theatre, London, in 1913. Designed to create opportunities for women in areas of theatre work on and off the stage, the season's two plays were, ironically, both written by men: Bjornstjerne Bjornson's *A Gauntlet* (a Norwegian drama which treats the double standard of sexual morality) and Eugene Brieux's *Woman On Her Own* (translated from the French by Charlotte Shaw, and focusing on women and employment).

The 1913 Women's Theatre season is important, however, because it shows women moving into professional theatre on their own terms, rather than either asking actor–managers to give them work, or only performing in non-theatre, oppositional, political contexts. Julie Holledge gives a fascinating account of how Bensusan raised the capital for her season through the suffrage network, with an advance booking system which made the season a financial success (*Innocent Flowers*, p. 93). It showed what could be achieved when women could draw on a national, feminist network.

For a relatively small number of women who had successful careers as actresses, it was possible to take up a hierarchical position such as that of manager, or a status position, such as that of writer. If women were able to access the male domain of theatre management, then they could be supportive of other women's work. For example, actress–manager and suffragette Lena Ashwell produced Cicely Hamilton's *Diana of Dobson's* (a comic-realist examination of the hardship facing unskilled middle-class women working as shop girls) during her management of the Kingsway Theatre in 1908. Given that, conventionally, women did not have the experience of, or access to, theatre to develop playwriting skills, it is perhaps not surprising to find some women playwrights emerging out of successful acting careers. Working as a performer was at least one way of discovering what would or would not work on the stage. Both Elizabeth Robins and Cicely Hamilton, for example, worked first as actresses and then as writers. While both women were involved in the AFL, they also had key roles in the WWSL (Women Writers' Suffrage league) which Cicely Hamilton co-founded in 1908, and of which Elizabeth Robins was president.

Elizabeth Robins's multi-faceted career – as actress, as political activist, as writer of journalism, plays, and fiction – is an interesting one to consider. American born, Robins spent much of her career in England, working in the theatre and for the 'cause'. Like other playwrights in this volume, her first playwriting success was at the Court, then under the progressive Vedrenne–Barker management (1904–7), concerned with promoting 'new drama'. Robins's full-length suffrage drama *Votes for Women!*, was staged at the close of this venture in 1907. Not only did *Votes for Women!* bring the suffrage campaign into the theatre, but a quarter of the fee which Robins was paid went to the two main suffrage parties.[6] That Robins's career as a writer was so wide-ranging does not just reflect personal choice or ambition, but demonstrates how hard it was to be financially self-supporting as a playwright, unless part of the commercial system, playing long runs to large audiences.[7] In our own time dramatists often combine playwriting with more lucrative writing for television and radio; Robins could not rely on her theatre contracts alone.

Yet her career as a performer had taught Robins the power of theatre as a live medium. Biographer Angela V. John explains how Robins, with the help of Cicely Hamilton, worked on turning her controversial but successful 1913 novel *Where are you going to . . . ?*, treating prostitution and the white slave trade, into a stage drama for a second Women's Theatre season in 1914 (*Elizabeth Robins*, p.192). The Lord Chamberlain refused to grant the play a licence, but, in any event, any plans for a second Women's Theatre season were overtaken by the outbreak of the First World War.

Votes for women and a backlash against feminism

It was not until 1928 that women were finally granted the same voting rights as men. In 1918 they achieved partial enfranchisement when women over thirty were given the vote. Although 1928 is, therefore, a landmark in women's history, feminist historians are quick to indict the social conditions and conservatism of the post-war years as creating a time of great hardship for women, and a backlash against feminism. Women had been sorely needed to work in industries during the First World War, but as soon as it was over and the men came home, women were expected to get back to their 'proper sphere' of domesticity – whether this meant being back in their own home, or working as a low-paid domestic servant in somebody else's. Irrespective of whether this was actually what women wanted to do – and many of them did not want to go back into the home – it was an impossible re-adjustment to make given the numbers of women needing to support themselves, and the incompatibility of industrial training with domestic employment.[8] The sense of social dislocation – for women and for men – was acute. Feminist historian Martha Vicinus explains: 'this takeover of male work left the men at the front feeling alienated and subtly emasculated. When they returned home, the women were forced out of their jobs; yet during the post-war economic dislocation many men could not find jobs nor could they regain their former ascendancy over women.'[9]

In consequence of these social conditions, the 1920s style of feminism was, as

Angela V. John describes, 'increasingly diffuse, even defensive', and 'the very word "feminism" became generally discredited' (*Elizabeth Robins*, pp. 206–7). It was in many ways a decade of contradictions, of gains and losses for women: on the one hand there were some legislative reforms which worked to the benefit of women, such as the 1925 Pensions Act (which provided Old Age Pensions, Widows' Pensions and Orphans' Pensions), and on the other hand the Marriage Bar for teachers (meaning a woman could not maintain her employment if she married) was widely accepted in the early 1920s.[10]

As women were no longer united by a single issue (the vote), they campaigned on a range of diverse issues generally concerned with social reforms from which women might benefit – such as the campaigning for birth control led by Marie Stopes. The Six Point Group, founded in 1921 by the Welsh suffragette Lady Rhondda, was a political pressure group which raised six points which it urged the government to address: satisfactory legislation on child assault, and for the widowed mother, and for the unmarried mother and her child; equal guardianship; equality of pay for men and women teachers; equality of pay and opportunity for men and women in the Civil Service. Peace was also an issue for women after the War, although many became critical of the League of Nations (inaugurated in 1918) for its marginalisation of women's involvement. Johns describes Robins's view of the league 'becom[ing] a League of Men, served by women in subordinate offices' (*Elizabeth Robins*, p. 211).

With regard to conditions in the theatre in the 1920s, we should remember that there was no public subsidy at that time, and that theatre was either commercially or privately funded (usually through subscription schemes). Edy Craig's women's theatre company, The Pioneer Players, set up in the climate of suffrage in 1911, showed how difficult it was to survive as a subscription theatre, giving one performance of a work at small London theatres. While Craig's company kept going throughout the War, lack of funds finally forced her to abandon regular productions at the beginning of the 1920s – although the company came together again to perform American playwright Susan Glaspell's *The Verge* in 1925.[11]

One opening for women who had been involved in the suffrage movement and suffrage drama was to continue their careers in regional repertory theatre, which begins to flourish at the turn of the century, in the wake of initiatives such as the Vedrenne–Barker management which produced *Votes for Women!* Although relying on the support of a wealthy individual or the backing of a community of civic dignitaries, repertory theatres were less commercially driven, and more receptive to new progressive drama. Annie Horniman of the Horniman tea family who used her private wealth to back the Gaiety Theatre Manchester from 1907 until 1917 is generally considered a pioneer of this movement. Her management encouraged new playwriting by men and women, and new playwriting which had a local flavour.[12] While Horniman's enterprise, and similar ventures – such as Alfred Wareing's attempts to establish a repertory theatre in Glasgow, Scotland – did not survive the War, the repertory initiative was sustained in two other major English cities – Liverpool and Birmingham.

The significance of an emergent repertory movement to women writers is exemplified by the playwriting career of Elizabeth Baker. Baker's socialist-feminist drama *Chains*, which premiered at the Court Theatre, London, in 1909, was revived at the Barker and Frohman's Repertory season at the Duke of York's, London, in 1910, at Manchester's Gaiety in 1911 and at Birmingham's Repertory Theatre in 1914. Subsequently, between 1915 and 1925 Baker had three new plays produced at Birmingham's Repertory Theatre. (Like the Manchester Gaiety, the Birmingham Rep. relied on the wealth of one individual – Barry Jackson.)

Women new to playwriting in the 1920s and 1930s also achieved careers on London's commercial West End stages, and, again, these women writers were often actresses before they became writers. Their writing was formally and ideologically conditioned by the 'malestream' of their theatrical and social lives; their dramatisations of women's lives raised a number of social issues but, like feminism itself, these were 'diffuse' and fragmented.

While the 1920s saw some cautious gains for women (the first English woman Cabinet Minister, Margaret Bondfield, was elected in 1929), Britain went into the 1930s in a financial crisis, bringing down the country's Labour government under Ramsay Macdonald in 1931.[13] While unemployed Glaswegians joined the hunger march down to England's capital in 1932, another movement was on the march: the British Union of Fascists was founded by ex-Labour Party member Sir Oswald Mosley in 1932, the year before Hitler became Chancellor of Germany.

The 'dual role' for women

The Second World War had a profound effect on the lives of women, but not exactly in the ways it is sometimes claimed. Women did experience new employment opportunities, a more open sexual climate, and greater independence in the absence of their fathers, husbands, and brothers. The British government instituted compulsory registration of women in order to assign them to essential war work, which included engineering and munitions. Not only did these jobs disappear after the war, but it was also the case that women received unequal pay for their work during the war. Barbara Caine writes, 'Women received less training and less payment during their apprenticeship than men and were shunted back into lower-paid female occupations even before the war ended.'[14] For example, Margaret Barraclough, retired company member of the socialist-feminist cabaret group The Chuffinelles (1986–93) and former crane-driver, recollects:

When I first started in the steel-rolling mills working with the tongs on red-hot steel ... there were lots of women doing these 'men's jobs', thousands, they were driving cranes and trucks and welding. However, this was during the war. As soon as the war was over and the men started coming back, they were out of a job, most of them anyway. By this time I'd been crane-driving a few years and I taught some of these men to drive the cranes, and their starting wage was much higher than mine was.[15]

Moreover, as Caine stresses, 'the war was followed by a powerful evocation of a traditional family, which ascribed to women a more domesticated role than they had ever actually undertaken' (*English Feminism*, p. 228). The consolidation of the family and the beginning of the baby boom had a profound influence on women's perceptions of their roles during the next decade. After the war, the 1,500 nurseries set up by 1944 to provide women with childcare were closed; they had served the temporary need of the nation (p. 228).

The Beveridge Report of 1943, which became the seminal document in establishing the post-war welfare state, was criticised by feminist groups still active from the earlier movement before the war. The Women's Freedom League organised twelve women's organisations to lobby the Ministry of Reconstruction:

Arguing that Beveridge denied women their rights as persons, they were particularly critical of women's loss of insurance rights made prior to marriage and of all the contributions they had made prior to marriage ... In the general climate of support for Beveridge, however, the critique of these equal rights feminists went largely unnoticed, especially as many women welcomed his proposals.[16]

There were, in fact, various organisations and societies that remained active after the war which were carry-overs from the more militant years of struggle for suffrage. The Six Point Group, for example, lasted until 1960. The militancy of the struggle for enfranchisement and equality, however, gave way to a post-war caution and concern with 'feminine matters', meaning the emphasis tended to be placed on individual women's adjustment to their particular circumstances, and to the dominance of domesticity as the chief arena in which women ruled. In an influential book published in 1956, *Women's Two Roles* by Alva Myrdal and Viola Klein, the feminist plea that women should be able to have both marriage and career is accompanied by a clear message that work must always take second place in their lives. 'This belief in women's "dual role"', Olive Banks writes, 'in which a woman's work must somehow be made to fit into her domestic responsibilities, continued into the 1960s, even amongst feminists' (*The Politics Of British Feminism*, p. 24).

This description of the circumscription of women's advocacy and advancement was, however, in tension with fundamental changes that were occurring in society. At the end of the war, the Marriage Bar for teachers was abolished (see

n. 10), and in 1945 women were first admitted into the police force. The Marriage Bar was abolished in the Civil Service in 1946, and in 1948 the British Nationality Act allowed British women to retain their nationality on marriage. The struggle for equality resulted in equal pay for men and women as teachers in 1952 and in the Civil Service in 1954. People married younger but also divorced more often. Divorce petitions increased by 20,000 after the war. One in fifteen marriages ended in divorce, compared to one in sixty in 1937.[17]

The empire was also breaking up: the botched attempt to overthrow the revolutionary government of Colonel Nasser in 1956 is often cited as the decisive event. The Cold War was creating a kind of paranoia and insularity which reinforced a strong ideology of internal security and external containment. Against this backdrop, it is not surprising that women were preoccupied with managing the rising tensions facing them in their daily lives. Enfranchised but not empowered, 'equal' in imagination more often than law, and genuinely perplexed by the 'dual role' dilemma, these women of the 1950s and early 1960s were very concerned about their quality of life in the context of the conservative climate of their times. Susan Bennett's perceptive essay in part 1 explains the dramas written by women grappling with these issues on their stages. While the differences between them and the generation of women who revolted in an open way in the late 1960s forming the 'Second Wave' of feminism seem to eclipse their similarities, it is worth stressing that the need for financial security, access to employment, protection and support for selves and children, and the desire for personal happiness have motivated women throughout the post-war period to seek to understand and to change their circumstances.

Happy Anniversary?

1968 is a year when a 'democratic opening' for different oppressed peoples was thought to be possible. As a decade the 1960s is characterised as a time of radical politics (sexual and political): the Black, New-left and anti-Vietnam movements in America; the 'Cultural Revolution' in China in 1966; and the anti-government protests of students in Paris 1968. Closer to 'home', 1968 saw an escalation of Civil Rights activism in Northern Ireland. While none of these movements in the 1960s were primarily concerned with women, they voiced the struggles of oppressed groups, communities, or countries in ways which women could relate to. In Northern Ireland specifically, for example, women involved in the Civil Rights activism would be instrumental in founding the Northern Ireland Women's Rights Movement in the mid-1970s.

For women in England, 1968 was the fiftieth anniversary of first being given the vote (albeit on unequal terms with men). Discontent with marriage, domesticity and motherhood was on the increase.[18] The year 1968 is also remembered in English women's history as the year in which working-class women machinists at a Ford's factory went on strike – significant because, as trade-union activist and Labour MP Audrey Wise explains, it was seen as the first women's strike since that of the match girls eighty years before.[19] Moreover, as Wise goes on to comment, with a Labour government in power (Harold Wilson was elected in 1964 with a slim majority of 4, and re-elected at the general election in 1966 with a majority of 97), there were expectations of better working conditions for lower-paid classes of men and women – although the women who went on strike at Ford's took seventeen years to achieve their original strike goals.[20]

The strike did, however, add pressure to campaigning for equal pay, which was one of the four basic 'demands' of the Second Women's Liberation Movement (WLM), formulated by women at a history workshop weekend at Ruskin College, Oxford: equal pay; equal education and opportunity; 24-hour nurseries; and free contraception and abortion on demand. In retrospective accounts of the Women's Movement this history workshop weekend is recorded as a seminal event (in this volume, see pp. 59 and 177). As Michelene Wandor recollects:

> As part of a generation who took over Ruskin College for a weekend in 1970, we were in at the beginning of a change in the consciousness of women in this country. For me, the most important overall legacy of that weekend was the realisation that, marginal as I very often felt, I was objectively a part of the historical process, and that I could help shape and change that history.[21]

Campaigning for equal pay met with some success in the passing of the Equal Pay Act in 1970 – although it did not come into force until 1975, along with the Sex Discrimination Act. That said, these acts could not legislate for occupational segregation, or the de-skilling of women which employers used to avoid awarding equal wages. Traditionally, trade unions had played a key role in fighting for better pay and conditions for low-paid workers, but as women often worked in non-unionised jobs they did not have this support. Asian women workers in the Grunwick dispute (1976–7), for example, went on strike because their employer dismissed workers wanting to join a union. Where women were able to join a trade union, they found themselves up against the masculinist bias which often meant collusion between management and union representation of the male workforce, at the expense of women workers.[22]

'Body politics', women's struggle to have greater control over their biological and, in consequence, their social lives, was crucial to the WLM campaigns, as reflected in the 'demands'. Like the suffragettes before them, feminist activists in the 1970s used the body to stage their politics: alternative 'body' shows were organised to protest at the Miss World contests (1969–71), and rallies, meetings, and demonstrations, such as the International Women's Day marches in 1971, made use of spectacle to make political points.

Out of these political street theatre beginnings, women interested in taking performance work further began to group together. Playwrights who contributed to the 'Women's Festival' hosted by Ed Berman's Almost Free Theatre in 1973 included two who appear in this volume: Pam Gems and Michelene Wandor. The season seeded two companies: the Women's Company (which did not survive) and the WTG (the Women's Theatre Group, currently our longest-running women's company, now renamed The Sphinx). The inception of the Women's Theatre Group was shortly followed by the socialist-feminist company Monstrous Regiment who, until the company disbanded in 1993, worked with a number of European and British women playwrights.

A number of women's companies followed in the wake of WTG and Monstrous including, for example, Siren, Spare Tyre and Clean Break (all 1979). Women set up their own companies because they knew that they would not be made welcome by the male-dominated theatrical establishment (at that time much preoccupied with acquiring a National Theatre, which opened on the South Bank, London in 1975). Even in socialist theatre companies such as Red Ladder, women found themselves subordinate to the men – both on and off the stage.

The explosion of feminist companies in the 1970s was important to women playwrights because these companies commissioned plays by women which might otherwise have been rejected by 'malestream' managements.[23] In addition to commissioning writers, the collaborative processes of devising issue-based theatre also meant that groups nurtured writing skills within their companies. For example, Tasha Fairbanks emerged as the playwright for the lesbian company Siren; Clair Chapman took on the main responsibility for writing Spare Tyre shows. The feminist movement meant that these women's companies and writers found women audiences through their networks, often performing in non-theatre spaces such as community centres, women's meeting spaces, or schools.

Theatre-in-education (which came with the expansion of regional theatre in the 1960s) was also important to feminist theatre practitioners as a means of taking issue-based theatre into schools: feminist theatre which would encourage young people – girls especially – to think about the social and political implications of their lives. Early 1970s productions by the WTG were group-devised TIE shows. Their 1974 production My Mother Says I Never Should, for example, was designed to promote discussion of contraception primarily (although not exclusively) among teenage audiences.[24] Inevitably not all schools were willing to listen, and even within the WLM the play was criticised for its recommendation of the Pill.[25]

In the late 1960s and the 1970s what appears to promise a more progressive future, socially and theatrically – and here we should also note the 1968 abolition of theatre censorship by the Lord Chamberlain's office – is in truth far more complex and contradictory. Although the 1967 Abortion Act had legalised abortion, providing a woman could get the consent of two doctors,[26] the rise of right-wing pro-life groups meant that throughout the 1970s there were counter attempts to restrict abortion. We noted earlier that the pay and discrimination acts were only partially successful in improving women's employment conditions and opportunities, and while there were a number of local initiatives for the organisation of child care in the 1970s, there was no high-profile national campaign.[27] In the theatre, although women formed a number of counter-cultural companies, the funding implications of this growth meant that in the long term these companies – and their commitment to women's playwriting – would not be sustainable.[28]

Similarly, as the decade progressed the WLM became increasingly fragmented. Internal debate focused on the communities and experiences of women overlooked by its middle-class, white agenda. In brief, what begins with the promise of a 'democratic opening', ends in reactionary closure, marked by the 1979 election of Margaret Thatcher – Britain's first woman Prime Minister.

'Top Girls'?

By 1987, Lynne Segal, one of the major socialist-feminist activists and thinkers of the 1970s, began her new book, *Is The Future Female?*, with this characterisation of 1980s feminists:

> I wanted to write this book because I was disturbed by what has been emerging as the public face of feminism in the eighties. The most accessible feminist writing today is one in which we are likely to read of the separate and special knowledge, emotion, sexuality, thought and morality of women, indeed of a type of separate 'female world', which exists in fundamental opposition to 'male culture', 'male authority', 'malestream thought', in opposition to the world of men. The central theme of this book, in contrast, is the inadequacy of such polarised thinking about women and men'. [29]

Segal goes on to comment that the notion of the social construction of gender – its contingency across class, ethnicity, and region – drops out of such analyses that return to a notion of innate difference through the back door of celebrating women's virtue, morality, and peace advocacy. She is particularly concerned that the absence of a strong feminist movement has caused the dilution of 1970s feminism and the rise of individualism and an over-emphasis on feminine experience: 'the dangers of such essentialist thinking have grown stronger within feminism as the women's movement itself has grown organisationally weaker and its perspectives more fragmented' (*Is The Future Female?*, p. xii).

In retrospect, what is striking is the irony of the similarity of the situation for women in the 1980s to both of the twentieth-century post-war periods, or, as Margaret Barraclough explained at the close of the 1980s: 'everywhere you look, history repeats itself. It's happening now – Thatcherite policy is about getting women back into the home' (Aston, *Feminist Theatre Voices*, p.163). While in each period quite distinct conditions accounted for the phenomena of the backlash, in all cases previously strong, aggressive women's movements had championed and pressed for equality between men and women, denying innate difference in order to secure opportunities. Early successes had led to later perceptions that the struggle for equality was over; women had achieved their goals (much evidence to the contrary notwithstanding). While the formal organisation and energy of the earlier movements dissipated, even self-identified feminists tended to lean towards concern with the personal, the domestic, and the 'feminine'. The problem of the 'dual sphere' reasserts itself as the 'two-career problem' for women, and in the resurgent backlash against feminism the fear of the 'bad mother' makes a strong reappearance. [30]

How was it possible to reverse such strong tendencies towards equality and open definition? The change in women's perception of their social and cultural situation has to be understood in the context of the Thatcher administrations. These years have been described as a revolution – and that is hardly too strong a description. Margaret Thatcher's success at what Stuart Hall termed 'Authoritarian Populism' combined a nostalgia for the imperial past with 'privatisation' and a regressive desire for the patriarchal family, while using the rhetoric of free markets and personal freedom as part of the appeal.[31] Thus, coupled with the xenophobia which lurks under the attack on the welfare systems as a response to the new waves of postcolonial immigration, we begin to see why, ideologically, the democratic aspects of feminism are displaced by the emphasis on 'personal choice'.

Margaret Thatcher is herself a highly ironic figure for women. Tough, uncompromising, and powerful, she is the monster strong woman, the feminist movement's shadow figure and nemesis. Caryl Churchill wrote *Top Girls* to question the extent to which Second Wave feminists were buying into Thatcher ideology to the detriment of a variety of real women. Marlene, her central character, thinks 'Maggie' is just fine while her sister Joyce begs to differ, and her daughter Angie suffers the fate of not being 'first-rate'.

It is important to remember, too, how hard these years were for the arts, especially those alternative, political, or experimental companies and artists who did not fall under the wing of powerful institutions like the National Theatre or the RSC. Immediately after Thatcher's re-election (1983/4), she cut the arts budget, did away with metropolitan authorities (including the Greater London Council), and circulated a major policy document entitled *The Glory Of The Garden*. This report worked on the metaphor of pulling the weeds and thinning the beds in order that 'excellence' might be cultivated. What this meant, of course, was the cutting of subsidies to many small and touring companies, a new emphasis on financial self-sufficiency, corporate sponsorship, and business planning and marketing. Many important theatre companies went under as a result of these policies: Joint Stock, 7:84 (England), Foco Novo were among the best-known general companies, and Siren, Monstrous Regiment, Spare Tyre were among the best-known feminist groups.[32] New groups started and worked, especially locally, without government funding or much corporate sponsorship. As observed by Aston in the editorial introduction to *Feminist Theatre Voices*:

> Closure has been a hallmark of the early 1990s, with many of the feminist theatre groups ceasing to tour, or ceasing altogether. However, the survival of feminist theatre is dependent upon change, and, despite the closures, the tenacious refusal of feminist practitioners to be silenced surfaces in other ways . . . Building on the past means moving in new directions.
>
> (p. 27)

New Labour: new directions?

With the election of a New Labour government in 1997, the first left-of-centre government to be in power in Britain for eighteen years, came the expectation of a more equitable society – both economically and socially. Reflecting on how bad things had become under successive right-wing governments, Gems, for example, talks of 'pinning' her 'hopes on the new government' (Stephenson and Longridge, *Rage & Reason*, p. 96). Yet, while the lyrics of New Labour's campaign song promised that their election would mean 'it can only get better', there is little sign that the change in government has brought with it a moment of 'democratic opening'. The advent of New Labour has not heralded improvements for state programmes of health, education, or welfare – nor has it improved the state subsidy of the theatre.

At the start of the decade Mary Remnant commented that 'ten years of Thatcherism have brought the wolf to the stage door',[33] and John Bull's figures presented in the final chapter of his 1994 *Stage Right*, show a troubling downward trend, which New Labour have done nothing to reverse. As Bull summarises: 'what this means is that it is getting harder and harder for even an established writer, let alone a new writer, to get a production on stage'.[34] To this we would add that it is even harder for women to have new works staged. As women have never had, as Gardiner's 1987 report concluded, a 'fair slice of the cake', have never had their own venues to manage (which Gardiner argues is a distinct advantage when it comes to competing for funds), they have inevitably found themselves with even fewer crumbs.[35] Men are the ones who have been predominantly in charge of the 'cake', in charge of theatres and theatrical production this century, deciding what gets put on.

2 Amelia Lowdell as Marie in Rebecca Prichard's *Yard Gal*

If there is one issue that most women playwrights, across different generations and social backgrounds, are currently agreed upon it is the relatively low levels of funding for their work, exacerbated by male control of theatre. Seasoned writer Pam Gems has commented throughout her career on the connections which men have in theatre which effectively keep women's writing, or a large portion of it, off the stage. Women coming more recently on to the theatre scene are also aware of the 'laddism' of their profession, as Phyllis Nagy describes it (Stephenson and Longridge, *Rage & Reason*, p. 28), and how this functions as a form of censorship. Playwright April de Angelis comments that 'all writers are dependent on the vagaries of whoever runs theatre, except it's often the vagaries of men because men still really do run theatres' (p. 58).

Struggling against the trend of safe revivals are a handful of companies, like the new writing companies Paines Plough and 7:84 (Scotland), or theatres such as the Traverse or the Court, which remain committed to the risky business of staging new work, relying on a combination of public and private sponsorship schemes, and seeking partnered arrangements.[36] Prichard's *Yard Gal* was a co-production between the Court and Clean Break – a company dedicated to working with women prisoners and ex-offenders. Clean Break manages the annual commissioning of a new play by a professional writer on issues related to women and crime (playwrights discussed in this volume who have worked with the company include, for example, Sarah Daniels and Winsome Pinnock).

Formed in 1979, Clean Break is unusual in so far as it is one of the few women's theatre companies to survive the Thatcher and the post-Thatcher decades.[37] Moreover, unless the current plans to secure a building base through the conversion of a former tie-factory in Kentish Town, London, are thwarted, Clean Break will be the first women's company to have its own building,[38] and the significance of this event, when it happens, given all that we have stated about the funding of women's work in the theatre, cannot be overstated.

For a young generation of writers like Kane and Prichard who joined the British theatre scene in the late 1990s, it means working in a context in which feminism retains an academic centrality (reflected, for example, in the way a *Companion* such as this is possible) but has no movement, which, as we observed in other moments of our twentieth-century history, was formerly able to support women's writing – providing venues, audiences, performers, and issues for dramatisation. Despite the absence of visible, feminist support, women's cultural activity – specifically women's playwriting – has not disappeared. As Mary Remnant commented in 1990: 'Despite the obstacles . . . it is apparent that women playwrights are gaining confidence, both in their work and in the notion that it *is* possible to be a woman and to write plays' (*Plays*, p. vii). If women are managing to get their plays on, it is not because things socially, culturally, theatrically, or politically have suddenly 'got better', it is because they are prepared, like Prichard's young women, or Kane's outcasts, to continue their struggle despite the odds stacked against them.

NOTES

1 Explained in Heidi Stephenson and Natasha Langridge (eds.) *Rage and Reason: Women Playwrights on Playwriting* (London: Methuen, 1997), p. 129.
2 *The Times*, 7 May 1998.
3 Honor Ford-Smith, 'Ring Ding in a Tight Corner', in M. Jacqui Alexander and Chandra Talpade Mohanty (eds.) *Feminist Genealogies, Colonial Legacies, Democratic Futures* (London and New York: Routledge, 1997), pp. 213–58, p. 217.
4 Sheila Rowbotham, 'The Vote', in *Hidden From History*, 3rd edn (London: Pluto Press, 1977), pp. 77–89.
5 For further details see Julie Holledge, *Innocent Flowers* (London: Virago, 1981), p. 62.
6 See Angela V. John, *Elizabeth Robins: Staging a Life, 1862–1952* (London: Routledge, 1995), p. 148.
7 For more on the financial arrangements of playwrights in commercial theatres, see Ian Clarke, *Edwardian Drama* (London: Faber, 1989), pp. 18–19.
8 See Ray Strachey, *The Cause: A Short History of the Women's Movement in Great Britain* (London: Virago, 1978), pp. 372–3.
9 Martha Vicinus, *Independent Women: Work and Community for Single Women: 1850–1920* (London: Virago, 1985), p. 282.
10 The Marriage Bar in teaching was not lifted until the 1944 Education Act. For a dramatisation of this issue see Charlotte Keatley's characterisation of Doris

Partington in her generational play *My Mother Said I Never Should* (London: Methuen, 1988).

11 For details see Holledge, *Innocent Flowers*, part 3, 'Edy and her Pioneers'. Holledge is cautious about the company's success in supporting women playwrights, writing that 'although the company recreated excellent work for actresses, it increasingly neglected women playwrights' (p. 144).

12 For example, actress and playwright Gertrude Robins was identified with the 'Manchester School' of writers, and had a number of works staged at the Gaiety, including her one-act play *Makeshifts* which looks at the lives of two unmarried sisters (1908).

13 This was only the second time a Labour government had been in power. The first, short-lived Labour government was in 1924, also under Ramsay Macdonald.

14 Barbara Caine, *English Feminism: 1780–1980* (Oxford: Oxford University Press, 1997), p. 227.

15 Quoted in Elaine Aston (ed.) *Feminist Theatre Voices* (Loughborough: Loughborough Theatre Texts, 1997), p.163.

16 Olive Banks, *The Politics Of British Feminism: 1928–1970* (Aldershot: Edward Elgar Publishing Ltd: 1993), p. 21. Other notes of feminist protest are to be found in seminal publications such as the first English translation of Simone de Beauvoir's *Le Deuxième Sexe* (1954).

17 Angela Holdsworth, *Out Of The Doll's House* (London: BBC Books, 1988), p. 147.

18 Key publications which gave voice to this discontent were Betty Friedan's *The Feminine Mystique* (1963) and Hannah Gavron's *Captive Wife* (1966). By the time of the Divorce Reform Act in 1969 the breakdown of marriage was recognised as the sole grounds for divorce in Britain, and in consequence petitions for divorce were up 50 per cent by 1971.

19 See Audrey Wise, interview in Michelene Wandor (ed.) *Once a Feminist: Stories of a Generation* (London: Virago, 1990), pp. 201–2.

20 *Ibid.*, p. 202.

21 *Ibid.*, p. 2.

22 The socialist company Red Ladder's first women's play in 1974, *Strike While the Iron is Hot*, used a Brechtian register to explore many of these work-related issues: the double oppression of working-class women as unpaid workers in the home and as low-paid members of a factory workforce. See Michelene Wandor's account of this production on p. 61.

23 Monstrous Regiment commissioned writers from the inception of their company, whereas the WTG began by devising shows and started to commission playwrights towards the end of the 1970s.

24 Published in Michelene Wandor (ed.) *Strike While the Iron is Hot* (London: Journeyman Press, 1980).

25 The contraceptive pill was first made in 1952. Contraception, previously only available to married women through the Family Planning Association, was made more freely available to women in the mid-1970s.

26 Lesley Doyal and Mary Ann Elston, 'Women, Health and Medicine', in Veronica Beechey and Elizabeth Whitelegg (eds.) *Women in Britain Today* (Milton Keynes: Open University Press 1986), pp. 173–208, state that 'by 1973 the number of legal abortions performed on British residents had risen to nearly 120,000' (p. 185).

27 For details of the child care campaigns in the 1970s see Joni Lovenduski and Vicky

Randall, *Contemporary Feminist Politics* (Oxford: Oxford University Press, 1993), p. 288.

28 Although WTG and Monstrous Regiment were funded by the Arts Council, women's companies set up in the latter part of the decade were less successful in gaining funding, given the by then reduced levels of subsidy, affected by inflation, and the increased number of alternative companies competing for funds. For further details see Stuart Laing, 'Institutional Change in the 1970s', in Bart Moore-Gilbert (ed.) *Cultural Closure: The Arts in the 1970s* (London: Routledge, 1994), pp. 29–56.

29 Lynne Segal, *Is the Future Female? Troubled Thoughts on Contemporary Feminism* (London: Virago Press, 1987), p. ix.

30 See Susan Faludi's *Backlash*, which first appeared in 1991 (New York and London: Anchor Books).

31 Stuart Hall wrote the best book on understanding the Thatcher era: *The Hard Road to Renewal* (London: Verso, 1988).

32 For a survey of feminist theatres in the period, see Lizbeth Goodman, *Contemporary Feminist Theatres* (London: Routledge, 1993), chapter 2.

33 Mary Remnant (ed.) *Plays by Women: 8* (London: Methuen, 1990), p. vii.

34 John Bull, *Stage Right: Crisis and Recovery in Contemporary British Mainstream Theatre* (Basingstoke: Macmillan, 1994), p. 208. Bull quotes David Edgar's figures which calculate a drop in the percentage of new work staged between 1985 and 1990 in London and regional main-house theatres to 7 per cent, as compared with the figure of 12 per cent for the period 1970 to 1985.

35 Caroline Gardiner, *What Share of the Cake?: The Employment of Women in the English Theatre* (London: Women's Playhouse Trust, 1987).

36 Timberlake Wertenbaker's *The Break of Day* (see chapter 9), for example, was a co-production between the Court and Max Stafford-Clark's Out of Joint company, also in association with Bristol Old Vic and Leicester Haymarket Theatre, and also in tandem with a 'classic' play to make it viable (*The Break of Day* toured and played with Chekhov's *Three Sisters*).

37 In England, the only other company to survive from the 1970s is the Women's Theatre Group, now touring as The Sphinx.

38 The WPT (Women's Playhouse Trust), a production company set up in 1981 to redress the inequalities of the theatrical profession, is also trying to raise the funds to secure a building base in London.

PART I

RETROSPECTIVES

Editors' note

Each of the chapters in this part is concerned with theatre history, and the histories of women's playwriting within it: with understanding the changing social, political, economic, and cultural contexts in which women have been writing for theatre during the twentieth century, and assessing how their work has been both forgotten and remembered.

Feminist theatre history has been primarily concerned with the recovery of women's playwriting previously 'hidden' by the canonical values which, for example, enshrined Shakespeare, Ibsen, and Brecht, but left out Aphra Behn, Susan Glaspell, and Marieluise Fleisser (see also our introduction to 'The Question of the Canon'). The values of an alternative, 'feminist canon', however, may also risk the elision of certain kinds of writers or writing. Thus, while feminist scholarship has been quick to claim the period of suffrage theatre at the turn of the century as a 'high point', it has, in consequence, paid far less attention to women's writing in the 1920s and 1930s, which is de-valued as less interesting, politically (viewed as conservative rather than radical) and formally (as playwriting in the dominant realistic, rather than alternative, experimental, tradition).

Maggie B. Gale's essay takes issue with the way in which the feminist focus on suffrage theatre has 'hidden' women's playwriting during the interwar years. Gale argues that we need to re-think a feminist approach which values the radical at the expense of the conservative. Rather, she proposes that what we need to understand are the changing circumstances of women's lives and their writing. For example, she lists a number of writers who wrote for the Edwardian theatre and then went on to write plays during the interwar years, stressing that their lives, their writing, did not stop when suffrage campaigning and theatre came to an abrupt halt with the war, but that they went through a process of social and theatrical change. In brief, Gale brings this 'lost generation' of women writers back into view.

Similarly, Susan Bennett's essay on women's playwriting in the 1950s challenges the dominant theatrical record of this decade as being mostly, if not exclusively, about John Osborne's *Look Back in Anger* (1956). Bennett charts the 1950s differently. Firstly, she revisits the very few women, or, more specifically, the two women playwrights – Ann Jellicoe and Shelagh Delaney – who manage to enter theatre history (albeit in the shadow of Jimmy Porter), under the 'angry' label. Both of these, Bennett argues, are dramaturgically more innovative than Osborne and his mode of socialist-realism (which remains deeply indebted to the well-made play), but are represented as marginal to, and as less important than, *Look Back in Anger* in the received version of 1950s theatre history.

Secondly, Bennett looks at a different kind of angry writing in women's playwriting in the more popular, commercial theatre context – focusing in particular on Lesley Storm's *Roar Like a Dove*. Gale's point that we re-assess the de-valuation of the conservative at the expense of the radical is relevant here too. Storm's anger may be different from that of other women playwrights, like Jellicoe and Delaney writing contemporaneously for a different kind of theatre and audience, but it ought, nevertheless, like Gale's 'lost generation', to be brought back into view; heard, rather than silenced by theatre history.

Just how plays come to be included in, or excluded from, theatre history is a complex question. Both Gale and Bennett indict the masculinist attitude of theatre reviewers as a significant factor in the writing 'out' of women's work in the moment of its production, and the male bias of theatre history which perpetuates its obfuscation. Michelene Wandor's account of women's playwriting and theatrical activity in the 1970s includes consideration of a further crucial point in relation to women's contemporary playwriting and theatre history: the issue of whether plays get published or not, which in turn determines whether they will be remembered, performed and studied in the future (see also our introduction to 'The Question of the Canon'). As Wandor's analysis of the 1970s – from the point of view of someone who, at that time, was highly engaged with feminist writing and reviewing for theatre – shows, it is much harder for women playwrights to get published than it is for male playwrights, given that it is the high-profile plays which are much more likely to get into print. As theatre is still predominantly male-managed, in effect this means the greater profiling of plays and performances by men. Although politically, theatrically, and socially the 1990s may be a far cry from the climate of feminist optimism in the 1970s, we still need feminism, Wandor argues, to meet the challenge of women's (under-)representation, both as authors of and subjects in contemporary theatre.

2

MAGGIE B. GALE

Women playwrights of the 1920s and 1930s

The play-going public suddenly . . . picked on a new type of comedy . . . predominantly female. It is completely undramatic . . . ran interminably . . . About? The ditherings of ordinary people seen through the magnifying glass of an observant sentimental humour. It is the vindication of the woman playwright, for it is usually written by a woman . . . the delight of mainly feminine audiences. It is with us still in 1945.[1]

In histories of British theatre, the 1920s and 1930s are traditionally presented as being unfruitful for women playwrights. However, the critical framing of their work by their own contemporaries leads us to see them as more prolific and significant than at first assumed – interwar women playwrights were clearly breaking into the male-dominated market. Rare acknowledgements of women writing for the theatre of the time, made by our own contemporaries, are often underpinned by comment on their seeming lack of a feminist perspective or innovative strategy: they were largely middle-class, writing for a commercially oriented theatre and so the assumption is that their work does not warrant serious examination. Women writing for the variety of theatres which produced plays during the 1920s and 1930s have in common their gender and more of a general leaning towards the conservative than modern feminist scholars would perhaps like.

Although for many 'realism' and 'domestic comedy' as dramatic forms contain serious inherent difficulties in terms of representation, for this lost generation of playwrights they were the perfect vehicle with which to place centre stage the issues directly effecting change in the lives of their female contemporaries. Some critics even saw their work as 'the dawn of the feminine influx and influence that's now filling the theatre',[2] and it is perhaps this, more than the use of dominant theatrical forms, which should prevail in any investigation of their work. Alison Light's observation that 'feminist work must deal with the conservative as well as the radical imagination' has great relevance here.[3]

From radical to conservative contexts

Explorations of the work of the Actresses' Franchise League (AFL), 1908–13, have established the links between feminism and theatre before the First World War [see 'A century in view', p. 1].[4] The AFL, rather than just promoting 'new forms' of drama, used performance and the processes of theatre as a means of discoursing the issues which grew out of and gathered support for the suffrage cause. Founded and run by women, the AFL originally advertised for membership amongst theatre professionals (Gardner, *Sketches*, p. 10). Membership was made up of known and little-known actresses, although Claire Hirschfield has suggested that, because 'many of its earliest members enjoyed celebrity status and public esteem, the AFL was perhaps the most successful of all "professional" women's organisations in drawing popular attention and sympathy to the cause of female enfranchisement' ('The Actresses Franchise League', p. 126). The actresses entertained at political meetings and trained non-professionals in the art of public speaking. Plays, not always written by women, were toured to both traditional and non-traditional theatre venues, with production profits donated to relevant political organisations. Most of the productions were largely ignored by the press, with exceptions, such as Cicely Hamilton's 1909 *A Pageant of Famous Women*, later titled *A Pageant of Great Women*, which provided an endless stream of star performers representing positive images of, amongst other things, exceptional women from history. For Winifred Holtby, 'one of the great virtues of the militant suffragette movement was its mastery of the art of ritual . . . pageants and processions'.[5] 'Pageants and processions', which the AFL staged so effectively, served to validate women's identity, history, and culture.

The AFL remains an important project in the history of women and theatre. Modern feminist theatre scholars are drawn to the links and parallels between First and Second Wave feminist theatres, and the AFL has become part of the 'new canon' of women's theatre history with an emphasis on its political basis. It is, however, interesting to note that, although it was not commercially oriented, there are many cross-over points between the legitimate theatre, the commercial theatre, and the AFL. A number of women writing or acting for the AFL, or writing feminist plays for the Edwardian theatre, continued their work during the interwar years in a far less 'political' and often more commercial context; such women would include Lena Ashwell, Cicely Hamilton, Auriol Lee, Elizabeth Baker, and Gertrude Jennings [see 'Chronology']. Although some arguably moved away from overtly propagandist arguments for greater equality, the threads of practical activism – larger female casts, plots centred around female heroines, woman as subject rather than object within the domestic sphere and so on – prevail. Thus the generation of women before the First World War who worked in an overtly feminist context did not simply stop producing woman-centred work once the vote was won.

Women playwrights of the 1920s and 1930s worked in a theatre system which was largely driven by economic forces: there was no real government subsidy for theatre production until well into the 1940s by which point the commercial theatres were owned by a small cartel of profit-oriented managers. Ironically, West End theatres often relied on the pioneering artistic outlook of the privately funded independent theatres, even though such organisations had been founded to combat commercialised attitudes to artistic production. Plays by women were produced in commercial mainstream, independent experimental and political theatres alike.

There was an explosive increase in the numbers of plays produced on the London stage during the early decades of the twentieth century. Over the 1920s and 1930s as a whole, there is a considerable variation, but the maximum (1930–5) is at least three and a half times the minimum. The average percentage of plays by women or female/male teams over the whole twenty-year period is 16% – figures for the London season of 1989–90 set the average at just over 10%.[6] Just as with male playwrights of the era, critical reception did not always correlate with box-office success. Critics often alluded to the fact that these women were 'amateur' or 'one hit wonders', that they were merely dabbling in the world of the professional playwright. If the critics and historians saw the interwar women playwrights as some kind of 'breed', it was also assumed that they served the interests of a certain type of audience. John Carey cites Louis MacNeice's condemnation of interwar female theatre audiences, 'who use theatre as an uncritical escape from their daily lives . . . the same instinct leads them which makes many hospital nurses spend all their savings on cosmetics, cigarettes and expensive underclothes'.[7] Even intellectuals and modernists like Virginia Woolf, Rebecca West, and Natalie Barney, however, were writing for an 'emerging women's market'.[8] The woman playwright, and by implication the female spectator, was usually referred to as having a penchant for sentimentality and domestic plots: the woman playwright was 'renowned' for the humour with which she treated the machinations of middle-class life, for the wealth of romance in her plays, and for her seeming lack of social critique.

Many of these playwrights began their careers as actresses and continued to perform as well as write and/or direct or manage productions or theatre companies. So we have a new generation of playwrights, trained as actresses, with significant experience of performance in professional theatre, who used playwriting as a vehicle for expression. Thus, in a market economy where her position as actress set her in competition with other out-of-work actresses all looking for employment in productions in which male characters predominated, the move from actress to playwright was, it would seem, a wise one. That many of the women playwrights had begun their professional lives as actresses may also have been a contributing factor to the predominance of female characters in their plays. Loren Kruger has pointed out that creating '"significant *stage* roles" . . . for women . . . neither challenges the traditional roles of women in the theatre . . . nor provides the means for women to run the show themselves'.[9] Running the show yourself is not always a viable option in the context of a theatre world largely driven by financial concerns. Similarly, for these playwrights the move from enactor of text to creator of text represented a challenge to existing traditional roles for women in the process of making theatre: women playwrights were not a new phenomenon but during the 1920s and 1930s they seem suddenly to have appeared in large numbers.

It was unusual for any playwright to have their plays first reach production under a commercial West End management. A less historically obscured playwright like Dodie Smith, who first wrote plays under the name 'C. L. Anthony', provides one of the few exceptions to the general rule in that all her plays saw their first productions under commercial West End managements. Smith had a sequence of West End hits in the 1930s, but had fewer London productions of her plays than a number of other female playwrights of the time, many of whom had their plays produced in independent theatres later transferring into the West End. Taking into consideration the female and female/male to male ratio of productions, women actually fared proportionately rather well in a theatre system where there was an influx of new plays by new playwrights. Over the period 1918–59 for example, three or more of the plays by Bridget Boland, Clemence Dane, Gertrude Jennings, Margaret Kennedy, Esther McCracken, Dodie Smith, Lesley Storm, Aimée Stuart, Joan Temple and Fryn Tennyson-Jesse ran for 51, and in many cases more, performances – and this does not include the many West End stage successes of their American female contemporaries [see 'Chronology']. Many of their plays were made into films or, later, television dramas. Plays by women do not dominate the London stage during the 1920s and 1930s but they have a fairly consistent place, and appear on average to have run for longer and thus been 'safer' investments for managements. Interestingly, during the Second World War there were fewer productions of plays by women but they were more popular. If one can assume that there were fewer men around in the years leading up to and during the war, perhaps it is possible to assume that the women left behind who went to the theatre were more inclined to go and see plays by women.

Realism as activism?

Many interwar women playwrights were once household names, working as actresses and journalists as well as successful playwrights alongside their male counterparts such as Somerset Maugham or Noel Coward. In terms of longevity of career some, such as Clemence Dane and Aimée Stuart, had their work produced throughout the interwar years and into the late 1950s. Theatre historians in general have failed to validate their work and feminist theatre historians have fallen into the trap of the 'censoring impulse'.[10] The 'censoring impulse' here is influenced by the fact that, along with the vast majority of playwrights of either sex, these women used realism – albeit often comic-realism – as a dramatic form. Identified by a number of recent theatre historians as a 'prisonhouse' form, one which endorses dominant ideology placing man as subject and woman as 'other', realism has become problematised.[11] That realism is a theatrical form which endorses the dominant ideology is contentious in many respects. As Patricia Schroeder has pointed out, critics of realism often neglect its adaptability as a form, and fail to assess their own tendency to assume passivity and complicity on behalf of the spectator.[12] Sheila Stowell has also been critical of anti-realist polemics in her analyses of feminist plays of the Edwardian period, pointing out that in fact 'dramatic forms . . . may be inhabited from within a variety of ideologies'.[13]

Most women writing for the theatres of the 1920s and 1930s did so within the boundaries of realism, the dominant form of the day. Their ideas about the female condition filtered through into their work with a frequent and direct correlation between the authors' choice of subject and theme and their cultural position as women, in a social environment where the women's movement took on a different shape and form from that of the years immediately preceding the First World War. In many ways realism was used by these women playwrights for what Eric Auerbach has identified as a 'serious treatment of everyday reality' – namely *their* reality as women living at a time when the *meaning* of 'woman' itself was constantly being negotiated.[14] Thus the 'woman question' in all its various mutations sustained a centre-stage position for many of the playwrights. One clear example is G. B. Stern, a significant and long-standing friend of the critic and novelist Rebecca West, who, like West, had originally trained as an actress (Scott, *Refiguring Modernism*, p. 225).

Stern's hit play *The Matriarch*,[15] based on her popular novel *The Tents of Izrael* (1924) and produced in 1929, was attended by such literary figures as Virginia Woolf. *The Matriarch* foregrounds questions of heredity, matrilinearity, femininity, gender, economic power, and the division of labour – thus keying into popular debate around women's social roles as well as making clear positive statements about the cultural validity of the female line. Stern's less successful but in many ways far more searching play, *The Man Who Pays The Piper*, first performed in London in 1931 with a cast which included Diana Wynyard and the young Jessica Tandy, is a serious attempt to analyse the relationship between gender and socio-economic power.[16] Daryll, the heroine, is friend to a suffragette who, her father thinks, has filled her up 'with all this fudge about votes for women – Suffragette processions and I don't know what' (Prologue, p. 9). Daryll, later juxtaposed with her less responsible 'flapper' sister, takes over the running of the family when the father and eldest brother are killed in the First World War. Her femininity is questioned by the male members of the family for whom she is a 'bit too lordly at times', although they admit that she's 'certainly got the best head of the family' (Act 1, p. 41). Daryll heads the family, refusing to marry her long-time fiancé because she is already a 'father' and, even though, as she herself observes, 'all the men come to me as man to man and thank me rather resentfully for what I've done', she sees her role as duty bound (Act 2, pp. 60–5). When her mother remarries Daryll agrees to give up her work, marry her fiancé and become 'feminine'. Of course after a few years, however, she is desperately bored and wants her old independent 'meaningful' life back: she wants to help her former suffragette friend whose business is faltering without her own business acumen. At the same time, Daryll sees how historical circumstances colour both her position and her ambitions: 'I'm no good for marriage . . . it's the war, we had to take over then . . . I expect there's a whole generation of us . . . we *fathers* of nineteen fourteen . . . we're all freaks my generation of girls' (Act 3, pp. 97–9). Her husband, a 1930s version of what we might call a 'new man', offers to become a house-husband – an offer she refuses. Finally they reach a compromise and Daryll leaves to save her old friend's fashion business.

For Bonnie Kime Scott it was Stern's depiction of relationships which received Rebecca West's 'particular admiration' (*Refiguring Modernism*, pp. 225–7). Certainly the levels of emotional and intellectual interaction between Stern's characters in this play are of the highest calibre. Her differentiation between the aspirations and needs of three close generations of women in terms of their attitudes to work and their social ambition is fascinating as is the implication that the rule of the patriarch is reliant on the fact that it is he who holds the *economic* power, that gender itself has a mutable social function.

Stern's sense that the First World War created a 'freak' generation of women connects with the notion of both a 'lost generation' and at the same time a new generation. The image of a generation of men lost through war is combined with the image of a new generation of women for whom work and career become either a necessity or simply a burning desire. After the First World War, work was seen by many young women as an alternative to the drudgery of married life and motherhood, some form of escape from traditionally prescribed roles for women. Some of the women playwrights of the era took this on board, although a few, like Aimée Stuart, who wrote a number of West End hits with her husband and continued to write successful plays after his death, saw questions of women, work, and career as cultural rather than emotional issues. Produced in 1930, *Nine Till Six*, about the various lives of women working in a fashion business, carefully integrates women from all classes questioning the relationship between class, gender, work, and power.[17] For one critic the historical significance of the play was obvious from first viewing:

> No play in modern times has presented so searching and fair-minded an analysis of women's place in the world of industry. There are those who say that this is a women's counterpart of *Journey's End*; its field of battle is the business world; its privations are the ruthless denials of ease and beauty; its sex problems, as incidental.[18]

Much of the talk between the shop girls is based on discussions of work conditions, pay, and prospects. Equally, the problems and dilemmas of the shop owner are discussed. *Nine Till Six* is clearly a play about a *woman*'s world of work, which places questions about women's working methods, class interaction, and women's relationship to the economy in the public arena.

Cultural shift: social change and the 'woman question'

The 1920s and 1930s represent an enormous social and cultural shift in British history. The old class system, although not completely collapsed, had been seriously undermined by the First World War. Death crossed all class barriers and traditional sexual divisions of labour were challenged as women moved *en masse* into the labour force during the war. Although many of these women were forced to return into domestic work after the war, middle-class women found themselves able to move into areas of work traditionally given over to men.[19] This caused much concern in the popular press, in particular during the late 1920s and early 1930s when women were thought to be taking 'men's work' at a time of economic depression. The many laws which were supposedly passed in favour of women were often formulated through bias grounded in an assumption of either women's 'natural' inferiority, or their irrationality or passivity. Thus the Sex Disqualification (Removal) Act of 1919 which stated that 'a person should not be disqualified by sex or marriage from . . . entering or assuming or carrying any civil profession or vocation' was no *guarantee* of employment for women.[20] In fact it was often used as a law to keep women out of the job market. The Marriage Bars, which meant that women, once married, were easily removed from employment, were regularly enforced until well after the Second World War. By 1935 married women were given the right to obtain, dispose of, and hold property as chosen, but it was not until well into the 1940s that matrimonial property rights were equalised, and, as was often the case, the benefit to middle- and upper-class women was often greater than that to working-class women. The Divorce Laws, which had gradually been changing since the late 1900s, were 'liberalised' by the late 1930s. Although the divorce rate rose continuously from an average of 832 in 1910–12 to 4,249 in 1930–2,[21] steadily rising as the law became more equal in its treatment of the sexes, divorced and unmarried women were often perceived as having somehow failed in their 'proper' duty as women.

Social and legal changes of the period are not necessarily overtly discoursed in plays by women but they often inform the general dramatic landscape. Thus, in Fryn Tennyson-Jesse's *The Pelican*, an adaptation of the famous Russell Baby Case of 1921 written with her husband Harold Harwood,[22] the question of marital separation is given a highlighted narrative position within a play about the transformation of a woman's life: society is seen through the eyes of the ex-wife, the rejected woman. Clemence Dane's *Bill of Divorcement* uses changes in the divorce laws as a narrative hook on which to hang debate on issues of generational differences in perceived levels of social and moral responsibility.[23] The play's heroine Sydney Fairfield, a feisty, intelligent, and independent young woman, encourages her mother to continue with her plans to remarry when the father returns from the insane asylum where he has been incarcerated since coming back from the First World War. Believing that her father is suffering from a congenital form of madness, Sydney rejects her lover in favour of looking after her own father. Her sense of moral responsibility is framed by a belief in eugenicist philosophy – at the beginning of the play she is very much the flapper girl, out dancing till three in the morning with no desire to work, rather she would like to marry and settle. Her mother is shocked that she should know so much about having children but, as Sydney says of her fiancé: 'Oh Kit's as keen as I am on eugenics. He's doing a paper for his debating society' (Act 1, p. 142). By the end of the play, fearful that she will have inherited her father's 'illness', she chooses career over marriage and childbearing. As with *The Pelican*, *Bill of Divorcement* has a somewhat traditional ending in that each of the heroines is haunted by the image of the 'Angel in the House' – a self-sacrificing, martyred middle-class woman. In the first play, however, the heroine sees her choice as a maternal duty (she gives up her own relationship to remarry her ex-husband as a way of legitimising her son), and, in the second, Sydney sees hers as primarily a duty to her nation – interestingly Dane here subverts the popular image of the flapper as irresponsible and selfish. Billie Melman gives an excellent account of the history of the word 'flapper' which moves from a euphemism for young prostitute to a term used to denote a young, independent, self-absorbed, and unattached woman. Such nomenclature became an inherent part of the popular press's scare-mongering about an impending 'petticoat government' after the initial franchise was granted to women in 1918.[24]

The question of social and moral responsibility is frequently foregrounded in plays by women in the 1920s and 1930s, which at times creates reactionary heroines who appear to care nothing for their own gender. Then again, heroines who seem overwhelmingly concerned with womankind often turn out to be more reactionary than it is possible to imagine. The most glaring example of this is in Marie Stopes's extraordinary play, *Our Ostriches,* where the young heroine Evadne Carillon, who belongs to the ruling classes, goes, as she puts it to her future husband Lord Simplex, 'slumming it' whilst visiting an old family servant.[25] During her visit she discovers to her horror that, as they have no access to methods of contraception, women already living below the poverty line are bearing one child after another, ruining their health and often producing still-born babies or children who are unhealthy. Her concern is very genuine in that she tries to expose the moral hypocrisy of the doctors and religious 'do-gooders' who proclaim to be helping these working-class women. During her discussions with the Health Commission, she even suggests sterilising women who have learning disabilities. Yet in her own words, 'woman must help woman – those poor women – . . . my heart is full of grief for poor women' (Act III, pp. 69–85). Stopes's play seems to the modern eye so bizarre in its moral logic that this totally undermines the fact that in its day it would have been shocking not for its lack of egalitarian politics, but for the fact that it foregrounds issues of birth control and, effectively, sex. For Stopes, birth control signified creating certain freedoms for women as well as providing a form of genetic engineering. It should be pointed out that the Eugenics Movement, founded on the notion that in order to prosper a nation must produce healthy babies of so-called 'good' stock, was initially applauded by *both* extremes of the political spectrum. Integral to the Eugenics Movement was a desire for population control, more than environmental improvement.[26] It is ultimately this desire for population control, as opposed to any real desire to improve life for the poor, which concerns the heroine of Stopes's play.

Cultural imperatives: for the good of the nation

Just as the promotion of votes for women was presented by the suffrage playwrights as ultimately beneficial to the whole of society, so too, in many of the plays by women during the interwar period, were gender-specific issues allied to an overriding concern with nationhood. This becomes stronger as the period progresses, but we can trace the integration of gender and nationalistic discourse back to Edwardian plays by women.

The playwriting of Gertrude Jennings, for example, reaches back to the Edwardian feminist theatre (her play *A Woman's Influence* was very popular with the AFL). Jennings saw domestic comedy as a way of looking at women's cultural and social positioning. Although historically positioned as writing predominantly for the amateur market, Jennings later achieved success in the West End with plays like *The Young Person in Pink* (1920), *Family Affairs* (1934), and *Our Own Lives* (1935). She foregrounded domestic issues and women's lives and always had an eye on current trends of thought, as evidenced, for example, in *Husbands For All* (1920), a farce in which the government decrees that, due to shortages of marriageable men, all men under forty must have two wives by 1925.

Originally directed by Auriol Lee and starring Lilian Braithwaite, *Family Affairs*[27] was one of her most successful West End plays. Here generational and gender differences are used as a way of looking at the family and its cultural significance. The official head of the family, Lady Madehurst, is fierce and determined, but she is also tolerant and forgiving, thus enabling the family to be adaptable. Again, as with many of Jennings's plays, the women are presented as more responsible, wiser, and stronger than the men who are often pompous or frivolous – in *Family Affairs* the mother risks breaking the law to protect the family, her charge. Although Jennings's comic angle on the family has to be acknowledged, she does present the family as women's power base – somewhere from which they can contribute to the well-being of the nation.

In 1926 Clemence Dane wrote of her great disappointment over those women who, having been given the vote, did not use it.[28] For Dane these women were evading the responsibilities of citizenship. She pointed out that: 'if they will not take their share of national housekeeping they run the risk of having their private housekeeping threatened by forces – laws, wars, strikes and revolutions – outside their control'.[29] Dane's concern that women should take social and moral responsibility was shared by many, and this is reflected in the issues discussed on the 'women's pages' in the national press during the 1920s. The fear of a 'petticoat government', however, meant that articles which suggested that women might be becoming politically powerful were juxtaposed in the popular press with articles on childrearing, home management, what to do without a servant, and so on. The interwar years represent a period in history where the whole experience of womanhood was changing. For Carl Jung, woman was clearly 'in the same process of transition as man . . . faced with a tremendous cultural task'.[30] Some of the women playwrights of the 1920s and 1930s took this 'cultural task' on board even though, just as there never was a 'petticoat government', they had no real power in what was a theatre system in transition but largely owned and run by men.

The overriding atmosphere in the commercial and mainstream theatre during the 1920s and 1930s was one of conservatism. Theatres had been largely taken over by investment managements during the First World War, and although women playwrights did relatively well under this system, Richard Findlater's observation in *The Unholy Trade*, that theatre was for most 'a holiday treat', implies that the theatre was largely middle-class.[31] Equally, middle-class women felt a renewed sense of social and moral responsibility in all its peculiarities, and a renewed sense of duty to the nation. It was this sense of national duty which was accentuated in many of the popular plays by women of the day, often through female characters whose desire to work was inspired by a need to 'serve the nation' outside, as well as inside, the home. The ways in which women's desire to work and still be considered as feminine were framed as culturally specific and historically significant have already been discussed. By the late 1930s the working woman as a dramatic character is no longer singled out for investigation in such a specific way. In Dodie Smith's *Dear Octopus* (1938)[32] working women are simply an expected part of the family set-up though still not always approved of. The play provides an extremely idealised picture of upper-middle-class family life and of Englishness, and as such contains innate statements about the necessity of the family unit and its indestructibility. The 'dear octopus' of the title symbolises the family, a treasured and feared institution which is, 'like nearly every British institution, adaptable' (Act III, pp. 378–9) – this at a time when the nation approached the Second World War, having not yet recovered from the First World War which tore its families apart so proficiently. The family, still viewed as the domain of women, is 'that dear octopus from whose tentacles we never quite escape' and signifies the nation and national well-being itself (pp. 378–9). Many women playwrights of the 1920s and 1930s, through an investigation of gender and power relationships within the family, locate the private sphere as having great *public* significance. If this meant writing for a particularly female market it also meant writing for an audience who had a renewed sense of their own social and cultural potential as contributors to the greater good of the nation. For Alison Light, 'something happened to middle-class femininity after the Great War which sees it taking on what had formerly been regarded as distinctly masculine qualities'. It is these qualities which are reflected in the seeming conservatism of much women's playwriting of the era suggesting a feeling of 'a new level of State recognition and of national inclusion' (*Forever England*, pp. 210–11).

Thus this 'lost generation' of women playwrights were often as concerned with the 'woman question' in its many different guises as their more radical forebears, even though they mostly worked within a commercial and conservative theatre system using popular as opposed to the more experimental forms of their day. Similarly, there are strong echoes of their concerns in much of the work of women playwrights of our own time.

For Rebecca West, to be a feminist was to express sentiments that differentiated a woman 'from a doormat or prostitute'.[33] Such plainly stated and trans-historically pluralistic notions of feminisms make it possible to see feminist concerns reflected in the majority of plays written by women during the inter-war years. Woman as a signifier is frequently problematised as is the experience of being a woman: questions of whether a woman should work or be financially dependent on her spouse, whether she should expect equal education and pay, or the same legal rights as men and so on, abound. The issues raised by the so-called 'woman question' are remarkably similar to those which face women today, and woman's role within society was consistently a point of public and private debate – it is the elements of this debate which dominate plays by women of the period.

FIRST PRODUCTIONS OF MAJOR PLAYS

Venues are in London's West End unless stated

Clemence Dane

Bill of Divorcement, St Martin's Theatre (1921)
Granite, The Ambassadors Theatre (1926)
Wild Decembers, The Apollo Theatre (1933)

Gertrude Jennings

Husbands For All, The Little Theatre (1920)
Family Affairs, The Ambassadors Theatre (1934)
Our Own Lives, The Ambassadors Theatre (1935)

Dodie Smith

Autumn Crocus, The Lyric Theatre (1931)
Service, Wyndham's Theatre (1932)
Call it A Day, The Globe Theatre (1935)
Dear Octopus, The Queen's Theatre (1938)

G. B. Stern

The Matriarch, The Royalty Theatre (1929)
The Man Who Pays The Piper, St. Martin's Theatre (1931)

Aimée and Phillip Stuart

Her Shop, The Criterion Theatre (1929)
Nine Till Six, The Arts Theatre (1930)
Sixteen, The Criterion Theatre (1934)

Fryn Tennyson-Jesse and Harold Harwood

Billeted, The Royalty Theatre (1918)
The Pelican, The Ambassadors Theatre (1924)
How To Be Healthy Though Married, Strand (1930)

NOTES

1 L. Hudson, *The Twentieth Century Drama* (London: Harrap and Co. Ltd, 1946), p. 59.

2 *Era*, 11 December 1935.

3 Alison Light, *Forever England: Femininity, Literature and Conservatism Between the Wars* (London: Routledge, 1991), p. 13.

4 See also Viv Gardner, *Sketches From The Actresses Franchise League* (Nottingham: Nottingham Drama Texts, 1985); Claire Hirschfield, 'The Actresses Franchise League and The Campaign for Women's Suffrage', in *Theatre Research International*, 10:2, 1985, pp. 129–53; and Julie Holledge, *Innocent Flowers* (London: Virago, 1981).

5 Winifred Holtby, *Women in A Changing Civilisation* (London: Lane and The Bodley Head, 1945), p. 96.

6 Ellen Donkin, *Getting into the Act* (London: Routledge, 1995), p. 188. For full details of interwar production runs, see Maggie B. Gale, *West End Women: Women and the London stage 1918–1962* (London: Routledge, 1996), p. 12.

7 John Carey, *The Intellectuals and the Masses* (London: Faber and Faber, 1992), p. 87.

8 Bonnie Kime Scott, *Refiguring Modernism,* vol. I: *The Women of 1928* (Bloomington, Indiana: Indiana University Press, 1995), p. 232.

9 Loren Kruger, 'The Dis-Play's the Thing: Gender and Public Sphere in Contemporary British Theatre', in *Theatre Journal,* 42, 1990, pp. 27–47, pp. 28–9.

10 Tracy C. Davis, 'Questions for A Feminist Methodology in Theatre History', in Thomas Postlewait and Bruce McConachie (eds.) *Interpreting the Theatrical Past* (Iowa City: University of Iowa Press, 1989), pp. 55–81, pp. 66–9.

11 Sue-Ellen Case, *Feminism and Theatre* (London: Macmillan, 1988), p. 124.

12 Patricia R. Schroeder, *Feminist Possibilities of Realism* (London: Associated University Presses, 1996), pp. 27–8.

13 Sheila Stowell, *A Stage of Their Own: Feminist Playwrights of the Suffrage Era* (Manchester: Manchester University Press, 1992), pp. 100–1.

14 Eric Auerbach, *Mimesis: The Representation of Reality in Western Literature* (Princeton: Princeton University Press, 1953), p. 491.

15 G. B. Stern, *The Matriarch* (London: Samuel French, 1931).

16 G. B. Stern, *The Man Who Pays The Piper* (London: Samuel French, 1931).

17 Aimée and Philip Stuart, *Nine Till Six* (London: French, 1930).

18 Letter from Constance Smedley to the editor of *The Times*, 2 March 1930.

19 Deirdre Beddoe, *Back to Home And Duty: Women Between the Wars, 1918–1939* (London: Pandora Press, 1989), p. 51.

20 Jane Lewis, *Women in England 1870–1950* (Brighton: Wheatsheaf Books, 1984), p. 199.

21 C. L. Mowat, *Britain Between the Wars* (London: Methuen, 1984), pp. 213–16.

22 J. Colenbrander, *A Portrait of Fryn: A Biography of Fryn Tennyson-Jesse* (London: Deutsch Ltd, 1984), p. 139.

23 Clemence Dane, *Bill of Divorcement* in *The Collected Plays of Clemence Dane* (London: Heinemann, 1961).

24 Billie Melman, *Women and The Popular Imagination in the Twenties: Flappers and Nymphs* (London: Macmillan, 1988), pp. 15–37.

25 Marie Stopes, *Our Ostriches* (London: Putnam, 1923).

26 Jeffrey Weeks and Sheila Rowbotham, *Socialism and The New Life* (London: Pluto Press, 1977), pp. 170–9.

27 Gertrude Jennings, *Family Affairs* in *Famous Plays of 1934* (London: Gollancz, 1934).
28 Melman has pointed out that when the vote was given to men over twenty-one and to qualifying women over thirty in 1918, 5.5 million females remained without the vote until 1928 (*Women and the Popular Imagination*, p. 1).
29 Clemence Dane, *The Women's Side* (London: Herbert Jenkins, 1926), p. 9.
30 C. G. Jung, *Aspects of the Feminine* (London: Ark, 1989), pp. 57–75.
31 Richard Findlater, *The Unholy Trade* (London: Victor Gollancz, 1952), p. 194.
32 Published in *Plays of the Thirties,* vol. 1 (London: Pan Books Ltd, 1966).
33 Jane Marcus (ed.) *The Young Rebecca: Writings of Rebecca West 1911–1917* (London: Virago, 1983), p. 219.

FURTHER READING

Primary sources: plays

Dane, Clemence. *The Collected Plays of Clemence Dane*. London: Heinemann, 1961.
  Recapture: A Clemence Dane Omnibus. London: Heinemann, 1961.
Jennings, Gertrude. *Love Among The Paintpots*. London: French, 1922.
  These Pretty Things. London: French, 1930.
  Family Affairs. In *Famous Plays of 1934*. London: Gollancz, 1934.
  A Woman's Influence. In Dale Spender and Carole Hayman (eds.) *How The Vote Was Won*. London: Methuen, 1985: 125–39.
Smith, Dodie ('C. L. Anthony'). *Service*. In *Famous Plays of 1932–1933*. London: Victor Gollancz, 1933.
  Call it a Day. In *Famous Plays of 1935–1936*. London: Gollancz Ltd, 1936.
  Dear Octopus. In *Plays of the Thirties*, vol. I. London: Pan Books Ltd, 1966.
  Autumn Crocus. In *Plays of the Thirties,* vol. II. London: Pan Books Ltd, 1967.
Stern, G. B. *The Man Who Pays The Piper*. London: Samuel French, 1931.
  The Matriarch. London: Samuel French, 1931.
Stopes, Marie. *Our Ostriches*. London: Putnam, 1923.
  A Banned Play (Vectia) and A Preface on Censorship. London: Bale, Sons and Daniellson Ltd, 1926.
Stuart, Aimée. *Jeannie*. London: Hamilton, 1940.
  Lace on Her Petticoat. London: French, 1951.
Stuart, Aimée, and Phillip Stuart. *Sixteen*. In *Famous Plays of 1933–1934*. London: Gollancz, 1934.
Tennyson-Jesse, Fryn, and Harold Harwood. *The Pelican*. London: Benn, 1926.
  How To Be Healthy Though Married. London: Heinemann, 1930.

Secondary sources

Alexander, Sally. 'Becoming a Woman in London in the 1920s and 1930s'. In David Feldman and Gareth Stedman Jones (eds.) *Metropolis London: Histories and Representations Since 1800*. London: Routledge, 1989: 245–71.
Beauman, Nicola. *A Very Great Profession: The Woman's Novel 1914–1939*. London: Virago, 1983.
Boyd, Alice K. *The Interchange of Plays Between London and New York, 1910–1939: A Study in Audience Response*. New York: Kings Crown Press, Columbia University, 1948.

Chothia, Jean. *English Drama of the Early Modern Period 1890–1940*. London: Longman, 1996.

Dane, Clemence. *Approaches to Drama*. London: Oxford University Press, 1961.

Davis, Andrew. *Other Theatres*. London: Macmillan, 1987.

Findlater, Richard. *The Unholy Trade*. London: Victor Gollancz, 1952.

Gardner, Viv. 'The Case for the Women Buccaneers: A Defence of Feminist Realism in G. B. Stern's *The Matriarch*'. In Maggie B. Gale and Viv Gardner (eds.) *Women and Theatre Occasional Papers 4*. Birmingham: University of Birmingham, 1997: 68–87.

Grove, Valerie. *Dear Dodie: The Life of Dodie Smith*. London: Chatto and Windus, 1996.

Marshall, Norman. *The Other Theatre*. London: John Lehman, 1948.

Morgan, Fidelis (ed.) *The Years Between: Plays by Women on the London Stage 1900–1950*. London: Virago, 1994.

Rose, June. *Marie Stopes and The Sexual Revolution*. London: Faber and Faber, 1993.

Sandison, G. *Theatre Ownership in Britain*. London: The Federation of Theatre Unions, 1953.

Smith, Dodie ('C. L. Anthony'). *Look Back With Mixed Feelings*. London: Allen, 1978. *Look Back With Astonishment*. London: Allen, 1979.

Smithers, David. *Therefore Imagine: The Works of Clemence Dane*. Tonbridge: The Dragonfly Press, 1988.

Spender, Dale. *There's Always Been a Women's Movement This Century*. London: Pandora Press, 1984.

Trewin, J. C. *The Gay Twenties*. London: MacDonald, 1958. *The Turbulent Thirties*. London: MacDonald, 1960.

Wandor, Michelene. *Understudies: Theatre and Sexual Politics*. London: Methuen, 1981.

Woolf, Virginia. 'Professions for Women'. In Michele Barrett (ed.) *Virginia Woolf: Women and Writing*. London: The Women's Press, 1979: 57–64.

3

SUSAN BENNETT

New plays and women's voices in the 1950s

The emergence of angry young theatre

In the ten years that followed the end of the Second World War, Britain instituted a wide range of social programmes commensurate with a general pattern of economic growth and development. The decade of the 1950s brought several key events: the return of a Conservative government in 1951, the coronation in 1953 of Queen Elizabeth II (described inevitably as the dawning of a new Elizabethan Age) and, in 1956, military crisis at the Suez Canal. In brief, these key events indicate some of the important characteristics of British social life at this historical moment in that this was a time of more or less general social and ideological stability (captured in adoration of the new Queen and her own young family), undercut by specific tensions brought about by external factors (such as the dismantling of the British empire, especially when it was forced through events such as Suez) and internal factors (a new wealth and mobility for a generation of young people who had been the first beneficiaries of the 1944 Education Act offering secondary education for all). It is against this social backdrop that the theatre of the decade must be read.

Histories of twentieth-century British drama have generally pointed to 1956 as the watershed year in theatrical production after the Second World War. The reason for 1956 receiving such especial attention, of course, is the première of John Osborne's *Look Back in Anger* on 8 May. The play centres on Jimmy Porter, a twenty-something lower-middle-class man, and his life with Alison, his wife, whose parents are decidedly upper-middle-class. For much of the play, Jimmy rails against everything – the classes above his own, women, culture. In this, he was seen as symptomatic of his generation in British social life. In Jimmy Porter's disaffection lies both frustration and rage brought about by the changing social conditions in England as well as a nostalgia for Britain's imperial might; in short, what Jimmy is upset about is the diminution of British male privilege through the political and cultural shifts in the post-war period. Most important was the fact that Jimmy Porter was young, at the crest of a new wave of attention given to the youth generation and the prospects they would (or would not) have in the economy of post-war Britain. This was, as drama critic Kenneth Tynan then championed and as subsequent theatre history has told us, the era of the angry young men. As John Russell Taylor put it in the introduction to his critical work *Anger and After* (first published in 1962): 'The whole picture of writing in this country has undergone a transformation in the last six years or so, and the event which marks "then" off decisively from "now" is the first performance of *Look Back in Anger* on 8 May 1956.'[1] He continues:

> For *Look Back in Anger* had a succès d'estime, a succès de scandale, and finally just a succès. It was constantly revived at the Royal Court, went on tour, was staged all over the world, made into a film, and in the end even turned up in a novelised version as the book of the film of the play. It was not just another play by another young writer, staged in a fit of enterprise by a provincial rep and then forgotten; it was something much more, something suspiciously like big business, and for the first time the idea got around that there might be money in young dramatists and young drama. *(Anger and After*, p. 9)

Look Back in Anger, then, might be seen as responding to a market shift, where there had been an exponential increase in the discretionary spending available for the under-30s. The reasons for the play's success, then, were as much economic as they were artistic.

It is nevertheless useful, however, to look at how the play realises the social anger that had suddenly found this commercial viability. As Stephen Lacey powerfully illustrates in his important reassessment *British Realist Theatre*, class resentment in *Look Back in Anger* is 'inseparable from an antagonism towards, and fear of, women . . . It is notable that one of the most oft-quoted remarks from the play, that "There aren't any good, brave causes left", comes in the middle of a long and vituperative attack on women.'[2] Lacey also notes, '[t]hat the Angry Young Men were men was self-evident, and worthy of considerably less critical attention than the fact that they were "angry" and "young"' (p. 30). More recently, Dan Rebellato has extended the revisionist critical context for *Look Back in Anger* with his important reassessment of '1956 and all that' (the book's title).[3] This chapter turns attention to women playwrights at this historical juncture and the venues and forms that they found to express their own responses to the British theatre (and, more generally, social) scene. In other words, I ask whether women playwrights were angry and, if so, were they angry like their contemporaries, the young men?

Cherchez Les Femmes: plays by Jellicoe and Delaney

First of all, it must be recorded that among the many artists working in theatre and other media who became clustered, deservingly or otherwise, under the rubric of the 'angry' were just a very few women. At the Royal Court Theatre (which had first produced *Look Back in Anger*), Ann Jellicoe's *The Sport of My*

Mad Mother ran for fourteen performances in February and March 1958. Jellicoe had come to the Royal Court's attention through a playwriting contest held by the *Observer* newspaper in that watershed year of 1956, where she had shared third prize with N. F. Simpson. *The Sport of My Mad Mother*, as Maggie Gale succinctly puts it, adopts a '"primitive" context' and an 'experimental form'[4] – unlike Osborne's retention of so many elements of the well-made play, Jellicoe's drama is much more innovative in terms of both dramatic structure and language. The play brings together violence and birth in scenes that rely as much on movement and style as they do on the emotions (indeed often angry) expressed by the central character Greta.

Jellicoe's attempts to institute new forms and patterns for her theatrical work can be well understood in terms of her own impatience at the characteristic performance of 'Angry Young Men'. In an interview, she states:

> You see, so many plays tell you what is happening the whole time. People don't act angry; they tell you they're angry. Now, my play is about incoherent people – people who have no power of expression, of analyzing their emotions. They don't know why they're afraid; they don't even know that they are afraid. So they have to compensate for their fear by attacking someone else; they're insecure and frustrated, and they have to compensate for that by being big, and violent. And all this is directly shown, instead of being explained.
>
> (cited in John Russell Taylor, *Anger and After*, p. 76)

It is telling, however, that Jellicoe's play has received very little attention from critics and historians. A few comment on *The Sport of My Mad Mother* as indebted to Melanie Klein's psychoanalytic readings of motherhood; others describe its balletic qualities. Judith Thompson's sensitive reading of the play focuses on embodiment, or non-verbal performance.[5] Most, however, ignore the play altogether and only cite Jellicoe in passing to indicate that the Royal Court Theatre did produce at least one woman during the reign of the 'angry'. (The statistics for the Royal Court Theatre are, as Lib Taylor records, rather depressing: 'between 1956 and 1968, out of over two hundred productions, only fifteen were plays written by women, six of which were single Sunday performances.')[6] Now, more than forty years later, it is possible to see Jellicoe – far more than Osborne – as rewriting the terms and conditions of British theatre practice through her attempts to match form to the social and psychic lives of her characters. Beyond this, *The Sport of My Mad Mother* is striking as a text which anticipates some of the impulses and directions of later (and especially French) feminist theory.

In fact, the only woman from the late 1950s explosion in new British drama who has received serious and extended critical attention is Shelagh Delaney for one of her plays, *A Taste of Honey*. Performed at the Theatre Royal in Stratford East (where Joan Littlewood had established a tradition of innovative stagecraft and socially conscious drama), her drama ran from May 1958 for some 27 performances. In January of the following year, A Taste of Honey transferred to the West End for another 368 performances. Such a success John Elsom conveys as 'a startling enough achievement from a nineteen-year-old girl from Salford'[7] – his praise is notably focused on the writer and her sex rather than the play itself. As well as this economic success, Delaney's play has also attracted significant interest from theatre critics and historians and, as Lib Taylor points out, it 'is often cited as an early example of a feminist text, and could be called feminine/reflectionist in its conscious focus upon women characters and the female condition' ('Early Stages', p. 19). In A Taste of Honey, a young working-class woman from the North of England, Jo, who has been in a sexual relationship with a black sailor and is pregnant, clashes with her mother and makes a new 'family' for herself and her impending child with her best friend, a gay man named Geof.

Sue-Ellen Case offers a persuasive description of A Taste of Honey as concerned with 'the moral and legal problems around the legitimate or illegitimate status of the child of a single mother, issues of domestic and child-care labour, the possibility of abortion, and the role or threat of homosexuality to the family unit'.[8] While this list of social concerns is impressive for any play of this period, Case is right in observing that the play 'doesn't really stage any critique of them or resolve them in any way. The nexus of social/sexual problems for women is there in the proto-posing of the assertion that "the personal is political"' ('The Power of Sex', p. 238). Lacey, on the other hand, draws attention to A Taste of Honey as one of the social-realist plays that was actually set in the North of England, a setting he argues connotes '"working class-ness" in a very direct way, helping to define a particular social and cultural landscape and to fix a pervasive stereotype, implying an authenticity of experience and attitude that could be contrasted with the narrow, shallow concerns of the South' (British Realist Theatre, p. 78). The point that I want to make with these brief accounts of the better-known women's plays from the 1950s is that both Jellicoe's and Delaney's plays push the boundaries of social-realism far further than Osborne's Look Back in Anger; both, however, as far as the (theatre) histories go, stand rather in the shadow of Jimmy Porter's legendary presence.

The forgotten success of Enid Bagnold

Simply, then, participation by women playwrights in the advent and success of the category of angry youth was limited. Moreover, with the exception of Delaney, their work has been under-represented in accounts of the new directions in British playwriting during the 1950s. This fact – the paucity of attention given to British women playwrights of the decade – is all the more disturbing when the emergence of the Angry Young Men is contextualised by its contemporary productions in mainstream London theatre. As Lib Taylor indicates, '[i]n 1956, the year that *Look Back in Anger* took the theatrical community by storm, a new play, *The Chalk Garden*, proved to be the most commercially successful play in London' ('Early Stages', p. 9). Its author was Enid Bagnold. Elsom describes *The Chalk Garden* as 'the high point in a West End season dominated (as before) by middle-brow, middle-class, middle-aged tastes' (*Post-War British Theatre*, p. 75), a description which points to the significance of age in the success of *Look Back in Anger* (in itself, ultimately, a middle-brow, middle-class look at the world). *The Chalk Garden*, nonetheless, appealed to a wide audience in 1956 – its plot turns on a series of secrets, more or less one for every character who appears in the house of the widowed, elderly Mrs St Maugham, descendant of a Governor of Madras. Within the demands of the well-made play, Bagnold produces a melo-dramatic comedy with a cluster of fascinatingly odd characters. The play's fine craftsmanship is admiringly conveyed in Michael Coveney's review of a 1992 revival: 'It is a mordant, beautifully written and rather subversive treatment of the stock Loamshire comedy of sunny mornings and French windows, every alternate well-honed line a morbid crack or funereal jest.'[9]

Since my objective in this chapter is to draw attention to the omissions of tra-ditional theatre history in regard to women's playwriting in the 1950s, it is useful to dwell briefly on the revival of interest in *The Chalk Garden* in the 1990s. If Jellicoe and Delaney have seen only passing attention to their plays, Bagnold has seen even less. To write about the British theatre of the 1950s has been, unfail-ingly, to write about *Look Back in Anger*. Yet it would appear, at least from the recent reviews of *The Chalk Garden*, that this imbalance is not only inappropri-ate, but undeserved. Charles Spencer writes of Bagnold's play:

> *The Chalk Garden* is an exotic bloom from the 1950s which miraculously retains its freshness more than 35 years after its première.
>
> When it opened . . . in 1956 Kenneth Tynan hailed it as perhaps 'the finest arti-ficial comedy to have flowed from an English (as opposed to an Irish) pen since the death of Congreve'.
>
> But less than a month later, John Osborne's *Look Back in Anger* arrived at the Royal Court, and elegant, well-made drawing-room plays like this were supposedly consigned to the dustbin of theatrical history. Yet it is Osborne's drama which now seems strident, sentimental and old-fashioned.[10]

Thus, it is important to remember that the group of plays (along with books and films) that were collected under the umbrella term of works by angry young men (along with one or two angry young women like Jellicoe and Delaney) were, in the ways they were critically received, exceptional. Yet in the more than forty years that have passed since this particular historical moment, the 'angry' have come to stand in for theatre history in Britain in the 1950s even though almost all of these plays had far fewer performances than any mainstream West End 'success'. This is, then, misleading to say the least and Rebellato has persuasively claimed 'that the Royal Court should not be simply opposed to the West End, that the criticisms of the West End were misplaced, and that the Court's success was not out of the blue, but was shaped by wider forces organizing the cultural life of the nation' (*1956 and All That*, p. 38.) This series of practices I want to argue, has had particular effects for our understanding of women playwrights' contribution to modern British theatre (it is they, in effect, who have suffered the fate of being 'consigned to the dustbin of theatrical history' as Spencer so charmingly puts it!). Rather than see women as exceptional and rather isolated contributors to the theatre (Delaney as typically 'Northern'; Jellicoe as a second-ranking angry), a more accurate account would show that there were many women with successful careers as playwrights, writing for all kinds of British theatres and, indeed, producing plays that were, like Bagnold's *The Chalk Garden*, the box-office hits of their season. Maggie Gale's important book *West End Women* has charted crucial territory here and lists forty-two plays by women appearing on the London stage between 1955 and 1958. We need to consider, then, why only *A Taste of Honey* generally merits more than a couple of lines of discussion in our theatre texts – even those dedicated to women's theatrical production – especially as, since the 1950s, both Delaney's play and Bagnold's *The Chalk Garden* have been revived as many times as Osborne's *Look Back in Anger*. Moreover, it is an oversimplification to see the plays that women wrote for the commercial stage as merely formulaic and, as such, uninteresting. What I propose here, then, is that we look much more seriously at those plays that achieved significant economic success and imagine not only what attracted audiences to see them but what, specifically, these plays might say to and about women.

Differently angry: Lesley Storm's *Roar Like A Dove*

Roar Like A Dove was first performed in 1957 at the Phoenix Theatre in London. Lesley Storm was already a successful playwright in the middle of a professional career which saw productions of her work not just in London but also in New York at key Broadway theatres. (Her first play was produced in 1934; her last in 1970 – an impressively long career by any standards. She also wrote several successful screenplays, one an Oscar-winner.) If *The Chalk Garden* had been the sell-out show of 1956 (658 performances between April of that year and November 1957), then *Roar Like A Dove* was a runaway stellar hit, opening on 26 September 1957 and running till March 1960 for a stunning 1,007 performances in total. This is not to say, however, that reviewers of the period had particularly positive things to say about Storm's play. In fact, it is precisely the kind of popular success that plays such as *Roar Like A Dove* achieved that caused (male) theatre reviewers to champion the cause of the Angry Young Men; the popular taste of London theatregoers was, as it tends still to be, despised by the reviewing community. In this connection, T. C. Worsley (writing in the *New Statesman* in response to Kingsley Amis's assertion that he would rather see a film than a play) argues that the British theatre desperately needs to bring in a new audience:

> If the theatre is to survive, it will survive not by virtue of the old class of patron – far too few of whom can any longer afford the price of a seat. It will survive by catering for, and drawing in, a new audience and making it feel that the theatre is worth paying more for than the cinema, both in money and trouble.[11]

While this *cri de coeur* sounds remarkably similar to claims made for contemporary theatres facing both funding and attendance crises, what is particularly revealing is Worsley's analysis of how this audience might be brought to see a play. Implicit in the 'old class of patron' is not only its antonymical status to 'the new' but also, surely, to 'the young'. Worsley continues:

> Naturally in appealing to this new audience the front of house management is only a small factor (but a not unimportant one). It is up to the managers (under the present system) to be alert to the new audience and its interests and to provide for them. This is by no means an easy thing to do, and I estimate that there is only one management in London at the moment who seems to be even trying to move with the times (just as Mr Osborne is the only playwright who is extending the audience at the moment). It is much easier for managements simply to overlook the new audience and play safe with the old. Take, for instance, Miss Lesley Storm's new comedy at the Phoenix. There are still enough of the older class of playgoers with money to spend to keep this sort of thing running happily and profitably, when it is as good of its kind as this is. But one cannot imagine Mr Amis and the new world he represents discovering the theatre as a new interest in life by being taken to see *Roar Like a Dove*.
>
> (p. 491)

It is tempting to imagine, however, that some of Mr Amis's female relatives might have happily bought tickets for *Roar Like a Dove* and perhaps several times. More seriously, although much of Worsley's polemic speaks for itself (and I have quoted it at length so that it might), it is important to underscore how quickly (within two years) Osborne had come to stand for all that was 'new' in British playwriting, while all the time he had more or less uncritically reproduced the conditions of the well-made play so easily dismissed by articles such as Worsley's. In a way, Worsley knows this; he concludes his review of Storm's play with more faint praise: 'Mind you, pieces like this have an honourable place in a commercial theatre and the old guard have as much right to their pleasures as the new' (p. 491).

The 'old guard' had indeed been making hits of Lesley Storm's plays for some time. Before *Roar Like A Dove*, Storm had, in the 1950s, had modest successes with *The Day's Mischief* and *The Long Echo* as well as, in 1949, the well-regarded *The Black Chiffon* which had run for 416 performances at the

Westminster Theatre before British and American tours. *Black Chiffon* is a fascinating family story which, while retaining all the dramatic conventions of the drawing room, draws interestingly on American ego psychology to explain the unhappiness and behaviours of the lead character Alicia Christie. In a dramatic climax, Alicia chooses to go to prison for shop-lifting (the black chiffon nightdress of the play's title), a crime she might easily be excused given her social status if she were to admit to psychological distress brought on by the triangulated jealousies within her family. Her motivation to refuse this escape route is to protect her son. Fidelis Morgan rightly suggests that in *Black Chiffon* '[t]he story-telling is compellingly handled and the dramatic opportunities are all there for a star turn by the leading lady'.[12] More directly, Gale describes *Black Chiffon* as a play about a 'dysfunctional' family (*West End Women*, p. 138) and, indeed, Storm might be seen as well ahead of her time – even before the 1950s, she is showing the kinds of emotional straitjackets put on women in the institution of 'appropriate' mothering and the entirely dubious and gendered uses, in this connection, of psychology. As the synopsis of the play in the Samuel French acting edition describes it: 'Once the black chiffon has been stolen, you cannot shake loose from the consequences.'[13] The use of a second person here works effectively to suggest how Storm's critiques of family mores and the psychiatric profession work not only on the play's characters but also on the spectators of her playtext. *Black Chiffon* is a drama that uses standard dramatic formulas to make a very disturbing and powerful commentary on women's social roles.

Unlike the melodramatic *Black Chiffon*, Storm's play almost a decade later, *Roar Like A Dove*, is a spirited and nimble comedy. Indeed, *Roar Like A Dove* painstakingly follows the standard trajectory of any well-made play: the explication, the complication, and a genre-appropriate *dénouement*. Unlike the sordid domestic scenes of Osborne's *Look Back in Anger* or Delaney's *A Taste of Honey* (in themselves evoking shock on the part of the old/new London theatre audiences), Storm's play is set in 'the library of Dungavel Castle, in the Western Highlands' moving chronologically through 'the present' from a morning in February to a closing scene at Christmas. The opening stage direction is predictably realist:

> A handsome room, lined – where the set permits – with dull volumes in uniform calf binding mellowed with age and methodically arranged as if they had not been handled for years . . . In the first and second acts and the last scene there are some decorative vases and bowls filled with flowers. In Act III, Scene I there are no flowers in the room.[14]

While the stage direction has much of an Ibsen drama (a heavy-handed symbolic component familiar from *A Doll's House* where Nora's waning interest in wifely and maternal roles is figured by the barren and stripped Xmas tree that opens the play's second act; in *Roar Like A Dove*, Emma's absence is similarly marked by the absence of fresh flowers), Storm is surely also playing into a fond fantasy for the romance of the Scottish Highlands. Whether we are looking at Joanna Baillie's early nineteenth-century tragedy *The Family Legend* or Mel Gibson's Oscar-winning *Braveheart*, what is self-evident is the on-going and irresistible appeal of a tartan drama. What Storm brings to the familiar romantic narrative of Scottish castle life is a lively 29-year-old American wife for Lord Dungavel. Emma, Lady Dungavel, is both young and angry: she has produced six daughters in a nine-year marriage and while her husband is obsessively desperate for a male heir, Emma wants none of it; instead she is determined to take her place in the London social scene and to exploit some of the cultural capital (literally and metaphorically) accruing to her aristocratic title.

As reviewers of the first performances pointed out, Storm's play, while guilty of some mechanical plotting, succeeds through the appeal and strength of its characters. Derek Conrad sums up his review with the declaration 'how pleasant to have at long last a comedy that takes us out of the depressing English drawing room'.[15] This, I think, is crucial to the appeal of Storm's play. What we see on stage is not a world that resembles our own (whether that is the drawing rooms of 'the old class of patron' that Worsley described or the one-room living with Alison at the ironing board in *Look Back in Anger* or the 'comfortless flat' of Jo in *A Taste of Honey*) but one which conjures up the story of a fairy-tale princess, whisked off to the baronial splendours of Prince Charming's stately home; as Emma describes it to her husband's Uncle Edward: 'Do you know it's nine years this month since I stepped aboard the Queen Elizabeth with Robert . . . married two weeks. Heading – this poor fool thought – for a romantic life in a romantic castle' (Act 1, sc. 1, p. 5). Using the familiar territory of the fairy-tale romance, however, Storm works that critical distance in order, precisely, to say something about the condition of women's lives in the 1950s.

What we see in Emma's interaction with the various characters who live at or come to visit Dungavel Castle is her progressive de-romanticisation of precisely that 'romantic life'. Simply put, Emma deconstructs the fairy tale for both herself and her audience. Albeit from the relatively comfortable location of the Castle's library, we are made witness to the social reality of Scottish rural life, including gale force winds that destroy 20–25 years' growth in Dungavel's surrounding forests along with the roof to Edward's house, as well as the endless work with the livestock (calving, foaling, slaughtering and so on). This is, as much as Osborne's one-room flat, an account of contemporary social-realism. In this context, Emma Dungavel demonstrates endless savvy about her situation: it may not be romantic, but she understands the power of history and its social leverage for a woman like herself. When Muriel, her mother, remarks 'You certainly hit the backwoods, didn't you' (Act 1, sc. 2, p. 19), Emma is quick to reply

'Depends how you look at it, mama. We're scheduled as an historical building' (Act I, sc. 2, p. 20). In Emma, Storm creates a strong character who is always self-aware and especially so, as a woman (wife and mother), in what opportunities she can draw from the expectations her husband, as well as British society, have of her. That she has an outsider status as an American serves particularly well to give Storm the opportunity for dismantling received notions of social responsibility. As an American, Emma cannot be expected to buy into Robert's belief system – or, at least, not automatically. From this vantage point, Storm is able to show her audience some of the ridiculous implications of tradition as well as its undoubted attractions.

In order to relieve Emma from the burden of producing more children in the hopes of a son and heir, her father contrives to bring Robert Dungavel's young cousin Bernard to the Castle. If Bernard can be persuaded to commit his life to the estate, then Dungavel Castle will stay in the family and a son would not be 'necessary' in the same way. Storm's critique of patrilineal heritage is wonderfully wrought. Bernard Taggart-Stuart could not be less suited for the life of an aristocratic farmer. He is, as one reviewer put it, 'the young man aesthete who is afraid of cows and shocked profoundly by farmyard obstetrics'.[16] Bernard's campy horror at a world diametrically opposed to the academic one he wants to pursue at Oxford is, indeed, conveyed by his hysterical reaction to Emma:

> Emma, don't you ever feel like going mad amongst this sickening fertility? When you think of those bleak wind-swept acres where nature never intended anything to live – and what goes on – cows having calves – horses having foals – hundreds of shivering little lambs popping out on those freezing hillsides – dogs having pups in the barns – cats having kittens in the lofts – my God, it's a nightmare! It's awful!
>
> (Act II, sc. 1, p. 38)

Bernard professes that, were he to inherit the estate, he would dispose of the livestock: 'Then I'd pull down this house – which you must admit is an anachronism – and build a small bungalow of the sort of Swedish type in its place' (Act II, sc. 1, p. 39). Here, then, Storm takes a stock character – the homosexual relative (and what better sign for non-reproductivity) – to point to the heteronormative assumptions that prescribe Emma's role as Lady Dungavel. Emma doesn't go mad, however, as Bernard suggests she might – far from it. After the second Act closes with a long seduction scene (crafted by Emma's father to bring Robert and Emma back together) and where Robert appears to win his wife back, we find, surprisingly, at the beginning of Act III that Emma has left Robert and taken her children back to America.

Much of Act III consists of reports of Emma's 'success' back in America, made available to Robert through the anonymous sending of newspapers from Boston. Interestingly, Tom (Emma's father) has stayed on at Dungavel while

Muriel (her mother) and Emma and the six daughters have fled. So, like Robert, Tom is an abandoned spouse. What this creates, then, is the weakened and depressed homosocial world of the Castle set in contrast to the energetic and potent public life of the women in the USA. The first scene of Act III has Tom and Edward *'sitting drinking gloomily'* (p. 68). With tears in his eyes, Tom reads from the American newspaper, '"At the reception given last night to the Daughters of the American Revolution at the Ritz-Carlton Hotel, Boston, the guests were received by Lady Emma Dungavel ... Lady Emma wore a white satin gown encrusted with pearls and a magnificent diamond tiara"' (Act III, sc. I, p. 69, ellipses in original). Emma, then, has achieved the social visibility that she so desired and the title she acquired through marriage does function, as she hoped it might, as a passport into the most elevated social circles of major cities.

As befitting a comedy, the women must return and a happily-ever-after ending be instated. Storm does give her audience precisely this typical conclusion but not without some contingencies. To start with, when Muriel and Tom are re-united, Muriel asks of Tom:

> Have you enjoyed your freedom?
> TOM *kneels beside her.*
> TOM: It's been hell, Muriel.
> MURIEL (*casually*): Too bad, I've enjoyed every minute of mine.
>
> (Act III, sc. I, p. 74)

What Storm suggests is that Tom's and Muriel's marriage will continue, but on newly conceived terms where Muriel's 'value' both to Tom and in the world will be mutually recognised. Similarly, with Emma's return to Robert, there is a dramatic shift in circumstances. It transpires that Emma is 'accidentally' pregnant from the seduction at the end of Act II and that she has hidden this until her fifth month when secrecy is no longer possible. When, at the conclusion of the Act's opening scene, she reunites with Robert in the knowledge of this seventh birth ahead, she comments 'It'll certainly be good for my morale to get the VIP treatment you hand out to those pedigree cows of yours' (Act III, sc. I, p. 85), her wit betrays exactly the terms of her marriage as well as her strengthened under-standing of the limits and latitudes of her role.

The final scene turns, inevitably, on the imminent birth of the seventh child. Storm's wonderful comic pointedness is at its most determined as she has Emma deliver the long-awaited son and heir – the estate's saviour as it were – on Christmas Day! On the one hand, the play's ending is loaded with sentimental-ity – Robert's anxiety that he is not allowed to see his wife during her long deliv-ery, through to the sound of the Highland piper, the traditional announcement for the birth of a son. On the other, Storm not only comments ironically on the Christian tradition but locates this specifically within Scottish history and women's treatment within that. Tom complains that the church bells are not ringing to mark midnight on Christmas Eve and Edward replies:

> Not in these western highlands – its popery.
>
> TOM: Well – what d'you mean it's popery?
>
> EDWARD: Before I went into that I should have to explain all about a man called John Knox.
>
> TOM (*animated*): I know. He was the one who said, 'The monstrous regiment of women'. (*He looks at ROBERT and begins to giggle.*) (Act III, sc. 2, p. 94)

The point, of course, is that Robert has his own 'monstrous regiment' to deal with and, even with the birth of a male child, the play is careful not to lose the characters' (and audience's) awareness of how Emma has ensured her own social presence and viability. This, Storm suggests, is what it means to roar like a dove. Emma Dungavel may have been angry, but she was also, unlike Jimmy Porter, an active agent in making life more engaging and palatable for herself. (It is hard, here, not to compare *Look Back in Anger* where Alison returns to her parents and there miscarries the baby she was expecting.)

Like *Black Chiffon*, *Roar Like A Dove* makes palpable the economic and emotional costs of marriage. Both plays, within their different generic sensibilities, show how marriage affects the women who try to meet the expectations of their socially inscribed roles. For Alicia, there is prison, and for Emma a seventh child – in both cases an extreme solution to the problem of the play. Within the particular examples of dramatic plotting, however, the point is self-evident that women who do not have such an exceptional failure or success slip from public view. Storm puts women's lives, by contrast, front and centre of the stage. The audiences for *Roar Like A Dove* clearly both enjoyed and endorsed the point of view that Emma so emphatically spells out. Even a contemporary male reviewer (J. C. Trewin) noticed that frame of reference: 'We can say, if it does not sound too pompous, that *Roar Like A Dove* is largely about women's duties and women's rights.'[17] Even while Trewin goes on to diminish the play's importance by characterising it as an 'attractive chatter-comedy' ('Thoughts', p. 608), it is important in our study of women dramatists not to understate the significant political and social issues that were given public visibility through the comic mode. Women did not – and do not – have to write passionate tirades to evoke social change. Lesley Storm, to take one example, shows women as 'differently' angry but the potential contribution to a cultural sense of self can be no less significant than that of a play like *Look Back in Anger*.

We might, then, take Emma Dungavel as emblematic for a broader consideration of women playwrights and theatre history. All the time Emma Dungavel was producing daughters, she was not doing her job – what she needed was to produce the exception, a son. In theatre history, we have relied far too readily on the exceptions and paid little attention to the continuities and the norms. Notwithstanding the vitriol poured onto the well-made play by Kenneth Tynan and other drama critics in the 1950s, the example of Lesley Storm's work shows that women playwrights could well use such a conventional form to bring serious issues – their issues – into a public forum. For theatre historians, however, perhaps Lesley Storm was not angry enough. In the context of this volume, it is crucial that we ask why theatre history does so little to record, celebrate and critique a full range of dramatic production so that successes such as Lesley Storm's plays are given, like Emma Dungavel, a valued role in the history of British social production.

FIRST PRODUCTIONS OF PLAYS

Venues are in London unless stated.

Enid Bagnold

National Velvet, Embassy Theatre, 20 April 1946.
The Chalk Garden, Haymarket Theatre, 11 April 1956.
The Last Joke, Phoenix Theatre, 28 September 1960.
The Chinese Prime Minister, The Royale Theatre, New York, 3 January 1964; Globe Theatre, 20 May 1965.

Shelagh Delaney

A Taste of Honey, Theatre Royal, Stratford East, 27 May 1958.
The Lion in Love, Royal Court Theatre, 29 December 1960.
The House That Jack Built, Cubiculo Theatre, New York, 7 October 1979.

Ann Jellicoe

The Sport of My Mad Mother, Royal Court Theatre, 25 February 1958.
The Knack, Arts Theatre, Cambridge, 10 October 1961.
Shelley; or, The Idealist, Royal Court Theatre, 18 October 1965.
The Giveaway, Garrick Theatre, 8 April 1969.

Lesley Storm

Dark Horizon, Daly's Theatre, 20 April 1934.
Tony Draws A Horse, Criterion Theatre, 26 January 1939.
Black Chiffon, Westminster Theatre, 3 May 1949.
The Long Echo, St James's Theatre, 1 August 1956.
Roar Like A Dove, Phoenix Theatre, 26 September 1957.
Times and Yellow Roses, St Martin's Theatre, 11 May 1961.
Look No Hands, Yvonne Arnaud Theatre, Guildford, 15 June 1971.

NOTES

1 John Russell Taylor, *Anger and After: A Guide to the New British Drama* (London: Methuen, 1962), p. 9.
2 Stephen Lacey, *British Realist Theatre: The New Wave in its Context: 1956–1965* (London: Routledge, 1995), p. 31.
3 Dan Rebellato, *1956 and All That: The Making of Modern British Drama* (London: Routledge, 1999).
4 Maggie B. Gale, *West End Women: Women and the London Stage 1918–1962* (London: Routledge, 1996), p. 136.
5 Judith Thompson, '"The World Made Flesh": Women and Theatre', in Adrian Page (ed.) *The Death of the Playwright? Modern British Drama and Literary Theory* (New York: St Martins, 1992), p. 40.
6 Lib Taylor, 'Early Stages: Women Dramatists 1958–68', in Trevor R. Griffiths and Margaret Llewellyn-Jones (eds.) *British and Irish Women Dramatists Since 1958: A Critical Handbook* (Buckingham: Open University Press, 1993), p. 21.
7 John Elsom, *Post-War British Theatre*, revised edn (London: Routledge and Kegan Paul, 1979), p. 83.
8 Sue-Ellen Case, 'The Power of Sex: English Plays by Women, 1958–1988', *New Theatre Quarterly*, 7: 27, 1991, p. 238.
9 Michael Coveney, review of Enid Bagnold's *The Chalk Garden* in the *Observer*, 5 April 1992; *London Theatre Record*, 25 March – 7 April 1992, p. 387.
10 Charles Spencer, review of Enid Bagnold's *The Chalk Garden* in the *Daily Telegraph*, 4 April 1992; *London Theatre Record*, 25 March – 7 April 1992, p. 385.
11 T. C. Worsley, 'Mr Amis Regrets', *New Statesman*, 19 October 1957, p. 491.
12 Fidelis Morgan, *The Years Between: Plays by Women on the London Stage 1900–1950* (London: Virago, 1994), p. 402.
13 Lesley Storm, *Black Chiffon* (New York: Samuel French, 1950), p. 3.
14 Lesley Storm, *Roar Like A Dove* (London: Heinemann, 1958), p. 1.
15 Derek Conrad, review of Lesley Storm's *Roar Like A Dove*, *Plays and Players* (November 1957), p. 17.
16 Anonymous review in *The Times*, 27 September 1957.
17 J. C. Trewin, 'Thoughts by the Way', *Illustrated London News*, 12 October 1957, p. 608.

FURTHER READING

Primary sources: plays

Bagnold, Enid. *The Chalk Garden*. London: Heinemann, 1956.
  Four Plays: The Chalk Garden, The Last Joke, The Chinese Prime Minister, Call Me Jacky. London: Heinemann, 1970.
Delaney, Shelagh. *The Lion in Love*. London: Methuen, 1961.
  A Taste of Honey. London: Methuen, 1989.
Jellicoe, Ann. *Shelly: Or, The Idealist*. New York: Grove Press, 1966.
  The Giveaway. London: Faber, 1970.
  The Knack and The Sport of My Mad Mother. London: Faber, 1985.
Storm, Lesley. *Tony Draws a Horse*. London, 1939.
  Black Chiffon. New York: Samuel French, 1950. (Also in Morgan, below, pp. 403–60.)

The Long Echo. London: Samuel French, 1957.
Roar Like A Dove. London: Heinemann, 1958.

Secondary sources

Anonymous. Review of Lesley Storm's *Roar Like A Dove*, *The Times* (27 September 1957).

Case, Sue-Ellen. 'The Power of Sex: English Plays by Women, 1958–1988'. *New Theatre Quarterly* 7.27 (1991): 238–45.

Conrad, Derek. Review of Lesley Storm's *Roar Like A Dove*. *Plays and Players* (November 1957): 17.

Coveney, Michael. Review of Enid Bagnold's *The Chalk Garden* in the *Observer* (5 April 1992); *London Theatre Record* (25 March – 7 April 1992): 387.

Elsom, John. *Post-War British Theatre*. Revised edn. London: Routledge and Kegan Paul, 1979.

Gale, Maggie B. *West End Women: Women and the London Stage 1918–1962*. London: Routledge, 1996.

Lacey, Stephen. *British Realist Theatre: The New Wave in its Context: 1956–1965*. London: Routledge, 1995.

Morgan, Fidelis (ed.) *The Years Between: Plays by Women on the London Stage 1900–1950*. London: Virago, 1994.

Osborne, John. *Look Back in Anger*. London: Faber, 1957.

Rebellato, Dan. *1956 and All That: The Making of Modern British Drama*. London: Routledge, 1999.

Spencer, Charles. Review of Enid Bagnold's *The Chalk Garden* in *Daily Telegraph* (4 April 1992); *London Theatre Record* (25 March – 7 April 1992): 385.

Taylor, John Russell. *Anger and After: A Guide to the New British Drama*. London: Methuen, 1962.

Taylor, Lib. 'Early Stages: Women Dramatists 1958–68'. In Trevor R. Griffiths and Margaret Llewellyn-Jones (eds.) *British and Irish Women Dramatists Since 1958: A Critical Handbook*. Buckingham: Open University Press, 1993: 9–25.

Thompson, Judith. '"The World Made Flesh": Women and Theatre'. In Adrian Page (ed.) *The Death of the Playwright? Modern British Drama and Literary Theory*. New York: St Martins, 1992: 2–42.

Trewin, J. C. 'Thoughts by the Way'. *Illustrated London News* (12 October 1957): 608.

Worsley, T. C. 'Mr Amis Regrets'. *New Statesman* (19 October 1957): 490–1.

4

MICHELENE WANDOR

Women playwrights and the challenge of feminism in the 1970s

It is over thirty years since the most important change in British theatre this century took place: the abolition of censorship in 1968. Without that significant development, it is arguable whether this book could have been written. The changes in the relationship between feminism, theatre, and women playwrights since then were predicated on two phenomena: first, the rise of a new theatre movement, variously called 'alternative', 'fringe', or 'political', which exploded in the late 1960s and generated an energetic debate about the relationship between theatre, society, and politics; and second, the development of a vigorous feminist movement.

Controversial ideas about the relationship between art and society were being widely discussed at the time, and many of us argued for a transformation in the gender balance and perspectives of theatre. The theatre industry, we argued, was dominated by men; most directors and writers and stagehands were male, most casts (and therefore theatre companies) consisted of more men than women. The 'classical canon' of plays were written from a male-centred point of view, unthinkingly considered 'universal' and the 'norm'. The stage world was generally male-dominated – the action driven by, and seen from, the perspective of the male protagonists – as was journalistic reviewing and academic criticism.

Given this gender imbalance, it was not surprising that it was women who first expressed dissatisfaction with the status quo. The time was right for a new critical approach to the understanding of the function of gender in the theatrical imagination. The influence of feminist ideas was the driving force, and various phrases were used to describe questioning approaches to the relative places and roles of men and women: sexual politics, gender and theatre, feminist theatre, each with a slightly different emphasis. These responses were not merely theoretical. Along with many others, I was deeply involved in theatre, initially as an actress, and then as both playwright and critic. At the same time I was also involved with feminism and socialism, and the interaction between all these different things lent an enormous excitement to everything we did. There was a tremendous sense of optimism. I think we all hoped that the advantages of radical cultural change would become so obvious that the transformation would come about in a generation, if not sooner. A theatre in which the balance between men and women was equal was an exciting prospect. Perhaps I exaggerate the optimisms, but, even at our most pessimistic, we thought things would change more than they actually have.

There is a serious and significant history of critical work which challenges conservative gender assumptions, and in the 1990s a small number of women playwrights appear on the theatrical map, some of whose work (e.g. Caryl Churchill's) has entered the contemporary canon. On the other hand, despite individual exceptions, we do not have a theatre world committed to parity based on gender, nor a broadly understood and accepted gender-based critique of drama. Male dominance, in terms of both actual jobs, and the critical and imaginative perspective of theatre, still prevails.

The reasons for this failure to achieve parity are complex; in part because attitudes to gender roles in society as a whole have not really shifted much (despite constant attempts by the popular media to persuade us otherwise), but also because conditions in the 1990s are very different from those in the 1960s. The political and cultural critiques of the 1960s and early 1970s were fuelled by a response to post-war conditions, in which work, private life, and a Labour government (which came into power in 1945) affected personal and social life in new ways.

After the Second World War, the welfare state took some basic socialist steps to enable access to education (at all levels), and health and housing to be available to everyone in the country, irrespective of class or wealth. The philosophy behind this was the idea of a genuine equality of opportunity, as a result of which, in theory, all the negative aspects of inequality (class, race, gender) would be ironed out, and everyone could benefit from society's resources.

By the late 1950s the first generations of ordinary people had been through university, and a professional class with new commercial and cultural aspirations was emerging. The influences of American popular culture – rock and roll, and the post-war Hollywood movie – spurred debates about 'high' versus 'mass' culture. At the same time, the new affluence, and a younger generation which had money to spend, raised ideological questions about the quality of life the new generations expected. At the level of world politics, the Campaign for Nuclear Disarmament (CND), with its concern for the post-war destructive aspects of nuclear power, and the university-based New Left, reflected a concern for more than material improvement in living conditions. The Parliamentary Labour Party began to be challenged by a broader-based set of socialist critiques. And – last, but not least – the voices of women began to critique the ways in which their lives were being affected after the war.

Wartime bombing resulted in vast areas of urban wasteland, and while the necessary rebuilding produced larger suburban areas with more comfortable housing, it also broke up working-class communities and family networks. Things we now take for granted – washing machines, vacuum cleaners, all the technology that simplifies housework – were newly available then, and while on the one hand they encouraged the self-sufficiency of each household, they also increasingly isolated women within their individual homes. At the same time, large numbers of women still worked outside the home, leaving them with two sets of responsibilities (so what's changed??). Women's magazines extolled the virtues of motherhood and wifehood, as post-war families reformed, but women who were benefiting from higher education alongside men now also began to develop their own career ambitions.

Methods of contraception, and in particular the freer availability of the Pill during the 1960s, meant that sexual choice and decisions about motherhood were – in theory, at any rate – greater for women than they had ever been. Books and articles wrestled with these new, and often also stressful, possibilities, discussing in particular the phenomenon of the 'graduate wife' who was caught between the old expectations of cosy wife- and motherhood, and aspirations in a world of work fully alongside men. In reality, women were still left with, in effect, two 'jobs'. Two books in particular discussed the way these questions manifested themselves: *The Captive Wife* (1966) by Hannah Gavron surveyed the way women felt in Britain, and *The Feminine Mystique* (1963) by Betty Friedan, undertook a similar, and very fiery, enterprise in the United States of America.

The material changes in family life and the changes brought about by new conditions for women were indirectly acknowledged by a series of legal reforms affecting personal life. Parliament had to keep up with the rapidly changing situation and people's needs. In 1967 an Abortion Act was passed, for the first time making abortion legal; in the same year an Act partially legalising male homosexuality came into force. In 1969 the Divorce Reform Act eased conditions for divorce, and in 1970 an Equal Pay Act set terms for equal pay for men and women (still far from fully implemented today). As tokenistic as some of these steps may have been, they at least recognised that greater personal and vocational freedoms were being demanded – particularly by women.

This climate of change affected all sorts of cultural phenomena. During the 1960s rock music and pop festivals contributed to a vibrant 'underground' youth culture, encouraging a superficially 'permissive' attitude to sexuality and challenging the lines of demarcation between audience and performers. At the same time, political activism, much of it based in the universities, fuelled a response to world events: the Chinese cultural revolution in the mid-1960s and the American war in Vietnam both united students and workers in transcontinental waves of protest.

In the arts, many students and young professionals, as well as older people who had been involved in socialist and Communist anti-fascist organisations, participated in this new questioning. The Campaign for Nuclear Disarmament agitated for an end to nuclear weapons in the interests of world peace, and the hippie movement demanded freedoms to enjoy the benefits of cultural self-expression, personal and artistic.

Theatre had its own particular focus for campaigning, since it was struggling under the handicap of a unique pre-performance censorship. Films and books could be prosecuted for obscenity or blasphemy, but only after publication or production. Indeed, during the course of the period there were a number of flamboyant challenges to censorship, including the trial of a book originally published privately in 1928, and which appeared in an unexpurgated edition in 1960: D. H. Lawrence's *Lady Chatterley's Lover*.

Theatre, on the other hand, as a live performance art, was different. Plays had to be submitted to the Lord Chamberlain in manuscript and could only go into rehearsal after he had given his permission. There were ways round this, by giving club, i.e. 'private', performances, but the journey from script to public performance was a long and tortuous one. Topical references, ad-libbing, satire, or adverse commentary on politicians, the church, and the royal family, were tabooed, as were references to, and representations of, sexuality, beyond the most chaste. However, even within these restrictions, a number of plays acerbically addressed post-war experience.[1]

At London's Royal Court Theatre and at Stratford East under the direction of Joan Littlewood (a rare female figure in artistic control), as well as in theatres outside London, such as Stoke-on-Trent, the experiences of ordinary people were beginning to become the subject matter of plays during the 1950s and 1960s. Greater interest in the work of European dramatists throughout the 1950s, including the absurdist Ionesco and the polemical Brecht, opened a fruitful channel for exploring new forms and approaches. The apocryphal watershed play by John Osborne, *Look Back in Anger* (1956), did not just appear out of the blue; it was part of a broader historical ferment where a mixture of working-class realism, absurdism, and didacticism was already influencing the theatre.

In 1968 the office of Lord Chamberlain was finally abolished, and theatre was no longer a censorship anomaly among the arts. Plays could now in theory address any subject, be topical, change from one performance to another, include improvisation, and have no restriction on language. Anyone could put on any play anywhere, to any kind of audience. Plays were now performed in rooms in pubs, in halls, in the streets, and many of the new theatres built during the 1960s included studio spaces which helped develop new and varied ways of staging. A genuine explosion of new groups produced the range of work which was variously categorised as 'fringe', 'alternative', and 'political' theatre.

With such a vital interchange between politics and culture, the voices of women began to be heard in a new way. This took the form of the rise of the Women's Liberation Movement, a broadly based umbrella spread of feminist protest from women. The first national conference took place in 1970 at Ruskin College in Oxford, and was initially intended as a conference on women and history, organised by women historians. About 500 women attended, and it soon snowballed into discussions which were as much about the contemporary position of women as about the position of women in the past.

From the beginning, theatrical self-expression was part of the feminist movement (as it was of the socialist). A Women's Street Theatre group provided pageants and images for street demonstrations, including a cartoon-like agitprop play in Trafalgar Square about the oppression of women within the family. They used a gigantic deodorant and sanitary towel to defy public taboos about references to intimate female body culture and to shock the audience into thinking about the position of women.

The broader 'political' theatre movement was already using performance to carry messages, along the lines of the so-called political movement earlier in the century. This style was based on a utilitarian idea of theatre as a device which could be used to raise consciousness, provoke debate, and spread propaganda. It was not necessarily just earnest and worthy; people used music, comedy, and broad visual images, alongside naturalistic scenes. Put at its simplest, entertainment and instruction alternated in these plays. One of the best-known (because it was one of the few 'political' plays published at the time) was *Sweetie Pie*, devised by members of the Bolton Octagon Theatre in Education team in 1972.[2] The play was structured in the form of a satirical fairy tale, in which a working-class woman began to understand the contradiction between the idealised path her life was supposed to follow (according to women's magazines) and the harsh realities of a life where she had to do two jobs, and was treated as a second-class citizen.

It took quite a long time before the debates and activities of the Women's Liberation Movement influenced many women playwrights. Caryl Churchill, for example, began writing stage and radio plays in the late 1950s, but it was not until the mid-1970s that her work (through collaborations with the Monstrous Regiment theatre company in particular) began to show evidence of radical thinking about relationships between men and women. Her work did not have wider impact until the end of the decade – *Cloud 9* in 1979, and *Top Girls* in 1982 – when she was no longer working with fringe theatre groups. It is not surprising that very few other women playwrights at this point were drawn to feminism at a self-conscious level. There were hardly any plays by women being produced on the professional stage, and while the earlier generations of radical writers at Stratford East and the Royal Court Theatre included Shelagh Delaney's and Ann Jellicoe's distinctive takes on female experience, it was pre-feminist, and by this point in time their playwriting careers had faded somewhat [for discussion of Delaney and Jellicoe, see pp. 39–41].

At the same time, the new radical theatre itself was, to an extent, suspicious of the 'individualism' of writing. Much of the general socialist approach to political organisation at the time involved intense debates about democracy, and the need to create structures where those in power were accountable to those lower down the hierarchy. The concept of the 'collective' was one of the thorniest and yet one of the most influential components of a philosophy of radical social change. Based on the assumption that people, across class, race, and gender determinants, were of equal value, the ideology argued that everyone should have equal input.

These ideas were applied to traditional theatre in two ways. First, it was argued, the dominant trend, especially in West End theatre, had been to represent the affluent middle classes, ignoring the lives of ordinary people. Second, within theatre practice itself, writer and director were seen as the 'authoritarian' figures. The writer was seen as a controlling force by virtue of producing the text – medium and message – and the director was seen as having excessive control over presentation. Within this scheme of things, performers were seen as mere puppets for the voices of writers and directors, with the stage crew as the voiceless manual workers.

Clearly, in traditional theatre, cast and crew did not make fundamental artistic or administrative decisions; but the analysis also begged all sorts of arguments about skill, expertise, experience, artistic vision – all the things that go into the inevitable social division of labour. The drive for democracy, however, did produce some interesting experiments with different working methods. Many of the political theatre groups aimed to work 'collectively', with everyone doing a bit of everything, discussing the content and message of the plays, writing scenes individually and bringing them back for comment, as well as directing the plays together during the course of rehearsal. Almost needless to say, it is not an approach which has survived to any great extent, since it is ultimately unworkable beyond a certain point, but it raised a fundamental question about control of working conditions, as well as the form and content of theatre work.

This ideology affected attitudes towards individual writers. There was a strong notion that the individual fictional voice was somehow reactionary, not sufficiently accountable either to fellow workers or to the audience. In response to this climate, a number of younger playwrights such as David Hare, Howard Brenton, John Mcgrath, and David Edgar all worked with some of the new fringe groups. David Hare was involved with director Max Stafford-Clark in founding the Joint Stock theatre group; David Edgar worked with the Welfare State; and John McGrath was one of the founders of the 7:84 theatre company, so called because 7% of the population owned 84% of the nation's wealth – a salutary statistic.

The same issues came up within feminism. To give a personal example, I was one of the editorial collective of a socialist feminist magazine called *Red Rag* where we discussed the content, wrote pieces (individually), and worked on layout and distribution together. It was heady, educational, full of argument and exhilaration. I remember one meeting where one of the women denounced poetry and novels as moribund bourgeois forms, since they did not make their message clear. (It was an ironic statement, since she later went on to write a novel!) For me this created something of a dilemma.

At the time I was writing in a range of genres – articles and reviews for *Time Out* (a radical weekly listings guide to cultural and political events in London); I was also writing a lot of open-form poetry, and performing some of it at poetry readings. Also, as someone who had always been passionate about theatre (acting as well as seeing), I had begun to write plays, which were then relatively easy to have produced in one of the many burgeoning new theatre venues. After going to the Ruskin conference in 1970, I not only 'caught' feminism, but also discovered that I had always been a kind of instinctive socialist. I wanted to bring ideas about women, social change, and art together in my writing, but I was already exploring rather more jagged forms which did not merely punch a message across. I was playing around with language and form instinctively, and did not gravitate towards writing fiction which was only interested in surface message. I also felt strongly about the importance of developing skills to as high a level as possible.

This placed me in something of a limbo situation – viewed with suspicion by the politicos since, despite my fascination with other people's work, it was not the way I wanted to write; and, on the other hand, viewed with suspicion by the theatricals because I was clearly interested in politics and ideas. Moreover, I was also reviewing plays; whereas it is generally accepted that novelists will review each other's work, playwrights who are also reviewers tend to be viewed with suspicion.

In 1971–2 I wrote a series of five short duologues called *To Die Among Friends*, which was commissioned by director Malcolm Griffiths, who was then running an experimental company called Paradise Foundry. Surreal and suggestive as they were, I knew that they were heavily influenced by feminism, but none of my feminist friends came – perhaps because the plays were being performed in pubs and studio theatres rather than as part of some overt political event. During this time I also wrote *The Day After Yesterday* which was about two couples watching the Miss World contest. The play explored the way ideas about men and women affect relationships. This was staged in a pub theatre in London, but again the audience did not include any of the people from whom I was deriving such political stimulus.

However, early in 1973 things began to change. A group of women were invited by Ed Berman, who ran the Almost Free Theatre in London, to put on a season of plays by women writers. Some women were already working in the profession, concerned to extend opportunities for women. Others had little theatrical experience and wanted to use theatre as a vehicle for propaganda, and, I suspect, also had something of an acting bug – nothing wrong with that; many of us love performing.

This mixed grouping produced a season of plays by women (among them myself and Pam Gems), directed and stage-managed by women. Theatre critics responded to the season with a mixture of jeering and interest. After the season, two groupings continued. The Women's Theatre Group developed work which combined some of the aims of the Theatre-in-Education movement with those of the adult touring groups. They devised their work collectively and performed mainly in non-theatre venues – halls, schools, etc. – and followed the plays with discussions about the issues. They performed plays about abortion and contraception, about women's position at work. The dramatic formula tended to consist of short naturalistic scenes, interspersed with songs to leaven the educational content with entertainment. It was not until 1978 that they began to work with individual women writers, commissioning plays which always had the subject matter pre-defined, and including work from Melissa Murray, Donna Franceschild, Bryony Lavery, and Timberlake Wertenbaker.

The very fact that the Women's Theatre Group was an all-female company provoked enormous argument. Why no men, challenged many? Why put on plays which presented a stage world peopled only by women? These questions in turn begged the very basic question of the way theatre was already unthinkingly organised – dominated by men, and with stage worlds in which women were almost always in a minority and where the perspective of the play was mainly from men's point of view. Implicitly this was considered the 'norm', and therefore anything which questioned the 'norm' was bound to provoke some annoyance and denial.

The second group which emerged from the Almost Free season was the Women's Company, which, though run by women, did include men in its casts – simply reversing the dominant convention of organisation. This group lasted only for a brief time, and in its composition it was a precursor to Monstrous Regiment, founded in 1975 by a group of actresses fed up with their secondary roles in socialist political theatre companies where, with a few exceptions, women still did not feel integrated on an equal basis. From the outset Monstrous Regiment commissioned women writers, including husband and wife team, C. G. Bond and Claire Luckham, and Caryl Churchill.

Caryl Churchill had already established a working niche with Max Stafford-Clark at the Royal Court Theatre, where, in 1972, her play *Owners* was produced. In *Owners* ideas about ownership and control (socialism) and about personal relationships and motherhood (feminism) mesh in a macabre, surreal story about a group of people who become embroiled in a series of helpless relationships. In the mid-1970s Churchill worked with both Joint Stock theatre company, directed by Max Stafford-Clark at the Royal Court Theatre and Monstrous Regiment. Indeed, during 1975–6 she worked on two plays for the groups, each demonstrating and feeding into the perspective of the other: *Light Shining in Buckinghamshire* for Joint Stock and *Vinegar Tom* for Monstrous Regiment. Both plays had mixed casts, but in *Light Shining* the emphasis was on the broad-based libertarian ideas with fed into utopianism in England in the seventeenth century, while in *Vinegar Tom* the focus was on witchcraft and the persecution of women during the same century.

Between 1971 and 1978 Arts Council theatre subsidy to fringe theatre increased from around £7,000 to about £1.5 million. This increase clearly recognised the new movement, and made it relatively easier for new groups to form and – at least for a while – to survive. After the marking out of new territory by the more polemically named groups such as the Women's Theatre Group, Monstrous Regiment, and Gay Sweatshop (also formed during 1976), the theatrical map grew. In the late 1970s a number of other small all-female groups formed, concentrating on cabaret and with more light-hearted names: Clapperclaw, Beryl and the Perils, and Cunning Stunts (be careful how you say it!). These groups wrote and performed their own material; they did not necessarily have explicitly formulated feminist intentions, but they were responding to a climate in which women were beginning to take greater control of the stage (albeit fringe).

Within the socialist theatre movement itself there were serious attempts to incorporate the critiques of feminism. A group called Red Ladder, initially London-based, began work on a 'women's play' in 1972, called *A Woman's Work is Never Done*, later titled *Strike While the Iron is Hot*. The play was, of course, interesting in its own right, but it was also telling in the way it drew on the work of Brecht. The play was modelled on Brecht's *The Mother*, in which a mother who has no sense of political commitment becomes a completely committed Communist. This play functioned as a sort of unofficial flagship during the 1970s – since it apparently gives heroine status to a woman at the centre of a play. However, this does not necessarily mean that she is treated as a figure in her own right or that she necessarily has any real control over the action of the play. In Brecht's play the Mother is placed on male territory, and her actions are judged in terms of the standards which are applied to male experience and politics.

At the start she is excluded from the political process – just a housewife concerned about whether her son is eating properly. In order to become a Communist activist, she has to relinquish all her motherly and so-called 'female' concerns. Brecht implicitly devalues the personal, domestic, and emotional in favour of the external, impersonal, and political, so that the very concept of 'politics' is still defined on male territory, which can only function effectively if it annihilates the emotional territory considered to be 'female'. Political action is outside the home, and so, although the Mother is genuinely heroic and self-sacrificing for the cause, she makes no demands in her own right as a woman – in crude terms, socialism is defined as a male-centred concern – and her achievement is to join it on its own terms. There is no space here for any feminist critique of the world in which she lives.

Red Ladder's play, however, although schematic and in many ways simplistic (no less effective for that), places the woman at the centre both as an active trade unionist, and as a wife and mother who challenges her husband at home. If both are to work and be politically active, then both need to share in responsibility for home and children. The 'struggle' is literally brought home, and the definition of 'politics' itself (unlike in *The Mother*) includes personal life as well as work and political activism. One of the slogans of the Women's Liberation Movement was that 'the personal is political', and Red Ladder's play attempted to reflect it by demonstrating that organising family life to create greater equality between the sexes is as important as the organisation of work – indeed, that the one cannot happen without the other.

The collectivist ideology described earlier had great advantages, but it was very largely responsible for the slowness with which women writers became involved with the theatre. There was also another factor. Women may have been writing plays, but very few of them were being professionally produced. (The amateur theatrical market is rather different – far more all-women plays and women playwrights there.) This phenomenon relates historically to the division of labour within theatre, and the idea of women playwrights having a more 'public' voice than women novelists or poets, because they are associated with live, public performance.[3] Unlike the male playwrights mentioned earlier, it was not a matter of there already being a large number of women writers who could be influenced by feminism. It took nearly a decade before a younger generation of women writers – among them Louise Page, Sarah Daniels, Timberlake Wertenbaker – were drawn to write for the theatre. Moreover, while some may have begun to write with the encouragement of women's groups and directors (e.g. Page and Wertenbaker), they would not have been able to continue writing professionally without inevitable male patronage – men being the artistic directors of major theatres, such as the Royal Court and the Royal Shakespeare Company.

Other chapters in this volume and publications elsewhere discuss the work of women playwrights which has been performed and published since the 1980s. Any work of research in years to come will reveal more plays by women written during this period than will have been published, and this is because commercial viability means that only the relatively high-profile plays produced in the larger theatres will see print. In the early 1970s I felt very strongly that many new plays by women should appear in print, since that was the only way in which (a) they stood a chance of further performance, and (b) they would be accessible as history. An anthology of three plays – *Strike While the Iron is Hot*, by Red Ladder; *Care and Control*, about women and custody, which I scripted for Gay Sweatshop; and *My Mother Says I Never Should*, by the Women's Theatre Group – was circulated to major play publishers and rejected because the work was not considered 'good enough'. At the level of sophisticated aesthetic judgement, in terms of the manipulation of language and theatrical form, this opinion was spot on. That said, they were all carefully and effectively crafted plays on burning issues of sexual politics, on matters that touched profoundly on questions of the social and sexual division of labour. They were very successful in terms of performances round the country and, in their own way, were symbolic of much other work which was going on.

Eventually the book was published by a small socialist outfit, the Journeyman Press; the discussions with Methuen (who also turned the book down) led indirectly to my being commissioned to write *Understudies* (1981; later revised as *Carry On, Understudies*, 1986), which is an account of the relationship between feminism, sexual politics, and contemporary theatre. This book was followed by the first four volumes of Methuen's *Plays by Women* series which I edited. The series began in 1982 and has proved invaluable in making plays by women available to a wider public, without their necessarily having to earn the cachet of performance by a major theatre company. Since then, as the small number of successful women playwrights has increased, publication of their individual work has been more assured.

This brief account of the interaction between theatre and women playwrights has focused on the 1970s because that is the decade in which the major changes took place. From 1979 onwards, the landscape has been rather different: with Thatcherism and a long period of Conservative government, individualism has become deeply entrenched in our social ideology. At the same time, the careers of individual women writers have followed their various trajectories, and there is at least a body of work which enables the concrete historical focus of a book such as this.

However, there is still the vexed question of feminism. Do we say that because there is no longer an identifiable feminist movement, we can no longer use terms which were developed during its existence? The ideas are still current, even though they have been subject to developments and modifications. There is another reason why it is important to use critical formulations which refer to feminism: in order to understand why – politically as well as aesthetically – the work of some women playwrights is taken up, patronised, and therefore influences which women playwrights become established as part of the cultural landscape. We need critical tools with which to understand the way gender, i.e. the distribution and relationships of male/female characters in a play, determines plot, structure, language, and the form of a piece.

In terms of the way women are represented onstage (still a thorny and minority area) we have to be able to take a strong critical stance in relation to the meanings of such representation. As we have seen in my brief analysis of *The Mother*, just because a woman is at the centre of a play (the 'heroine'), it does not mean that the play encodes a feminist or woman-centred position. She may be partially – or wholly – a cipher for the concerns of men, able to symbolise other meanings more poignantly precisely because she is relatively marginal – an 'outsider' – to the action. The same problem is there in some modern plays, such as David Edgar's *Maydays* (1983), where the character of Amanda is emotionally strong, reassuring, and carries the torch of emotional hope. It is still there in Michael Frayn's *Copenhagen* (1998) in the character of Margrethe, who is both intellectually and emotionally assured in the face of shifting certainties in the lives of two male scientists. Here are apparently 'strong' women in terms of realistic representation (and, concomitantly, 'good' parts for actresses); but in the fictional world of the play they are dynamically weak and powerless. The action does not follow their concerns, and they are not subject to emotional flux and contradiction. They do not change during the play, nor do they transform. They operate as relatively marginal commentators ('outsiders'), and are thus (in a sense) de-gendered, and, by implication, devalued as women.

This is, of course, not a moral judgement on the writer – but it is a small example of the complexity of the relationship between gender ideology and the fictionalising imagination. As a crude rule of thumb, it tends to be true that male playwrights are male-centred in their concerns, while women playwrights tend to be female-centred, whether they consider themselves feminists or not. Indeed, while it may be interesting to know whether a woman playwright considers herself a feminist, in the end her work will consist of a mix of conscious and unconscious impulses which derive from all sorts of ideas which are in the air. Fiction is not journalism, to put it at its simplest, and the workings of the imagination cannot be reduced to analysis at the level of conscious intent. However, we can test the gender dynamic in a play against the three main political tendencies within feminism.[4]

Act I of Caryl Churchill's play *Cloud 9* (1979)[5] is set in Victorian colonial Africa. The values of an authoritarian British imperialism are linked with repressed sexualities and rigid male/female roles. Act II, in London in the 1970s, shows a group of men and women (ostensibly the 'same' characters) living more openly libertarian lifestyles, with social and sexual roles based on what they desire rather than on what they are constrained to choose.

Where the first half demonstrates the dynamic interplay between political, social, and sexual roles (class and gender, and therefore a socialist-feminist dynamic), the second half merely 'shows' us men and women living as they wish, based on individual choice – a bourgeois, or bourgeois feminist dynamic. At a relatively simple level, bourgeois choices are seen as those made by individuals without necessary reference to circumstance or environment, while socialist choices are those in which the interaction between individual and social context is inevitable and symbiotic. The socialist-feminist approach, then, I would argue, is fuller, because it accounts for more elements and shows the way the world really works, while the bourgeois feminist dynamic either asserts the survival of the most successful, or is merely utopian.

In Nell Dunn's *Steaming* (1981),[6] a group of women become friends in a Turkish baths threatened with closure. The territory is all-female – no man is allowed into the women's baths. However, men control the structure of this world: by both maintaining the works, and controlling whether the building remains open. The play focuses on the friendship, conflict, and support generated among the women – along the radical feminist principle of women establishing relationships independent of men. This solidarity is precarious, however, because the very territory which makes it possible is controlled by men, and is under threat. The radical feminist idea which places great importance on female solidarity and strength is shown by implication to be a stronger version of a more traditional feminine dynamic where in the final instance women are still dependent on men.

Even if a play consists of mixtures of feminist dynamics, there is likely to be a dominant structural drive, and it is important to analyse this, rather than allow surface symptoms, such as a central female character, or an all-female cast, to appear to answer the need for redressing both gender-imbalance and gendered perspective.

Parity between male and female playwrights is a pre-requisite for a fuller and more varied set of representations of women onstage (in form and content), and consequentially of gender relations between men and women. The success of a small number of women playwrights is vital, but they are the bourgeois feminist tip of the iceberg (whatever their personal politics). They will always be the exceptions who prove the rule that male playwrights control our imaginative stage worlds. We still, therefore, need feminism in the theatre (as we do elsewhere in our society) at a time when there is no real feminist movement. Cultural and intellectual feminism keeps ideas alive, providing insights into the work of women playwrights and helping to boost political argument.

Perhaps a final few words about my own critical/playwriting career are in order here. By the end of the 1970s a small number of women writers had become nationally and internationally visible (some, such as Caryl Churchill and Timberlake Wertenbaker are discussed elsewhere in this book). This, it has to be said, was largely due to male patronage in influential theatres such as the Royal Court and the Royal Shakespeare Company. For the rest, fringe groups and small theatres were still options, but do not yield enough income to enable writers to survive professionally.

Although I began in theatre and have never lost my passion for it, from the end of the 1970s I have written mainly for radio – with the occasional exception, such as my dramatisation of *The Wandering Jew* at the National Theatre in 1987. I have found that, on the whole, radio producers have been more receptive than theatre directors (male and female) to both the subjects and the more experimental/impressionistic forms which have always interested me. Yet radio, which commands a far larger audience for a single performance than the vast majority of stage plays, rarely results in publication, and has a far lower profile.

Live performance captures a communal vividness not shared by the individually consumed radio and television. Whether we like it or not, theatre is still likely to be seen as the cutting edge of significant, if not radical, drama. All the more reason, then, to be campaigning and rigorous about the imperatives of feminism, and the gender dynamic in both the industry and the art. Theatre still needs feminism and its insights.

FIRST PRODUCTIONS OF PLAYS BY MICHELENE WANDOR

Venues are all in London.

You Two can be Ticklish, Lamb and Flag Theatre (1970)
The Day After Yesterday, Act Inn Theatre Club (1972)
Spilt Milk and *Mal de Mère*, Portable Theatre (1972)
To Die Among Friends, Paradise Foundry (1974)
Care and Control, Gay Sweatshop, Drill Hall (1977)
Floorshow (with Caryl Churchill and Bryony Lavery), for Monstrous Regiment (1977)
The Old Wives' Tale, Soho Poly Theatre (1977)
Penthesilea (version of Kleist's play about the Queen of the Amazons), Salt Theatre (1977)
AID thy Neighbour, Theatre at New End (1978)
Scissors, Almost Free Theatre (1978)
Whores D'Oeuvres (1978) Institute of Contemporary Arts (ICA) (1978)
Correspondence (adaptation of own radio play), ICA (1979)
Rutherford and Son (adaptation of play by Githa Sowerby), Mrs Worthington's Daughters, Royal Court (1980)
Aurora Leigh (dramatisation of verse-novel by Elizabeth Barrett Browning), Mrs Worthington's Daughters, Royal Court (1979); National Theatre (1981)
The Blind Goddess (adaptation of play by Ernst Toller), for Red Ladder Theatre Company (1981)

Future Perfect (with Paul Thompson and Steve Gooch), Wakefield Tricycle (1981)
Whose Greenham and *Mal de Mère*, Early Stages, Royal Shakespeare Company, Barbican (1986)
The Wandering Jew (dramatisation of novel by Eugene Sue), National Theatre (1987)
Wanted, Arc Theatre Company, Drill Hall (1988)

NOTES

1   For further discussion of theatre censorship see Michelene Wandor, *Look Back in Gender: Sexuality and the Family in Post-War British Drama* (London: Methuen, 1987).

2   *Sweetie Pie: A Play About Women in Society*, devised by the Bolton Octagon Theatre in Education Company, with an introduction by Eileen Murphy (London: Methuen, 1975).

3   For further discussion of this point, see Michelene Wandor, 'Finding a Voice: Women Playwrights and Theatre', *Carry On, Understudies* (London: Routledge and Kegan Paul, 1986), pp. 121–9.

4   This is more fully developed in *Carry On, Understudies*. See chapter 8, 'Political Dynamics: the Feminisms', pp. 130–9.

5   Caryl Churchill, *Cloud Nine* in *Plays: One* (London: Methuen, 1985).

6   Nell Dunn, *Steaming* (Oxford, Amber Lane Press, 1981).

FURTHER READING

Primary sources: plays

Wandor, Michelene. *Sink Songs*. London: Playbooks, 1975.
   Care and Control. In Wandor (ed.) *Strike While the Iron is Hot*. London: Journeyman Press, 1980.
   Mal de Mère and *Spilt Milk*. In Robin Rook (ed.) *Play Nine*. London: Edward Arnold, 1981.
   Aurora Leigh. In Michelene Wandor (ed.) *Plays by Women: 1*. London: Methuen, 1982.
   Five Plays: To Die Among Friends, Whores D'Oeuvres, The Old Wives' Tale, Scissors, AID Thy Neighbour. London: Journeyman Press, 1984.
   The Wandering Jew (dramatisation of Eugene Sue's novel). London: Methuen, 1987.
   Wanted. London: Playbooks, 1988.

Secondary sources

Other chapters in this book carry bibliographies of books covering feminism/women and theatre, and the work of women playwrights. More detail about some of the issues raised in this chapter can be found in the following publications.

Wandor, Michelene (ed.) *Strike While The Iron Is Hot: Sexual Politics In Theatre*. Journeyman Press, 1980. The volume has an introduction, and contains three plays by Red Ladder, Gay Sweatshop, and the Women's Theatre Group, respectively, each with a preface from a member of the group.

Carry On, Understudies: Theatre And Sexual Politics. London: Routledge and Kegan Paul, 1986. A mixture of history, theory, and criticism, covering the work of theatre groups, and men and women playwrights between 1968 and the early 1980s. Presents an outline of different feminist dynamics to help analyse the 'take' on gender in individual plays.

Look Back in Gender: Sexuality and the Family in Post-War British Drama. London: Methuen, 1987. A series of analyses, based on gender dynamics, of plays by twenty-eight playwrights (male and female), from John Osborne to Caryl Churchill. The study stresses the way the family (real and symbolic) is represented, accompanied by an analysis of the way the imaginative concepts of the 'personal' intersect and interact with concepts of the 'political'.

Drama Today: A Critical Guide to British Drama 1970–1990. London: Longman, British Council, 1993. Analyses key themes of writers and plays on contemporary British stage.

PART 2

NATIONAL TENSIONS AND INTERSECTIONS

Editors' note

The political, cultural, theatrical, and feminist matrix is very different in the 1980s from that of the 1970s that Michelene Wandor charts at the close of the last part. In terms of the Women's Movement specifically, a major shift by the end of the 1970s was constituted by thinking about difference, rather than sisterhood; acknowledging that not all women are oppressed in the same way, but, for example, are affected by different economic, class, or ethnic factors. Susan Bassnett's chapter which opens this part looks at 'the politics of location' as a site of difference in 1980s and 1990s politics and culture, arguing that where you are, where you live, is inextricably bound up with issues of who you are – with issues of gender, identity, and oppression. This is particularly true in Britain which, as Bassnett describes, has constituent national cultures in Wales, Scotland, Northern Ireland, and England. The politics of these national cultures and locations will create very different stage pictures, arguments, and feminisms. Chapters in this section examine women's playwriting in relation to the various 'politics of [national] location'.

Wales, Scotland, and Northern Ireland all have histories of seeking separate national identities from England. In Wales in the late 1960s the assertion of identity was marked by the campaigning of the Welsh Language Society and the bomb outrages committed by the Welsh Home Rule Group. When it came to the referendum on devolution in 1979, however, the vote went convincingly against a national assembly. This, coupled with the election of Margaret Thatcher had, as Anna-Marie Taylor describes in the introduction to *Staging Wales*, 'a bearing on our lives well on into the 1990s. We were all for a long time and in many ways contemporaries of our 1979 selves.'[1] In her chapter in this volume, Taylor is particularly concerned with how the first generation of Welsh women playwrights have been 'staging Wales' in combination with gender politics. Taylor identifies the tropes of memory, exile, and home as ones through which these women playwrights are able to challenge and to revise dominant, masculinist representations of Wales and Welshness.

Scotland charts a similar pattern of growing nationalism in the 1960s, and increased support for the Scottish National Party in the 1970s. While the 1979 pro-devolution vote was greater in Scotland than in Wales (in percentage terms), it was still not enough to secure Scottish devolution. Therefore, for contemporary Scottish women writers feminist concerns with gender or sexuality continue to combine with the broader issue of national identity. Adrienne Scullion's essay introduces a number of these Scottish women playwrights, including Liz Lochhead, Rona Munro, and Sue Glover, to detail how their feminist dramaturgy mixes (formally and ideologically) with Scottish culture and politics.

Here, we can index what is a key concern in Scullion's chapter, with an additional example of our own: the critical reception in England of Rona Munro's *The Maiden Stone*. Written in the dialect and rhythms of Munro's native North-East Scotland, *The Maiden Stone* was commissioned by and performed at the Hampstead Theatre, London, in 1995, and was the winner of the first Peggy Ramsay Award. Reviewing in England, Michael Billington tried hard to fathom the play's meaning, but confessed he was thwarted by 'the language so often couched in difficult dialect' and was 'hopelessly lost in a dense Scots myth',[2] while Benedict Nightingale patronised Munro as 'the little-known Scots dramatist' (Munro had been writing since 1982), with a 'bold imagination' if only you could get beyond the 'play's thick Celtic mists and the production's even thicker Highland accents'.[3] What these reviewers actually reveal is a colonialist attitude towards Celtic culture, myth, and language.

While the separatist impulse in Wales and Scotland was contained by the voting against devolution in 1979, the struggles in Northern Ireland, on the other hand, escalated into increased violence. After armed forces were brought in in 1969 to deal with the violence, fighting continued until the 1994 cease-fires by the IRA (Irish Republican Army) and the Combined Loyalist Military Command. As stand-up comedian Sandra, at the close of Christina Reid's *Clowns* (1996), jokes:

> We're a nation of comedians. The best ones are offstage. On the day the Loyalists declared their own cease-fire, two wee Belfast women were standing at a bus stop. And one turns to the other, and she says, 'Bloody typical isn't it? You wait twenty-five friggin' years for a cease-fire and then two come along one after the other.'[4]

Women organising in Northern Ireland have had to contend with the violence of the political struggles; have had to try and reach each other across the sectarian divide. Mary Trotter examines the work of Northern Irish women playwrights, seeing how they 'look at gender through the lens of the national question', but also drawing our attention to how complicated that 'national question' is, given the diverse geographical, religious, cultural, and political positions involved. Crucially, Trotter argues, these playwrights have been concerned with 'voicing' the struggles of Northern Irish women, noting moreover that their 'within and without' position as writers – officially recognised as being within the borders of the UK, but working with the hybridity of Irish and Northern Irish cultures – echoes the highly complex matrix of oppression and marginalisation staged in their theatre.

Reid's Sandra observes that in English politics people 'don't know where Belfast stops and Dublin begins. It's all Ireland to them', but that, likewise, in Northern Ireland, people are unaware of 'conditions in places like Moss Side and Toxteth', or 'the thousands of homeless sleeping rough on London's streets'.[5] Arguably, it has become increasingly impossible, however, to remain divorced from the violent realities of our national/local and international/global geographies. In Judith Johnson's *Uganda,* performed at the Royal National Theatre Studio in 1994, for example, a widowed father tries to make sense of the war in Yugoslavia through newspaper and television reports, but his understanding is restricted by his isolationist outlook – what Johnson describes in her afterword to the play as an 'island mentality'.[6]

Other contemporary women playwrights, across different generations, have felt similarly drawn to challenging the 'island mentality' – most controversially, perhaps, in Sarah Kane's *Blasted* (1995) which visually brought the war in Bosnia to a hotel setting in Leeds in the North of England, but most particularly in the theatre of Timberlake Wertenbaker. As Susan Carlson argues in her chapter, Wertenbaker dramatically represents 'a new sense of community', one which takes us 'beyond a stable identity in gender, class, race, or nation'. In *The Break of Day* (1994), which crosses between a former Communist, East European country and an English country setting, Carlson explains that Wertenbaker's characters can no longer hide out in their 'lovely English country garden'. On the contrary, they must seek to understand their lives, identities and responsibilities in the context of 'global issues and events'.

It is because, as Carlson traces in her chapter, Wertenbaker problematises the issue of national identity (not least because of her own cultural hybridity) that we situate this chapter at the close of this part (when we might, alternatively, for example, have presented Wertenbaker in the section 'The Question of the Canon', or indeed in our final part on identity). By so positioning Wertenbaker, we hope to problematise the concept of 'British'; to interrogate (as Bassnett proposes) this adjective, whose imperialist overtones are problematic for all of the women playwrights discussed here.

NOTES

1 Anna-Marie Taylor (ed.) *Staging Wales: Welsh Theatre 1979–1997* (Cardiff: University of Wales Press, 1997), p. 6.
2 *Guardian,* 1 May 1995, p. 14.

3 *The Times*, 1 May 1995, p. 13.
4 Reid, in *Plays One* (London: Methuen, 1997), Act I, sc. 2, p. 343.
5 *Ibid.*, Act I, p. 309.
6 Judith Johnson, afterword to *Uganda*, in Pamela Edwardes (ed.) *Frontline Intelligence 3: New Plays for the Nineties* (London: Methuen, 1995), p. 133.

5

SUSAN BASSNETT

The politics of location

A new phenomenon is increasingly apparent in contemporary British women's theatre: from relatively parochial origins, there is an increased internationalism, that reflects major changes in the culture of the British Isles. This internationalism is apparent both in the choice of material from which to create theatre, whether scripted or devised, and in the broader base of performance styles that reflects a greater traffic and exchange of skills in theatre as a whole. It also reflects the shift towards a more integrated idea of Britishness, that is no longer premised on assumptions about ideals of (predominantly male) English behavioural models.

Feminist theatre in Britain from the 1970s to the end of the 1990s has gone through a series of quite distinct shifts of emphasis. Mid-way through the 1970s, women's theatre began to shift away from its initial socialist agenda to an exploration of broader debates about gender and sexuality. The subjects of women's performances also changed. From plays looking at motherhood, wages for housework, equal pay, exploitation of women in the workplace, and a general emphasis on women's work, attention shifted to more personal explorations of incest, domestic violence, and then to questions of sexual identity and preference. By the early 1980s, gay and lesbian theatre was increasingly important, and there was a marked increase in the number of solo performers and performance artists. This emphasis on the body, which was directly connected to feminist politics in general, was also accompanied by a growing interest in exploring theatre form.

In 1986 the first festival of women's experimental theatre, known as Magdalena '86 (which later became the Magdalena Project), took place in Cardiff, Wales. Two points are of particular significance: firstly, the project was funded by a combination of different bodies, including the Cardiff Laboratory Theatre, the Welsh Arts Council, and the Calouste Gulbenkian Foundation. That such a project should have received monies from sources such as these is an indication of the seriousness with which the enterprise was perceived. Secondly, the festival strongly asserted its internationalism, and a primary task was the

bringing together of women from different countries and different theatre traditions to share their work.

The internationalist agenda of Magdalena marked a new phase in British
women's theatre. Despite accusations of elitism, most notably by Margaretta
D'Arcy, who claimed that there was excessive emphasis on the visual and not
enough connections made between performers and audiences, the project established a solid base in Cardiff, and set up a series of workshops that followed the
format of the first festival.[1] It is worth noting that none of the performers had
any interest in agitprop theatre, and several would best be described as performance artists. Many of the women who took part in the 1986 event came from
the Third Theatre community, those who on the whole have chosen to distance
themselves from the commercial theatre. However, by 1988 that distinction had
broken down, and Magdalena participants included professional performers,
directors, academics, and writers as well as Third Theatre workers.

It would be unfair to over-emphasise the importance of the Magdalena Project
at the expense of other developments in women's theatre practice, but with hind-
sight it does appear to have been a development that happened at exactly the
right time and so served as a focal point and meeting place for a very wide range
of women working in some form or other of theatre. Patrice Pavis has described
theatre in the last decades of the twentieth century as standing 'at the crossroads
of culture', a metaphor that is particularly appropriate when considering the
Magdalena Project and its impact.[2] The crossroads can be seen as a meeting
point, a place where travellers from different cultures encounter one another and
exchange information. It is also a place of great danger, however, an unstable site
in-between, traditionally the place where those who could not be buried in sanc-
tified ground were hastily shovelled into shallow graves. There is something
about the image of the crossroads that disturbs, and the notion of the unholy
encounter serves as a useful metaphor for post-modern women's theatre of the
1990s.

Early feminism was all about alternatives to the existing social order. Women
called into question all kinds of received ideas and practices and challenged the
fundamental patriarchal notion of binary oppositions that saw woman as the
opposite of man. Hélène Cixous famously argued against the idea of the binary
divide, positing a third way that celebrated the space in-between polar oppo-
sites.[3] Alternative concepts of artistic excellence began to be debated, and the
traditional canon, dominated by male authors, with women relegated to the
margins, began to be reconceived. This stage of feminist thinking and creativity
was concerned with the establishment of alternative models for women, and the
task of rewriting cultural history to give greater priority to the contributions
made by women was undertaken by women around the world.

There was a flaw, however, in 1970s feminist thinking in the tendency, particularly among Anglo-American women, towards a notion of universalism, best expressed in ideas of sisterhood that might in some way transcend other boundaries. The fallacy of such a position was quickly pointed out by black women and by women from outside the Euro-American white mainstream. Differences came to be marked more fiercely and the terms of the debate widened. The Iranian revolution of 1979 showed clearly the gulf dividing women from different cultures. Western feminists who deplored the imposition of the veil on Iranian women failed to look at the function of the veil in traditional Islamic society. Similarly, it became clear that simply deploring female circumcision as a barbaric practice would not lead to its disappearance in cultures where tradition is seen as a protective wall that keeps the wolves at bay, and where a girl's market value, and assurance of survival, depends on evidence of virginity. Universal sisterhood, the utopian ideal of women in the late 1960s and early 1970s gave way under the pressure of difference. The subaltern began to speak, to paraphrase Gayatri Spivak, and what she said was not always recognisable or acceptable to all other women.[4]

What was happening was the reassertion of cultural difference, together with differences of class, race, and gender; nor is it accidental that the concept of post-colonialism should have come into its own at roughly the same time as feminism was discovering the fallacy of universalism. An event like Magdalena '86, therefore, illustrated ways in which women in theatre were moving in diametrically opposite directions. On the one hand, there was a great deal of discussion about similarities, about sharing, about the search for a common language, about the possibility of there being a discernible feminine aesthetic that would be manifest in performance. On the other hand, there were great differences in working practice, goals, attitudes, and traditions. While some women saw themselves as feminists, others vehemently opposed the term. Significantly, the next workshop, in 1987, entitled 'A Women's Language in Theatre?' opened its doors to men. The notion of a women-only Magdalena had been debated by the advisory board, and, though there was some opposition, the general consensus was that it would be in the best interests of theatre practitioners as a whole, regardless of gender, if events were open to all. In fact, very few men chose to attend, and of those who did, the majority were either partners of women taking part in the workshop or academics.

In a few decades' time, when the history of British theatre in the 1980s comes to be written, there will be absolutely no consensus. If we focus on festivals, such as Magdalena (which is international in emphasis, though based in Wales), the London International Theatre Festival, the Edinburgh Festival and countless other major regional arts events, then this will be seen as the decade when British theatre finally became truly international. There is another way of interpreting events, however. The success of playwrights such as David Edgar, David Hare,

Howard Brenton, Pam Gems, and Caryl Churchill in the 1970s had resulted in the epithet of the 'new Elizabethan age' being used by broadsheet reviewers. By the 1980s that era had come to an end, and the market-driven Britain under Margaret Thatcher's Prime Ministership was marked by a move away from their brand of theatre. The era of the block-buster musical that celebrated the wealth and flashiness of the new order had begun. Small companies went to the wall. Funding was directed increasingly at large-scale companies with assured audiences. If it was not by Andrew Lloyd Webber or playing at the National Theatre it did not count. Historians might therefore want to say that this was a time that did not favour experimentation. Yet it was also a time when an alternative culture of women comedians began to emerge, when cabaret and stand-up acts came back strongly in alternative venues, when performance artists increased in number and popularity, when writers like Carla Lane, Lynda La Plante, Trevor Griffiths, and Alan Bleasdale wrote not for the theatre but for television. It was also the time when British cinema was starting to move again and was, despite grave financial difficulties, preparing the ground for its huge international successes of the 1990s.

What we can say about the 1980s with some degree of confidence is that it was a time when homogeneity in British theatre ceased to exist. The New Elizabethan age had been dominated by a group of playwrights, men and women, characterised by their Left-wing politics and their deference, in different ways and to different degrees, to a theatre loosely based on that of Brecht. The primary differences explored by these writers were differences of either class or gender, both of great significance at the time. The 1980s, however, were a decade of internationalism, characterised by multinational take-overs, developments in computer technology, and the concept of the global village. Debates about class in 1980s Britain began to seem outdated, belonging to another age altogether, for although class divisions remained as strongly as ever, indeed were exaggerated by large-scale unemployment, what changed radically was the perception of class distinctions. The extent of those changes could be seen most clearly in 1997, when Diana, Princess of Wales, died in a car crash in Paris with her Egyptian lover and millions reacted with expressions of grief at the loss of a woman 'just like us'. In some mysterious way, people had been able both to acknowledge the great class gulf that divided them from Diana in their everyday lives and at the same time to perceive her almost as a member of their own families. The fact that no British social historian of the day was able to explain this phenomenon serves to strengthen the suggestion that this was a manifestation of a process that had been underway for a long time, probably since the combined national crises of the Falklands War in 1982 and the Miners' Strike in 1984.

In 1989 the collapse of the Berlin Wall and the removal of the Iron Curtain forced the British Left to confront its own identity crisis. For identity could no longer be assured to reside in assumptions about class, political position, or authority conveyed by clearly determined gender roles, nor could there be any solace in ideas of universal sisterhood or universal socialism. At this point, however, what became clear was that an alternative politics of identity was already well established and it now began to emerge: the politics of cultural identity which has taken a particular form in the British context.

Anyone following trends in Scotland, Wales, and Northern Ireland could not fail to notice that during the 1980s there had been a steady increase in artistic creativity in these regions, not only in the performing arts but also in literature, music, and the visual arts. Funding from regional Arts Councils and from the European Community assisted the process, and the EEC funding also underlined the fact that traditionally Scotland, Wales, and Ireland had long-standing links with various European cultures. The remaking of the Republic of Ireland, one of the great success stories of the eighties and nineties, led to a surge of popularity of all things Celtic, music in particular. Pan-Celticism, regarded more as a joke than a serious artistic movement in Britain as a whole, re-emerged in new forms. Writers, musicians, actors, artists, and film-makers from the Celtic environment began to acquire international prominence. At the same time, however, this emergence of national cultural trends was accompanied decisively by internationalism, because the expanding national culture was also prime material for export. Standing at the crossroads, with roads leading to London, Europe, the rest of the world, and their own native locality, Scottish, Welsh, and Irish theatre practitioners bartered, exchanged, and borrowed from everywhere. Lists of leading British writers, produced by the Arts Council and the British Council, increasingly featured writers from Scottish, Irish, Welsh, Afro-Caribbean, or Indian sub-continent backgrounds. It is also not accidental that many of the finest translators in the British Isles are based in Scotland, Wales, or Ireland, where the link between national culture and language is a powerful one. When Peter Brook's *Mahabharata* came to Britain, it went not to London, the metropolis, but to Glasgow, the city that is home to the Glasgow Citizen's Theatre which has one of the most international repertoires of any regional theatre in the United Kingdom. Following precedents set by the Cardiff Laboratory Theatre, Magdalena established a permanent base in Wales, enabling companies like Bryth Gof to perform in Welsh to international audiences.

Another group of performers also met at the crossroads, only this time the signs pointed in other directions: to India, Uganda, the Caribbean, Bangladesh, Nigeria, as well as to London, Birmingham, Leicester, or Edinburgh. For Britain had been steadily becoming more culturally diverse, and by the 1980s the extent of the transformation wrought upon urban society in particular was apparent (see chapter 13). With over 500 mosques in London alone, the dominance of Christianity was challenged. Moreover, unlike the United States that favoured a policy of conscious discrimination in favour of a model of multiculturalism, in the more pragmatic British context the impulse for change came from the grass roots. Writers like Jackie Kaye, Adele Saleem, Meera Syal, and Moniza Alvi take as their material the multiplicity of their own cultural backgrounds and heritage, rejecting binary oppositions in favour of a new notion of cultural hybridity. For if internationalism is to have any serious impact upon artistic creativity, it has to be more than mere borrowing from alternative sources. It has to connect with elements in the native tradition, and here the resurgence of Irish, Scottish, and Welsh political autonomy has immediate repercussions in artistic terms. Not only are playwrights and other writers looking back into their own traditions, seeking, for example, a line of Scottish women writers distinct from the powerful English mainstream, but they are also challenging the dominance of standard English as a language.

In a book that has the adjective 'British' in its title, it might appear incongruous to question the validity of such a term, yet question it we must. For the term itself has undergone a mysterious transformation in recent years, from a catch-all that encompassed within itself the English, Scots, Welsh, Irish, and all those from different parts of the empire who were fortunate enough to hold British passports, to something else. In her book, *Britons Forging the Nation 1707–1837*, Linda Colley argues that Britishness was formed in this period of intense nationalistic fervour in Europe by being opposed to other nations.[5] Britishness is therefore a relatively recent concept, and one linked inexorably to empire. It follows that with the end of empire, and a redrawing of political and cultural boundaries, there should be a major rethinking of identity and Britishness. What, at the end of the twentieth century, does it mean to be British? We seem to be witnessing a move away from the illusory homogeneity conveyed by the term 'British' towards a reassertion of diversity, that is being manifested in different ways. So we have pan-Celticism, we have an increasing assertion of English identity – though this is proving more difficult to define than Scottishness or Welshness or Irishness – and we have the post-colonial hybridity of those who feel confident in more than one culture and are able to move between languages, traditions, and rituals.

The question of how these changes are being manifested in the theatre is difficult to answer. Liz Lochhead, for example, is concerned in her work with Scottishness, but also with the broader spectrum of power relations. Timberlake Wertenbaker is one of the playwrights who takes as her primary material the politics of identity in the British context, and she is in a special position by virtue of being both inside and outside the culture. Two aspects appear striking, however. The first is the return not only to history but also to myth. History, like myth, though in different ways, provides a framework within which explorations of identity can be made without the restrictions of a naturalistic context. A play set in West Belfast, for example, is grounded in the realities of the circumstances of the characters who live in that environment, whereas a play that uses the myth of Medea or Philomel can be both general and particular at the same time. Moreover, the use of myth reinforces the notion of hybridity, since myths transcend national boundaries and become part of a shared inheritance.

History provides us with a trace of events that have taken place in the past, events that can be reconsidered and reassessed, but which nevertheless have a point of origin. Hence when Liz Lochhead returns to the story of Mary, Queen of Scots, she is using material that compels a rewriting, because the basic elements of Mary's life are generally known. To some extent, a process of evaluation of that original historical material is bound to take place and in consequence the audience cannot avoid being made to rethink what they know. When Timberlake Wertenbaker uses the myth of the rape of Philomel, however, she is using a myth premised on an idea of metamorphosis that serves as a device for inviting the audience to think through questions of transformation and change. Here the task demanded of the audience is slightly different, for what is involved is not so much a process of re-evaluation, but rather a process of re-interpretation. In this similar but different use of primary materials, Lochhead can be seen as representative of the new Scottish writer, who re-examines her history of links with the English and draws attention to the relationship between the past and the present, while Wertenbaker is representative of the post-colonial writer, calling upon us to consider the ways in which power relations in the world have been shaped by the language imposed by the dominant power.

Secondly, and of equal significance, is the emphasis on the body of the performer in contemporary theatre. This is, of course, a truism, for the body is always in evidence in the theatre. What has happened with increasing frequency over the last decade or so is that the body has become not only the focus of attention but the locus of performance. Companies such as DV8 who cross boundaries between drama, dance, and gymnastics have devised a form that complements their refusal to conform to norms and boundaries of sex and gender. For the performance artist, the body is the signifying presence, and the relationship of the audience with that body takes place in a space that is decidedly not the same as the space of interaction between traditional theatre and an audience. For the playwright, the actor's body is, of course, the channel through which the play comes to life, but at a time when physicality is of such significance in theatre and cinema, it is not surprising that there should be a strong emphasis on the body in the work of many playwrights. No longer merely a vehicle for speaking the words written in the script, the body becomes the site of another theatrical language. We can see this as a logical development from the debates about the body propounded by gender theorists, but it is also an indication of a change in conceptions of place and space. It is also, of course, a further indication of the internationalisation process, for in a theatre where a single language cannot be taken for granted, the body can speak both in its own language and in ways that transcend verbal language altogether.

In the 1990s we are witnessing a double-faced pattern of movement: towards increased globalisation on the one hand, and towards a reassertion of national cultures on the other – a double movement towards a sense of identity through a mythicised culture of unification and an insistence nevertheless on plurality. That process is particularly apparent in contemporary Britain, when the old homogeneous idea of Britain as a single, unified society is no longer tenable. That society is dissolving into separate entities that define themselves once again as nations and are in the process of setting up their own parliaments. Britain as a federation of diverse national groupings is also a space in which peoples from the former imperial territories have settled, bringing great cultural diversity and integrating those diverse practices into all aspects of British life. Without the United States' concept of the melting pot that premised homogeneity as a model, British interculturalism is developing quite differently, and plurality is seen as desirable rather than as reprehensible. This is interesting, given the spread of English at the present time as a global language. The insistence of different groups of British citizens on exercising the right to use their own languages as well as their own variety of English, in short to be bilingual as well as bicultural, is bound to have an impact on the next generation of playwrights. Whether they will want to describe themselves as *British* playwrights, however, remains to be seen.

NOTES

1 For details of Margaretta D'Arcy's position, see Susan Bassnett, *Magdalena: International Women's Experimental Theatre* (Oxford: Berg, 1988), pp. 67–9.
2 Patrice Pavis, *Theatre at the Crossroads of Culture*, transl. Loren Kruger (London: Routledge,1992).
3 Hélène Cixous, 'Le rire de la méduse', in *L'arc*, 61, 1975, pp. 39–54. English version, 'The Laugh of the Medusa', transl. Keith Cohen and Paula Cohen, *Signs* 1 (Summer 1976), pp. 875–99.
4 Gayatri Spivak, *In Other Worlds: Essays in Cultural Politics* (London: Routledge, 1988).
5 Linda Colley, *Britons: Forging the Nation 1707–1837* (New Haven and London:Yale University Press, 1992).

FURTHER READING

Bassnett, Susan. *Magdalena: International Women's Experimental Theatre*. Oxford: Berg, 1988.
(ed.) *Studying British Cultures: An Introduction*. London and New York: Routledge, 1997.

Cutler, Anna. 'Abstract Body Language: Documenting Women's Bodies in Theatre'. *New Theatre Quarterly* 14 part 2, no. 54 (May 1998): 111–19.

Goodman, Lizbeth. *Contemporary Feminist Theatres: To Each Her Own*. London and New York: Routledge, 1993.

Feminist Stages. Interviews with Women in Contemporary British Theatre. Amsterdam: OPA. Harwood Academic Press, 1996.

Griffiths, T. R. and M. Llewellyn-Jones (eds.) *British and Irish Women Dramatists Since 1958*. London: Open University Press, 1993.

Harvie, Christopher (ed.) *Regional Cultures. The Difference Between*. Special issue of *Journal for the Study of British Cultures*, 2 (1995).

Melrose, Susan. 'My Body, Your Body, Her-His Body: Is/Does Some-Body (live) There?' *New Theatre Quarterly* 14 part 2, no. 54 (May 1998): 119–25.

Stephenson, Heidi, and Natasha Langridge (eds.) *Rage and Reason: Women Playwrights on Playwriting*. London: Methuen, 1997.

Stratmann, Gerd (ed.) *National Identities*. Special issue of *Journal for the Study of British Cultures* 5, no.1 (1998).

6

ANNA-MARIE TAYLOR

Contemporary Welsh women playwrights

Women and drama: the Welsh context

It is no exaggeration to state that women have been 'hidden' from historical, cultural, and literary production in Wales.[1] It is also not an overstatement to maintain that Welsh cultural experience in Britain has tended to be strait-jacketed into a small repertoire of imaginative possibilities. These possibilities usually foreground masculine activity – male-voice choirs, rugby playing, mining, bardic proclamations, chapel ministry, and political radicalism. Although there is no denying that these behaviours existed (and are still resonant in Welsh cultural life), recent academic work in the social sciences and humanities in Wales has attempted to illuminate our clouded female past and to indicate new ways of representing 'Welshness'.

In Welsh historical studies, with their strong tradition of local and labour history, there has been a flourishing of work on women's lives, often supported by community publishing ventures.[2] This interest in female experience, centred in particular on women's work and domesticity, was prompted in part by women's increased visibility in the public sphere, as shown, for example, in the miners' support groups during the strikes of the mid-1980s, and the establishment of agencies to promote women's presence in the workforce, such as Chwarae Teg (Fair Play) founded in 1992. From the late 1950s onwards, changes in the Welsh economy – specifically a gradual and eventually seismic shift away from the heavy industries of coal, steel, and slate to service and light industries – have served to make women more prominent in public life. Indeed, nowadays in some (re)industrialised areas in South Wales there is a higher proportion of women in the work force than of men. However, it must be said that these jobs are often part-time and not highly skilled, and surveys indicate that the official face of Wales remains a masculine one, with key positions in Welsh public, political, and commercial life still held by men.[3]

Imaginative writing can provide a space for marginalised groups to intervene in public debate. However, it is depressing to note that participation here (and certainly publication) has again been overwhelmingly masculine. For example, the University of Wales Press's lengthy 'Writers of Wales' series features a bare half-dozen women authors. While there have been several attempts to raise the profile of popular female writers, such as turn-of-the-century best-selling novelist Allen Raine (Anne Adaliza Puddicombe),[4] and although writers such as novelists Kate Roberts, Siân James, and Bernice Reubens, and poets Gillian Clarke, Menna Elfyn, and Gwynyth Lewis, may be becoming increasingly well known, both inside and outside Wales, the canon of Welsh literature, in both the Welsh and the English languages, remains that of a brotherhood of writers, often referred to in familiar terms, such as 'R. S.' or 'Dylan' (R. S. and Dylan Thomas, respectively).

These writers' particular inclusion in the canon as poets (and not in Dylan Thomas's case as short-story writer and dramatist) indicates also the elevation of poetry within Welsh literary tradition. The status accorded poetry is consequent upon a number of factors. These include a bardic tradition of writing and reciting verse through Eisteddfod competitions; a ruralist emphasis on landscape and ecology in Welsh literature; the suitability of poetry to express inward emotion in a country whose inhabitants can place greater emphasis on religious observance than in other parts of mainland Britain; as well as the proliferation of small presses across Wales due to the lack of a centralised publishing industry.

The situation that promotes poetry as a literary form also accounts for why drama has been underrecognised and is the least published genre of literature in Wales. Western drama has usually prospered in a professionalised, urban, and secular context, sited around particular metropolitan performance spaces. Therefore it is not surprising to note that a fully professionalised theatre developed much later in Wales than elsewhere in Europe. Because of Wales's hilly geography and linguistic 'internal difference',[5] which divides south from north and west from east, its demography – the population thins out the further north you travel – and its Nonconformist past which frowned on dramatic entertainment, professional theatre-making has only been fully established here since the late 1960s and early 1970s.[6] Since the late 1970s, professional drama has rooted itself across Wales largely through community touring and locally based initiatives. This dissemination of theatrical activity has allowed companies to establish themselves in remotely located rural places, as illustrated, for example, in the case of the community drama groups Theatr Powys in Llandrindod Wells, Arad Goch in Aberystwyth, and Theatr Bara Caws in Caernarfon.

So, by way of an introduction to playwriting in Wales, these two factors – the erasure of women from public and literary life and the late development of a professional stage – do not bode well for a discussion of drama by Welsh women. Despite these obstacles, Welsh women playwrights have, as I shall argue here, made a powerful contribution to contemporary theatre, both extending dramaturgical models and contributing to debates on Welsh identity and nation-hood. It is difficult to find a unifying critical approach to present what is a very diverse body of work, but I propose to place Welsh women's drama in what are familiar Welsh literary locations: those of memory, exile, and home.

Women's drama in Wales as memory and exile

If you go into any library housing collections of Welsh books, you will encounter the *cofiant*, the memoir, a widely used form, often adopted by clergymen in the last century to recount their own spiritual lives and ministries, or those of famous clerics. The masculine act of remembering found in the *cofiant* is feminised by leading Welsh poet Gillian Clarke in her long poem of the same name.[7] This substantial and accomplished piece takes us on an epic journey through generations of Clarke's family: beginning with her departure from a suburban Cardiff home, through Edwardian memories and Victorian family tragedies, and leading eventually to the writer's familial origins in the warrior kingdoms of ancient Welsh-speaking North Wales. This personal journey of remembrance is holistic, for the poet's initial sense of severance from place and history becomes in the final verses a reconnection with family origins and tribal belonging. Private memory and domestic incidents merge with a wider ancestral past.

This relocation of a personal history within an ancestral past is shared by writers who see themselves as part of a diaspora; most notably with black American novelists such as Alice Walker, Jamaica Kincaid, and Paule Marshall. What may seem unusual about Clarke's epic poem is that she experiences severance from her past within her own country. Such dislocation, however, is not uncommon in Welsh literature, as exile from an authentic Welshness, more often than not centred around displacement from the Welsh language and the countryside, is a condition voiced by several modern Welsh writers.[8]

In her discussion of the meaning of home in modern drama, Una Chaudhuri observes that:

> In the theater, environmental realism was a precise reflection of this figuration of home, producing a stage furnished on the principle of immediate spatial intelligibility ... around the actions of arriving, staying, leaving, returning, and so on ... The dissolution of that homogeneous idea of culture redefines the problem of home as problematic; something that does not simply pose personal problems for individuals and groups but something that conflicts with their overall cultural outlook and expectations ... An emblem of this difference is the shift of focus in drama from actions of leaving home to homecomings.[9]

Chaudhuri's observations are pertinent to women's stage writing in Wales where the act of homecoming – whether in the form of a re-entry into a shared female history or of a more complex understanding of belonging to Wales – has become the central concern of many of this first generation of women playwrights.

Lucinda Coxon's *Waiting at the Water's Edge* (Bush Theatre, 1993; Made in Wales Stage Company, 1995) takes her own family's desire to return *home* to Wales (her grandmother and two sisters had gone to work in domestic service in England in the 1920s) as the starting point for her drama about the precariousness of linguistic and social identity. As Coxon explains, 'what had begun as a straightforward economic migrancy became translated into a far more complex dynamic'.[10] *Waiting at the Water's Edge* is the story of two maids – one from the North Wales coast, the other from the mining communities of the South – who find employment in London. Although marred somewhat by over-busy plotting, this drama of escape from domestic service and from a gendered identity foregrounds questions of cultural belonging with theatrical skill. At the end of the play, the maid Vi who, disguised as her employer's son, has broken free to work in the mining territories of Nova Scotia, is heavily pregnant and sets sail for Wales. As she gives birth to her child in the boat, 'the stars in the sea and fish in the sky' are reflected in the water and guide her 'south . . . east . . . home'. This final image of mother and baby drifting off Newfoundland is shared by Su, the maid left behind in London, and points to the complex conditions of homecoming. Vi is literally at sea with her identity; Su is stranded in England, but nature is beckoning both women homewards to Wales.

Coxon's play, like Gillian Clarke's poem *Cofiant*, appeals to a desire for authentic Welshness through returning to the shores of home. Tracey Spottiswoode in *Dare!* (Made in Wales, 1998) looks at a different idea of exile in her Theatre-in-Education play which contrasts two waves of migration: the settling of poor Italians in the South Wales valleys in the early years of the twentieth century, and the aspirations of a modern-day rock band in Aberdare who see their music as the only way out of what is no longer a thriving community. Afshan Malik's *Safar/Voyage* (Made in Wales, 1996)[11] continues this dissection of cultural identity by stressing the hybridity of Welsh personhood. This hybridity is referred to by Chaudhuri as the 'post nostalgic' condition of contemporary life,[12] meaning that we are all exiles from home, that there is no authentic point of origin in an increasingly globalised world – a view of identity that is at odds with the assumed authenticity of ethnic and linguistic belonging found in some versions of Welshness.

In Malik's *Safar*, Ismaat, an Urdu-speaking Cardiffian, negotiates her identity as 'immigrant/ . . . /exile/Welsh/traveller/Pakistani'. Ismaat has neither Ur-Welshness nor original Pakistanihood with which to reconnect. She has 'a short memory because there are no holes for [her] past to fit into'; her identity is a void because she lost her parents in a car accident and is, therefore, severed from her cultural heritage. Liberated by Rhiannon, a Welsh-speaking spirit guide and

Celtic goddess in the guise of a librarian, Ismaat uncovers her parents' grief at leaving Pakistan and their frustration at life in Britain. However, Malik's play ends optimistically: Ismaat is welcomed into her hybrid cultural position through active story-telling. She is reassured that 'where she was and wherever she was, was home'. This is a notion of belonging which echoes the words of eminent historian Gwyn A. Williams, quoted earlier in the play: 'Wales in many ways never was, but has always been now.'[13] In Williams's view, Wales has never existed in its own, independent right and, with each wave of political and economic change, has been forced to reinvent itself and its citizens' identity. Wales may be weighed down by ideas of its heroic past, but Welshness has always existed in the present tense. Thus Malik's drama uncovers another face to Welshness: a multi-cultural Wales not divided by the binarism of language.[14]

In its shifting historical identity and lack of confirmed nationhood, Wales may always have been now, but perpetual contemporaneity does not of course necessitate cultural and historical amnesia. Like historians working on Welsh women's history, women playwrights have investigated the past reality of women's lives in Wales. Bringing women out of historical exile is often dramatised at a personal level, as for example in Sêra Moore Williams's *Trais Tynor / Tender Violence* (Y Gymraes, 1994), which looks at the way memories and experiences are transmitted over generations of women; the Magdalena Project's collection of personal testimonies, *Canu o'r Brofiad / Voices of Experiences* (1992); and Sharon Morgan's *Ede Hud / Magic Threads* (Dalier Sylw, 1997) which dramatises the lives of women in her family. The pronounced use of autobiographical narratives in Welsh-language work is linked to a desire to reclaim a doubly silenced female voice: women rendered mute through the anglicisation of Wales from the nineteenth century onwards and the overwhelmingly patriarchal structures of Welsh society. Moreover, as playwright and actress Sharon Morgan observes, the concentration on nationalist politics and on the language issue in the 1960s and 1970s may have resulted in 'the tremendous contribution of the feminist movement, – its analysis of the repressive aspects of sexuality and the family, its reassessment of the social roles of women and men . . . passing us by, at a crucial time in our history'.[15] Thus staging the politics of *home* through family history constitutes an important feminist reclamation of the past, as in Morgan's own *Ede Hud / Magic Threads*.

Some playwrights have retold better-known women's lives, filling in the silences and crevices of history, as for example in Siân Evans's *The Journey of Mary Kelly* (Theatr Clwyd, 1998) which concerns itself with Jack the Ripper's last victim who travelled from Wales to London for work. Historical lives are dramatised in Kaite O'Reilley's account of the suffrage campaign in Wales, *Shrieking Sisters* (Welsh College of Music and Drama / Made in Wales, 1998), and in Lucy Gough's *Joanna* (Made in Wales, 1990; BBC World Service, 1997) which examines the life of Gough's ancestor, the nineteenth-century religious divine, Joanna Southcott. In *Y Forwyn Goch / The Red Virgin* (Dalier Sylw, 1992), Menna Elfyn explores the life of French activist Simone Weil, using the dramatic device of Weil's interrogation at Liverpool docks on landing in Britain. On a more contemporary note, Christine Watkins's *Queen of Hearts* (Made in Wales, 1998) historicises the figure of Diana, Princess of Wales, through the narration of events in the life of a Diana look-alike whose livelihood comes to an end on Diana's death.

Mothers and home

Although it is difficult to draw parallels between dramatic form and cultural experience, it may be as a result of Wales's own incipient duality – its shifting identity between borders of language, of rurality and urbanisation, of ancient myth and (post-)industrial reality – that work by Welsh women playwrights has rejected naturalistic presentation. This rejection of naturalistic verisimilitude may also be due to the more tangible influence of experimental performance on contemporary theatre in Wales. There has been a lively experimental scene in Wales since the 1970s, and innovative theatrical presentation, as well as a concern with the complexity of Welsh identity, can be seen in the work of companies such as Moving Being, Earthfall Dance, Volcano Theatre and Brith Gof, and in the Magdalena Project [see pp. 73–5].

An example of such innovative practice is to be found in the scripted performance text *8961: Caneuon Galar a Gobaith / Songs of Grief and Hope* (Brith Gof, 1985–7) created by Lis Hughes Jones, founder member of avant-garde company Brith Gof and highly active contributor to events organised by the Magdalena Project. This one-woman show was conceived, scripted, and acted by Hughes Jones (see plate 3). In a series of powerfully enacted scenes and songs she created a stirring lament for those who disappeared under the Argentinean military regime in the late 1970s. This brave and often painfully poignant performance (which, incidentally, was the first British drama to be toured in Argentina after the Falklands War) commemorated those political suspects who were tortured and went missing under Galtieri's rule, and remembered the mothers' campaign to reclaim their children. Furthermore, Hughes Jones's enactment of the grief of the mothers, girlfriends, and other female relatives was complexly located within the politics of exile and home. Not only did it recognise a present-day, brutal separation from mother and home in Argentina, but its Welsh-language performance connected with the histories of economic and religious migrants from nineteenth-century Wales to Patagonia in southern Argentina.

Hughes Jones structured *8961: Caneuon Galar a Gobaith* in a Brechtian-styled series of short scenes. Each scene portrayed specific social gestures typifying the

3 Lis Hughes Jones in *8961: Caneuon Galar a Gobaith / Songs of Grief and Hope*

emotions of the relatives of *los desaparecidos*. Individual scenes were interrupted by songs based on Argentinean popular ballad and dance forms, and sung in Welsh. Some of the songs extended the emotion of the scene; the sometimes histrionic quality of Latin American popular music was transformed into raw emotion and genuine sorrow. Other songs dislocated the action. A love song of hope, for example, stood in ironic contrast to the reality of the loved one's death in internment. Because of Hughes Jones's own 'Third Theatre' training, which at this time was highly influenced by Jerzy Grotowski's and Eugenio Barba's work, these social gestures were often taken to their limits, and Hughes Jones's committed performance embodied extreme feelings, raw grief, as well as, most poignantly, the ecstasy of hope. Thus Brechtian demonstration of socially conditioned behaviours was married to a highly intense embodiment of emotion.

Hughes Jones's performance might have been received as exploiting the grief of relatives – especially as the performance was toured less than a decade after the brutalities of the regime. However, what is interesting is that *8961: Caneuon Galar a Gobaith* indexed a complex cross-cultural exchange which gave an alternative and (for audiences in Argentina) partially liberating perspective. Welsh is still spoken in Argentina, albeit by a very small minority, and the performance in a minority language with no obvious attachment to any powerful nation state or system of hegemonic rule, meant that in this instance Welsh, a marginalised language, became the voice of the bereft women: an alternative domestic expression of family, lovers, and home. This was in contrast to the public patriotic announcements by the regime which were delivered in Spanish, and the cool, super-rational 'voice' of the BBC reporting on the atrocities in English. In addition, the performance of grieving and loss in a Welsh context connected with a long history of losing relatives – in particular the emigration of male relatives to the Americas.

Exile from home and mother is also dramatised in Hughes Jones's libretto/text *Llythyron o'r Nefoedd / Letters from Heaven* (Brith Gof, 1990). This 'étude' which was later developed into the operatic *Pax* (Brith Gof, 1991–2) has at its core a series of letters between an astronaut and his Welsh-speaking mother. After her involvement in the internationally acclaimed *Disasters of War* (1987–90), a physically audacious series of performances based upon Goya's portraits of the horrors of warfare, Hughes Jones's aim in *Llythyron o'r Nefoedd* was to stage peacefulness. Here, the astronaut looked down from the skies (the vaulted ceiling of a mediaeval church) upon a poisoned world. In their letters, mother and son bonded anew in a child-like wonderment at stars and angels in a desire for ecological peace on Earth.

The wish to reconnect with a parent figure – especially with a mother – as illustrated in both of these works by Hughes Jones, is a recurrent motif in modern Welsh drama.[16] In Siân Evans's *Little Sister* (Made in Wales, 1996), the absence of a mother forces its central figure, a young girl who has a job as a hostess in a club and a fraught relationship with an older man, to make her way independently in the world. Rather like Marlene, the business-woman in Caryl Churchill's *Top Girls*, Evans's young woman is portrayed as having to reject maternal and tender qualities in order to survive. The lack of a mother results in a search for an alternative female identity, that of the survivor not the nurturer. In other plays parental absence is used not only to emphasise the quest for individual identity but, as in Malik's *Safar*, to invoke cultural and national *anomie*. In some plays, this imaginative search for parentage can be seen as corresponding to Wales's own identity as a stateless nation: the country's social self writ metaphorically large as orphaned or illegitimate.

Christine Watkins's *The Mother House* (Made in Wales, 1990) continues a search for origins, this time in the context of Wales's religious history. Set in a convent at the time of the Tudor dissolution of the monasteries, Watkins dramatises the story of a novice nun who has an illicit affair with a soldier. The nun's story is observed by three pre-Christian goddesses who, rather like Wim Wenders's angels in the film *Wings of Desire*, can travel through time, here carrying the 'burden of souls' that is Wales's religious legacy. The imagery of the play is strongly pagan – ravens, holly trees, stones. In the shape-shifting abilities of her goddesses, Watkins suggests a more emotionally expansive version of Welsh femaleness that goes well beyond the received images of tall-hatted chapel attenders abrim with moral fury. Instead, she portrays a feisty, vulgar, and passionate connection with the earth and with life, revealing more woman-centred Celtic and Catholic religious observances which were erased by Nonconformism.

The nuns in *The Mother House* have taken 'a vow of perpetual enclosure'. Religious imprisonment is also used by Lucy Gough in *Crossing the Bar* (Fallen Angel, 1994). Inspired by the suicide of young men on remand in Swansea Jail, *Crossing the Bar* explores the relationship between a prisoner and a mediaeval nun who are sharing the same cell. Similarly, Gough's *Our Lady of Shadows* (BBC Radio Three, 1995) reworks Tennyson's 'The Lady of Shalott' as a tale of religious confinement, with the heroine recast as anchoress, walled up and locked away from the world. Again, like the dramatic motif of lost parents, these images of religious enclosure have a national dimension: the legacy of moral strictness and emotional control associated with Wales's religious background.

Christine Watkins returns to questions of women's spiritual experience in *The Sea That Blazed Fire* (Made in Wales, 1996) again to suggest a counter-tradition to the dour severity associated with Nonconformism. As with many of the plays discussed in this chapter, this work uses different time scales, and juxtaposes the religious ecstasy of Ann Griffiths, an eighteenth-century hymnist, with the enervation of a present-day ME sufferer. This drama hints at the miraculous, and, like *The Mother House,* attempts to open up a more generous space in Wales's religious and emotional legacy.

Performing Welshness

Victor Turner has alerted us to the way in which extended images and metaphors can be fruitfully employed in the absence of consolidated group behaviours, collective identifications or recognised rituals – for example, when we enter liminal stages of the life cycle such as adolescence or old age.[17] Many of us involved in contemporary Welsh cultural activities are concerned with creating new perceptions of Wales. We would like to break free from reducing the manifold experience of Welsh people into just a few imaginative possibilities, which, in the main, are based on outdated images of masculinist experience. It is important to find other expressions of Welshness that are more flexible, less anachronistic, and also woman-centred. Although the professional theatre is still young in Wales, it has rapidly developed a sense of itself as a public forum: a space in which to weigh up and to debate issues of Welsh identity. Historians have uncovered the past realities of women's domestic and public lives that could not and cannot be accommodated in the traditional, masculine projections of Welshness. In the newly created forum of theatre,[18] Welsh women playwrights have begun to extend the historical recovery of female experience into emotional and spiritual spheres. Theatre is remarkable for 'the creation of presence',[19] and it is hoped that these various enactments of memory, exile, family, and religiosity can help us to conceive more commodious, imaginative locations for women in Wales.

FIRST PRODUCTIONS OF MAJOR PLAYS BY WOMEN PLAYWRIGHTS IN WALES

Very few modern Welsh plays are published, but many are archived. Individual companies keep collections of their scripts. Made in Wales Stage Company based at Chapter Arts Centre in Cardiff, for example, has an extensive collection of plays, and the Welsh Drama Association, also in Cardiff, houses an archive of contemporary Welsh plays in its library. This production chronology offers a further guide to the location of unpublished scripts.

Branwen Cennard, *Mysgu Cymylau / Blending Clouds* (available from Dalier Sylw, Cardiff) (1991)
Lucinda Coxon, *Waiting at the Water's Edge*, Bridgend, Seren (1992)
Menna Elfyn, *Y Forwyn Goch / The Red Virgin* (available from Dalier Sylw, Cardiff) (1992)
Meg Ellis, *Cyn Daw'r Gaeaf / Before Winter* (available from author) (1987)
Siân Evans, *Little Sister* (available from Made in Wales, Cardiff) (1996)
    The Journey of Mary Kelly (available from Theatr Clwyd, Mold) (1998)
Lucy Gough, *Joanna* (available from Made in Wales, Cardiff) (1990)

Crossing the Bar (available from the author) (1994)

Our Lady of Shadows (available from BBC Radio Three) (1995)

Helen Griffen, *The Ark* in *Act One Wales*, Bridgend, Seren, 1997.

Lis Hughes Jones, *8961: Caneuon Galar a Gobaith / Songs of Grief and Hope* (available from Brith Gof, Cardiff) (1985)

Llythyron o'r Nefoedd / Letters from Heaven (available from Brith Gof, Cardiff) (1990)

Afshan Malik, *Safar/Voyage* in *New Welsh Drama*, Cardiff, Parthian, 1998.

Sharon Morgan, *Ede Hud / Magic Threads* (available from Dalier Sylw, Cardiff) (1997)

Kate O'Reilley, *Shrieking Sisters* (available from Made in Wales, Cardiff) (1998)

Mari Rhian Owen, *Hyn Oll yn Ei Chalon / All That's in her Heart* (available from Arad Goch, Aberystwyth) (1993)

Tracey Spottiswoode, *Dare!* (available from Made in Wales, Cardiff) (1998)

Siân Summers, *Un Funud Fach / One Little Minute* (available from the author) (1993)

Angharad Tomos, *Fel Paent yn Sychu / Like Paint Drying* (available from the author) (1988)

Tanddaerol / Underground (available from the author) (1992)

Christine Watkins, *The Mother House* (available from Made in Wales, Cardiff) (1990)

The Sea That Blazed Fire (available from Made in Wales, Cardiff) (1996)

Queen of Hearts (available from Made in Wales, Cardiff) (1998)

Sêra Moore Williams, *Byth Rhy Hwyr / Never Too Late* (available from the author) (1992)

Trais Tynor / Tender Violence (available from the author) (1994)

NOTES

1 See Deirdre Beddoe, 'Images of Welsh Women', in Tony Curtis (ed.) *Wales: The Imagined Nation* (Bridgend: Poetry Wales Press, 1986), pp. 227–38.

2 Our understanding of Welsh women has been enhanced by studies such as Angela V. John (ed.) *Our Mothers' Land: Chapters in Welsh Women's History 1830–1939* (Cardiff: University of Wales Press, 1991); Jane Aaron, Teresa Rees, Sandra Betts, and Moira Vincentelli (eds.) *Our Sisters' Land: The Changing Identities of Women in Wales* (Cardiff: University of Wales Press, 1994); as well as oral histories such as Leigh Verill-Rhys and Deidre Beddoe (eds.) *Parachutes and Petticoats: Welsh Women Writing on the Second World War* (Cardiff: Honno, 1992) and Carol Williams and Siân Rhiannon Williams (eds.) *Struggle or Starve: Women's Lives in the South Wales Valleys Between the Two World Wars* (Cardiff: Honno, 1998).

3 See Nickie Charles, 'Women – advancing or retreating', in Richard Jenkins and Arwel Edwards (eds.) *One Step Forward: South and West Wales Towards the Year 2000* (Llandysul: Gomer, 1991), pp. 83–97. Recent reports on women's careers in higher education in Wales and in political organisations point to a low rate of advancement and participation.

4 See Katie Gramich's introduction to Allen Raine, *Queen of the Rushes* (Cardiff: Honno, 1998).

5 M. Wynn Thomas's *Internal Difference* (Cardiff: University of Wales Press, 1992) opens up a debate on the relationship between the two language literatures of Wales.

6 For a discussion of Welsh theatre in general, see Cecil J. Price, *The Professional Theatre in Wales* (Swansea: University of Swansea, 1984); Elan Closs Stephens, 'A Century of Welsh Drama', in Dafydd Johnson (ed.) *A Guide to Welsh Literature 1900–1996* (Cardiff: University of Wales Press, 1998), pp. 233–71; and Anna-Marie Taylor (ed.) *Staging Wales* (Cardiff: University of Wales Press, 1997).

7 In Gillian Clarke, *Letting in the Rumour* (Manchester: Carcanet, 1989).

8 These include Bobi Jones, Saunders Lewis, and R. S. Thomas. See Rob Humphreys, 'Images of Wales', in Trevor Herbert and Gareth Elwyn Jones (eds.) *Post-War Wales* (Cardiff: University of Wales Press, 1995), pp.133–60.

9 Una Chaudhuri, *Staging Place: The Geography of Modern Drama* (Ann Arbor: University of Michigan Press, 1997), pp. 91–2.

10 Lucinda Coxon, *Waiting at the Water's Edge* (Bridgend: Seren, 1995), p. v.

11 Unpublished playscript. I am grateful to Made in Wales Stage Company for allowing me to pillage their archive of plays.

12 Chaudhuri, *Staging Place*, p. 92.

13 Gwyn A. Williams, *When Was Wales?* (Harmondsworth: Penguin, 1985).

14 See Glenn Jordan and Chris Weedon, *Cultural Politics: Class, Gender and Race in the Postmodern World* (Oxford: Blackwell, 1995), for a critique of Welsh cultural myopia.

15 Sharon Morgan, 'Hidden Treasure', in Anna-Marie Taylor (ed.) *Magdalena: Newsletter*, no.21, October 1996. Special issue devoted to 'Women of Theatre in Wales'.

16 Plays include Gwyn Thomas, *The Keep* (1960), Ed Thomas, *House of America* (1988), and Dic Edwards, *Wittgenstein's Daughter* (1992).

17 Victor Turner, *Dramas, Fields and Metaphors: Symbolic Action in Human Society* (Ithaca, NY and London: Cornell University Press, 1974).

18 This is not to deny an influential pre-existent amateur theatre.

19 Edward L. Schieffelin, 'Problematizing Performance', in Felicia Hughes-Freeland (ed.) *Ritual, Performance, Media* (London: Routledge, 1998), pp. 194–208.

FURTHER READING

Aaron, Jane, Teresa Rees, Sandra Betts, and Moira Vincentelli (eds.) *Our Sisters' Land: The Changing Identities of Women in Wales*. Cardiff: University of Wales Press, 1994.

Bianchi, Tony. 'Aztecs in Troedrhiwgwair: Recent Fictions in Wales'. In Ian A. Bell (ed.) *Peripheral Visions: Images of Nationhood in Contemporary British Fiction*. Cardiff: University of Wales Press, 1995: 44–77.

Chaudhuri, Una. *Staging Place: The Geography of Modern Drama*. Ann Arbor: University of Michigan Press, 1997.

McElroy, Ruth. 'Cymraes Oddi Cartref?: Welsh Women Writing Home and Migration'. In Tony Brown (ed.) *Welsh Writing in English*. Llandysul: Gomer, 1997.

Taylor, Anna-Marie (ed.) 'Women of Theatre in Wales'. Special Issue. *Magdalena: Newsletter* no. 21 (October 1996).

Staging Wales: Welsh Theatre 1979 to 1997. Cardiff: University of Wales Press, 1997.

7

ADRIENNE SCULLION

Contemporary Scottish women playwrights

The dynamics of identity and community, marginality and self-reflection, inclusion and exclusion, are key themes across a range of writings by contemporary Scottish women playwrights. At root is a concern with the idea and the representation of the 'nation' that is Scotland.

In arguing for the efficacy of the 'imaginary' – of the nation as 'an imagined political community' – Benedict Anderson outlines a version of belonging that is eclectic, multifarious, and resists closure.[1] He allows for a version of the nation, a version of community, that is open, egalitarian, and pacific. In opposition, and in practice, the application of the idea of the nation may be less tolerant; for nations also define themselves as exclusive and sovereign, building barriers (both literal and metaphoric) to limit access and regulate membership, determinedly separating the elect from the ostracised. It follows that nationalism will prefer, prioritise, value, and reward one grouping over another. The point in the establishment of society, of community, at which one group, one identity, is legitimised and the other disenfranchised, marginalised, cast, however crudely, as 'other', is a result of the socio-cultural development of the community, a conjunction of historical, economic, social, and political factors but defined in the nation's traditions, myths, and collective imagination, and replayed in its cultural texts. One might suggest that, whilst nations emerge as a geo-political phenomenon, developing through an interaction of socio-economic, cultural, and political factors, gender is a similar construction, a bio-political system whose meaning is as dependent on shared moments of recognition and rites of passage as is that of national identity and nationalism.

A Marxist reading of gender-based analyses of culture – with women being used and exploited as a symptom of and/or metaphor for colonial exploitation – has been a particularly potent symbol within Scottish representations, often linking with the idea of the woman character as the personification of natural, physical Scotland. In some measure Scottish culture's tendency towards patriarchy and the phallocentric, and its general introspection and self-criticism resists Anderson's 'imaginary' and has not yet found a consistent way of moving beyond these myth-based models. Increasingly, however, counter-criticism and readings constructed by and through textual analyses and cultural heritage have done much to reset a traditional repertoire of images and responses to them. If Scottish culture has been seen to be obsessively attracted to a set of easily transferable character stereotypes, ubiquitous images, and predictable politics, Scottish criticism has merely added to the myopia by validating and perpetuating debilitating and constraining versions of national and gender identities. However, such easy assumptions, predicated upon patriarchal and colonial models of experience, do not go unopposed. One might now point to a group of writers and practitioners who, while using and referring to the defining myths and recognisable semiotics of Scottishness, aim to produce a revisionist account of ourselves and our culture. It seems increasingly possible for the audience and the critic to follow the example of these writers and engage with Scottish drama in an analogous spirit of socio-cultural contextualisation, adapting a new framework of criticism and representation within a praxis that remains distinctively our own. In this we can see Liz Lochhead's dramaturgy as a key reference point, with the plays and screen plays of Rona Munro, Sue Glover, Donna Franceschild, and A. L. Kennedy providing new and necessary twists in the tail.

Increasingly, writers of drama are responding by adopting a dramaturgy reassessing and recreating the existing cultural codes and conventions, thereby exposing the emotional uncertainties beneath totemic structures and, most importantly, taking knowing responsibility for the nature and the effects of our own culture. It is only with an awareness of the social and political importance of this shared responsibility to the meanings of Scottish culture that the drama can confront its cultural heritage, that criticism can find fresh impetus to reassess its orthodoxies, and that the contemporary Scottish theatre industry can prepare itself for the new millennium.

Nation and gender: the case of Liz Lochhead

The best-known – both within and outwith Scotland – of contemporary Scottish women playwrights is Liz Lochhead. She has built an enviable career as a writer of poetry and drama and, increasingly, of commentary and criticism, with a distinctive voice as a broadcaster of experience and wit. Her work has found a significant place in the repertoire and in the academy. Her prominence among Scottish playwrights is, in some measure, the result of her deliberate use of and engagements with the key socio-cultural tropes of history and myth, national and sexual identity, popular, traditional, and 'high' cultural forms, and a deliberate deployment of strategies of politicised deconstruction and feminist revisioning. What makes her work particularly pertinent is her explicit

4 Alison Peebles as Elizabeth in Liz Lochhead's *Mary Queen of Scots Got Her Head Chopped Off*

engagement with and paralleling of gender (specifically women's) and national (specifically Scottish) identities throughout her writings and in her theatre-making generally.

Contemporary Scottish drama – and, with significant frequency and success, especially that written by women – has found a useful paradigm in the recreation of the history play. Several Scottish writers have very deliberately applied classic feminist strategies – recovering women's stories and histories, and reinterpreting folk tales and legends – to historical events, figures, and tropes in a bid to recreate Scottish drama: different as they are, Ena Lamont Stewart's *Business in Edinburgh* (1977), Sue Glover's *The Straw Chair* (1988) and *Bondagers* (1991), Rona Munro's *The Maiden Stone* (1995) and Lara Jane Bunting's *Whispers of Water and Yarn* (1997) are versions of the history play, and their recovery of lost or marginalised biographies reinterprets and critiques the roles of women within contemporary society. In this process Lochhead's plays have proved to be of central importance, combining a tangible feminist dramaturgy with an overt engagement with issues of nationalism, imperialism, and colonialism. Lochhead's *Mary Queen of Scots Got Her Head Chopped Off* (1987) has emerged as an important centre-piece in subsequent dramatic and critical considerations of the relationship between history and historiography, national identity and nationalism, and gender identity and feminism.[2]

Lochhead uses the past to make clear and political comment on the present.

Her 'history play' is littered with anachronism and incongruity: she makes use of twentieth-century props (prams, telephones, and bowler hats), music, rhymes, and games; draws deliberate and explicit parallels with contemporary British politics (in particular in the figure of Margaret Thatcher reworked in the representation of Elizabeth I as arch-politician); and the dramaturgy itself, the structure, the language, and the narrativity of the play, borrows from across the centuries to create a rich tableau of theatrical forms to debate the ideas and representations of 'Scottishness'.

Lochhead's plays retell the familiar and fantastical stories of Mary Shelley and Frankenstein, of Mary Queen of Scots and Elizabeth I, of Tartuffe and Dracula. She recounts them with a compelling mix of traditional Scots, contemporary vernacular, and a subtle lyricism that recent theatre writing often effaces in favour of bald realism. Lochhead is unafraid to mix the prosaic and the poetic in the one play, the one scene, the one character, the one speech. This mix can bring to her already credible and recognisable characters new heights of tragedy or pathos.

History, myth, and memory interconnect, are analysed and deconstructed in a body of work that finds reference in both literary and popular culture. Lochhead has been particularly attracted to the images and the conventions of the Gothic and has discovered in fairy tales and in childhood rhymes a new set of metaphors for the role of women in society. Like Angela Carter, Lochhead twists the familiar to find a dark and bloody unconscious with new perspectives on the assumed truths of our society. Lochhead's plays hint at themes of corporeality and body horror, and they toy with the grotesque and the ambiguous. Within the Scottish folk tradition these images flit into and haunt the unconscious and the imagined. Fantasy and the fantastic are key features of many of the most influential works of Scottish literature, but Lochhead's plays make a significant modern use of these tropes, paralleling the unnatural with debates around potency, creativity, and empowerment.

Lochhead's writing uncovers society's fears of the *unheimlich* aspects of the feminine, focusing, in part, on the experiences of women in history and in literature. Her plays foreground the social and domestic, sexual and creative roles of women within societies which politically and culturally marginalise and devalue their work and lives. Lochhead takes the common view of these women – in *Mary Queen of Scots* Elizabeth as scheming politician and Mary as *femme fatale*, in *Blood and Ice* (1982) Mary Shelley as daughter of more famous parents and lover of a more famous man – and peels back the mythology, drawing out the essential humanity of the person. She strives to find in each of her creations a more empowering identity than has traditionally been represented.

Lochhead's plays reset the role of women in history and in contemporary society within a dramaturgy that draws on her skills as poet and performer. The subjects of her plays may be historically diverse but they are united by an energetic, vibrant, and precise use of language. *Blood and Ice*, her first full-length play, is as much a memory play as it is a history play, with characters and spirits emerging from the life and imagination of Mary Shelley, 'in whose consciousness', Lochhead states, 'my *entire play* takes place'.³ Time, place, and degree of 'reality' are all signalled in the language – the prose and the verse – of the text. In a play dealing with Mary Shelley's creativity and the writing process, with commentary on the lives of both Percy Shelley and Lord Byron, there is a deliberate over-emphasis on the significance of words. Language is used to mark shifts in time and space, memory and imagination. Variations in tone suggest in turn the lyricism of the idyll of Lake Geneva, the artificiality of the conversation and society of Mary's Romantic companions, the prosaic language of domestic duties and responsibilities, and the obsessive and violent aspects of her imagination and her creativity.

The nature and value of creativity is examined by presenting alternative visions of Mary Shelley as mother and as author. The process of writing the novel is mirrored in Mary's role as mother (to her children, certainly, but also developed in the maternal role she is forced to adopt in her relationships with Shelley and her half-sister Claire) and as creator of the fiction of *Frankenstein*. This is further compared to the character of Victor Frankenstein bringing life to his monster – the reproductive transgression of Frankenstein resulting in warped progeny daring audiences to recognise a socially constructed comparison to Mary Shelley's and the woman's 'transgressive' progeny of the novel, the work of art. Jan McDonald offers a particularly bold reading of these parallelings arguing that 'She [Mary Shelley] *is* "Frankenstein".'⁴

As in *Blood and Ice*, the demands of society upon woman to be wife and mother are a central politic of *Mary Queen of Scots*. In this play, however, the dramatic conflict is not played out in private places, nor in the psyche of one woman but in the public sphere and in the political conflicts of two nations. The debate is, on one level, predicated on the public/private responsibilities and roles of women, on another it is about nationhood and national identity: explicitly questioning 'when's a queen a queen / And when's a queen juist a wummin', and 'whit like *your* Scotland is'(Act I, sc. III, p. 16 and Act I, sc. I, p. 11).⁵

Mary Queen of Scots is typical of Lochhead's dramaturgy in its re-presentation of the cherished and even hegemonic myths of Scottish national identity, its explosive feminist re-setting of both 'legitimate history' and 'popular culture', and its activation of metaphors of playing, acting, and story-telling: 'Once upon a time', La Corbie (the play's fantastically grotesque narrator, chorus, and sometime-conscience) begins, 'there were *twa queens* on the wan green island' (Act I, sc. I, p. 12). The two queens are, of course, the Catholic Mary of Scotland and the Protestant Elizabeth of England, and the play is an elaborate charade based on their stories and their mythologies, their lies and their legends. Just as the received images society holds of Mary Shelley are dissected in *Blood and Ice* so, in *Mary Queen of Scots*, Lochhead deconstructs the mythology associated with both Mary and Elizabeth, and again finds disturbing parallels between the demands made of the women in the play and the prejudices that still limit their expectations and ambitions.

Lochhead re-examines the history, mythology, legends, and even the iconography of Reformation Scotland, presenting an iconoclastic version of one of the 'privileged moments' of Scotland's past. The play's beginning distils some of the key elements of Lochhead's unravelling of the shibboleths of Scottish history: it is traditional and familiar but simultaneously can be read as aggressive and unexpected; the haunting tones of fiddle music and Scots dialect are richly evocative but, even in the context of theatre-making within Scotland, strikingly unexpected. While the audience attunes to the heady mix of Lochhead's eclectic version of sixteenth-century Scots and her expert application of standard English, the 'legitimate' theatre space itself is transformed into a diabolical circus ring, with La Corbie as ring-master and barker: '*Alone*, FIDDLER *charges up the space with eldricht tune, wild and sad, then goes. Enter into the ring, whip in hand, our 'chorus', La* CORBIE. *An interesting, ragged ambiguous creature in her cold spotlight*' (Act I, sc. I, p. 11).

La Corbie's long opening monologue is a sardonic deconstruction of the pop semiotics of Scotland, undercutting the sentimental effect of the fiddle music and interrogating the audience's perceptions with her wild interpretations and commentaries. The other characters begin to appear as a fantastic circus parade not a royal entry – '*our characters, gorgeous or pathetic, parade*' (Act I, sc. I, p. 12). The audience's spectating is immediately and radically altered from that of theatre-goers to that of freak-show voyeurs. Lochhead's characters are stripped of their historical and political significance to be recast within an absurd menagerie, with the audience positioned in paradoxical uncertainty with the action. Overseeing this ambiguity La Corbie functions at a dual level – to some degree within the play's complex diegesis but still able to transgress narrative, theatrical, and historical convention. The role of La Corbie alone points to Lochhead's determination to problematise Scottish history as both subject and ideology: the repertoire of narrative techniques she employs overtly deconstructs a dominant, legitimate historiography while her incongruous vocabulary of performance styles underlines her counter-hegemonic dramaturgical agenda. This is particularly caustic in her use of popular performance techniques.

The background of popular entertainment, of music hall and of pantomime, is essential in histories of Scottish theatre, where it attains a significance as an indigenous and alternative tradition. It is certainly a style and an idea rediscovered and redeployed within contemporary Scottish theatre-making: in 1996 Femi

5 Alison Peebles as Elizabeth and Anne Lacey as Mary in Liz Lochhead's *Mary Queen of Scots Got Her Head Chopped Off*

Folorunso observed that 'in nearly every modern Scottish play, recognisable bits and pieces of music-hall aesthetics can be found . . . the impact of music hall is everywhere discernible'.[6]

The circus motif emphasises Lochhead's self-reflexive theatricality and encourages us to seek further parallels, or reference points, within the popular tradition. Among the most significant features of popular and variety theatre is the stagecraft of the performer and the shocking presence of the performer to the spectator, a relationship that goes beyond immediacy to encompass collusion with the audience and to embody a range of performance techniques predicated on a dramaturgy – direct address, audience participation, topical referencing – which cannot permit a fourth wall. Within the context of Scottish popular theatre the direct address and interrogative technique of Lochhead's La Corbie are, therefore, familiar. One might argue that a Scottish dramaturgy *is* a popular one and it is certainly the case that this popular tradition can easily and effectively slip into a political discourse.[7] In her reassessment of patriarchal society and its approved history, Lochhead's use of the popular is just as political, just as radical, as that embodied by John McGrath's quintessential Scottish politicisation of the popular, *The Cheviot, the Stag and the Black, Black Oil* (1973).

Scottish theatre certainly uses history and, specifically, the nation's history, but it is also criticised for its essential nostalgia. *Mary Queen of Scots* is a play about the past *and* the mythology of Scotland's socio-political and cultural development. However, the play also energises the discourse of nostalgia through a distinctive dramaturgical iconoclasm and sophisticated linguistic play, notable in the use of rhymes and games. Lochhead sets out with political (feminist) intent to reinterpret the past and to draw out a new and radical agenda for the contemporary audience. She mixes the introspection of much of Scottish culture with a desire to develop a new set of images and a new system of metaphors for the depiction of domestic and psychological drama. The activation of memory – possible because of the play's use of anachronism and incongruity – as well as history is again reflected in her use of language. Using *doppelgängers* for all the main players in the drama, the omnipresent narrator, who speaks in an eclectic, ironic version of sixteenth-century Scots, and introducing parallel scenes played within a twentieth-century diegesis, Lochhead's use of the past is very much more precise and focused than is the case with plays that offer a more straightforward version of historical drama. Lochhead uses doubling with psychological intent, actors being required to play two, three, or even four different but fundamentally linked characters. Mary and Elizabeth are matched at each step by parallel and complementary characters, each time played by the same actors. The pairings of the maids Marian and Bessie, the beggars Mairn and Leezie, and the children Marie and Wee Betty each reveal another facet of Lochhead's project to show the similarities in the dilemmas and the problems faced by Mary and

Elizabeth, in particular, but also by other women in hugely different economic circumstances and both within the time-frame of the drama and in our own. Anne Varty describes a nexus of characters who are 'Constantly paired, up and down the social scale, these women complement and complete each other. Masculine and feminine, Protestant and Catholic, repressed and oppressed, adult and child, English and Scottish, virgin and whore, imprisoned and free, the binaries of the argument, multiply, swop [*sic*], and converge.'[8]

This dynamic is underlined in the play's ending which certainly undercuts its historicity and affirms its engagement with epic structures as the characters of the drama are transformed into children playing a demonic game in which Mary/Marie is again the victim of centuries of prejudice and group hysteria. The scene parallels the opening parade as '*Through the back curtains, one by one, come all our characters, stripped of all dignity and historicity, transformed to twentieth-century children by the rolling up of trouser legs, addition of a cardigan or pair of socks*' (Act II, sc. VII, p. 63). The characters play children's games, sing children's songs but they soon turn on the stranger, on Mary/Marie, attacking her because of her Catholicism. The prejudice continues and it is what society defines as the unknown or unfamiliar woman who is most easily victim. Lochhead's reassessment of the myths of Scottishness shows that the old prejudices still prevail, locking the disenfranchised into set patterns of exploitation and oppression.

Gender and community: Sue Glover and Rona Munro

Scottish drama is habitually concerned with the nature and politics of the community, with the moment of inclusion in, or exclusion from, that community as recurrent narrative spine. Contemporary Scottish drama's particular interest in the depiction of communities of women has indeed found moments of exclusion, disillusionment, and disenfranchisement. Whilst it is true that female communities may be subject to socio-economic austerity and marginalisation, within that locus Scottish writers, and in particular Scottish women writers, have found cause for pleasure in the recognition of shared identities and common interest. In plays ranging in tone and style from Donna Franceschild's *And the Cow Jumped Over the Moon* (1990), and Sue Glover's *Bondagers* and *Sacred Hearts* (1994) to Rona Munro's *Bold Girls* (1990), the unity of female community is affirmed. Although the moments of release may be fleeting, such experiences are dramatically poignant, transcending the individual and insisting upon group participation and collective action. Within communities of women, belonging is assumed and implicit in the simple acknowledgment of sisterhood, not constructed and restricted within the exclusive cabals of masculine structures. Indeed, within the female community the pleasures of sharing are potentially more egalitarian than are the hierarchical structures which connote masculinity.

The women of Scottish drama are only occasionally fully empowered and independent of a phallocentric economic order, more often being on the edges of or dependent upon groups of men and patriarchal communities. The conceits used to bring women together may be politically motivated (as in *Sacred Hearts*), or socially and economically imposed (as in *Bondagers*) in ways that seem not to be the case in connection with communities of men, where there is a dominant ethos around the dignity of labour. Women's work patterns seem to efface such discourses and, while one might find these representations of the exploited and disenfranchised limited and limiting, their communion is manifest with a democratic egalitarianism that celebrates and empowers where masculine communities exclude and humiliate.

Sue Glover has found the history play to be a particularly ubiquitous genre and her play *Bondagers* has become one of Scottish theatre's most popular pieces – successfully revived by the Traverse, toured widely and produced internationally, published and anthologised, and studied within secondary education. As Glover explains, 'Bondagers were the women workers of the great Border farms in the last century. Each farm worker was hired on condition that he brought a female worker to work alongside him – if not his wife or daughter, then some other girl that he himself had to hire at the Hiring Fair, and lodge and feed with his own family in his tiny cottage.'[9] The play recounts one year – from one February Hiring Fair to the next – in the lives of six women working the land under this system. Told in a vivid, energetic, and poetic style, it too draws on Scottish popular traditions of story-telling, song, dance, and music, adding stylised physical movement and choral elements to investigate gender and history, women's work and families, social and agricultural improvement, industrialisation and emigration. Glover confronts difficult issues of class, land, ownership, and belonging, and parallels the agricultural exploitation of the land with the economic and, in one brutal rape, the sexual exploitation of the women. The play is, however, more than a dramatisation or metaphor of colonialism: it is also a vibrant domestic drama of women subject to economic 'bondage' but also revelling in female 'bonding', the women finding strength and communion even within a context of subjugation: 'I want a place on a big farm. Plenty lassies for the crack. Plenty plooman for the dancing!' (Act I, sc. I, p. 8).

The play centres on the community of women bondagers: Sara and her 'daftie' daughter, Tottie; Ellen, a former bondager now married to the master of the farm; Maggie, a woman married to one of the farm workers, with numerous young children; Jenny, a young bondager; and Liza, the play's narrator, whose independence of spirit challenges the accepted class and gender conventions of the society. The women's work is hard and laborious, described in the play through a compelling mix of poetic language, and elaborate, ritualised movement sequences re-enacting the women working the fields, and paralleled by

6 and 7 The all-female community in Sue Glover's *Bondagers*

strange visionary sequences described by Tottie, foreseeing the industrialisation of agriculture and the inevitable displacement of the people. Throughout, the play uses music and song and dance – the agricultural calendar is marked out by fiddle music and dances in the barn, by improvised and traditional songs for hoeing, sowing, and harvesting. In this the women celebrate their labour and their identity close to the land and linked to its cycles.

The play's dramatic climax sees Tottie raped by the most seductive of the ploughmen and taken away from her extended family to an asylum. The community of women is then dispersed with the end of the agricultural year: the improving master of Blacksheils is put off his farm by the laird; the farm workers lose their security and are returned to the dwindling open market of an industry in long-term decline; the bondagers are left to the uncertainty of the Hiring Fair and their sustaining, but increasingly desperate, friendships. These conclusions prefigure the end of a whole way of life.

The theme of female community and celebration, so vivid in *Bondagers*, is also significant in Munro's lesser-known work *The Straw Chair*, a play set in the first half of the eighteenth century on the tiny island of St Kilda (or Hirta as it is known to its population and in the play). It is a piece of significant depth, worthy of more serious attention from theatre-makers and audiences, and often overlooked in favour of the more obviously entertaining *Bondagers*.

The narrative centres on the women of the island – a local woman, Oona; the noble Lady Rachel, the alienated wife of James Erskine, the Lord Advocate; and the middle-class Isabel, the young wife of the minister, Aneas. Rachel is a sophisticated, intelligent, worldly woman, but she has been banished from her Edinburgh home for threatening to expose her powerful husband as a Jacobite and a traitor. She is at least mistrusted, and in some measure feared, by the locals because of her otherness from them, a separateness marked by her class and her language: at points their descriptions of her come close to naming her 'witch'. More than anything Rachel is a victim to the power of men – her husband, her family, the lieutenants who carried her away, the vassals of the lairds Lovat and McLeod who first imprisoned her and then abandoned her on Hirta. Isabel too has been taken to the island by her marriage, by the power of patriarchy. On the island, however, she finds a freedom, an authority, and even an awakened sexuality that escaped her in her uncle's house in Edinburgh. Her freedom is represented in two related acts of patriarchal transgression: she tries to help Rachel send a letter to her lawyer cousin in Edinburgh; and she travels with the other young women to the neighbouring island of Boreray for a week relieved from their usual domestic responsibilities, 'just talking and song' (Act II, sc. III, p. 139). The latter is thrillingly escapist, but unexpectedly it also draws her closer to Aneas. The former is disastrous, as the letter is discovered and the minister is judged guilty of disobeying the authority of Erskine. The play ends with the couple being removed from the parish and returning to Edinburgh facing a future of much uncertainty: Aneas's hopes for a permanent living are in crisis, but their love and mutual respect are affirmed. Rachel is left on Hirta in physical and mental collapse. The play's final image is of her writing an imaginary letter on invisible paper in a vain attempt to draw attention to her plight: the tale of a forgotten woman exists only as an ephemeral oral story not as a written document.

One can also find such commonalities and continuities – women acting together, women protesting against their invisibility and powerlessness, the use of Celtic mythology and imagery – in the diverse writings of Rona Munro. Active throughout the 1980s, when some memorable early plays were written, including *Fugue* (1983), *Piper's Cave*, and *Ghost Story* (both 1985), Munro came to particular prominence with *Bold Girls* – a play at the very centre of the new canon of contemporary Scottish plays. This is an evocative and haunting play set in Belfast and against the backdrop of the Troubles. Like Lochhead, Munro makes purposeful use of folk, traditional, and popular culture to assess the roles available to women in a determinedly patriarchal environment. The play negotiates a complex path between realism and expressionism and is full of heavy portent and symbolism. It tells of a group of women facing up to and living with the emotional and practical ramifications of the violence of Northern Ireland. The play has a strong narrative core – exploring and explaining the relationships between Marie, Cassie, Nora, and Deirdre, the mysterious, spirit-like figure who seems to haunt Marie – but this merely serves Munro's incisive feminist analysis of contemporary, urban, patriarchal society. Like Lochhead and Glover, Munro facilitates this through an analysis of the mythologies and images of that society, weaving a text full of references to both folk and popular culture. Munro has returned to folk mythologies and, more particularly, Celtic legend to deepen the resonances of many of her dramas and *Bold Girls* is littered with references to or engagements with the fantastic and the imagined: for example, in the naming of the characters there is explicit reference to Deirdre of the Sorrows, the tragic heroine of Celtic mythology, the inspiration of great kings and heroes. The references are also topical and current, however, the women watch and provide mordant comment on both the television programme *Blind Date* and the film *The Accused*; they dance to popular music and enter a raffle in their local social club; they discuss the loss of their men folk to the violence around them. *Bold Girls* confronts the idea of the urban hardman, but contextualises it much more widely, extending the theme so that the politically and religiously motivated violence of Northern Ireland is read as an extension of domestic violence, with women as the ultimate victims: indeed the moral is also extended away from the Irish locus to all violent societies.

Unlike her other plays, the Belfast setting of *Bold Girls* removes Munro from the linguistic world of North-East Scotland which she captures so effectively in

Fugue, Piper's Cave, Saturday at the Commodore (1989), and *The Maiden Stone*. She has, in fact, set a determined example by writing in the numerous dialects and ages of Scots – Alisdair in *Piper's Cave* speaks a recognisable but curiously heightened Scots; Lena, the narrator of *Saturday at the Commodore*, in a rich and evocative Aberdonian; the characters of *Your Turn to Clean the Stair* (1992) in the vernaculars of contemporary Edinburgh; while *The Maiden Stone* is filled with a range of voices of the North-East of Scotland which, despite being set in the nineteenth century, she describes as 'the native dialect as I remember it . . . in no sense [an] historical but a living language'.[10] She, therefore, demonstrates the utility of Scots for telling stories of fantastical possibilities, contemporary relevance, and emotional worth. As Munro says: 'I am a Scottish playwright, a woman playwright, and an Aberdonian playwright, not necessarily in that order. All of these facts inform my writing but don't define it.'[11]

Munro's career significantly encompasses the other media: single plays and continuing drama for radio, and a similar diversity in her television commissions including the single dramas *Biting the Hands* (1989) and *Men of the Month* (1994). Her high-profile filmed successes include Ken Loach's *Ladybird, Ladybird* (1994) and *Bumping the Odds* (1997). Both these texts are dark visions of contemporary urban decline. Quite different from the historical settings or folkloric references of her stage plays, both films are grimly naturalistic, reflecting domestic violence, drug culture, and urban decay. The worlds of these texts are bleak and at times hopeless but, as with *Bold Girls*, her characters can reveal a mordant gallows humour. *Bumping the Odds* is a sombre and unrelenting tale of loan-sharking and barely contained violence but offers some hint of relief in the camaraderie of young men trading on the fringes of the black economy and the more desperate society of women clinging together through the fragile order of friendship and mutual dependency: Terry, concealing from her female friends a relationship with a violent loan-shark, sums up the women's situation with the bleakly aphoristic 'Men are for shags. Friends are for life.'

Emigrants and immigrants: Marcella Evaristi, Anne Marie Di Mambro, and Sharman Macdonald

All the writers considered in this chapter have some kind of relationship with the fact and the image of Scotland. For some it is a source of ideas, inspiration, representations, and narratives. For others it represents an industry and a culture within which they have found a means of production and system of distribution. For others it is in many ways a place to escape and to react against. For this latter group the identity of 'Scottish' is simultaneously destructive and inspirational.

Through the 1980s Marcella Evaristi wrote a group of popular plays for the theatre and honed her skills in the generally undervalued expertise of writing for radio. All her writing is archetypally personal, at least hinting at autobiography, and certainly rooted in her own experiences of being, according to Ned Chaillet, 'part Italian Catholic, part Jewish, altogether Glaswegian'.[12] Most of Evaristi's work engages to some degree with these identities and debates the individual's responsibility to and separateness from the socio-cultural certainties they connote. Her dissection of her characters' inner selves and the unblinking attention she gives to their every turn and every motivation create memorable but hugely complex figures. The painstaking minutiae of her character portraits set the foundations for plays that investigate and interrogate the complex roles of the individual within society.

Set in Scotland and Italy, *Commedia* (1982) confronts the stereotypes of both national identities focusing, in particular, on the idea of the mother: an identity as central to twentieth-century Scottish drama as it is rooted within Italian socio-cultural forms. *Commedia* presents a strong central woman/mother at the centre of a community of other women in a way that undercuts the misogynistic mythology of urban Scotland. *The Hat* (1988), Evaristi's most mature piece of radio drama, has been described as 'a feminist pastiche of Oscar Wilde's *The Picture of Dorian Gray*'[13] and certainly she uses the play to debate ideas around art, inspiration, and creativity. It is a complex piece, perfectly formed as a radio play, in which the inanimate objects of Marianne's home and life are given voices to comment on what they have observed of her character and, in particular, on what they have observed of her relationship with her artist lover Crispin. Some objects, including her compact mirror and her cloche hat, actually converse with Marianne, adding another dimension to a rich aural world of contrasting voices. Paralleling Lochhead's Mary Shelley, Evaristi's Marianne interrogates the role of woman as muse and potential artist.

Like Evaristi, Anne Marie Di Mambro has also described the immigrant experience, in particular the Italian immigrant experience, in Scotland. Although she has written extensively for Scottish Television's long-running soap opera *High Road*, she still focuses her attentions on the stage and has produced plays marked by a clear-eyed yet subtle undercutting of the mythologies of community so significant within Scottish culture. Her theatre work is broadly realistic, set in urban Scotland, generally contemporary but with occasional forays into Scotland's recent past. Most successful of this kind is *Tally's Blood* (1990), a play set around the Second World War and telling of Italian immigrants running a confectionery and ice-cream shop near Glasgow, with the action, as in Evaristi's *Commedia,* shifting between Scotland and Italy.

Di Mambro's *The Letter-Box* (1989) is a powerful dramatic monologue depicting the struggle of a woman, Martha, brutally beaten and thrown out of her home by her husband, trying to explain the situation to her young daughter through the letter-box of the front door. The play deconstructs the mythologies of working-class, urban Scotland by interrogating its two quintessential myths, the community spirit of the tenement and the appeal of the hardman: the neighbours 'Jack' and 'Jill' embarassedly ignore Martha declaring her 'Pissed'; while Martha herself excuses the actions of her husband by saying 'Maybe when he was out tonight something made him mad, then when Mum burnt the toast it just set him off.'[14] The play eschews any hint of the sentimentality discernible in some of Di Mambro's other work – for example, *Tally's Blood*; in contrast, *The Letter-Box* is one of Scotland's best short plays, succinct and powerfully focused.

Like *Tally's Blood*, Di Mambro's *Brothers of Thunder* (1994) is dramaturgically very straightforward, but benefits from a familiar personal quality to the writing. With only partial success – it unravels into a predictable politics of prejudice and ignorance – it is about society's response to AIDS. The two characters are a Catholic priest and the young gay student he allows to live in his presbytery. The play hints at wider themes of trust, faith, responsibility, and openness but the specifics of the drama contain rather than universalise its relevance. At the centre of the play is a moral debate between the two men, which, although it may lack passion and sensuality, is unquestionably handled with determination and commitment.

For both Evaristi and Di Mambro the idea and the representation of Scotland are far from the inferiorist or psychotic discourse which is often highlighted in criticism. Sharman Macdonald, however, has a significantly more problematic relationship with Scotland. In contrast to those writers working predominantly within a Scottish theatre industry, Macdonald's career is predominantly metropolitan. Although many of her plays are set in Scotland, she has achieved much more by way of production success in England, both in the West End and, more recently, in Leeds – *When I Was a Girl, I Used to Scream and Shout* (1984) premiered at the Bush, *When We Were Woman* (1989) at the Cottesloe, *All Things Nice* (1991) at the Royal Court, *Shades* (1992) in the West End, *Borders of Paradise* (1995) at Watford Palace, and *The Winter Guest* (1995) at West Yorkshire Playhouse. The lack of production success in Scotland is at least intriguing as not only are many of her plays set in Scotland but her characters speak a shockingly realistic, completely familiar Scots-English, the subtlety of which marks it as both affectingly truthful and achingly poetic, rooting her characters to Scotland linguistically and geographically. Thematically, too, her plays touch on issues deeply resonant within Scottish culture – complex mothers in strange and even destructive relationships with their children (particularly their daughters), absent or problematic fathers, confused adolescents, an immediate and deeply affecting physical world, and the nature of memory, nostalgia, and regret are all common themes in her work.

Macdonald's first play, *When I Was a Girl, I Used to Scream and Shout*, is set in a small seaside town on the Scottish East coast. It shifts easily and movingly between the past and the present, between 1983 (the play's present) and 1955, 1959, 1960, and 1966. It charts three sets of relationships: that between Fiona and her mother Morag; between Fiona and her friend Vari; and between Fiona and her boyfriend Ewan, who only appears in the earlier flashbacks. The play is something of a rites-of-passage narrative, with Fiona's relationship with Ewan at the centre of that. However, and despite the significance of that relationship, the play's focus is on the mother/daughter relationship, exploring the secrets they keep from each other and the compromises necessary within families.

Her more recent piece, *The Winter Guest*, adopts a much more classical temporal structure – one day in the lives of the characters – but is equally and highly evocative; all but plotless, it is an assured study in mood and feeling. It is set one February day in a seaside town on the West coast of Scotland, when the beach is covered with a chilly layer of frost, a forthright metaphor for the stalled relationships the play describes and the characters' preoccupations with death. Again at its core is the relationship between Elspeth, a mother, and Frances, her adult, recently widowed daughter. Their conversation is locked in a cycle of adolescent petulance and nostalgic regret, but tempered by feelings of love and responsibility. It is a wholly human play, with a chilly *dénouement* of innocence lost.

Macdonald's reputation within Scotland may be shifting: in 1996 Perth Theatre produced *When We Were Women*, in 1997 the Brunton produced *When I Was a Girl*, while the film version of *The Winter Guest* (1998) won a significant degree of interest in the Scottish press. A more meaningful link may have been forged with the 1998 stage première of Macdonald's *Sea Urchins* – a play previously produced with marked success on radio – by the Tron Theatre, Glasgow, in association with Dundee Rep.

Sea Urchins is again about a remembered childhood past. It is set in Wales in June 1966 on a coved and pebbled beach below a precipitous cliff. The play reveals family secrets and passions through the eyes of eleven-year-old Rena, the daughter of Scottish mother Ailsa and Welsh father John. Each year the family go on holiday with John's brother David and his family. In the course of one hot day the façade of familiarity, the habits, rituals, and traditions that hold the family together, are tested to breaking point: John's less-than-secret affair with his sister-in-law Dora is exposed, hastening the revelation that John is the father of two of Dora's children, Rhiannon and Noelle; we learn of the death at birth of Rena's twin brother, a tragedy which continues to affect Ailsa and John; and we see Rhiannon's departure to live with her married lover in London. The play is, then, about the lies and the concessions, and the negotiations that keep all relationships going.

The convention of the childish voyeur and narrator has been a significant and successful feature of Macdonald's work. Very frequently her plays are about children watching adults, with much of the drama resting on the vision and the telling of children. Although this is certainly the key structuring theme of *Sea Urchins* – Rena and, to a lesser degree, Noelle carry the full weight of the drama – one might also detect in the play a straining at this convention. The deeply felt crises in the play are not for the children and they are not seen or overheard by, or told to, them. Instead there are private moments where adults struggle to achieve communication with each other and this struggle is the stuff of real and difficult and demanding drama.

Macdonald's is a unique and oddly distanciated voice within Scottish theatre. By conjuring and representing hugely personal memories, her plays achieve a distinctive emotional immediacy, geographical localism, and linguistic specificity. They are utterly assured in their narrativity, occasionally breathtaking in their emotional ruthlessness, but always utterly honest in their representations of family.

Institutions

Like Femi Folorunso, Audrey Bain has commented on the pervasiveness of the popular tradition within contemporary theatre practices, developing her position by arguing that women, in particular, have turned to this popular and populist tradition with political (again feminist) intent, and she points to the fact that many of the leading Scottish women writers have parallel, or at least complementary, careers within popular (if not quite 'illegitimate') theatre: so Liz Lochhead found early success writing and performing revues and entertainments such as *Sugar and Spite* (1978) with Marcella Evaristi, later providing material for the actor Siobhan Redmond and musician Angie Rew with *True Confessions* (1981). She has performed her verse and monologues, such as *Quelques Fleurs*, on formal and informal stages, sometimes working alongside and with musician Michael Marra, and she deliberately mixes popular verse, narrative, and song with new writing in productions for her company, Nippy Sweeties. Independently of Lochhead, Evaristi has performed her own distinctive one-woman show, *The Offski Variations* (1990). The playwright Rona Munro and performer Fiona Knowles have worked together as the MsFits in cabaret and in a series of themed and politicised entertainments including *Batquine and Roberta* (1987–9), *Everyone's Gone to Dunoon* (1990), and *Rabbie Burns, Yer Tea's Oot* (1993). More recently Deirdre Heddon and Rachel Jury have collaborated in creating cabaret material for lesbian and gay events in Glasgow including the pastiches *Are You Being Serviced?*(1996), and *EastBenders* (1997). All these interventions suggest the diversity of work occurring in Scotland and hint at the range of skills and repertoire of styles that Scottish writers must draw upon in order both to establish themselves and to forge a viable career within a relatively small theatre industry.[15]

The goal is not just to expand the production base and to encounter new media and new genres but, pragmatically, to supplement the sometimes limited incomes possible as a theatre writer in Scotland. Many of the writers already mentioned in passing have, at one time or another, written for radio and television. For all, the broadcast media provide a welcome security of income, for some, they also offer much more significant possibilities: the opportunity to learn a new discipline, a new form, and to prepare for future work. Aileen Ritchie, for example, eased her transition from theatre writer – her plays for Clyde Unity Theatre include *Shang-a-Lang* (1989) and the trilogy *Ma Mammy's Story* (consisting of *Can Ye Sew Cushions?* (1988), *Will Ye Dance at my Wedding?* and *All the Time in the World* (both 1990)) – to the screen-writing course at the National Film and Television School, and a burgeoning film-making career, by writing for *High Road*. Lochhead has also written for television (*Sweet Nothings* in 1984) and for film (*Latin for a Dark Room* for the Scottish Film Council's prestigious *Tartan Shorts* scheme in 1994), Sue Glover has written for *High Road* and *Strathblair*, while Evaristi and Catherine Lucy Czerkawska have written some of their best material for radio – although Czerkawska has recently returned to theatre writing with *Wormwood* (1997), a poetic and bleak play responding to the Chernobyl disaster.

Many of the women considered in this chapter have made productive links with Scottish theatre companies – Munro and Glover with the Traverse, Liz Lochhead with Communicado and, earlier in her career, Borderline, while 7:84 (Scotland) have premiered Munro's *Saturday at the Commodore*, Di Mambro's *The Letter-Box* (these as part of a successful 1989 tour of new short plays, *Long Story Short: Voices of Today's Scotland*), Jackie Kay's *Twilight Shift* (1993) and Bunting's remarkable community project *Whispers of Water and Yarn*. Even the composer Judith Weir benefited from a partnership with Scottish Opera, who commissioned *The Vanishing Bridegroom* (1990), the libretto of which is a complex, multi-layered retelling of traditional Scottish folk tales.[16] Over several years, Anne Downie has written a significant number of plays and adaptations for the Radio Scotland drama unit in Edinburgh, while American-born, but Scotland-resident, Donna Franceschild has written two remarkable television series – *Takin' Over the Asylum* (1994) and *A Mug's Game* (1996) – for BBC Scotland.

In Scotland the established companies who subscribe to the new writing agenda are the touring company 7:84 (Scotland) and the building-based Traverse – responsible for the première of Franceschild's deeply moving play about a group of women living with and receiving treatment for breast cancer, *And the Cow Jumped Over the Moon*, Glover's *Bondagers*, Di Mambro's *Tally's Blood*, and, later in 1998, Lochhead's *Perfect Days* and Nicola McCartney's *Heritage*. Both these companies maintain writers' groups and have staff committed to supporting them: the Traverse works with a dramaturge and a literary manager advising several writers' groups (including one dedicated to women writers and one offering support for 'Young writers') and an enviable bill of short-play programmes, rehearsed readings, and platform events. Until recently, 7:84 had a permanent literary manager and an annual summer school, co-ordinated by the playwright Iain Heggie. The Traverse certainly has the more high-profile record of new writing, going back to its inception in the early 1960s, but 7:84 have made significant interventions in this area: the *Long Story Short* tour, Kay's *Twilight Shift*, Stephen Greenhorn's *The Salt Wound* (1994), their new adaptation of Peter Sichrovsky's *Born Guilty* (1995), David Greig's *Caledonia Dreaming* (1997), Bunting's *Whispers of Water and Yarns*, the devised piece *Talking Bollocks* (1995/6/8) and, in late 1998, another première, *Dissent* by Greenhorn.

In addition to these two major companies, a number of smaller touring companies have made strong commitments to new writing by women. Clyde Unity was launched in 1986 with a production of a neglected Scottish masterpiece, Benedict Scott's *Lambs of God* (1948). Since then they have set upon a policy of making relevant Scottish drama reflecting real lives, often featuring lesbian and gay characters. They have mounted more than fifty productions – numerous community projects and more than thirty new plays by Aileen Ritchie and by John Binnie. A more recent addition to Scottish theatre, Stellar Quines declares its commitment to writing about women and providing roles for women. They have achieved early success with *The Refuge* by Janet Paisley (1997) and *The Clearing* by Helen Edmundson (1993, for Stellar Quines 1998).

Look Out, formed in 1993, have staged five plays, four by writer/director Nicola McCartney – *Laundry* (1994, revised 1996), *Easy* (1995), *Entertaining Angels* written with actor Lucy McLellan (1996), and *The Hanging Tree* (1997). McCartney's declared commitment is to writing strong female characters and addressing social and political issues from a personal perspective. The company's appealing and topical eclecticism certainly reflects this policy with investigations of urban decay, rape, and, at root, an on-going interrogation of family and familial relations. McCartney's strong sense of character and talent for dynamic naturalistic dialogue insist upon the general relevance of theatre to a wide-ranging audience. Her work-in-progress – *Transatlantic* for Look Out and *Heritage* for the Traverse – investigates the Celtic diaspora, and her assessment of issues of belonging and community, of emigration and loss, will add a welcome contemporaneity to themes of perennial interest in Scotland.

Molly's Collar and Tie (1996, revised 1997), the first production by the eponymous mct Theatre Company, told stories from Scotland's lesbian and gay past. Collected and organised by Christopher Deans, some stories were fictional, others historical, some autobiographical personal testimony, with the speaker talking directly to the audience. This element was achieved by working with a group of lesbians and gay men and unlocked a remarkable range of stories which were recounted with calmness, wit, and humour. The company's commitment to these non-professional performers continues with a lesbian drama group – 'Finger Licks' – working and writing together.

Such productions, writers, and companies demonstrate the trend that Peter Zenzinger celebrates in recent Scottish writing when he argues that: 'while the new works are informed by an artistic vision that is distinctively Scottish, they have largely moved beyond the self-conscious Scottishness of the earlier dramatic tradition, which often hampered its artistic realisation and limited its appeal outside Scotland'.[17]

On 11 September 1997 the people of Scotland voted in a two-part referendum which, at root, was to decide on the definition of Scotland in the next millennium. The so-called 'Yes. Yes' outcome – 'Yes' for a devolved assembly and 'Yes' to giving that assembly tax-varying powers – ushered in the 1997 Scotland Bill, laying the foundations for legislation which will allow Scotland a degree of legislative autonomy unknown since the Act of Union in 1707.[18]

For us living in Scotland, the implementation of the Scotland Act will alter our whole understanding of and relationship to government, bringing decision-making closer and encouraging a more immediate sense of responsibility and, perhaps, empowerment. In a country with a population of a little over 5.1 million, government will be a more tangible and personal thing than ever before, politicians more accountable and the electorate more liable. As a consequence of all this, the constitutional but also, surely, the 'imagined' nature of Scotland will necessarily change. Scottish culture has been much preoccupied with issues of colonialism, marginalism, and parochialism but, in a context in which at least some aspect of political independence has been achieved, the dynamic must shift from aspiration and desire to definition and responsibility.

This period of transition, creation, and recreation coincides with the more widespread socio-cultural reassessments inevitable in the *fin de siècle*, presently heightened by radical expectations of the end of the millennium. In this complex nexus of chronologies a conspicuous acknowledgement of history and tradition has emerged as a necessary foundation for building new forms and allowing new narratives. In this process of reassessment and recreation the role of the Scottish artist has never been more significant, for the artist is never more necessary than at the point at which a long-desired goal has been reached; and, when boundaries are changing and institutions adapting, it is the role of the artist to retain the vision of what is longed-for and to be critical of the processes and elaborations of what is possible. Even in the short term, Scottish writers will be vital in debating and describing our new social and cultural responsibilities.

The writers of new Scottish drama have demonstrated that they are capable of the task. Liz Lochhead, Rona Munro, Sue Glover, Sharman Macdonald, Jackie Kay, Donna Franceschild, Nicola McCartney, and their male counterparts Iain Heggie, John Clifford, Chris Hannan, Simon Donald, David Greig, David Harrower, and Stephen Greenhorn, have set themselves a very different agenda to the fashion-victim, nihilistic 'shopping and fucking' introspection of London, perhaps more aware of the significance of representation within a culture in political flux and with limited financial resources.

FIRST PRODUCTIONS OF MAJOR PLAYS

Anne Marie Di Mambro

The Letter-Box, Sabhal Mor Ostaig, Isle of Skye (1989)
Tally's Blood, Traverse Theatre, Edinburgh (1990)
Brothers of Thunder, Traverse Theatre, Edinburgh (1994)

Marcella Evaristi

Wedding Belles and Green Grasses, Tron Theatre, Glasgow (1981)
Commedia, Crucible Theatre, Sheffield (1982)
The Hat, BBC Radio (1988)

Sue Glover

The Seal Wife, Little Lyceum, Edinburgh (1980)
The Bubble Boy, Tron Theatre, Glasgow (1981)
The Straw Chair, Traverse Theatre, Edinburgh (1988)
Bondagers, Traverse Theatre, Edinburgh (1991)
Sacred Hearts, Dundee Rep, Dundee (1994)

Liz Lochhead

Blood and Ice, Traverse Theatre, Edinburgh (1982)
Dracula, Royal Lyceum Theatre, Edinburgh (1985)
Mary Queen of Scots Got Her Head Chopped Off, Lyceum Studio Theatre, Edinburgh (1987)
The Big Picture, Dundee Rep, Dundee (1988)
Jock Tamson's Bairns, Tramway, Glasgow (1990)
Perfect Days, Traverse Theatre, Edinburgh (1998)

Sharman Macdonald

When I Was a Girl, I Used to Scream and Shout, Bush Theatre, London (1984)
When We Were Women, Cottesloe Theatre, London (1989)
All Things Nice, Royal Court Theatre, London (1991)
Shades, New Victoria Theatre, West End (1992)
Borders of Paradise, Palace Theatre, Watford (1995)

The Winter Guest, West Yorkshire Playhouse, Leeds (1995)
Sea Urchins, Tron Theatre, Glasgow, and Dundee Rep, Dundee (1998)

Rona Munro

Fugue, Traverse Theatre, Edinburgh (1983)
Ghost Story, Tron Theatre, Glasgow (1985)
Piper's Cave, Soho Poly Theatre (rehearsed reading), London (1985)
Saturday at the Commodore, Sabhal Mor Ostaig, Isle of Skye (1989)
Bold Girls, Cumbernauld Theatre, Cumbernauld, near Glasgow (1990)
Your Turn to Clean the Stair, Traverse Theatre, Edinburgh (1992)
Men of the Month, BBC Television (1994)
The Maiden Stone, Hampstead Theatre, London (1995)

NOTES

1 Benedict Anderson, *Imagined Communities: Reflections on the Origin and Rise of Nationalism* (1983. London: Verso, 1990), p.15.
2 The critics Ilona Koren-Deutsch and Anne Varty have made significant contributions in this area, with Varty's formulation that 'It is a play with a history rather than a history play' being particularly succinct. See Ilona Koren-Deutsch, 'Feminist Nationalism in Scotland: *Mary Queen of Scots Got Her Head Chopped Off*', in *Modern Drama*, 35, 1992, pp. 424–32; and Anne Varty, 'The Mirror and the Vamp: Liz Lochhead', in Douglas Gifford and Dorothy McMillan (eds.) *A History of Scottish Women's Writing* (Edinburgh: University of Edinburgh Press, 1997), pp. 641–58, p. 651.
3 Liz Lochhead, 'Afterword' to *Blood and Ice* in Michelene Wandor (ed.) *Plays by Women: 4* (London: Methuen, 1985), pp. 81–118, p. 118. Lochhead's play first appeared, directed by Michael Boyd, as *Mary and the Monster* at Belgrade Theatre, Coventry, in 1981; rewritten, it then appeared as *Blood and Ice*, directed by Kenny Ireland, at the Traverse in the context of the 1982 Edinburgh Fringe Festival; being later revised and played, as first published, by a small company called Pepper's Ghost at a pub venue, New Merlin's Cave, in London in 1984.
4 Jan McDonald, 'Scottish Women Dramatists since 1945', in Gifford and McMillan, *A History of Scottish Women's Writing*, pp. 494–513, p. 495.
5 All quotes come from Liz Lochhead, *Mary Queen of Scots Got Her Head Chopped Off and Dracula* (Harmondsworth: Penguin, 1989).
6 Femi Folorunso, 'Scottish Drama and the Popular Tradition', in Randall Stevenson and Gavin Wallace (eds.) *Scottish Theatre Since the Seventies* (Edinburgh: Edinburgh University Press, 1996), pp. 176–85, p. 176.
7 A position succinctly theorised by David Mayer in his essay 'Towards a Definition of Popular Drama', in David Mayer and Kenneth Richards (eds.) *Western Popular Theatre* (London: Methuen, 1977), pp. 257–77.
8 Anne Varty, 'The Mirror and the Vamp: Liz Lochhead', in Gifford and McMillan, *A History of Scottish Women's Writing*, p. 652.
9 Sue Glover, *Bondagers* in *Bondagers and The Straw Chair* (London: Methuen, 1997), p. 2.
10 Rona Munro, 'Author's note' to *The Maiden Stone* (London: Nick Hern, 1995), p. v.

11 Rona Munro, 'Comment', in K. A. Berney (ed.) *Contemporary Dramatists,* 5th edn (London: St James Press, 1993), p. 477.

12 Ned Chaillet, 'Marcella Evaristi', in Berney, *Contemporary Dramatists,* pp. 172–3, p. 172.

13 Jan McDonald, 'Scottish Women Dramatists since 1945', in Gifford and McMillan, *A History of Scottish Women's Writing,* p. 497.

14 Anne Marie Di Mambro, *The Letter-Box,* in Alasdair Cameron (ed.) *Scot-Free: New Scottish Plays* (London: Nick Hern, 1990), pp. 99–104, p. 104, p. 102.

15 See Audrey Bain, 'Loose Canons: Identifying a Women's Tradition in Play Writing', in Stevenson and Wallace, *Scottish Theatre Since the Seventies,* pp. 138–45, p. 140. The two examples of collaborative writing teams mentioned – Munro and Knowles, and Heddon and Jury – suggest that some of the feminist working methods and writing strategies identified by Lizbeth Goodman within a London context are just as pertinent in Scotland: Goodman, *Contemporary Feminist Theatres: to Each her Own* (London: Routledge, 1993), pp. 107–13.

16 While it is at least unfortunate that this commissioning has not been repeated – with Weir's subsequent work finding a home with the English National Opera – nevertheless Scottish Opera has produced new work including James McMillan's 1996 opera, based on John Clifford's 1989 play, *Inez De Castro.*

17 Peter Zenzinger, 'The New Wave', in Stevenson and Wallace, *Scottish Theatre Since the Seventies,* p. 125.

18 The result of the poll was overwhelmingly in favour of devolution: to having a Scottish Parliament 1,775,045 (74.3%) voted 'Yes' and 614,400 (25.7%) voted 'No'; to giving that Parliament tax-varying powers 1,512,889 (63.5%) voted 'Yes' and 870,263 (36.5%) voted 'No'.

FURTHER READING

Primary sources: plays

Di Mambro, Anne Marie. *The Letter-Box.* In Alasdair Cameron (ed.) *Scot-Free: New Scottish Plays.* London: Nick Hern, 1990: 99–104.

Evaristi, Marcella. *Commedia.* Edinburgh: Salamander Press, 1983.

Glover, Sue. *Bondagers and The Straw Chair.* London: Methuen, 1997.

Lochhead, Liz. *Blood and Ice.* In Michelene Wandor (ed.) *Plays by Women: 4.* London: Methuen, 1985: 81–118.

Tartuffe: A Translation into Scots from the Original by Molière. Edinburgh: Polygon and Third Eye Centre, 1985.

Mary Queen of Scots Got Her Head Chopped Off and Dracula. Harmondsworth: Penguin, 1989.

Macdonald, Sharman. *Shades.* London: Faber and Faber, 1992.

Plays: One – When I Was a Girl, I Used to Scream and Shout; When We Were Women; The Winter Guest; Borders of Paradise. London: Faber and Faber, 1995.

Sea Urchins. London: Faber and Faber, 1998.

Munro, Rona. *Piper's Cave.* In Mary Remnant (ed.) *Plays by Women: 5.* London: Methuen, 1985: 109–44.

Saturday at the Commodore. In Alasdair Cameron (ed.) *Scot Free: New Scottish Plays.* London: Nick Hern, 1990: 193–200.

Bold Girls. In Matthew Lloyd (ed.) *First Run 3.* London: Nick Hern, 1991: 183–257.

Your Turn to Clean the Stair and Fugue. London: Nick Hern, 1995.
The Maiden Stone. London: Nick Hern, 1995.

Secondary sources

Berney, K. A. (ed.) *Contemporary Dramatists.* 5th edn. London: St James Press, 1993.

Craig, Cairns (ed.) *The History of Scottish Literature*, vol. IV: *The Twentieth Century.* Aberdeen: Aberdeen University Press, 1987.

Crawford, Robert, and Anne Varty (eds.) *Liz Lochhead's Voices.* Edinburgh: Edinburgh University Press, 1994.

Di Cenzo, Maria. *The Politics of Alternative Theatre in Britain, 1968–1990: The Case of 7:84 (Scotland).* Cambridge: Cambridge University Press, 1996.

Findlay, Bill (ed.) *A History of Scottish Theatre.* Edinburgh: Polygon, 1998.

Gifford, Douglas. 'Making them Bold and Breaking the Mould: Rona Munro's *Bold Girls'. Laverock* 2 (1996): 2–8.

Gifford, Douglas, and Dorothy McMillan (eds.) *A History of Scottish Women's Writing.* Edinburgh: Edinburgh University Press, 1997.

Harvie, Jennifer. 'Desire and Difference in Liz Lochhead's Dracula'. *Essays in Theatre / Etudes Thèatrales* 11.2 (May 1993):133–43.

Koren-Deutsch, Ilona. 'Feminist Nationalism in Scotland: *Mary Queen of Scots Got Her Head Chopped Off'. Modern Drama* 35 (1992): 424–32.

Maguire, Tom. 'When the Cutting Edge Cuts Both Ways: Contemporary Scottish Drama'. *Modern Drama* 38.1 (Spring 1995): 87–96.

McDonald, Jan. '*Dracula*: Freudian Novel to Feminist Drama': In Peter Reynolds (ed.) *Novel Images: Literature in Performance.* London: Routledge, 1993: 80–104.

Munro, Rona. 'Sex and food'. *Theatre Scotland* 3 (Autumn 1992): 15–21.

Nicolson, Colin. 'Liz Lochhead: The Knucklebones of Irony'. In Nicholson (ed.) *Poem, Purpose and Place: Shaping Identity in Contemporary Scottish Verse.* Edinburgh: Polygon, 1992: 203–23.

Scullion, Adrienne. 'Feminine Pleasures and Masculine Indignities: Gender and Community in Scottish Drama'. In Christopher Whyte (ed.) *Gendering the Nation: Studies in Modern Scottish Literature.* Edinburgh: Edinburgh University Press, 1996: 169–204.

Stephenson, Heidi, and Natasha Langridge. 'Sharman Macdonald.' In Stephenson and Langridge (eds.) *Rage and Reason: Women Playwrights on Playwriting.* London: Methuen, 1997: 61–70.

Stevenson, Randall, and Gavin Wallace (eds.) *Scottish Theatre Since the Seventies.* Edinburgh: Edinburgh University Press, 1996.

See also the following:

Chapman 43–4 (1986). A special edition on Scottish theatre.

Theatre Research International 17.2 (Summer 1992). A special edition on Scottish theatre.

Theatre Scotland (1992 to 1995).

8

MARY TROTTER

Women playwrights in Northern Ireland

In Anne Devlin's *Ourselves Alone*, a Belfast Catholic woman is harassed for moving into the 'neutral,' university area of town. Her socialist roommate, however, does not believe she is being victimised until a brick flies through the window of their flat. In Christina Reid's *The Belle of Belfast City*, a carefree woman exacts a joking revenge on her Protestant, ultra-loyalist brother by serving him 'Republican' sausages she had smuggled out of the Republic of Ireland. A Belfast Protestant man in Marie Jones's *A Night in November* overcomes his sectarian anger as he cheers for the Irish team in the 1994 World Cup with Irish people from the Republic and the USA in a New York sports bar. These three instances from contemporary Northern Irish drama reflect one of the constant dilemmas facing people in Northern Ireland: the negotiation of identity in a region crossed and recrossed by a web of geographical, religious, cultural, economic, and political fault-lines. With the range of national identities co-existing in Northern Ireland's borders, each person in Northern Ireland finds her/himself on shifting political and cultural sands, negotiating her/his own identity through relationships both within and without that area's borders.

For Northern Irish writers, writing in the interstice between Eire and the UK, and finding their work influenced by both British and Irish cultural traditions and politics, the notion of national identity becomes complex indeed. Many Northern Irish playwrights have received funding from the Arts Councils both in Great Britain and in the Republic of Ireland, and their works are regularly anthologised and critiqued as Irish, rather than British, dramas. Since many Northern Irish writers are generally considered (and consider themselves) part of an Irish cultural tradition, discussing Northern Irish women playwrights in an anthology of *British* rather than *Irish* writing is a problematic, and even volatile, endeavour. Their inclusion here, however, enriches our view of how Northern Irish women playwrights, like many other groups within the official borders of the United Kingdom, negotiate a voice simultaneously within and without, resistant to and in co-ordination with, the aesthetics, politics, and economics of the contemporary British theatre scene. Other chapters in this part examine how Welsh and Scottish playwrights have similar struggles with their double marginalisation as women on the Celtic Fringe, while the final section of this volume explores how black and lesbian playwrights in England also seek a space despite their marginalisation in mainstream feminist playwriting. Such dilemmas are not unique to women writers in Britain, however, and many Northern Irish artists and activists, feeling alienated in both Irish and British camps, have often looked to the experiences of marginalised women in other societies to understand and to create change in their own situation.

One helpful allegory for understanding the Northern Irish woman writer's dilemma is the experience of women of colour in the USA, who find themselves excluded from women's canons for being writers of colour, and African-American or Latina/o canons because they are women. US critic Patricia Hill Collins, for example, calls for a new way of theorising about marginalised groups which throws out strictly binary distinctions for understanding identity conflicts (African-American vs Euro-American, coloniser vs colonised, gay vs straight), in favour of thinking of people's experiences in terms of a 'matrix of domination'.[1] This model is useful for women in Northern Ireland, where the national question influences all other issues, including the fight for gender equality. English feminist performance groups like the Women's Theatre Group (now renamed The Sphinx) look at gender issues through the lenses of race and class, but from a relatively stable (albeit imperfect) political and national system. Northern Irish feminism, however, is ultimately subordinate to what the larger Northern Irish community sees as the more pressing issue of national identity. While groups have had some success addressing local issues, like opening women's centres in working-class neighbourhoods, feminist campaigns for systemic change have been more difficult. Rosemary Sales points out that '[t]he construction of politics around community loyalties gives little space for raising other forms of inequality', further noting that 'this is particularly problematic for feminists, whose demands may conflict with established values within the community'.[2] Northern Irish theatre groups that deal specifically with women's issues may shy away from calling their plays 'feminist' so as not to alienate their local audiences, even if their plays deal with women's social, cultural, and political oppression in society, and call for reforming gender discrimination. Charabanc's Eleanor Methven said of her all-women company's work in the late 1980s:

> We deal with political issues. It would be stupid to say we're not 'feminist', but every time someone says 'feminist' I want them to define it for me. It has a bad ring to it . . . We can't deny the fact that we are women and because we're women we write from a woman's point of view. But [our work is] not meant to be agitprop. It's more like human rights than women's rights.[3]

Methven's comment in its Northern Irish context reflects Charabanc's commitment to being a working-class company, addressing its community's issues in that community's language. It also reflects, however, the anxiety for performers as well as audiences around the very term 'feminist' in a community struggling to define itself on multiple political fronts.

Northern Irish women also fight deep-seeded cultural expectations for their gender. Nationalist women in both Northern Ireland and the Republic battle not only their communities' everyday gender biases, but also the mythic stereotypes of woman as nation within Irish nationalist discourse. Women are either helpless victims, like the *Shan Van Vocht* or *Roibin Dubh*, or mother figures like Hibernia or Mother Ireland. The Protestant roles for women are not as mythic, but their image as keepers of the family hearth is equally restricting. In Maria M. Delgado's words, 'in Catholicism we see woman as angelic virgin figure reworked by the nationalist movement into Mother Ireland; in Protestantism, woman as loyal steadfast servicer and nurturer of men willing to die for Queen and country'.[4] Each image limits women to auxiliary roles within their communities, their agency subordinated by their roles as inspirers or helpers of men. Northern Irish women playwrights are helping to change these restricting gender roles by embodying on the stage new points of view and radical possibilities for women, and for all of Northern Irish society.

This chapter explores in detail the work of some of the most prominent women playwrights currently working in Northern Ireland: Anne Devlin, Christina Reid, and Marie Jones. It also examines the now disbanded performance group Charabanc. While each playwright or group presents a unique artistic voice, there are some common threads in their work. Each of these writers portrays life in Northern Ireland from both Catholic and Protestant viewpoints. They have all created strong, central roles for women actors. Perhaps most importantly, they explore how Northern Irish women seek their own private and public voices amid the clamour of political, cultural, and gender identity expectations. These three factors enable the plays to reflect the divisions between the North and the Republic, the North and Great Britain, and the deep sectarian, economic, and gender gaps within Northern Ireland itself.

Anne Devlin

Anne Devlin is one of the most internationally visible woman playwrights in Northern Ireland or the Republic. Part of her success emerges from her relationship with England's Royal Court Theatre (two of her plays have been produced there) and her work writing for television. She won the Samuel Beckett Award for her teleplay, *The Long March*, in 1984, the Susan Smith Blackburn Prize in 1985 and was a co-winner of the George Devine Award in 1986. Much of Devlin's work deals with Northern Irish women struggling to assert their own voices as they negotiate their political and personal lives.

Voice is a striking, recurring symbol in Devlin's first play, *Ourselves Alone*, which recounts the lives of three Northern Irish women whose experiences are shaped by both their own ideologies and those of their fathers, brothers, and husbands. The very title is a kind of play on words. It is the English translation of *Sinn Fein*, an Irish nationalist motto and the name of the most prominent nationalist political party. It also refers, however, to the other ways these women are isolated from the mainstream – as women, as Northern Irish, as Catholics in Belfast, as affiliated to the IRA. Conflicted ties to family, religion, political party, and nation force these women often to sacrifice their personal dreams for community duty. Yet these women perpetually seek to make their voices rise – literally and figuratively – beyond their restricted, gendered spheres.

The play begins in an IRA-controlled club where Frieda, the youngest and wildest of the characters, is practising a revolutionary song. Although she works in the club, she is more interested in a singing career than national revolution, and she pesters the reluctant bandleader to let her sing one of her own compositions. Part of Frieda's rebellious rejection of her family's politics stems from her caretaking responsibilities to her two maiden aunts. Her Aunt Cora became blind, deaf, and dumb and lost her hands when some defective explosives she was stowing detonated in her face. Cora's sister, Bridget, never married as she looked after her sister, and now Frieda takes care of them both. Frieda, however, has no intention of following either of her aunt's self-sacrificing footsteps. She describes the role her disfigured Aunt Cora plays in the movement: 'They stick her out at the front of the parades every so often to show the women of Ireland what their patriotic duty should be. But I'll tell you something – it won't be mine!'[5]

Her sister-in-law, Donna, plays a more traditional role for women linked to the IRA, as she raises her infant child and waits for her partner, Liam, to be released from prison. Donna must handle not only the economic and emotional demands of raising her child without the help of its father, but also her partner's unjustified jealousy and distrust, despite his own affairs. Josie resides in a kind of political middle ground between Frieda's radical spirit and Donna's faithfulness, as she is one of relatively few women actually working in the IRA. While Josie is committed to her IRA work, some of her involvement stems from her close relationship with her father, Malachy, a leader in the organisation. In fact, she finds herself drawn to revolutionaries like her father, first as the mistress of an IRA leader, then as the lover of a new, elite recruit.

At first it seems that these women are escaping familial and social oppression and finding their voices through liaisons with men. Liam is released from prison to return to Donna; Frieda moves out of the nationalist neighbourhood, Andersonstown, and lives with John McDermot, a childhood friend who is now in the Socialist Party; and Josie becomes pregnant by Joe Conran, her new, revolutionary lover. All these men, however, prove to be kinds of traitors. Liam leaves Donna for another woman, John uses physical force to coerce Frieda to stay with him, and Joe, an actual traitor to the IRA, disappears. All three women survive these 'treasons', relying on their individual and communal strength as women to see them through these personal and political crises. There is no question that these women will continue to fight: in fact, the loss of their men gives them more freedom to, as Frieda puts it in Act I, 'have a chance to be [themselves]' (p. 21). Josie, beginning to break free from her need to be aligned with a heroic man, will have her child and will 'never be lonely again' (p. 84). Donna finally lets go of a man whose jealousy has kept her in an abject position for years. Frieda, in the tradition of Stephen Daedalus, decides to leave Ireland to pursue her dream of being an artist. Devlin leaves uncertain, however, whether they will truly express their own voices in these new roles, for the economics, politics, and rigid patriarchy of their world still remain in place.

Almost ten years later, Devlin wrote another play about sisters from Belfast, *After Easter*. Unlike the family of *Ourselves Alone*, the sisters are a little older, better-off financially, and unaffiliated with any nationalist group. Yet sectarian violence and the presence of the soldiers still infiltrates the characters' experience while they are in Belfast. By showing the pervasiveness of the Troubles in everyday life, even in a drama ostensibly dealing with questions of faith and family, Devlin exposes the inextricable links between family, nation, religion, politics, class, and gender that continue to bind individuals from Northern Ireland at every identity position.

While *Ourselves Alone* deals almost exclusively with the politics of Northern Irish Catholicism, *After Easter* looks at religion from a more mystical perspective. Greta, a declared agnostic married to an English Marxist historian, finds herself the recipient of holy visions, culminating in the sight of a flame on Pentecost Sunday. Her visions lead her husband to have her committed to a mental hospital, and separation from her new baby causes her to disown the child. While such a plot could become maudlin, Devlin's acerbic wit has her characters confronting their crises with a satirical, defiant smirk.

Contacts with her family begin to liberate Greta from both the physical restriction of the hospital and the repression of her spiritual experience. Her sisters take her to one of their homes in London on an Easter holiday from the hospital, and while in the flat Greta experiences a religious revelation: 'My voice has come back to me. After all these years . . . Do you know what this means? . . . It means that I'm back. It means that from now on everything I say will be true.'[6] Again, Devlin makes voice a central theme of her play, but in a more proactive way than in her earlier drama. The women in *Ourselves Alone* never fully free their voices from the cultural and political oppressions around them. When Greta finds her 'voice', however, she experiences both personal liberation and the power to speak out for social justice, as she unabashedly speaks the truth to her family, to her community, and to herself throughout the rest of the play. In Act II, Greta and her sisters return to Belfast after her father has a heart attack, and Greta is able to see and speak out about her family's resentments and insecurities. Throughout this segment of the play, Devlin reveals the banal horror of the Troubles, as Helen deals with the inconvenience of a gang breaking her windshield outside the hospital, and Manus, Greta's brother, runs a road block and leads three soldiers into the family backyard, their guns raised and ready. Manus is adamant that he was right to run from the soldiers, but Greta's admonition reflects the 'truth' she has discovered in all aspects of her life. If the soldiers had killed them, the family 'wouldn't be alive to tell it . . . all we have to do is stay alive and tell the truth' (p. 53). Greta has learned the importance of survival, witness, and testimony in the midst of crisis – the need to see and speak of things as they truly are. Greta's voice, however, is not only one for personal expression, as is Frieda's quest in *Ourselves Alone*, but also for community change.

Along with the link between the personal and the political in Northern Ireland, Devlin's works also reflect the vital role of class, although economic issues are often cloaked in religious and/or political ideologies. In *Ourselves Alone* Josie remembers Dublin as an ideological dream to her as a child, a place she once visited by getting a lift from a pig lorry. Her middle-class friend, however, knew Dublin as a place where she went to buy shoes, divorced from the political dream by her economic security. And when Greta's storekeeper mother in *After Easter* decides to stop buying hand-made christening gowns from a Catholic woman in favour of cheaper, machine-made gowns from a Protestant, Devlin shows how the expediencies of money can erase cultural and religious considerations on both sides of Northern Ireland's religious fence.

Christina Reid

A Belfast native, although she has lived in London since the 1980s, Christina Reid captures women's experience in Northern Ireland from both Protestant and Catholic perspectives in her radio dramas and stage plays. She has served as Writer-In-Residence at the Lyric Theatre, Belfast (1983–4), and the Young Vic, London (1988–9), and has won such literary honours as the Thames TV Playwright Scheme Award (1983) and the George Devine Award (1986). In the Northern Irish dramatic tradition, Reid displays a shrewd wit in her dramas, as she explores how individuals struggle to make meaningful lives for themselves and their families in the midst of political and economic crisis. Reid's plays often reveal how family and political histories are intertwined. In *My Name, Shall I*

Tell You My Name? a Protestant woman seeks personal freedom, while reconciling her grandfather's love for her with his religious bigotry. In her dramas *Tea in a China Cup* and *The Belle of the Belfast City*, Reid develops a matrilineal narrative that recounts Northern Irish women's private and public lives over the past century. Political events like war affect the lives of the women in this play, yet Reid punctuates the narrative with such private, familial events as birth, marriage, and death, pointing out how those personal experiences are marked by external events.

Tea in a China Cup tells of three generations of Protestant Belfast women between 1939 and 1972. Although Beth, the third generation and the narrator, has broken away from the gender, class, and religious biases of the previous generations, she still feels an integral part of their stories. 'I've heard . . . all the other family stories so often that I can remember and see clearly things that happened even before I was born', she claims.[7] From the beginning of the drama, Reid points out how the 'united' Protestant front is in fact divided on distinct gender and class lines. In Act I, Beth recounts how, when she was four months old, her mother took her to the historic July marches, and a man praised her mother for bringing her baby. His hard hat and white gloves let her know he was a gentleman and '[s]he was very proud that a man like that had stopped to pay the likes of her such a compliment' (p. 10). Although the marches are designed to bring Protestant unionists together, the class rifts continue to be self-enforced by the community.

Appearances are important for Beth's mother and grandmother, who take pride in their scrubbed front steps and spotless homes. In Act II, when Beth's grandmother's house is under threat of being burned down by paramilitaries, she refuses to leave her home, filled with the things the women of her family have collected over the years. 'I'm not leavin' my wee house', Sarah declares, 'I won't abandon them' (p. 56). By 'them', she ostensibly refers to the objects in her house, but actually 'them' implies the loved ones who worked to bring those things into the family. When Beth tells her mother, 'Mum . . . they're only . . . things . . . bits and pieces . . . they can all be replaced', her mother replies, 'They're my life!' (p. 57). For the women in the family, linen, photographs, and china cups serve as history, relics of love and labour passed matrilineally down the generations.

Beth's childhood experiences, along with those of her Catholic friend, Theresa, expose the preconceptions segregation has developed between the two tribes. Both Theresa and Beth believe that persons of the other religion have more closely set eyes. Theresa assures Beth that nuns do not always go about in pairs because some nuns are men. The girls also wonder where babies come from and why the local slang calls their school uniform underwear (Beth's are navy blue, Theresa's are deep green) 'passion killers'. Both Beth and Theresa are kept in the dark about the sexual and the sectarian. They struggle naively to make sense of the silences about both issues in their households, not comprehending that true knowledge of either subject is a potential threat to the political and/or gender social status quo.

Reid fills the 'silences' in women's history by metatheatrically interjecting a range of styles into her works. *Did You Hear the One About the Irishman?* counterpoints the black humour shared between a star-crossed mixed-religion couple in Belfast with the tired and brazen anti-Irish jokes told by a Comedian who performs his jibes '*directly to the audience as if he is performing in a club*'.[8] In *The Belle of the Belfast City*, Reid punctuates the narrative with music-hall numbers and traditional Protestant tunes.

Reid employs this musical element in *Joyriders*, a drama that uses songs written by actual residents of the Divis Flats where the play is set. *Joyriders* is perhaps her most didactic play, a much more heavy-handed account of gender, race, and class on Belfast's violent streets than that found in her other works. In this drama Kate, a middle-class social worker in her mid-thirties, runs an employment training project for Belfast's working-class youth. Facing daily violence and chronic unemployment, the participants in the scheme often resort to sniffing glue or joyriding, stealing cars and driving them around town. Kate tries to reach the students, but she finds herself confronting the ultimately trivial gesture of the employment scheme, which does not attack the systemic problems underlying Belfast's unemployment and poverty rates. Plus, the scheme complies with the restrictive gender and class roles that pervade Belfast society. Sandra, one of the students, complains that while she wants to learn auto mechanics, she has been assigned a more 'feminine' job on the knitting machines. Arthur, another student, is teased for learning commercial cooking. As Sandra puts it, 'They're all the same. They ask ye what ye want to be, an' then they tell ye what yer allowed to be.'[9] The students are well aware of this futility, and fight it in subversive, funny ways, like sneaking slang insults into signs 'welcoming' officials visiting their project.

The play ends on an uncertain note regarding the future of these youths. Arthur, on one hand, seems on the brink of middle-class respectability as he plans to invest his government settlement (he was accidentally shot by British soldiers) into a restaurant. Sandra, however, shaken by the shooting of her friend Maureen by soldiers pursuing her joyriding little brother, is more wary of buying into the social system that perpetuates these kinds of economic, personal, and political oppressions. Both choices have personal and social costs.

In 1996, Reid responded to recent developments in Northern Ireland with her sequel to *Joyriders*, entitled *Clowns*. Many of *Joyriders*' characters, now in their twenties, appear in this drama. The old Lagan Mill, which was the site of the employment scheme in *Joyriders*, is now a new shopping mall, a symbol of Belfast's burgeoning economic growth at the eve of the cease-fire. Yet the pristine mall, with its culturally non-specific stores and romanticised statue of a millworking woman and her child in the middle of a fountain, reflect the way Belfast's true history – and the history of its workers – is being smoothed over by the hands of global capitalism.

Arthur is now married and opening a café in the new mall. Sandra has returned from London, where she works as a stand-up comic, to perform at the opening ceremonies. She is haunted throughout the play by the presence of Maureen's memory/ghost. Jimmy, Maureen's little brother, has moved from joyriding to selling drugs. 'I'm the king of the only scene in Belfast that has nothing to do with religion, class or creed', Jimmy boasts.[10] Sandra knows, however, that Jimmy is replacing one corrupt order with another: 'The darlin' boy's a dirty dealer. The ultimate joyride. You do the driving, and the passengers get killed' (p. 329).

The play ends on a note of optimistic uncertainty about the new Belfast, as Sandra, back in England, performs her stand-up act at a Christmas party. Her jokes about the cease-fire are optimistic but tinged with a sense of ambiguity. Sandra raises her glass of champagne to Northern Ireland's future, replacing the slogan 'Ulster Says No', with 'Ulster says Ho Ho Ho!' (p. 343), but what new social order will slouch towards Belfast?

Charabanc

Charabanc was founded in 1983 by five Belfast women actors who were frustrated by the absence of adequate parts for women and decided to form their own company. These Catholic and Protestant women, Marie Jones, Carol Scanlan, Eleanor Methven, Maureen Macauley, and Brenda Winter, collaborated not only with each other and other theatre workers like Martin Lynch and Pam Brighton, but with the very communities about which they were writing, the very audiences for whom they performed. Charabanc usually wrote their dramas collaboratively, or group member Marie Jones wrote them, but they did perform adaptations and plays by other playwrights. Charabanc's work performed a vital service for the Belfast community by recovering women's experience in Northern Ireland during the twentieth century, from public events like the linen mill strikes of 1911 to private crises, like the lack of birth control and prenatal care in the 1940s. The actors in the troupe spent months interviewing men and women who had lived through the historical events they dramatised before developing their stories into stageable scenes. In their first three years, Charabanc managed to cover eighty years of Irish history in their three plays, *Lay Up Your Ends, Oul Delf and False Teeth*, and *Now You're Talkin'*. The first play examines the vital role of women workers at the York Street Mill in unionising Belfast labour and founding the first branch of the Irish Transport and General Workers' Union.

The ITGWU became extremely important to both the labour movement and Irish nationalism throughout the early twentieth century. The final play, *Now You're Talkin'*, takes on women's roles in the current crisis, as a group of Protestant and Catholic women are sent on a reconciliation retreat, led by a very handsome but overly idealistic American man. The women, who come from an array of class and ideological as well as religious backgrounds, become frustrated by Carter's patronising activities – at one point he has them dancing to Rogers and Hammerstein's 'The Farmer and the Cowman Should Be Friends' – but they rebel. While some go home, others insist on staying the full weekend, locking themselves in a bedroom. While the press revels in the women's self-barricading, the women actually get a chance to talk.

Perhaps the most riveting of Charabanc's collaborative efforts is their anarchic political farce, *Somewhere Over the Balcony*, an examination of life in the Divis Flats – the Belfast housing project said to be the worst in Europe. Like many of their dramas about contemporary Belfast life, *Somewhere Over the Balcony* questions the long-term effect of perpetual violence on the streets, to the point that the warlike conditions seem 'normal': 'the parameters of sanity shift and the idea arises that violence has reached an acceptable level'.[11] The three homemakers who lead us through a day in the Divis Flats encounter such characters as Rambo McGlinchey, a one-eyed dog who bites British soldiers; a soldier who jogs around the deck of his observation tower for exercise; and an IRA man who has to sneak into his own wedding. In true comedic form, the play does indeed end with a wedding, as old Granda Tucker, along with two other generations of his family and a pet tortoise, hijacks a helicopter and holds a British army major hostage. Granda uses his advantage to insist the marriage ceremony take place, and Charlene MacAldooney gets her wedding before her baby is born.

Although an overview of their work reflects some leaning towards nationalist rather than unionist points of view, Charabanc went to tremendous lengths to maintain their non-partisan identity, refusing to allow their work to be appropriated by any sectarian side. When Charabanc first performed *Now You're Talkin'* at the Belfast Civic Arts Theatre, they continually changed the finale, partly in a struggle to 'perfect' the piece, but also to stop the audience from pigeonholing the group into a particular ideological position on the current Troubles, based on the play's ending.[12] Charabanc's unique gift of reflecting the polyvocality of Belfast life, playing to sectarian audiences in Catholic, Protestant, and mixed performance spaces as they embodied the silenced experiences of Northern Ireland's working-class women, epitomises the collaborative spirit theatre collectives struggle to achieve. Collaborative relationships, however, are difficult to maintain, as personal and professional pressures often draw individuals to other projects. Jones left the troupe in 1991 to pursue her own playwriting career, and in 1995 the group officially disbanded, although its members continue to work independently.

Marie Jones

Since leaving Charabanc, Marie Jones has continued to employ her sharp, satirical wit to expose the absurdity of sectarian strife and its economic and cultural underpinnings in contemporary Belfast. She has collaborated with colleagues from Charabanc days, like the director Pam Brighton, and new groups, like DubbelJoint and Replay Theatre Company (the Belfast TIE group), and she has written for radio and television. Her recent play, *A Night in November* is a surprising departure for Jones: a one-person show lasting two and a half hours about Kenneth McAllister, a Belfast Protestant man deeply committed to his sectarian roots. Events at a local football match and encounters with his Catholic supervisor, however, make him question for the first time the cultural and personal assumptions that have shaped his life. He drives his Catholic supervisor home from work one day, thus entering the Falls Road area for the first time, and remembers how he felt:

> nervous, like a stranger in a foreign country . . . knowing I was the enemy but no-one paid a blind bit of notice, I fitted into the normality just like the soldiers . . . I felt a sudden rush of inexplicable anger . . . those soldiers look more at home here than me and this is my country . . . what was I saying . . . Jesus . . . then suddenly I began to laugh out loud.[13]

Ultimately, he finds personal peace by escaping his identity in the Belfast Protestant community by selling his golf clubs and running away to New York to watch the Irish play in the 1994 World Cup. By leaving his family and literally relying on the kindness of (Irish Catholic) strangers for a place to stay, Kenneth retraces the experience of Irish emigrants escaping prejudice and starvation during the famine. Only Kenneth is trying to escape his own bigotry and find food for a spiritual, rather than physical, hunger. He finds it on a New York street, sharing an embrace with a Catholic Irishman, Mick, after hearing of the killing of six Catholics by a Unionist paramilitary group. He thinks to himself, 'I am not of them anymore . . . no, no one can point the finger at Kenneth Norman McAllister and say, these people are a part of you . . . tonight I absolve myself . . . I am free of them Mick . . . I am free of it, I am a free man . . . I am a Protestant Man, I'm an Irish Man' (p. 47).

While Jones continues to write compelling comedies with women protagonists, like *Women on the Verge of HRT*, her analysis of the 'normality' of the Northern Irish crisis through the eyes of a Protestant man reflects both her range as a writer and her insight into the rigidity of class, gender, and religious identity positions for all individuals caught in the current status quo. Kenneth's abnormal behaviour, abandoning his Belfast life to run away to New York, actually reveals the abnormality of his 'normal' life, with its golf club memberships, Jammy Dodgers, and sectarian social and physical violence. He can only change his position by first removing himself from it, crossing over the borders of the Falls Road, the Irish Republic, the Atlantic Ocean, to find sympathetic camaraderie with the other side.

Northern Irish women on both sides of the political struggle do think about their identities outside the binary framework of Catholic/Protestant, but in the context of a 'matrix of domination'. They contest Northern Irish gender stereotypes through both public political activism and the private choices they make in their lives. Some groups, like the NI Women's Rights Movement in the 1970s and 1980s and the Women's Support Network in the 1990s, have united diverse Northern Irish women's communities on class lines, and the Northern Irish Women's Coalition, founded in 1996, has already gained enough strength to have two members at the recent Peace Talks.[14] The national question, however, has ultimately coloured almost all attempts at feminist solidarity, either by dividing the women on sectarian lines or by subordinating all other community concerns. The vast majority of Northern Irish plays by women, likewise, look at gender through the lens of the national question, just as Northern Irish feminism finds itself circumscribed by sectarian politics. Belfast's Just Us theatre company, for example, seeks to give women from the Northern Irish Republican community non-traditional training and jobs in the theatre, but their recent plays *Just a Prisoner's Wife* and *BinLids* reflect the prominence of the national question in their artistic work. Outside the country, plays by Northern Irish women, like Anne Devlin's productions at the Royal Court in London, are also hailed more for their analysis of nation than their exploration of gender. These plays speak eloquently of women's experience in Northern Ireland through the varied political and national contexts in and against which these women write. Yet they also reflect the inescapable spectre of the nationalist question which looms over all aspects of Northern Irish experience.

Still, contemporary Northern Irish drama by women vigilantly resists accepting the violence and oppressions of the current situation as 'normal', constantly questioning and reframing the political status quo. Warring ideologies, like Unionism and Nationalism in Northern Ireland, can only survive in their purest states by enforcing rigid senses of self on their practitioners, subsuming all other cultural and social concerns to the main political goal. With the inflammatory, binary rhetorics employed on both sides of the national struggle, and the oppressive absurdity of the political stalemate, simply to articulate the complexity of Northern Irish identity – the 'matrix of domination' in which Northern Irish negotiate their lives – is to cut through it, opening up a space for redefinition, re-evaluation, and reconciliation on the personal and social levels. The women discussed in this chapter, along with other women playwrights like the brilliant Northern Irish resident Jennifer Johnston, uncover the previously silent histories of women's experiences on both sides of the nationalist struggle. Despite the national, gender, religious, and class boundaries which typically exclude their voices from many mainstream critiques – and even some discussions of marginalised dramatists – these playwrights and their collaborators shout above the cacophony of conflicts, giving an authentic theatrical voice to women in Northern Ireland.

FIRST PRODUCTIONS OF MAJOR PLAYS

Charabanc

Charabanc's scripts are available at the Linen Hall Library, Belfast, and the Irish Writer's Centre, Dublin. All of these plays were written collaboratively, but credit Marie Jones as the main playwright, with the exception of *Lay Up Your Ends*, attributed to Martin Lynch and the Company.

Lay Up Your Ends, Belfast Civic Arts Theatre (1983)
Oul Delf and False Teeth, Belfast Civic Arts Theatre (1984)
Now You're Talkin', Belfast Civic Arts Theatre (1985)
The Girls in the Big Picture, The Theatre by the Lake, Enniskillen (1986)
Gold in the Streets, Belfast Civic Arts Theatre (1986)
Somewhere Over the Balcony, Drill Hall, London (1987)
The Hamster Wheel, Arts Theatre, Belfast (1990)

Anne Devlin

Ourselves Alone, Liverpool Playhouse Studio (1985)
Heartlanders (with Stephen Bill and David Edgar) Birmingham Repertory Theatre (1989)
After Easter, RSC at The Other Place, Stratford (1994)

Marie Jones outside Charabanc

A Night in November, West Belfast Festival, Whiterock (1994)
Women on the Verge of HRT, Féile an Phobail, Belfast (1995)

Christina Reid

Tea in a China Cup, Lyric Theatre, Belfast (1984)
Did You Hear the One About the Irishman . . . ?, Royal Shakespeare Company USA Tour (1985)
Joyriders, Tricycle Theatre, Belfast (1986)
The Belle of the Belfast City, Lyric Theatre, Belfast (1989)
My Name, Shall I Tell You My Name? Dublin Theatre Festival (1990)
Clowns, The Room at the Orange Tree, Richmond, London (1996)

NOTES

1 Patricia Hill Collins, *Black Feminist Thought: Knowledge, Consciousness, and the Politics of Empowerment* (New York: Routledge, 1991), p. 225.
2 Rosemary Sales, *Women Divided: Gender, Religion and Politics in Northern Ireland* (London: Routledge, 1997), p. 170.
3 Carol Martin, 'Charabanc Theatre Company: "Quare" Women "Sleggin" and "Geggin" the Standards of Northern Ireland by "Tappin" the People', *Drama Review* 1: 2, 1987, p. 97. Similarly, England's Black Theatre Cooperative declined replying to Lizbeth Goodman's Feminist Theatre Survey because they 'had no "feminist" theatre involvement and [were] specifically a black company, not a women's company'. Explained in Lizbeth Goodman, *Contemporary Feminist Theatres: To Each Her Own* (London: Routledge, 1993), p. 150.
4 Maria M. Delgado, Introduction, Christina Reid, *Plays: One* (London: Methuen, 1997), pp. xiv–xv.
5 Anne Devlin, *Ourselves Alone*, in *Ourselves Alone, with A Woman Calling and The Long March* (London: Faber and Faber, 1986), p. 29.
6 Anne Devlin, *After Easter* (London: Faber and Faber, 1994). p. 17.
7 Christina Reid, *Tea in a China Cup*, in *Plays: One*, p. 10.
8 Christina Reid, *Did You Hear the One About the Irishman?*, in *Plays: One*, p. 69.
9 Christina Reid, *Joyriders*, in *Plays: One*, p. 175.
10 *Clowns*, in *Plays: One*, p. 330.
11 Programme, *Somewhere Over the Balcony*, Charabanc Theatre Company, 1987, p. 3.
12 Martin, 'Charabanc Theatre Company,' p. 92.
13 Marie Jones, *A Night in November* (Dublin: New Island Press; London: Nick Hern Books, 1995), p. 24.
14 Begonia Aretxaga, *Shattering Silence: Women, Nationalism and Political Subjectivity in Northern Ireland* (Princeton: Princeton University Press, 1997), pp. 171–2.

FURTHER READING

Primary sources: plays

Devlin, Anne. *Ourselves Alone, with a Woman Calling and The Long March*. London: Faber and Faber, 1986.
    After Easter. London: Faber and Faber, 1994.
Devlin, Anne, Stephen Bill and David Edgar. *Heartlanders*. London: Nick Hern Books, 1989.
Jones, Marie. *The Hamster Wheel. The Crack in the Emerald*. In David Grant (ed.) *New Irish Plays*. London: Nick Hern Books, 1990.
    A Night in November. Dublin: New Island Press; London: Nick Hern Books, 1995.
Reid, Christina. *Plays: One*. Intro. Maria M. Delgado. London: Methuen, 1997.

Secondary sources

DiCenzo, Maria R. 'Charabanc Theatre Company: Placing Women Center Stage in Northern Ireland'. *Theatre Journal* 45.2 (May 1993): 175–84.
Etherton, Michael. *Contemporary Irish Dramatists*. New York: St Martin's Press, 1989.

Harris, Claudia. *Inventing Women's Work: The Legacy of Charabanc Theatre Company.* London: Colin Smythe, forthcoming.

Johnson, Toni O'Brien, and David Cairns (eds.) *Gender in Irish Writing.* Philadelphia: Open University Press, 1991.

Lojek, Helen. 'Difference without Indifference: The Drama of Frank McGuinness and Anne Devlin'. *Eire/Ireland* 25.2 (Summer 1990): 56–68.

Martin, Carol. 'Charabanc Theatre Company: "Quare" Women "Sleggin" and "Geggin" the Standards of Northern Ireland by "Tappin" the People'. *Drama Review* 31.2 (1987): 88–99.

McMullan, Anna. 'Irish Women Playwrights Since 1958'. In T. R. Griffiths and M. Llewellyn-Jones (eds.) *British and Irish Women Dramatists Since 1958.* Philadelphia: Open University Press, 1993: 110–23.

Roche, Anthony. *Contemporary Irish Drama: From Beckett to McGuinness.* New York: St Martin's Press, 1995.

Roll-Hansen, Diderik. 'Dramatic Strategy in *Tea in a China Cup*'. *Modern Drama* 30.3 (1987): 389–95.

Weekes, Ann Owens. *Unveiling Treasures: The Attic Guide to Published Works of Irish Women Literary Writers.* Dublin: Attic Press, 1993.

Wilmer, Steve. 'Women's Theatre in Ireland'. *New Theatre Quarterly* 7.28 (1991): 353–60.

9

SUSAN CARLSON

Language and identity in Timberlake Wertenbaker's plays

Consistent in all of Timberlake Wertenbaker's writing has been a problematisation of the global politics of identity, a problematising marked by characters – from ex-expatriates to middle-class professionals – struggling through a crisis of identity. She offers on-stage a view of late twentieth-century 'Great' Britain in which she examines the multiple and conflicting subjectivities of the world and brings to life the various 'others' created by hierarchies of gender, race, and nation. In her 1990s play, *The Break of Day*, Mihail, a disenfranchised Eastern European trying to strategise his way out of communism to capitalism, places his hope in what he calls 'cross-border children', children who 'will be wilfully international, part of a great European community'.[1] Broadly conceived, such cross-border children – with their multiple cultural heritages, their welcoming of fluid identity, and their consciousness of both future and past – are at the heart of Wertenbaker's drama. In her varied plays, she examines the problems and triumphs of living in a world of porous cultures and shifting identities.

I would like to explore the powerful energies of Wertenbaker's plays with a focus on two issues. First I will detail her attention to language, a focus most obvious in her characters' self-consciousness about words; Wertenbaker's own self-consciousness is clear in her building of intertextual relations between her plays and other texts, and in her sensitivity to the conscriptions of language by those persons or institutions with power. Second, I will analyse her forceful investigations of identity in the realm of various institutions and ideologies, from colonialism to politics to capitalism. With a focus on half a dozen of Wertenbaker's most influential plays, I hope to outline a drama which begins with a focus on women, and then shakes assumptions about our lives in the contemporary world on the way to conclusions which offer an enticing and disturbing openness.

Language

Wertenbaker's *The Love of the Nightingale* is perhaps the most forceful example of her alertness to the nuances of language. The play opened in 1988, at the

Royal Shakespeare Company's The Other Place in Stratford-upon-Avon and later transferred to the RSC's small London theatre, The Pit. Just one month after the uplifting *Our Country's Good* had opened in London, this dark meditation on violence opened in Stratford. Together, the two plays marked Wertenbaker's new prominence in English theatre. The one, *Our Country's Good*, grew out of workshops with actors and director and saw Wertenbaker profiting from the collaborative generation of ideas in a play that would move from the Royal Court to the lucrative West End. The other, *The Love of the Nightingale*, allowed Wertenbaker to use the intimate space of the small non-proscenium theatres of the RSC. Thus, while I am grouping the two plays together to study their treatment and use of language, they are notably different in tone and structure as well as genesis and venue.

The Love of the Nightingale is marked by its tough and raw treatment of rape and violence as well as its spare stylisation of the mythical story of Philomele, Procne, and Tereus. The play's poetic, philosophical conversations challenged audiences to scrutinise their assumptions about gender and power, as well as language. Although the play follows the bleak inevitability of its mythical source in documenting the rape and mutilation of Philomele by Tereus, it is enlivened by its ruminations about language and voice, ruminations energised by feminist awakenings in Philomele and Procne.

From the beginning of the play, young idealistic Philomele is distinguished by her respect for and agility with words. As she trades interpretations of a performance of *Hippolyta* with her brother-in-law Tereus early in the play, she specifies the power of language, 'When you love you want to imprison the one you love in your words, in your tenderness.'[2] Later, when she accompanies Tereus on the long sea-trip from her home in Athens to his in Thrace, she continues aggressively and even obsessively to explore the epistemological potential of language with the captain, with Tereus, and others. After Tereus rapes her and cuts out her tongue, however, the play exposes the open spaces of silence and contemplates the loss of power and control that accompanies the loss of language. Left alone in Thrace, with neither husband Tereus nor sister Philomele, Procne laments 'Where have all the words gone?' (sc. 4, p. 297), and the inadequacy of language she feels is echoed by the female chorus – 'I have trouble expressing myself. The world I see and the words I have do not match' (sc. 9, p. 316). This gap between the meaning words promise and their frequent failure to carry that meaning dominates the troubled second half of the play. Philomele is – literally – silenced, and other characters come to find parallel ways in which their language is stolen from them. In the staccato proclamations of the women's chorus near the end of the play, as the chorus members move from general statements about language ('Without the words to accuse', 'There are some questions that have no answers' [sc. 20, p. 348]) to specific commentary on paradigms of difference ('Why do white people cut off the words of blacks?' 'Why are little girls raped and murdered in the car parks of dark cities?' [sc. 20, p. 349]), they link one's access to language to one's position in a hierarchy.

Wertenbaker's atomising of language comes also through her self-conscious borrowings from the Greek literary tradition. Not only does she take her story from the realm of mythology (and her inter-text from *Hippolytus*), but she speculates about the revelations such literary models can bring to our late twentieth-century world. For example, the male chorus insists on the continuing power of myth: 'There is no content without its myth. Fathers and sons, rebellion, collaboration, the state, every fold and twist of passion, we have uttered them all. This one, you will say, watching Philomele watching Tereus watching Philomele, must be about men and women, yes, you think, a myth for our times, we understand' (sc. 8, p. 315). In this passage, Wertenbaker broadcasts the power of myth; and her play constantly reminds us that both language and its absence are integral to such lasting narratives. As Wertenbaker herself notes, the play is about 'the violence that erupts in societies when they have been silenced for too long'.[3] Wertenbaker explains that she is drawn to Greek literature because the Greeks, as the first great humanists, wrote 'about being human, not about private, individual psychology'.[4] The Greeks faced these large issues at 'a very raw stage. They were very interested in the use and abuse of power: Creon misjudges and abuses his power when he condemns Antigone. As do the "democratic" Greeks in *Hecuba* by sacrificing Hecuba's daughter' (unpublished interview, 1997). Such perceptiveness offers an almost blindingly pure look at human struggle. *The Love of the Nightingale* is a linguistically sensuous play in which the women of the Philomele myth search for a voice, for words which will account for the horrific play of desire, power, and position at the heart of this play. Although the play ends with a burst of bacchanal frenzy and fury (when Philomele and Procne kill Procne's son), it refuses answers, ending with a question which could have come directly from Wertenbaker to her audience, 'Didn't you want me to ask questions?' (sc. 21, p. 354). In *The Love of the Nightingale*, as in her translations of Sophocles' *The Theban Plays* and Euripides' *Hecuba*, Wertenbaker offers a relentless examination of the ways in which language controls and is controlled.

Like *The Love of the Nightingale*, *Our Country's Good*, Wertenbaker's most well-known play, privileges meta-commentary on language and is based on the interplay of Wertenbaker's drama with both an established theatrical text – George Farquhar's *The Recruiting Officer* – and historical fiction, *The Playmaker* by Thomas Keneally. While I could just as easily examine this play in my second section of the chapter (on identity), I have chosen to deal with it here, because its lively debates about theatre, power, and nationality all turn on linguistic ingenuity and linguistic colonisation.

Director Max Stafford-Clark commissioned Wertenbaker to write a play based on Keneally's novel, which recounts the early days of Britain's first penal colony in Australia. It would be the first of several fruitful collaborations between author and director (Stafford-Clark also directed *Three Birds Alighting on A Field* and *The Break of Day*). The play was to run in repertory at the Royal Court with Farquhar's *The Recruiting Officer* (1706), the play convicts had actually staged in the penal colony to celebrate the King's birthday in 1789. In the preliminary efforts on this piece, Wertenbaker worked intensively in workshops with the actors who would play in both *The Recruiting Officer* and *Our Country's Good*. She found such a collaborative process 'very rich, because you get a huge canvas [of ideas and responses] from which you then choose' in writing the play (unpublished interview, 1997). Wertenbaker's openness to the multiple voices of workshop collaboration is also played out in the intertextual fabric of the play which has 'more than one voice' as it draws from Farquhar and Keneally.[5] These are not just voices from the past, however, as these many voices seemed to have spoken to and of the 1980s. As Christine Dymkowski notes, the play seemed very much about its own times: '1980s Britain, a time during which the ruling Conservative government steadily dismantled the welfare state, destroyed the country's manufacturing base, disempowered the trade unions, and sold off public utilities, and whose leader, Margaret Thatcher, even declared that "There's no such thing as society"'.[6] Let me analyse the play's commentary on language as well as its ending to explore this rich text so central to Wertenbaker's career.

As Wertenbaker's motley collection of convicts tackles the unlikely feat of performing eighteenth-century comedy, Wertenbaker is able to make her double theatre a double forum for words. Many of the characters, for example, have a heightened sensitivity to language – from convict John Wisehammer, who is in love with the dictionary, to Liz Morden, who perceives of language so literally that it takes on a new materiality. As such experientially based paradigms of language are put into practice in the convict's production of Farquhar, however, language becomes a site of cultural and institutional power struggle, for at the heart of this play is a debate over the power of theatre and its heightened language to civilise and/or control. Governor Phillip sees theatre as a way to level differences of education and class: 'And we, this colony of a few hundred, will be watching this [play] together, for a few hours we will no longer be despised prisoners and hated gaolers. We will laugh, we may be moved, we may even think a little.'[7] Phillip defends theatre as a site for cultural redemption while his colleagues remain sceptical of the civilising power of theatre on the convicts. The greatest share of the play, however, is devoted to demonstrating the ways in which the performing of this play does change the lives of those involved, from Second Lieutenant Ralph Clark, the director, to the men and women convicts. Wisehammer, for example, is encouraged to develop his linguistic talents and even writes a prologue for the production of Farquhar; convict Mary Brenham and gaoler Clark use Farquhar's love scene to give voice to their own love; and Liz Morden, in what many see as the play's most triumphant scene, gives up her silence and adopts the particularity of Farquhar's language to reclaim her dignity before a group of men ready to hang her.

Language is not, however, an unproblematic presence in the play, for as Wertenbaker alerts us to the way power is exercised in the colony, particularly the way class, gender, and race predict who holds power, the audience must acknowledge how language is controlled by those with power. Liz Morden keeps silence for so long, for example, because her words hold little value since she is so low in the hierarchy; as she puts it, speaking 'wouldn't have mattered' (Act II, sc. 10, p. 271). Liz's language is devalued because she is a woman and a convict; Wisehammer's because he is a Jew and a convict. 'The Aborigine', whose brief appearances punctuate the colonists' actions, is most severely marginalised due to his race, and allowed only a few poetic responses to the British intrusion on his land. So while one might recognise the regenerative power of language in this play, another way to understand the language is to see that those with institutional power control language, and that the only way to challenge such power is to become fluent in the very language which oppresses you. Thus, the issues of language and silence so powerful in *The Love of the Nightingale* reverberate throughout this play.

The play's tension between these oppositional possibilities for language has often been a pivotal factor for those judging the work. While initial reviewers, in England especially, saw the play's language as the triumphant expression of community and of the civilising empowerment of theatre, a significant portion of recent commentary has criticised the play for participating in the very colonisation it purports to expose.[8] In particular, critics have looked to the play's ending as a marker of its efficacy as a social document. Those critics who have foregrounded the play's progressive portrait of theatre read the end of *Our Country's Good* – an end in which the convicts giddily take the stage to perform Farquhar's play – as a valorisation of the power of theatre, of its power to carry over into real life.[9] Wertenbaker endorses this positive reading of the conclusion, noting that:

> *Our Country's Good* was a plea for the value of Theatre and because the characters discovered this value for themselves, it ended up an up note. *Three Birds* was a plea for the value of Art, but showed how Art is also corrupted by the price put on it by a cynical society. The ending was more tentative although Biddy was definitely transformed and deepened by her encounter with painting.
>
> (unpublished interview, 1997)

But a more negative reading of the conclusion of *Our Country's Good* finds that the ending underwrites the inequities of colonialism. In other words, the play ends by reproducing the dominant ideology at the expense of a social critique.[10]

Our Country's Good stands at the centre of Wertenbaker's work to date, fortified by an ebullient debate over theatre, a debate which begins with characters on stage and continues in critical debate off stage. The play's continuing production in theatres around the world and its prominent place on school reading lists attest to its continuing influence. In this play, as in all of Wertenbaker's work, language is not just a vehicle for ideas; it is at the centre of both our oppressions and our liberties. The kind of linguistic alertness in both *The Love of the Nightingale* and *Our Country's Good* is also present in *New Anatomies*, where Wertenbaker's historical figure Isabelle Eberhardt seeks permeable borders between language and culture; in *The Grace of Mary Traverse* where patriarchal control of language constantly intrudes upon Mary's search for autonomy; and in *The Break of Day* where both Wertenbaker's 1990s characters and their counterparts in Chekhov's *The Three Sisters* must make do with a language 'depleted by this terrible century' (*Break of Day*, Act I, p. 24). As I will outline below, the intensity of Wertenbaker's language as well as the scrutiny she brings to its use are intimately connected to her consistent preoccupation with issues of identity.

Identity

In each of Wertenbaker's plays, she offers forceful investigations of the constructed nature of identity, and offers various glosses on the ways social and political institutions as well as their hierarchies of difference play into individual lives. In her early play, *New Anatomies*, written for the Women's Theatre Group in 1981 (and her first published play in 1984), she offers her most exotic exploration of these issues, depicting her main character's subversive attempts to create her own racial and sexual identity. Isabelle Eberhardt is Wertenbaker's focal character, the European woman whose love of Arab culture and whose rejection of conventional sexuality led her to rattle the hierarchies of colonial Algeria in the early twentieth century. The play's succession of scenes is marked by a Brechtian presentational quality as four of the five women in the cast take on at least three roles, each playing a Western woman, an Arab man, and a Western man.[11] The fifth plays Isabelle, a woman whose openness to the multiplicity of her own identity brings most other assertions of identity into question. When the play was revived in 1990 at London's Man in the Moon Theatre, reviewers who were fresh from the high-profile success of *Our Country's Good* in 1988 tended to see the play as pre-echoing 'the later work'.[12] Several were critical of the spare dialogue and episodic construction of the play. The most notable response, however, was the reviewers' acknowledgement of the enduring toughness of Wertenbaker's early play.

Out of her need to see the world from perspectives not native to her, Isabelle, a white, European woman, spends the play learning how to live and think as an Arab, how to desire as a man, and how to understand the creation of nation. Chronicling Isabelle's attempts to understand both Arab culture and French attempts to colonise it, the play is an inventive, episodic investigation into the languages and social structures which create identity in such a cultural amalgam. Early on in her quest, as Isabelle has, for the first time, exchanged her clothes for those of an Arab man, she articulates the desire to erase her identity as a European woman and to adventure into the possibilities open to her in male, Arab dress. Dismissing the terms 'foreigner', 'European', 'woman', and 'Isabelle' that might be used to hail her, she claims only the desert freedom of her chosen Arab name, 'Si Mahmoud' (Act I, sc. 5, p. 26).

Isabelle pursues several existential issues simultaneously, but two quests predominate: (1) her search to re-define desire and sexuality without having to accept the stereotypes of European female behaviour, and (2) her search to understand Arab culture and let its social and institutional structures replace those constraining European ones under which she has operated. Wertenbaker establishes in early scenes that Isabelle has always chafed under what seem to her arbitrary definitions of male and female, but in the provocative scene that opens Act II the playwright brings together a group of women all of whom have lived their lives outside the boundaries of traditional womanhood. In a Parisian salon, they trade stories of their adventures dressing as men, loving women, and creating new selves. Lydia, a writer, prophesies that the sexual aberrations they represent will lead to a 'revolution greater even than the French Revolution', and Isabelle follows with her crude, though precise, vision of gender-bending: 'I am not a woman. I'm Si Mahmoud. I like men. They like me. As a boy, I mean. And I have a firm rule: no Europeans up my arse' (Act II, sc. 1, p. 40). As Ann Wilson notes, the scene clarifies the performative nature of gender, and toys with threatening inversions to the status quo.[13] While the compacted events of Isabelle Eberhardt's short life offer her no realisation of her dream to have a sexual desire freed from culturally imposed restraints, the pressure of her search brings both European and Arab practices into question. The unfinished quality of Isabelle's search was unsettling to reviewers of the 1990 production, with one noting the 'sullen truculence' of the heroine.[14]

This unresolved quest for a reconceptualising of gender identity is not completely separable from Isabelle's simultaneous interrogation of nation-based identity. French colonisation in Algeria is present from the play's opening scene, and as Isabelle aggressively seeks admission to Arab society she looks for alternatives to the European position of power she was born into. She states her desires directly to her Arab friends – 'I wanted to possess this country. It has possessed me' (Act II, sc. 2, p. 42) – and her acceptance into male religious sects is extraordinary evidence of their sanction of her dream. Yet Isabelle never finds peace in the binary of European/Arab on which she shuttles back and forth. When a colonial judge finds her 'offensive masquerade' as an Arab male intolerable, Isabelle articulates the threat her slippery identity poses – 'It's not even what I am doing, is it? It's what I am. You hate what I am' (Act II, sc. 3, p. 49). Events suggest that she is othered in *both* cultural realms; a self-created cross-border child, Isabelle is always an outsider. Julia Clancy-Smith's analysis of the historical Isabelle Eberhardt captures the dangerous hybridity Wertenbaker's Isabelle lives: 'Gender transvestism permitted her [Isabelle] to engage in cultural transvestism, which ultimately rendered her marginal to both cultures – the hybrid European community of French Algeria and Muslim North African society. Isabelle Eberhardt was an extreme example of cultural hyphenation.'[15]

The play ends with Isabelle's ironic death by drowning in the desert – a bleak commentary on her frenetic efforts to move outside the gender, race, and culture to which she was born. As this play explores the possibility of a cultural mobility we may or may not have in this century, Wertenbaker marks out an intercultural territory with which her name has become synonymous. Wertenbaker's own heritage is a confluence of British, American, and French, and while she is cautious about encouraging connections between her plays and her own biography, she does often refer to her being brought up in Basque country as a major influence on her thinking. It was an experience which imprinted on her a consciousness of destabilised selves:

> I was brought up with a complicated cultural mix: Basque, French, Anglo and American and always felt slightly outside any one of them. I think I can identify with outsiders imaginatively. What it means to be an outsider has always interested me whether it is Isabelle Eberhardt or the characters in *Our Country's Good* or Procne in *The Love of the Nightingale* – that feeling of being estranged from your childhood and your roots. Women often feel they are outsiders anyway.
>
> (unpublished interview, 1997)

Indeed, the focus of Wertenbaker's plays is often on 'a woman who has been radically dislocated from the culture into which she was born' (Wilson, 'Timberlake Wertenbaker', p. 2496). In the differences of gender and culture which swirl around Isabelle Eberhardt's search for a self she can accept, Wertenbaker establishes early in her career an interest in exposing the complex forces which shape contemporary selves. As Wertenbaker herself notes, this play is unusual for her in that it ends on a 'dark' note.[16] Its combustible dialectical energies, however, urge audiences and readers to accept the philosophical challenge of experimenting with new selves.

With *The Grace of Mary Traverse*, Wertenbaker revisits the issues of identity which drive Isabelle Eberhardt, this time in England of the 1780s. In a play often described as a woman's 'rake's progress', Wertenbaker shows how Mary Traverse's hunger for knowledge and experience forces her to confront restrictive institutional structures of family, class, and gender. The play is set in the late eighteenth century, at the time of the Gordon riots, through, as with *Our Country's Good*, its subject matter was an contemporary as the Brixton riots through which Wertenbaker was living as she wrote. The play opened at the Royal Court Theatre in 1985, where Wertenbaker had been a Writer-in-Residence, and it won her the *Plays and Players'* award for most promising playwright. This play first brought Wertenbaker's work to large audiences, an important prelude to the prominence of *Our Country's Good* and *The Love of the Nightingale* three years later.

While I plan to focus on the ways this play pursues issues of female identity, such issues are inseparable from Wertenbaker's scrutiny of the impact of language on such identity. At once blunt and poetically charged, the spare dialogue is self-conscious and exact. When, for example, Mary seduces and then confronts her father in the first scene of Act III – at this point she is pregnant, diseased, and impoverished – she carefully distinguishes the variant meanings of words. She tells him that the two of them no longer share his conventional understanding of what 'father' and 'daughter' mean: 'The father I want cannot be the father of "your" daughter. And yet, I want a father. Could you not be "my" father? Could you not try?'[17] While Mary's language suffers in the shadow of male hegemony, Jack finds his working-class linguistic heritage similarly inadequate. Though he wants to 'tell people about freedom', he is 'cursed' and 'silent' (Act III, sc. 5, p. 129). Both characters recognise the power that language can carry, a power over-determined, in this play's world, by class and gender. As Mary strips herself of the comfortable middle-class, bourgeois, female identity her father has worked so hard to imprint on her, she uses a language never quite in her grasp to explore hierarchies of class and gender which have delimited her self and her world.

Several characters in the play join Mary to voice a critique of the class system and its ability to freeze identity. Angered by his limited education and stunted life options, Jack not only identifies his linguistic inadequacies, but is also instrumental in fomenting community riots to protest economic privilege. Mrs Temptwell, with a smouldering anger over her family's economic demise, is taking a more personal revenge on Mary and her family by tempting Mary out of privilege. These two more conventional critiques of class hierarchies are, however, joined to a third, more novel commentary which comes in the character of Sophie, a young working-class woman who stays with Mary after saving her from a rape by substituting herself as the victim. Ever loyal, Sophie remains with Mary to the end, enduring not only the rape but also the death of her child, the hanging of her husband Jack, and, in general, her objectification by Mary.

Through the relationship of Sophie and Mary, Wertenbaker explores the stubborn resilience of the class system, even for a character like Mary who imagines her will alone can remove her from the hierarchy. For while Mary rejects her life of privilege and throws herself into the radical political protest of her time, she unconsciously (and contradictorily) assumes that some degree of privilege remains hers: for instance, as she campaigns for liberty, she continues to treat both Mrs Temptwell and Sophie as servants. Most critically, Sophie's elemental life, though it endures to the end of the play, and though it spawns the most genuine vision in the play, remains an unarticulated hope for a different world, a hope that is incomplete in a world still constructed by hierarchies of class.[18]

These critiques of the class system are joined to Wertenbaker's interrogation of gender and its configurations of power. The play's opening scenes quickly establish that Mary's life as an eighteenth-century young woman is dictated by the goal of remaining an 'unruffled landscape' of value in the marriage market (Act I, sc. 2, p. 71). Mary is lured out of this facile world of manners by her Faustian desire for knowledge and experience, and, through a series of crude encounters, learns that her womanhood is not a refined essence but a construction of cultural and political forces. In the first stage of her education, Mary analyses the power of sexual desire. After she escapes her own rape, she makes Mr Hardlong a study in heterosexual desire, makes Sophie her study in homosexual desire, and turns the seduction of her father into a study of incest. Frighteningly, Mary experiences the multiplicity of human sexuality as if she were conducting a laboratory experiment. In the second stage of her education, she learns how political institutions dictate the experiences and desires that can command power. Mary's quest for personal self-knowledge moves her towards a 'resistant, mobile subjectivity' (Dahl, 'Constructing the Subject', p. 156), and her study of political power leaves her with an understanding that though identities are fluid, the power to effect that fluidity lies in the hands of a very few men.

In the last scene of the play, Mary, her father, her daughter Little Mary, and Sophie have created a fragile, new community in the country. Still seeking to understand her world, Mary stakes a hopeful claim on the future – 'One day we'll know how to love this world' (Act IV, sc. 3, p. 160). Sophie's insistence, however, on remembrance of the past – 'We must not forget' (Act IV, sc. 3, p. 160) – Mrs. Temptwell's unrelenting claim to the Traverse land, and Little Mary's ephemeral presence remind us that the future, like the past, will offer options, not answers. In the course of the play, Mary gains political power and voice; she learns, however, that 'there are very few solutions to society and to the abuse of power'.[19] This play works through the intertwined issues of identity and power; with its open ending, it challenges us to define and position ourselves responsibly in a world while conscious of the forces around us. In two plays from the 1990s, Wertenbaker explores similar quandaries in contemporary settings.

Wertenbaker's *Three Birds Alighting on a Field* (in *Plays 1*) which won the 1992 Susan Smith Blackburn Prize for playwriting, explores the high-powered and often corrupt world of contemporary art. Three years after the première of *Our Country's Good*, Wertenbaker returned to her productive alliance with director Max Stafford-Clark and the Royal Court Theatre to produce this influential and acclaimed play. Like *Our Country's Good*, this play began in workshops with director and actors; and the play Wertenbaker wrote used the art world as the launch pad for investigations of English identity in a global context. Wertenbaker offers an intense exploration of a changing world in which ideologies like capitalism and nationalism are collapsing, and she studies 'how the world is going to function in a non-ideological age' (unpublished interview, 1997). Indeed, the play was well received initially as a 'drama about the way we live now and the moral code that conditions Britain today', as a play about 'multiplicity and uncertainty'.[20]

It is also a play focused on the idea of English identity; and as she explores the lives of characters who bring together English, Greek, Romanian, Asian, and American backgrounds, she offers a play about contemporary England, a place in which the concept of nation is problematised and 'English' identity is consequently destabilised. In the final scene, the main character Biddy – a middle-aged, middle-class woman who has spent the play expanding her intellectual, political, and sexual horizons – poses semi-nude for artist Stephen; and as her body stands in for the English landscape he normally paints, it emblematises the contemporary English 'landscape'. Biddy represents what is both good and bad about the privileged English approaching the end of the twentieth century: she does good works and has a good heart, but is only marginally cognisant of the issues of race, class, nation, and privilege which are reshaping her world. All around her are characters who force this middle-class woman with a tendency to complacency into a recognition of the intense psychological pressures on a Greek man (her husband) who would be English; of the shell of an identity left to a woman whose Indian father denies his racial heritage; and even of the way a failed capitalism in Romania impacts individual lives. The resolution that can be brought to the many issues of the play through Biddy's recognitions is small, however; Wertenbaker offers yet another open ending in which the audience is challenged to come to terms with the multiplicities of English social identities and with the corruption of cultural institutions. This play's middle-class existential angst and millennial readjustments are also at the heart of Wertenbaker's *The Break of Day*.

Drawing from Chekhov's *The Three Sisters*, *The Break of Day* chronicles the middle-age adjustments of three 'feminist' sisters whose friendship grew out of the heady 1970s. Almost a decade before the writing of the play, Wertenbaker noted her debt to Chekhov: 'I adore Chekhov, and although it is not obvious, he has influenced me very much' (unpublished interview, 1986). In 1995, Chekhov's disintegrating culture, his 'slit of hope' (*Break of Day*, Act II, p. 61), and his reflective characters offered an appropriate starting point for Wertenbaker's own end-of-the-century musings. One of Wertenbaker's three sisters, Tess, is married to Robert, an actor who takes on the part of Chekhov's Vershinin and brings Vershinin's philosophical musings into his late twentieth-century world. Over and again, Robert makes Chekhov his touchstone for understanding the turmoil of his personal life and the confusions of his cultural moment. In particular, he uses Vershinin to voice his own hope for the future: 'In *Three Sisters*, the characters contemplate the end of their century with that same sense of waste, of being outside history, but Vershinin intoxicates himself with a vision of a better future' (Act I, p. 24). With her own focus on the future, Wertenbaker's description of the play is congruent with Robert's: 'I wanted to write an absolutely contemporary play about everybody's situation: the end of the century . . . you know, the fatigue at the end of the century, the breakdown of a lot of ideals, particularly for women, and this notion of the future and what the future is, what sort of future we are providing for others' ('Interview' in *Rage and Reason*, pp. 143–4). With this contemplative emphasis on the fissures and future of a once powerful culture, Wertenbaker returns once again to the issues of late twentieth-century existence and identity in an increasingly global community. In this play about several cross-border 'children', she points to a future beyond the nation-based individual. As Wertenbaker herself explains, we are in a 'post-political age', beyond post-colonialism, where we experience 'the shift of cultures and the shift of people through several cultures in their lifetime, in one or two generations' (unpublished interview, 1997).

The play is rich with reference to contemporary issues – the dismantling of National Health, the de-funding of university education, the political reshaping of Eastern Europe, the false promises of capitalism, the roller coaster of infertility treatments, and the marketing of popular culture. In this issue-conscious context, the play's three middle-aged women who have promised themselves a feminist future, examine the power and position they have accumulated by the 1990s. Tess, the editor of a women's magazine, chillingly acknowledges and accepts her privileged empowerment by a once 'heroic empire' (Act I, p. 5); and Nina, a popular recording artist, adds her recognition that any power she has is but a factor of historical happenstance (Act I, p. 7). These women, however privileged to have a position and a voice denied women through most of history, have not resolved the issues of gender and power which troubled Isabelle Eberhardt and Mary Traverse. They are simply looking at the issues from a new point of view. Both childless, Nina and Tess are, in fact, fixated on maternity, and their longings for motherhood are counterpointed in the long and episodic second act. As Nina and her husband pursue a labyrinthine Eastern European adoption and as Tess gyrates among various infertility treatments, the play explores the contemporary politics of motherhood. The presence of their friend April (who has no interest in children) keeps the play from tilting completely into a manic quest for children. As it dominates the play, however, the quest fills out a facet of female identity that Isabelle Eberhardt ignored and Mary Traverse shunned; Wertenbaker urges that any rethinking about female identity must accommodate women's options for motherhood. Mothering, then, is not a biological issue here, but an economic, cultural, and political one. Both Tess and Nina are face-to-face with their relative privilege; their complicity in class and national power bases is exposed in their attempt to buy motherhood.

When *The Break of Day* opened in London in November of 1995, it earned negative, sometimes hostile reviews; this play meant to reflect on the state-of-the-nation was begrudgingly digested. Some reviewers were offended by the women characters' baby lust, some found the play a hollow tract, some were disappointed in what they found to be an ineffectual use of Chekhov. Wertenbaker found herself puzzled by the 'vitriol' (unpublished interview, 1997), but notes that the open-ended nature of the play's discussion, its inconclusiveness, left people discontented: 'I think people left the theatre feeling a little bit puzzled, slightly dissatisfied' (unpublished interview, 1997). Wertenbaker notes additionally that the play's profusion of ideas is part of the point:

> I think contemporary life in the West is like that: you can be driving in a city, reading signs, talking on a mobile, listening to the news on the radio, eating your lunch sandwich, trying to digest a novel you finished the night before and coping with a general anxiety about the year 2000 all in the same minute. We can no longer pretend to have long evenings in Norway or in the remote provinces of Russia. We are assailed by information, often contradictory and that chaos is part of the modern landscape. (unpublished interview, 1997)

Wertenbaker's refusal to contain an idea, her acceptance of the indeterminate nature of experience, is at the centre of the play. Wertenbaker urges a new sense of community which moves us beyond any certainty, beyond a stable identity in gender, class, race, or nation. While they attempt to hide out in their lovely English country garden, all of the characters in *The Break of Day* are touched by global issues and events and must acknowledge both their privilege and their responsibility. I would argue that Wertenbaker asks of her audience what she asks of these characters, that they recognise their lives as 'cross-border', and think about themselves as people trying out, performing those aspects of themselves that seem truest to their multiple experiences of the world.

In her series of intelligent, original plays, Timberlake Wertenbaker has carved out an important space for herself on the contemporary stage. With her work in the 1980s, she was able to make her distinctive poetic voice and her exciting exploration of topical issues of identity a significant part of women's presence on the London stage. In the late 1990s, troubled by the diminished presence of women writers and women characters on that stage, Wertenbaker has felt called upon to take up, again, her part in re-establishing women's theatre:

> I made a fuss about it recently because I felt women's plays were being marginalised again. There have been some bad years recently when not only could you not see any plays by women on the main stages you no longer even saw women appear on those stages. And in so far as theatre holds up a mirror of some sort, you began to feel women had no reflection.
>
> In the Royal Court classics season of 1996, out of some thirty odd characters appearing across three plays, only one was a woman.
>
> I do think this is changing again. (unpublished interview, 1997)

Wertenbaker promises to remain a significant woman playwright into the next century – one who will speak to audiences not only in London, but also in Europe and around the world. As her writing helps us map out various trajectories into a new century, Wertenbaker's drama will continue challenging audiences to acknowledge their complicities and celebrate their possibilities, across borders.

FIRST PRODUCTIONS OF MAJOR PLAYS BY TIMBERLAKE WERTENBAKER

Venues are in London unless stated.

New Anatomies, Edinburgh Theatre Workshop, Edinburgh Festival; ICA, Women's Theatre Group (1981)
The Grace of Mary Traverse, Royal Court (1985)
The Love of the Nightingale, Royal Shakespeare Company, The Other Place, Stratford-upon-Avon (1988)
Our Country's Good, Royal Court (1988)
Three Birds Alighting on a Field, Royal Court (1991)
The Break of Day, Out of Joint, Leicester Haymarket and Bristol Old Vic (October 1995); Royal Court (November 1995)

NOTES

1 Timberlake Wertenbaker, *The Break of Day* (London: Faber and Faber, 1995), Act II, p. 82.
2 Timberlake Wertenbaker, *The Love of the Nightingale*, in *Timberlake Wertenbaker: Plays 1* (London: Faber and Faber, 1996), sc. 5, p. 305.
3 Timberlake Wertenbaker, 'Introduction' to *Timberlake Wertenbaker: Plays 1*, p. viii.
4 Timberlake Wertenbaker, unpublished interview with author, November 1997.
5 Jim Davis, 'A Play for England: The Royal Court Adapts *The Playmaker*', in Peter Reynolds (ed.) *Novel Images: Literature in Performance* (London: Routledge, 1993), p. 177.

6 Christine Dymkowski, '"The Play's the Thing": The Metatheatre of Timberlake Wertenbaker', in Nicole Boireau (ed.) *Drama on Drama: Dimensions of Theatricality on the Contemporary British Stage* (London: Macmillan, 1997), p. 127; see also Davis, 'A Play for England', p. 178.

7 Timberlake Wertenbaker, *Our Country's Good*, in *Timberlake Wertenbaker: Plays 1*, Act I, sc. 6, p. 206.

8 See Ann Wilson, '*Our Country's Good*: Theatre, Colony and Nation in Wertenbaker's Adaptation of *The Playmaker*', *Modern Drama*, 34: 1, March 1991, pp. 22–34.

9 See Dymkowski, 'The Play's the Thing', pp. 128–9; and Jim Davis, 'Festive Irony: Aspects of British Theatre in the 1980s', *Critical Survey*, 3: 3, 1991, p. 349.

10 See for example, Esther Beth Sullivan, 'Hailing Ideology, Acting in the Horizon, and Reading between Plays by Timberlake Wertenbaker', *Theatre Journal*, 45, 1993, p. 144.

11 Timberlake Wertenbaker, *New Anatomies*, in *Timberlake Wertenbaker: Plays 1*, 'Notes on the Staging', p. 4.

12 Lyn Gardner, review of *New Anatomies*, in *City Limits*, 15 March 1990; *London Theatre Record*, 26 February – 11 March 1990, p. 324.

13 Ann Wilson, 'Timberlake Wertenbaker', in Frank M. Magill (ed.) *Critical Survey of Drama*, revised edn (Pasadena, CA: Salem Press, 1994), p. 2497.

14 Martin Hoyle, review of *New Anatomies*, *Financial Times*, 9 March 1990: *London Theatre Record*, 26 February – 11 March 1990, p. 325.

15 Julia Clancy-Smith, 'The "Passionate Nomad" Reconsidered: A European Woman in L'Algérie Francaise (Isabelle Eberhardt, 1877–1904)', in Nupur Chaudhuri and Margaret Strobel (eds.) *Western Women and Imperialism: Complicity and Resistance* (Bloomington: Indiana University Press, 1992), p. 73.

16 Timberlake Wertenbaker, unpublished interview with author, May 1986.

17 Timberlake Wertenbaker, *The Grace of Mary Traverse*, in *Timberlake Wertenbaker: Plays 1*, Act III, sc. 1, p. 119.

18 See Ann Wilson, 'Forgiving History and Making New Worlds: Timberlake Wertenbaker's Recent Drama', in James Acheson (ed.) *British and Irish Drama Since 1960* (New York: St Martin's Press, 1993), pp. 154–5. See also Mary Karen Dahl's use of the play as a paradigm for cultural critique, 'Constructing the Subject: Timberlake Wertenbaker's *The Grace of Mary Traverse*', *Journal of Dramatic Theory and Criticism* 7: 2, Spring 1993, pp. 149–59.

19 Timberlake Wertenbaker, 'Interview', in Heidi Stephenson and Natasha Langridge (eds.) *Rage and Reason: Women Playwrights on Playwriting* (London: Methuen, 1997), pp. 136–45.

20 Sheridan Morley, *Herald Tribune*, 18 September 1991, in *London Theatre Record*, 10–23 September 1991, p. 1116; Clare Bayley, *What's On*, 18 September 1991; *London Theatre Record*, 10–23 September 1991, p. 1118.

FURTHER READING

Primary sources: plays

Wertenbaker, Timberlake. *The Break of Day*. London: Faber and Faber, 1995.

    Timberlake Wertenbaker: Plays 1. London: Faber and Faber, 1996. (Contains *New Anatomies*, *The Grace of Mary Traverse*, *Our Country's Good*, *The Love of the*

Nightingale, and *Three Birds Alighting on a Field*.)
trans. *The Theban Plays*. London: Faber and Faber, 1992.

Secondary sources

Carlson, Susan. 'Issues of Identity, Nationality, and Performance: The Reception of Two Plays by Timberlake Wertenbaker'. *New Theatre Quarterly* 9.35 (August 1993): 267–89.

Dahl, Mary Karen. 'Constructing the Subject: Timberlake Wertenbaker's *The Grace of Mary Traverse*', *Journal of Dramatic Theory and Criticism* 7.2 (Spring 1993): 149–59.

Davis, Jim. 'A Play for England: The Royal Court adapts *The Playmaker*', in Peter Reynolds (ed.) *Novel Images: Literature in Performance*. London: Routledge, 1993: 175–90.

Dymkowski, Christine. '"The Play's the Thing": The Metatheatre of Timberlake Wertenbaker'. In Nicole Boireau (ed.) *Drama on Drama: Dimensions of Theatricality on the Contemporary British Stage*. London: Macmillan, 1997: 121–35.

McDonough, Carla J. 'Timberlake Wertenbaker'. In William W. Demastes (ed.) *British Playwrights, 1956–1995: A Research and Production Sourcebook*. Westport, CT: Greenwood Press, 1996: 406–14.

Rabey, David Ian. 'Defining Difference: Timberlake Wertenbaker's Drama of Language, Dispossession and Discovery', *Modern Drama* 33.4 (December 1990): 518–28.

Sullivan, Esther Beth. 'Hailing Ideology, Acting in the Horizon, and Reading between Plays by Timberlake Wertenbaker'. *Theatre Journal* 45 (1993): 139–54.

Wilson, Ann. '*Our Country's Good:* Theatre, Colony and Nation in Wertenbaker's Adaptation of *The Playmaker*'. *Modern Drama* 34.1 (March 1991): 22–34.

'Forgiving History and Making New Worlds: Timberlake Wertenbaker's Recent Drama'. In James Acheson (ed.) *British and Irish Drama Since 1960*. New York: St Martin's Press, 1993: 146–61.

PART 3

THE QUESTION OF THE CANON

Editors' note

As we began to plan this volume – what and who to include, how to present the material, what categories would be most workable – we kept stumbling over what we came to refer to as the 'question of the canon'. Defined as the 'indispensable' works which must be included under the subject matter of the title, one way of understanding canonicity is to ask what plays simply could not be excluded from this discussion of modern British women playwrights. However, that approach already begs the question of the canon because it presupposes an established and undisputed authoritative list of such works that has widespread consensus. As the Women's Movement has been militant in pointing out, 'canons' are highly questionable constructs, historically set by men and power elites to ensure repetition and perpetuation of works which reinforce the dominant ideology of a given culture. One of the early tasks, therefore, of Second Wave feminism's academic women has been to challenge received notions of the canon. They worked to recover, and to insist on the acknowledgement and study of, women's history, literature, art, and other accomplishments that had previously not enjoyed prominence or even discovery because of the emphasis on 'great works' by famous men (see Bennett, chapter 3, for an extended discussion of this point). Of course, the notion of 'great works' is no less fraught, since taste is as much a matter of fashion and power relations as it is of inherent value. In fact, as this book has argued as one of its premises (see our main introduction), value is a constantly changing matter, negotiated between the work and the historical moment from which it is viewed, not a fixed, timeless quality.

A further irony is that any book billed as 'A Companion' itself inevitably participates in canon formation. What is the purpose of this volume if not to serve as a guide for the formulation of class syllabi, study lists, references to 'the most important' modern British women playwrights? In addition, if the book is successful, it will aid in reinforcing the canonicity of whatever it includes. A final irony appeared when we volume editors turned out to choose for the subjects of our own contributions two women, both of whom would be widely considered canonical – perhaps even the most canonical of the writers discussed here (Caryl Churchill and Pam Gems). In the end, we decided to meet this problem head-on by including a section which addresses the problem, as well as by elsewhere striving to include material that critiques the adequacy of our enterprise.

Apart from the presumptuousness of a claim to establish the canonical, there are often exclusions that are practically demanded and yet inexcusable. If this volume is intended to serve as a companion to the works themselves, but the works are not available in print or inadequately represented by print format (in the next section see MacDonald's discussion of experimental work in chapter 14 and Case's focus on ephemeral solo performances in chapter 15), it becomes difficult to justify their inclusion in such a volume. The inclusion of some work that is unfortunately *not* readily available, however, was accepted as indispensable – precisely in order to insist on this issue as well as its specific contribution to the overarching topic.

The three writers we finally chose to group together are playwrights whose work is generally viewed as canonical. For many years, Gems and Churchill were the only two contemporary women playwrights to be endorsed by the theatre academy.[1] Daniels is arguably the most controversial and the most successful representative of a younger generation of women playwrights to emerge in the 1980s – a generation which includes, for example, Louise Page and April de Angelis. Moreover, there are other playwrights who do appear in this volume who might also have been placed in this section: Timberlake Wertenbaker, who seemed better located in the previous section; Michelene Wandor, who wrote her own contribution to the volume, and Liz Lochhead, a study of whose work appears in chapter 7, all meet many of the criteria we established for being considered, for better or worse, canonical.

Caryl Churchill, Pam Gems, and Sarah Daniels are not 'canonical' for purely capricious reasons. Their work does share several attributes that account for why they are widely viewed as canonical writers. It is anthologised and readily available in print; it has received productions by the most prestigious and well-funded of Britain's theatres, the Royal National Theatre, the Royal Court, and the Royal Shakespeare Company; and some plays have had extended runs in the West End. Not that these women have only or always had their plays produced in these theatres – all three and most of the contemporary women in this volume have received consistent support from smaller, alternative theatres, and women's companies. Mainstream production and publishing are directly linked, however, and the combination of having a play put on and perhaps simultaneously published (as is often the case in the Royal Court Writers Series, for instance) goes a long way towards insuring public attention, future productions, inclusion on study lists, and at least some longevity.

In fact, a number of women writers have produced a vast body of work which has had little 'life' beyond the moment of theatrical production. Lesbian play-wright Bryony Lavery, for example, has a prolific output, working for a range of companies which includes Gay Sweatshop, the Women's Theatre Group / The Sphinx, Monstrous Regiment, and Clean Break, but she has never achieved mainstream recognition. Commenting on the relative playwriting careers of Caryl Churchill and Bryony Lavery, Mary McCusker of Monstrous Regiment observed that while Churchill was fortunate 'to find a relationship with the Royal Court', Lavery 'has suffered from lack of public profile', adding that 'there's only so much you can do on a cardboard box at the back of the garage!'[2] Similarly, over the ten-year period in which Tasha Fairbanks developed as the writer for Siren (1979–89), she never gained a high public profile. This was because, as Sandra Freeman explains, Siren 'were always on the fringe', working with a 'lack of recognition and lack of money'.[3] Only in the 1990s has Lavery been published in collection, and a volume of Siren plays scripted by Fairbanks finally appeared in print.[4]

After the explosion of women's theatre work in the 1970s (see Wandor, chapter 4), it is perhaps surprising to discover that relatively few plays by women were published. Mary Remnant, the second series editor of Methuen's *Plays by Women*, observed that of the seventy-five playwrights listed in Methuen's 1981–2 catalogue, only two of them were women.[5] In 1982, Methuen launched the *Plays By Women* series initially edited by Michelene Wandor. Remnant explains that, while it was difficult to publish single playtexts by women, the idea of a women's anthology of plays was a much more marketable proposition, given the general publishing expansion in women's writing in the 1980s.[6] In 1987 and 1989, Jill Davis edited Methuen's two volumes of *Lesbian Plays* on the grounds that, as Davis argued in the introduction to the first volume, relatively little work by lesbian playwrights was published, and that 'by comparison with the number of plays by gay men accessible in print and in Britain's larger theatres, lesbian theatre might be thought not to exist'.[7] Also in the mid-1980s Cheryl Robson set up the Women Writers Workshop at The Drill Hall Arts Centre and inaugurated Aurora Metro Press to nourish women's playwriting and to create the opportu-nity for more women to see their work in print. In spite of these new opportu-nities to publish plays coming from non-mainstream theatres, Methuen's 1998–9 catalogue for the Contemporary Dramatist series only lists nine women among its forty-seven playwrights. Daniels and Churchill are among those nine;[8] Gems has a Penguin collection.

In her introduction to the play collection *Female Voices Fighting Lives,* Cheryl Robson argues that 'theatre publishers are not only looking for good plays but also bankable writers who'll be writing plays in ten years time, so they can recoup their initial publishing investments. Women playwrights are often con-sidered to be unsuitable for long-term investment because they may take time out of their writing career to have children.'[9] Gems and Churchill both contradict this assumption, since both developed their careers as writing mothers, and many other women have managed to juggle these roles (e.g. Timberlake Wertenbaker, Michelene Wandor, and Bobby Baker).

What is significant both for the prospect of publication and also for any eventual designation as canonical is a certain longevity. Churchill, Daniels, and Gems may be considered canonical not only because of strong production and publication records, but also because their work now spans at least two generations, if not three. They are, in a sense, the senior stateswomen of post-war dramatists, whose work has helped to pave the way for new writers in the 1990s – like Phyllis Nagy or Sarah Kane – and whose major plays, just like Pinter's and Stoppard's, enjoy international productions and even major revivals (in 1997, both *Light Shining in Buckinghamshire* and *Cloud 9* had high-profile productions at the National and Old Vic). Longevity, however, is itself the product of several factors. Instead of affirming a timeless essence of excellence, even in the work of these three celebrated women, we think it is useful to consider their relationship to the historical transitions through which they have lived and about which they write.

The playwriting of Churchill, Daniels, and Gems spans a period of significant change in the social conditions of women. All three lived as young and middle-aged women through the Second Wave feminist movement, and survived the Thatcher reaction. Although marking a too-tidy dialectical relation, it does seem significant to point out that the tensions between old and new notions of what is appropriate for women have formed a dramaturgical dynamic that parallels the social dynamics of those decades. The 'house-wife' (Gabriele Griffin's name for the dilemma of 'women now in their 60s and 70s . . . who might be described [as sharing] a long-term investment in heteropatriarchy, whereby economic dependence on their husbands, long-term marriage and conformity to the demands of men and conventions of society have made it difficult for them to envisage change or a different life'), the working mother, and the 'damaged' daughter are three repeating persona in the plays of all three. Conflict frequently deals with women's ability to negotiate between and among these roles. The first productions of plays like *Top Girls, Dusa, Fish, Stas and Vi,* and *Ripen Our Darkness* dramatised these conflicts as actual British women were living through them. They have reappeared in 1990s versions in plays like *The Skriker, Stanley,* and *Beside Herself.* This is not to say that the themes are 'eternal' or timeless; rather it is to suggest that the work of Churchill, Gems, and Daniels allows a historically specific examination of how women have imagined their conditions during a highly volatile and contradictory post-war era, and that the duration of their writing careers itself allows historical changes to show amidst the continuity.

NOTES

1 In Christopher Innes, *Modern British Drama 1890–1990* (Cambridge: Cambridge University Press, 1992), only Gems and Churchill have entries as 'major women writers' (p. 452).

2 Quoted in Elaine Aston (ed.) *Feminist Theatre Voices* (Loughborough: Loughborough Theatre Texts, 1997), pp. 71–2.

3 Sandra Freeman, *Putting Your Daughters on the Stage: Lesbian Theatre from the 1970s to the 1990s* (London and Washington: Cassell, 1997), p. 65.

4 Bryony Lavery *Her Aching Heart* (with *Two Marias* and *Wicked*; London: Methuen, 1991); *Bryony Lavery Plays:1* (London: Methuen, 1998); and Tasha Fairbanks, *Pulp and other Plays* (*Curfew* and *Now Wash Your Hands Please*; Amsterdam: Harwood Academic Publishers, 1996).

5 Mary Remnant, Introduction, *Plays By Women: 5* (London: Methuen, 1986), p. 7.

6 *Ibid.*

7 Jill Davis, *Lesbian Plays: I* (London: Methuen, 1987), p. 9.

8 The other seven are Bryony Lavery, Phyllis Nagy, Louise Page, Christina Reid, Ntozake Shange, Sue Townsend, and Victoria Wood.

9 Cheryl Robson, Introduction, *Female Voices Fighting Lives* (London: Aurora Metro, 1991), p. 5.

10

ELAINE ASTON

Pam Gems: body politics and biography

Now in her seventies, Pam Gems's life-time almost coincides with the time-line of this volume. While she has a prolific output – Gems is the author of some twenty plays and has adapted a number of European classics by writers such as Duras, Chekhov, Ibsen and Lorca – her life in the theatre spans a much briefer period, with her work for the stage not gaining recognition until the 1970s. Hers is not a success-glamour-story, but – similar to the narratives of so many of the 'great' women, and occasionally men, whom Gems explores in her revisionist style of biographical theatre – is one of hardship and struggle; of a life, in and out of the theatre, disadvantaged by both class and gender.

Born in 1925, Gems was raised by her widowed mother in harsh material circumstances. She left school at fifteen, held a variety of jobs, and served as a Wren during the Second World War, which entitled her to a university place. Like so many women in the 1950s, Gems gave up work (she had a research job with the BBC), and was kept busy raising a family of four children, which, like Churchill, she combined with writing for television and radio. Only when the family moved back up to London from the Isle of Wight in 1970 was she able to begin writing for theatre, as the move to the capital brought her into direct contact with the Women's Movement and with fringe theatre.

Although acknowledging the importance of the Women's Movement to her life, specifically because it brought her into contact with other political theatre women, it is significant that Gems was also aware of her difference; a difference rooted in age, class, and appearance. She recognised that she was older than the women she was meeting in the 1970s; that she came from a working-class rather than middle-class background, and was plainer than the more glamorous women she encountered: 'I felt the movement was for younger women – flat-bellied, tough radical women. I was fat, flabby and a failure.'[1] When asked if she saw her early work as feminist, Gems replied 'to me it's just the point of view of a woman' (Wandor, 'Uncharted Territory', p. 12).

Reflecting on my research and reading for this chapter, I have begun to realise just how important Gems's own life is to her theatre. Her drama is underpinned by her experience of living through a time prior to the second Women's Liberation Movement, when women had far less reproductive control over their bodies, were encouraged back into the home when jobs were scarce in post-war years, when, in brief, they had far fewer opportunities available to them (especially if they were working- rather than middle-class). This contrasts with her experience of the post-Liberation, post-Pill, and now so-called 'post-feminist' years, in which women have gained certain economic and sexual freedoms. Gems works with this dual vision: she brings her 'before' and 'after' experiences to bear on the complications which greater choice and opportunity mean for women, and resists the temptation to write polemically about a world which has suddenly got 'better' for women since the late 1960s and 1970s.

Dusa, Fish, Stas and Vi

A good example of her dual vision is to be found in the play which first brought Gems recognition: *Dusa, Fish, Stas and Vi* (originally titled, *Dead Fish*). Here, Gems dramatises a community of four very different young women who find common ground in their struggle to survive in a 'man-made' world. Although we never see the men in the lives of these women, their absent presence haunts the on-stage domestic interior of Fish's flat in which the women take refuge. In Gems's dramatisation of intra-sexual relationships it is Fish who does not survive (as signalled in the original title). When Fish loses the man she loves to another woman, and realises she has lost her chance to have his child, she breaks down and commits suicide.

At the time of the play's production in the feminist climate of the 1970s, Gems described Fish as the 'pathfinder', as a 'woman attempting to break out a new, equitable way of living'.[2] In retrospect it is also helpful to characterise the other three women as 'pathfinders': Dusa surviving a failed marriage and a battle to get back her abducted children; Stas working as a hostess to fund her training as a marine biologist; and Vi, whose protest against the feminine body is registered in her refusal to eat. Each of the three women represents a complex corporeal site of 'damaged' resistance; the bodies of the divorced mother, the prostitute, and the anorexic are all bodies violated by a man-made world, but their unorthodoxy signals the will to resist and to survive – if only just. Fish, the political activist, however, does not survive because she fails to connect the politics of her middle-class feminism to the 'body politics' of her personal life. Although she was criticised by some feminist reviewers for the death of Fish, Gems countered that she did not see herself as a writer of polemic, but as a dramatist who wanted to show 'women . . . trying to live the revolution with their fellers, and so often getting knocked back in what is still so inexorably a man's world' (Wandor, 'Uncharted Territory', p. 13).

The 'gap' between struggling for the 'revolution' and fighting for her 'feller' is visually encoded in Fish's costuming. When Fish first appears she is dressed in '*government surplus clothes*' (Act I, p. 50), signifying political activist. Later, much to the surprise of her flatmates, she puts on the conventional costume of femininity, '*dress, jacket and makeup*' (Act II, p. 61), although she cannot make this 'fit' – her make-up is crooked. She cannot present herself in a way which makes sense of these different aspects of her life. The 'gap' between the political and the personal is further illustrated in the biographical monologue sketching the life of Rosa Luxemburg, delivered by Fish speaking directly to the audience as if from a platform (Act I, p. 54). In this monologue Gems draws our attention to the way in which biographers write only about Luxemburg's political life. They fail to mention the woman who never had the child she so longed for: 'Usually when people write about her nowadays they leave all that out. They are wrong' (Act I, p. 55).

In her own biographical writing for the theatre, which is the main focus of my chapter, Gems has been concerned not to 'leave all that out'. In the 1970s she was already working on biographical subjects (see production list for details), and had her second major stage success in 1977 with a dramatisation of the life of Queen Christina.

Queen Christina

Originally *Queen Christina* was to have been performed by the Royal Court. Playwright Ann Jellicoe who saw *Go West, Young Woman*, Gems's play about pioneer women crossing America, performed by the Women's Company in 1974 at the Roundhouse, offered Gems a Court commission. Gems wrote *Queen Christina*, but by the time it was ready Jellicoe had left the Court and the new (male) management rejected the play on the grounds that it was 'sprawling unattractive' and 'appealed, more to women than men'.[3] *Queen Christina* was finally taken up by the RSC in 1977 and was the first play by a woman to be staged by the company in Stratford. Moreover, Gems managed to secure a woman in the roles of both director (Penny Cherns) and designer (Di Seymour).

Described by Gems as 'a very uterine play' ('Uncharted Territory', p. 46), *Queen Christina* takes a historical subject as a vehicle for contemporary feminist issues, and, like *Dusa, Fish, Stas and Vi*, is centrally concerned with the issue of reproduction and choice. Where, however, *Dusa, Fish, Stas and Vi* examines motherhood in a post-Pill society, *Queen Christina* continues the debate in a historical context where women do not have choice or control over reproduction; where pregnancy is a life-threatening experience for the mother whose socially and culturally determined goal is to produce a male heir. When the play opens, Christina the child is imaged in the on-stage world of men as the King and

Chancellor discuss the issue of succession, which is set against the off-stage sobbing of the Queen whose baby boy has died in childbirth. The dilemma of the child caught between the masculine world, embodied in her father the King, and the feminine, registered in the maternal anguish of her off-stage mother, brought close to death in childbirth, pre-figures the life-long struggle for Christina the woman-monarch. Gems's representation of the Swedish Queen is of a woman caught between the trappings of masculine power and the disempowered body of a woman: the warring between 'the manly qualities of a king, and the fecundity of a woman' (Act I, sc. 5, p. 29).

Central to her exposition of masculine and feminine identities is the *gestus* of the cross-dressed body. Commenting on Garbo's 1933 film performance as Christina, cultural critic Roland Barthes observed that 'Garbo does not perform . . . any feat of transvestism; she is always herself, and carries without pretence, under her crown or her wide-brimmed hats, the same snowy solitary face'.[4] By contrast, Gems uses the device of the cross-dressed body towards a more subversive end: not a harmonious, androgynous vision of two sexes in one, but a 'misfit' body which invites us to question gender roles, identity, and behaviour. When Christina first appears as an adult woman in the play, she is mistaken for a man. Accompanying her female lover, Ebba, and described as '*a battered figure in hunting clothes*' who '*appears to be slightly crippled*' (Act I, sc. 2, p. 18), Christina is unrecognisable to her prospective royal suitor. Her masculine appearance, swagger, and bravado, as Christina's friendly 'thump' knocks her suitor off-balance, disguises her sex and her royal identity. Yet Christina the warrior 'King' who fights the 'bloody war', is also Christina the woman, at war with her own body, gesturally represented as Christina clutches at her stomach because of her 'bloody period' (Act I, sc. 2, p. 19).

Confused by the contradictory demands made on her to rule and to reproduce, Christina abdicates. The abdication scene brings Act I to a close, and Christina presents herself for this ceremony in a wedding dress. The *gestus* of the wedding dress points to the role required of her should she remain monarch: the subservient female required to produce an heir. Underneath the wedding dress, however, she wears a riding costume, revealed at the close of the act as Christina tears off the dress. The final stage directions for this scene state: '*she throws the dress across the space onto the throne, whirls round, her arms out in ecstasy, and leaves at the run*' (Act I, sc. 6, p. 33). The wedding dress, abandoned on the throne, images the gender-based conflict between marriage, reproduction, and disempowerment on the one hand, and monarchy, non-childbearing body, and power on the other.

The freedom which Christina embraces at the end of Act I, however, continues to elude her throughout Act II. When she re-appears in the Paris salon of the Blue Stockings, for example, she tries to 'fit' in by draping a skirt awkwardly over the top of her riding clothes (Act II, sc. 1, p. 33). In addition to the visual costume devices, Gems also stages the issue of gender and identity through a series of verbal encounters in which Christina talks through her various personal and political difficulties. With the Pope, for example, she debates the issue of pro-creation and her rejection of a woman's 'sacred destiny': the reproduction of a male heir (Act II, sc. 2, p. 37).

Further, in the exchanges between the Pope and Christina the issue of Christina paying for her lovers is raised. When asked to give a reason for this, Christina replies 'my face' (Act II, sc. 2, p. 36). The reference to the face, coupled with the cinematic style of writing – the collage of short, talking-head scenes – indexes Garbo's 1933 Christina. Garbo, whom Gems describes as mis-representing Christina as 'a shining, pale, intellectual beauty, who had, romantically, chosen freedom' (afterword, *Queen Christina*, p. 47), was famous for the cinematic close-ups which 'deified the face' and 'plunged audiences into the deepest ecstasy' (Barthes, *Mythologies*, pp. 56–7). Gems challenges this through her representa-tion of Christina as a woman who is both conventionally unattractive and bisex-ual (thereby undermining the cinematic emphasis on the heterosexual romance quest). Ultimately, Christina's inability to secure a loving and lasting relationship (with either a man or a woman) results in her breakdown. While the play ends with Christina showing signs of a recovery, and Azzolino and Lucia extolling her virtues, Lucia's final comment to Azzolino dismisses Christina as a woman who is 'nothing to look at' (Act II, sc. 7, p. 46). Thus Gems underlines her point that a woman who is 'nothing to look at' has no value in the sexual economy.

Gems has always argued that writing is a difficult career choice for both men and women, but especially for women 'who have few positions of power in the theatre' (afterword, *Dusa, Fish, Stas and Vi*, p. 72), and who need to be suppor-tive of each other if they are to 'survive' and not to 'succumb to careerism'.[5] She has given her own support to other women in concrete ways – for example, as a founding member of the Women's Playhouse Trust, set up in the 1980s to create opportunities for women in theatre. Gems's own work has been produced in a number of venues or at festivals supportive of new, Left-wing, or specifically fem-inist work, such as the Soho Poly, Hampstead Theatre, or Almost Free Theatre. Her career as a playwright has also benefited from her association with the RSC as a high-profile company, with whom she had a second success in 1978 when the company staged her revisionist biography of *Piaf*.

Piaf

Like *Queen Christina*, *Piaf* uses a large cast with a 'starring' female role. Stylistically and thematically the two plays have much in common: both set out to historicise the lives of 'great' women and to portray women struggling in a man-made world. Christina and Piaf are both insecure about their physical appearance in a world where women are judged by their looks, and both are desperate to secure loving relationships in which they are loved for themselves, rather than for what they represent, or can be used for. Unlike Christina, however, Piaf offers Gems the opportunity to dramatise a working-class, rather than a royal, subject.

In *Piaf* Gems stages the gap between the star image of the French cabaret singer as 'the little sparrow' and the hardship of her working-class life, originating in destitution and prostitution. Jane Lapotaire, who played Piaf in the original RSC production, was costumed throughout in the familiar Piaf black dress, but the iconic representation of the diminutive figure in the little black dress was critiqued in performance by the Brechtian-styled biographical narrative, pointing to the 'gap' between image and reality. For example, the play opens with an episode from much later in Piaf's singing career when she is already famous, but on the verge of a breakdown. A manager appears on stage to announce Piaf to his audience: 'I give you . . . your own . . . Piaf!'.[6] The Piaf who appears, however, falters at the microphone and has to be taken off. Using a metatheatrical device – opening with a Piaf concert to open the play – highlights the mythologising dynamic of the image, culturally 'owned' ('your own . . . Piaf') both by the fictional spectator of the concert and the real spectators of Gems's play, but demythologised in the moment of the failed introduction.

Moreover, Gems also uses this short opening scene to underline Piaf's gender and class resistance to a male-dominated world. When Piaf falters at the microphone the manager physically tries to remove her from the stage, but, '*struggling*', she yells and swears at him 'get your fucking hands off me, I ain't *done* nothing yet' (Act I, sc. I, p. 11). Surviving in a man's world is represented as a physically brutal and brutalising experience. Gems captures this in the *gestus* in which Piaf is struck across the face by different men: by the Inspector who arrests her after she is implicated in the murder of the club owner Louis Leplée (Act I, sc. 5, p. 21); by the club manager (Act I, sc. 5, p. 22); and, later in her career, at the point of breakdown, by a male attendant (Act II, sc. 6, p. 61). As a club manager, in conversation with Piaf's agent, explains, 'there's only one thing to do with a woman who makes trouble . . . Hit 'em in the face' (Act II, sc. 5, p. 51).

Piaf is regarded as 'a woman who makes trouble' because she refuses to modify her behaviour to an acceptable feminine 'norm'. Although she benefits from the material comforts which her singing career brings her, she rejects the values, behaviours, and niceties of middle-class femininity. Gems underlines this in Act I sc. 3 when Piaf is fed by Leplée in his restaurant. Pretending to know how to behave in a restaurant, Piaf's 'performance' is exposed as she '*sips delicately from the finger bowl*' (p. 15). However, when she is laughed at and corrected by a young waiter, Piaf does not accept the correction, rather she retaliates with 'All

right, clever cock. Seen me drink – now you can watch me piss. [*She does so . . .*]'
(p. 16). Swearing and urinating in public signal Piaf's refusal to conform to an
acceptable standard of 'feminine' behaviour.

Where the cross-dressed body is central to the exploration of gender issues in
Queen Christina, in *Piaf* Gems centrally counterpoints a visual text of disintegrating corporeality with the aural text of the singing voice as a way of highlighting the divorce between star image and private reality. In Act I the songs which
Piaf later made famous are used to cut across the scenes depicting less affluent
times. For example, Piaf has sex with a legionnaire (and gets her friend Toine to
take over when she's 'pegged out') to the music of *Un sale petit brouillard* (Act
I, sc. 4, pp. 16–17). In Act II both aural and corporeal texts are marked by
moments of breaking up to suggest the decline of both the star performer and
the woman. Car accidents, for example, were a contributory factor in Piaf's dete-
rioration, and Gems brings one of these into her dramatic frame by working the
sound of a car crash into the music of a song, followed immediately by a Piaf
'*looking very much the worse for wear*' (Act II, sc. 6, p. 57). The aural 'collision'
suggests the impact of the crash on the performer. In a reprise of the opening
scene, visual and aural registers suggest a failing Piaf, as she breaks down, misses
her cues, and, finally, has to be carried off-stage.

The play ends with the death of Piaf in her wheelchair. As the lights fade to
black this moment of closure immediately gives way to the voice of Piaf singing
'Non, je ne regrette rien'. The mortality of the woman is juxtaposed with the
immortality of the star. The lyrics point to the woman who regrets nothing of
her life; the scene shows the more painful reality of an early death – although in
performance the emotional appeal of the song may reaffirm, rather than deconstruct, the legend.

Camille

The commercial success of *Piaf* is evident from the play's subsequent West End
and Broadway transfers. Gems's playwriting career continued with her producing both original new plays and translations of the classics (see list of first productions of plays for details). In 1984 she had a further success at the Other Place
with *Camille*, in which she sets out to revise the nineteenth-century novel and
stage play *The Lady of the Camellias* by Alexander Dumas *fils*. Inspired by the
real-life courtesan Marie Duplessis, Dumas's drama stages the doomed love-
affair between the consumptive courtesan, Marguerite Gautier, and her bourgeois lover, Armand Duval. Marguerite has need of her aristocratic lovers to pay
for her material comfort, whereas Duval has neither the money to support her,
nor a father who will tolerate the liaison. The narrative ends with the death of
Marguerite. The emotional appeal of the 'saintly sinner' attracted many of the

nineteenth-century star actresses to the role (including, for example, Sarah Bernhardt and Eleonora Duse), and Garbo played a film version in 1937.

In his critical commentary on the mythologisation of Dumas's Marguerite Gautier, Barthes argues that the Marguerite who 'lives in the awareness of her alienation' is not yet the 'revolutionary' figure who is able to 'bring . . . criticism to bear on her alienation'. 'At bottom' Barthes continues, 'she would need very little to achieve the status of the Brechtian character, which is an alienated object but a source of criticism' (*Mythologies*, pp. 104–5). Although Gems's revisioning dramatises a harsher social reality than the Dumas original (one in keeping with the harsh social reality of the mid-1980s in which the play was produced), her Marguerite does not fully 'achieve the status of the Brechtian character' and is only a partial 'source of criticism'. On the one hand, Gems de-glamorises the prostitute world of the *demi-monde*, replacing the allure of forbidden sex with a world which is characterised by brawling (between women as well as men), swearing, vulgar songs, gambling, drinking, and trading in flesh. On the other hand, it is ultimately the case that Marguerite's tubercular body, infected by the social and material concerns of poverty and class, is re-infected by the patriarchal disease of the tragic, romantic love-object.

A clear example of the latter occurs in Act I, sc. 4, in Marguerite's salon. Marguerite leads her guests in singing a 'vulgar song' and dancing. When Armand challenges her choice of song, Marguerite rebukes his sentimental view of her, and asks him 'what would you like me to sing? Something more elevated? Don't delude yourself, Monsieur'.[7] At this moment, however, Armand is also demonstrating concern over Marguerite's coughing fit, and although linguistically Marguerite refuses to be romanticised, visually this is overshadowed by Armand's attendance on her tubercular body, visibly weakened by the spasms of coughing.

That said, Gems attempts a number of theatrical techniques to try to counter the sentimentalisation of the tragic-romance narrative. The metatheatrical device of an off-stage opera, for example, is used for the on-stage *demi-mondaines*, gathered in the foyer of the opera house, to question the ideological closure of the operatic text and the object-victim positioning of the tragic 'heroine' whose fate is death. 'Why can't they leave her alone', questions one; and 'I've seen it before, she kills herself' explains another to her companion who is vexed she will miss the ending (Act II, sc. 4, pp. 137–8).

The masculinist fantasy of tragic love-object is formally critiqued by Gems through the narrative structure of *Camille*. At the close of Act I, Marguerite, weakened by a consumptive attack and coughing up blood, finally agrees to Armand's suggestion that they leave Paris for their rustic idyll. Armand's fantasy that Marguerite's wasted body will be 'cured' by this romantic escape is exposed as he recoils from her embrace 'aghast' that he cannot see her eyes (Act I, sc. 6,

p. 114): the moment in which Armand possesses her, she vanishes; she is 'dead'. The point is reinforced in the opening to Act II when, chronologically, we are returned to the present and are witness to a grieving Armand, situated by Marguerite's graveside, awaiting her exhumation. For the exhumation to take place Armand must identify the body, but when he finally sees her stinking corpse (the object of his desire), he backs away in horror, refusing to identify her, and repeating the line 'I can't see her eyes!' (Act II, sc.1, p. 118).

There is no romantic reconciliation between Armand and Marguerite as in Dumas's original play. Instead of romance there is anger as Armand reacts violently, throwing money in Marguerite's face, when she suggests that she sleep with her Russian prince in order to bring him a dowry (Act II, sc. 5, p.149). This is the action which 'kills' her. As Marguerite had warned in Act I, 'the day that you pay for me I'm a dead woman' (Act I, sc. 6, p. 111). Gems's Marguerite does not, therefore, die a romantic death in the arms of Armand (à la Sarah Bernhardt), but in the presence of a creditor making an inventory of her room. Her dying words do not whisper the name of Armand, but that of her child, Jean-Paul.

The difficulty for women of choosing between maternal interest and self-interest is a recurrent theme in Gems's theatre.[8] In Camille Gems stages this dilemma in the encounter between Armand's father and Marguerite in Act II, sc. 3. In Dumas's play Marguerite is persuaded by Armand's father to give up his son for the good of the (bourgeois) family name, and for the sake of the impending marriage of Armand's sister into a respectable middle-class family. Gems re-works the encounter so that Marguerite chooses for her child, rather than for Armand's (aristocratic) family. However, the revisioning of this moment is undermined by the melodramatic narrative twist in which Armand's father is identified as the father of Marguerite's child. Important issues about social background, poverty, childhood rape, maternity, and so on are negated by the discourse of familial melodrama. In brief, set against the 'evil' father-figure, Marguerite is re-cast as the object of audience sympathy.

In the closing moments of the play, demi-mondaine Prudence suggests to Armand that Marguerite may have 'preferred her freedom' to his coming to the 'rescue' (Act II, sc. 7, p. 152). On the one hand the demi-monde is presented as a 'space' in which women conduct business, friendship, and sex with each other, using men merely for financial gain; on the other it is not represented as a viable alternative to heteropatriarchy. The fissures in which women connect with other women are similar in other plays: Christina loses Ebba to her male lover and future husband; Piaf's friendship with Toine gets left behind as she becomes a star; and Marguerite does not, despite Prudence's suggestion, choose the alternative, sub-cultural demi-monde (which includes a lesbian relationship with Sophie) over Armand. She 'lives' the myth and dies. I would argue that this reflects Gems's concern to portray the ways in which heteropatriarchal and capitalist structures dominate and damage women's lives. She demonstrates how, given these structures, it is much harder for women to connect socially, politically, and sexually. Hence, although alternative, intra-feminine possibilities are glimpsed and represented as desirable, they cannot overturn the dominant masculine order. (This contrasts, for example, with the lesbian relationships and utopian 'escape' routes for women which Sarah Daniels portrays in her theatre and the endings to her plays [see chapter 12, p. 205]).

The Blue Angel and *Marlene*

For a woman to succeed in a man's world (which, usually, as Churchill dramatises in *Top Girls* (1982), means playing a man's game), she must surely be exceptional. Exceptional women are evidently central to Gems's theatre – especially those women like Piaf, Garbo, and, as we shall see in this section, Dietrich, who became successful at a time earlier this century when opportunities for women were far more restricted than they are now. Gems herself acknowledges the influence of the movie star on her generation who grew up with cinema, rather than television.[9]

Her interest in Dietrich is first evident in *The Blue Angel* (The Other Place, 1991), a version of Heinrich Mann's *Professor Unrat* (1905), rather than a remake of Josef von Sternberg's 1930 movie, *Der Blaue Engel*, which was the film which brought Marlene Dietrich international recognition. That said, as in the film, the action of the play is transposed to the Weimar period, foregrounding the corruption of a nation and the rise of 1930s fascism. Like *Camille*, *The Blue Angel* gives dramatic treatment to a well-known narrative, and is further evidence of Gems's pragmatic practice: 'You've only got two hours – I think you're a fool nowadays if you try and make people sit for longer for new stuff – and if you start with someone from history, you start with a known pallet.'[10] *The Blue Angel* details the story of a schoolmaster, who cannot resist his passion for nightclub singer Lola, thus bringing about his social disgrace and downfall (like many of the Conservative ministers in British government who suffered similar fates in the 1980s). To this modern version of a Greek Hippolytus, Gems added her revisioned figure of Lola so that she appeared 'not [as] Mann's almost passive figure of temptation, but [as] a successor to . . . Piaf and Camille: a bruised but proud victim of a predatory society'.[11] Publicity shots of actress Kelly Hunter in the role of Lola image a scantily clad, sexually provocative night-club singer, with the look of Dietrich in a finger-on-lips Monroe pose.

While the presence of Dietrich haunts *The Blue Angel*, in *Marlene*, staged at the Oldham Coliseum in 1996 and transferred to the Lyric Theatre in 1997, Gems chooses her as the subject. Given the repertoire and style of Gems's earlier biographical work, in *Marlene* you expect to find the narrative behind the 'beauti-ful face' which Dietrich, like Garbo, made famous in the cinematic close-up. However, where plays like *Piaf* or *Queen Christina* operate formally and ideolog-ically in deconstructive mode, *Marlene* is re-constructive in its representation of Dietrich.

Marlene has just three roles: the star role of Marlene and two supporting roles – a silent elderly dresser and a boyish secretary. The role of the dresser, a survi-vor of the concentration camps, is used to refer to Marlene's war-time struggles: the Germany she abandoned in the war against Hitler. The role of the secretary is a device which suggests the possibility of a lesbian love-interest (again, this remains an undeveloped possibility).

Marlene is written in two parts: preparation for a cabaret concert and the concert. Both parts are, therefore, meta-theatrical in mode. The backstage scenes create the opportunity to impart biographical detail and to hear about other famous stars Dietrich knew and worked with (Garbo's acting is described by Dietrich, for example, as though she 'was suffering from some female problem down below'). The private woman and the star performer are juxtaposed in Dietrich's backstage monologuing, or are represented visually in the woman with an obsession for cleanliness who puts on rubber gloves and kneels on her fur coat to scrub her dressing-room floor.

In the preparations for the concert it is made clear that Dietrich pre-planned every detail of her performance, including, for example, her direction of the theatre usherettes in the presentation of bouquets to herself. That Gems sets *Marlene* in the cabaret-concert period from Dietrich's later life and career is sig-nificant from a feminist point of view for two reasons. Firstly, by this time Dietrich had gained a working knowledge of lighting, staging, and direction, which she could use to produce herself in cabaret performances. This mode of self-management and -production contrasted, for example, with Sternberg's direction of her earlier film career. Secondly, presenting an older rather than a younger Dietrich affords an older actress the opportunity of a major role. (The play briefly thematises the difficulties for women of ageing and performing, as the backstage Dietrich is troubled by pain to her leg, which she works to conceal in her 'performance'.)

The final part of *Marlene* is the Dietrich concert. Where in *Piaf* songs are used to punctuate the narrative as the body of the performer disintegrates, in *Marlene* the songs do not invite the spectator to question the illusion of the star – rather to 'believe' in it. Actress Siân Phillips who took the role of Dietrich appeared in Dietrich drag: the glittering sheath dress, Dietrich make-up, and hairstyle (see pl. 8). Facially, vocally, physically, and gesturally Phillips offered the illusion of Dietrich for the audience. The pleasure in this illusion was evident from audi-ence reaction, although just who or what is applauded in the Phillips/Dietrich

8 Siân Phillips as Pam Gems's Marlene

concert is a complex question. How you 'read' this masquerade of a masquerade
of femininity will depend on what you 'see', conditioned by the cultural, sexual,
political, generational, etc., position from which you are viewing. To give an
example: if, as Gems claims, Dietrich's own concert performances were an illusion, a 'memory' of songs associated with wartime,[12] then it may be that the
memory of a memory of wartime surfaces most strongly for spectators of
Gems's generation. On the other hand, the masquerade also captured the

popular, post-modern imagination of the 1990s, trading in images rather than the 'real' (just like Madonna's re-creation of Eva Peron in Alan Parker's film *Evita*). Finally, in her tribute to Dietrich, one might also argue that Gems is pleasuring herself in exploring her self-confessed 'fascination with beautiful women', in contrast to what she describes as her own 'ordinariness',[13] and, moreover, that that fascination is one which also holds many (often contradictory) spectatorial pleasures for 'ordinary' women.

Stanley

Given the woman-centred direction of Gems's theatre, *Stanley*, her biographical portrait of the twentieth-century painter Stanley Spencer, which opened at the Royal National Theatre's Cottesloe in 1996, may come as something of a surprise. For Gems, the connection between *Stanley* and some of her other biographical subjects is class rather than gender. Gems likens Spencer to Piaf, 'both little squits but both geniuses', and, as with Dietrich, makes no attempt to disguise her own affection for him as a subject: 'I Love him.'[14] She also wrote the play for actor Antony Sher, who had taken the title role in her revised translation of *Uncle Vanya*, staged at the National's Cottesloe in 1992.

While *Stanley* is Gems's first original stage play to be performed at the Royal National Theatre, it is not the first time she has placed masculinity centre-stage. In *Franz in April* (1977), she looked at pioneer *Gestalt* therapist Fritz Perls. *Aunt Mary*, which had a rehearsed reading with the RSC, and a production at the Warehouse in 1982, explored gender through the lives and relationships of two male transvestites. *The Project* (1976), subsequently revised as *Loving Women* (1984), examined the triangular relationship between one man and two women. As in *Dusa, Fish, Stas and Vi*, Gems set *Loving Women* in a contemporary scene to explore the issue of political projects and personal lives. In *Stanley* Gems returns to a triangular relationship, but within the biographical framework of Stanley Spencer and his two wives: Hilda Carline and Patricia Preece.

The play opens in the aftermath of the First World War. Stanley is first seen in his studio talking over wartime experiences with his wife Hilda. The recollections cause his body to shake, and Hilda comforts and nurses him like a child.[15] Later, he explains to her: 'Men aren't brave, you know. They try to be. I don't want to see all that again. Friends – people you sleep next to in the trench turned into convolvulus – entrails hanging on the wire' (Act I, sc.1, p. 4). In a persuasive analysis of male hysteria and the First World War, feminist critic Elaine Showalter argues that 'if the essence of manliness was not to complain, then shell shock was the body language of masculine complaint, a disguised male protest not only against the war but against the concept of "manliness" itself'.[16] Stanley's shaking body and admission to men's lack of manliness point to a historical moment when masculinity was in crisis, and it is against this crisis in Western masculinity that Stanley's personal, obsessive sexual behaviours and his treatment of women are set.

Gems's stage biography portrays Stanley's most pressing obsession as his painting, but further dramatises the complexity with which his painting is interwoven with the relationships with his two wives. Stanley's deep love and affection for his first wife Hilda is gradually displaced by his growing sexual obsession with Patricia. He divorces Hilda to marry Patricia, but this second marriage is never consummated. Patricia desires Stanley for his money and artistic connections; her body she keeps for her lesbian lover, Dorothy Hepworth. Much of Act II is taken up with the attempted reconciliation between Stanley and Hilda, and traces Hilda's decline in health, her mastectomy, and her death.

Gems's directions indicate that the tensions of this triangular relationship are to be acted out in the fictional playing space – staged for the Cottesloe production in a church-like setting, in the style of Spencer's painting. As Stanley switches backwards and forwards between 'his' two women in Act I, Hilda becomes an increasingly isolated figure, pushed out of the stage space (just as she is eventually pushed out of her home by Patricia). She occupies the margins with only her handbag left to cling on to. The triangular tensions structure the climax of Act I, sc. 9, which ends in the divorce of Hilda and the marriage to Patricia. Stanley's sexual 'climax', however, is denied, as Patricia pushes him away and leaves with her lesbian lover. The final image of this act is of Stanley who stacks his painting materials into an old pram and exits alone. Gems uses this biographical detail – the painter trundling around his village of Cookham with his materials in an old pram – metonymically: the pram stands-in for the absent Hilda, the maternal love-object (the mother who mothers both the artist and his children) of whom Stanley is dispossessed but whom he fetishistically desires to repossess. After Hilda's death in Act II Stanley remains alone with the pram, and the play's final image is of Stanley as '*he packs up his things, puts them on the pram. And goes*' (Act II, sc. 14, p. 88). Although Gems is treating a biographical subject belonging to a post-war period which she herself experienced, the issue of marital breakdown is one which also connects with Britain in the 1990s where increasing divorce figures, lone mothers, and 'new' families undermine the 'myth' of marriage and family.

Patricia's heterosexual role play is for material rather than physical gain. In her 'gaze' it is Stanley who is the victim; Patricia 'sees' no one but herself. At a party hosted by the Spencers in Act I, sc. 5, it is suggested that identity for Stanley and Hilda is bound up in each other, as they cross-dress in each other's clothes, whereas Patricia arrives at the party costumed as Narcissus (pp. 26–7). In Act I, sc. 7, the boutique scene, Patricia dresses up as Stanley's fantasy sex-object for which she is rewarded with an expensive necklace. While Stanley '*mesmerised*' feasts his gaze on Patricia, she, on the other hand, gazes '*on the necklace, absorbed and unaware of him*' and '*fingers the necklace gently, with a small, rare smile into the glass*' (p. 36).

The portraits of Patricia and Hilda may be difficult and painful for lesbian and heterosexual feminist spectators. The narrative demonisation of Patricia is problematic, even though there may be pleasures in her heterosexual masquerade as a means towards a lesbian end; the destruction of Hilda in a narrative of masculine obsession makes for uncomfortable feminist viewing. Although some feminist spectators in the 1990s might, therefore, be as disappointed with the death of Hilda as some feminists were with the death of Fish in the 1970s, it is clear that it is passion rather than polemic which continues to motivate Gems; biographical 'truths' rather than political ends remain her theatrical objective. Twenty years after *Dusa, Fish, Stas and Vi*, the critical 'gaze' on masculinity may seem like a new departure. On closer inspection, however, the canvas of *Stanley* emerges as a different perspective on a familiar landscape: the damaging consequences for women of an unequal world which prioritises the masculine sphere of material, cultural, and sexual production, over women's lives, creativity, and maternal reproduction.

FIRST PRODUCTIONS OF PLAYS BY PAM GEMS

Venues are in London unless stated.
Betty's Wonderful Christmas, Cockpit Theatre (1972)
The Amiable Courtship of Miz Venus and Wild Bill, Almost Free Theatre (1973)
My Warren & After Birthday, Almost Free Theatre (1973)
Sarah B Divine! (contributor) Jeanetta Cochrane Theatre (1973)
Go West, Young Woman, Roundhouse (1974)
Up in Sweden, Haymarket Theatre, Leicester (1975)
Dead Fish, Edinburgh Festival (1976)
Dusa, Fish, Stas and Vi, Hampstead Theatre (1976)
Guinevere, Edinburgh Festival (1976)
My Name is Rosa Luxemburg (adaptation: Marianne Auricoste), Soho Poly (1976)
The Project (subsequently *Loving Women*), Soho Poly (1976)
The Rivers and Forests (adaptation: Marguerite Duras), Soho Poly (1976)
Franz in April, ICA (1977)
Queen Christina, The Other Place, Stratford (1977)
Piaf, The Other Place, Stratford (1978)
Ladybird, Ladybird, King's Head Theatre (1979)
Sandra, King's Head Theatre (1979)
Uncle Vanya (adaptation: Anton Chekhov), Hampstead Theatre (1979)
A Doll's House (adaptation: Henrik Ibsen), Tyne Wear Theatre, Newcastle (1980)
Aunt Mary, Warehouse Theatre (1982)
The Treat, ICA (1982)
Camille, The Other Place, Stratford (1984)
The Cherry Orchard (adaptation: Anton Chekhov), Haymarket Theatre, Leicester (1984)

Loving Women, The Arts Theatre (1984)
Pasionaria, Playhouse Theatre, Newcastle (1985)
The Danton Affair (adaptation: Stanislawa Przybyszewska), Barbican Theatre (1986)
The Blue Angel, The Other Place, Stratford (1991)
Uncle Vanya (revised adaptation: Anton Chekhov), Cottesloe, RNT (1992)
Ghosts (adaptation: Henrik Ibsen), Sherman Theatre, Cardiff (1993)
Yerma (adaptation: Federico García Lorca), Battersea Arts Centre (1993)
Deborah's Daughter, Library Theatre, Manchester (1994)
The Seagull (adaptation: Anton Chekhov), Olivier, RNT (1994)
Marlene, Oldham Coliseum (1996)
Stanley, Cottesloe, RNT (1996)
The Snow Palace, Wilde Theatre, Bracknell (1998)

NOTES

1 Gems, quoted in Michelene Wandor, 'Women are Uncharted Territory', *Spare Rib*, September 1977, p.12.
2 Afterword to *Dusa, Fish, Stas and Vi*, in Michelene Wandor (ed.) *Plays By Women: 1* (London: Methuen, 1982), p. 71.
3 Afterword, *Queen Christina*, in Mary Remnant (ed.) *Plays by Women: 5* (London: Methuen, 1986), p. 47.
4 Roland Barthes, *Mythologies*, trans. Annette Lavers (London: Granada, 1973), p. 56.
5 Gems, quoted in Lyn Gardner, 'Precious Gems,' *Plays and Players,* April 1985, p. 13.
6 *Piaf* in *Three Plays: Piaf, Camille, Loving Women* (Harmondsworth: Penguin, 1985), p. 11.
7 *Camille* in *Three Plays*, p. 101.
8 For a more extensive treatment of this issue see the mother–daughter relationship in Gems's *Deborah's Daughter* (London: Nick Hern Books, 1995).
9 See programme notes, *Marlene*, Lyric Theatre, 1997.
10 Quoted in Georgina Brown, 'Something Out of the Ordinary', *Independent,* 31 January 1996, p. 7.
11 John Peter, 'The RSC's New Place to Flex its Muscles', *Sunday Times*, 1 September 1991, p. 4.
12 See programme notes, *Marlene*, Lyric Theatre, 1997.
13 Quoted in Georgina Brown, 'Something Out of the Ordinary', p. 6.
14 Gems, quoted in Michael Simmons, 'Marks of Spencer', *Guardian*, 22 January 1996, p. 40.
15 *Stanley* (London: Nick Hern Books, 1996), p. 2.
16 Elaine Showalter, *The Female Malady* (London: Virago, 1987), p. 172.

FURTHER READING

Primary sources: plays

Gems, Pam. *Dusa, Fish, Stas and Vi*. In Michelene Wandor (ed.) *Plays By Women: 1*. London: Methuen, 1982.
    Aunt Mary. In Michelene Wandor (ed.) *Plays by Women: 3*. London: Methuen, 1984.
    Three Plays: Piaf, Camille, Loving Women. Harmondsworth: Penguin, 1985.

Queen Christina. In Mary Remnant (ed.) *Plays By Women: 5*, London: Methuen, 1986.
(Adaptation) *Uncle Vanya*. London: Nick Hern Books, 1992.
(Adaptation) *The Seagull*. London: Nick Hern Books, 1994.
Deborah's Daughter. London: Nick Hern Books, 1995.
Stanley. London: Nick Hern Books, 1996.

Secondary sources

Barthes, Roland. *Mythologies*. Trans. Annette Lavers. London: Granada, 1973.
Brown, Georgina. 'Something Out of the Ordinary'. Interview with Pam Gems, *Independent* (31 January 1996): 6–7.
Carlson, Susan. 'Revisionary Endings: Pam Gems's *Aunt Mary* and *Camille*'. In Lynda Hart (ed.) *Making a Spectacle*. Ann Arbor: University of Michigan Press, 1989: 103–17.
Colvin, Claire. 'Earth Mother From Christchurch'. Interview with Pam Gems, *Plays and Players* (August 1982): 9–10.
Franey, Ros. 'Women in the Workshop'. *Plays and Players* (November 1973): 24–7.
Gardner, Lyn. 'Precious Gems'. *Plays and Players* (April 1985): 12–13.
Gems, Pam. Interview. In Heidi Stephenson and Natasha Langridge (eds.) *Rage and Reason: Women Playwrights on Playwriting*. London: Methuen, 1997: 88–97.
Hemming, Sarah. 'Falling in Love Again'. Interview with Pam Gems, *Independent* (20 May 1992): 19.
Keyssar, Helene. *Feminist Theatre*. Basingstoke: Macmillan, 1984.
McFerran, Ann. 'The Theatre's (Somewhat) Angry Young Women'. *Time Out* (21–27 October 1977): 13–15.
Reinelt, Janelle. 'The Politics of Form: Realism, Melodrama and Pam Gems' *Camille*'. *Women and Performance* (1989): 96–103.
Rose, Helen. 'A Woman's Place'. Interview with Pam Gems, *Plays and Players* (August 1991): 11–13.
Wandor, Michelene. 'Women are Uncharted Territory'. Interview with Pam Gems, *Spare Rib* (September 1977): 11–13, 46.

11

JANELLE REINELT

Caryl Churchill and the politics of style

Caryl Churchill is arguably the most successful and best-known socialist-feminist playwright to have emerged from Second Wave feminism. Her plays have been performed all over the world, from the UK and the United States to Korea and Japan. She is routinely included in anthologies of contemporary drama and her plays regularly appear on student reading lists. Within theatre studies, her work has provided the basis for five books and numerous articles. Often linked to theoretical debates about representation in feminist performance, Churchill has stimulated and provoked some of the most important feminist thinking about the theatre since coming to critical attention in the mid-1970s. She came to prominence concurrently with the development of Second Wave feminism in Britain, both its activism and its academic thrust; and at the time when Marxism was being re-thought in the academy in light of Althusser and Lacan, and challenged by feminists for ignoring gender and, later, sexuality. She is still writing in the so-called 'postfeminist', 'postsocialist' nineties; while not abandoning her commitments, she has reflected the historical transformations of the eighties and nineties in plays which stage the central preoccupations and contradictions of these movements as they have shifted and changed.

Her theatre practice similarly mirrors a series of challenges and changes in hegemonic producing modes over this period. She began as a solitary writer who only came to consider herself a woman writer belatedly: 'For years and years I thought of myself as a writer before I thought of myself as a woman, but recently [1977] I've found that I would say I was a feminist writer as opposed to other people saying I was.'[1] She started writing radio plays in the 1960s [see Chronology] while she was house-bound with young children. She was the first woman to have a residency at the Royal Court (1975), London's premier writers' theatre. In these ways, she appears to be a lone woman breaking through the male-dominated theatre world as an isolated phenomenon.

On the other hand, over the years she has developed a collaborative style of writing which involves making plays with collectives (Joint Stock and Monstrous Regiment), working with musicians, choreographers, and directors as equal partners (e.g. David Lan and Ian Spink), and regularly involving actors in workshops which have significantly contributed to the final script (*Cloud 9, Fen,* and *Mad Forest*). At the same time, she engaged in activism: in fact she met the women from Monstrous Regiment, a feminist theatre collective, on an abortion march.[2] She is a socialist-feminist intellectual; serious historical and philosophical reading forms the background of her work and often enters the workshops. (Acknowledged sources include Marxist historian Christopher Hall, Frantz Fanon, Michel Foucault, and feminist writers Eva Figes, Barbara Ehrenreich, Kate Millett.)

The years 1976 and 1977 mark a watershed in Churchill's work.[3] She found a community of artists who shared her intellectual and activist commitments and developed various working methods that created a theatre practice which was democratic and experimental, and which could challenge dominant modes of representation. She worked collaboratively with a group of writers on *Floorshow* for Monstrous Regiment, with whom she also produced *Vinegar Tom*. During that time she also worked for the first time with Joint Stock on *Light Shining in Buckinghamshire*. This company became known for its workshop process in which the group held an initial period of research, exploration, and improvisation followed by a writing interval in which writers typically went away and created a script which was then brought back into rehearsal. While not a feminist company, Joint Stock was arguably socialist, by which I mean the members argued all the time about what was meant by 'socialist'.[4] Indeed, *Vinegar Tom* and *Light Shining in Buckinghamshire* remain two of her strongest feminist and socialist plays, benchmarks for the 1970s movements they recall, when the conviction and clarity of these plays seemed intimately connected to a historical moment of great promise.

At a time in the 1970s when many feminist explorations in theatre, literature, and life were preoccupied with personal experience, represented often in realistic terms, Churchill was resilient in developing a social, multivalenced approach to representing women's experiences. Using an epic dramaturgy many have linked to Brecht,[5] Churchill placed her characters as social subjects at the intersection of economic, religious, and political forces which disciplined their sexuality and prescribed their gender. *Vinegar Tom* treated the witch hunts of the seventeenth century as manifestations of a historical conjuncture where the professionalisation of the health industry clashed with midwifery and 'cunning women's' curative practices. Combining religious misogyny with emergent capitalism to construct poor women, unmarried women, and old women as scapegoats for this historical enactment of new power configurations, the authorities in this play confine, torture, and ultimately hang women whose unruly bodies/behaviours they cannot control. Churchill intercuts her schematic historical scenes with contemporary songs which mock the proceedings and ensure that the modern parallels to contemporary sexism, ageism, and capitalism cannot be ignored.

Light Shining in Buckinghamshire was also written with an eye to the link between the English Civil War of the 1640s, when the Levellers, Diggers, and Ranters struggled for an alternative revolution which never happened, and the new social movements of the 1970s which were fuelled by various forms of utopian socialism. In an interview about the play, Churchill noted the similarity of 'the emergence of many popular movements and small groups on the left today, also concerned about taking control of your own life'.[6] Unlike *Vinegar Tom*, there was no overt reference to the present, but the parallels were obvious to spectators. One hostile critic wrote, 'A group of free loving, pantheistic communists . . . set their standard against the false revolution of Cromwell's parliamentarians.'[7] Churchill's dramaturgical techniques in both plays eschewed protagonists in favour of multiply cast roles which represented the different subject positions in the depicted society, and historicised the events of the narrative to enable spectators to see how these events were similar to and different from present-day circumstances, similar to and different from received historical traditions. While her narratives constituted logical outcomes of a series of events, these were not portrayed as inevitable – it might have been otherwise: therein lies the 'hope' for the future borne on the back of the failure of the past. While less overtly feminist than *Vinegar Tom*, in *Light Shining* Churchill again represented the discipline of uppity and poor women by a public flogging, and the internalised oppression of middle-class women through fear and self-hatred.

These productions seemed to signal a watershed in Churchill's work both thematically and theatrically. She developed techniques for staging the multiple intersections of identity caught at historical crossroads which continue to distinguish her writing through the nineties, and she also embarked on creative methods of collaboration and theatrical devising which produced her hybrid identity as a writer, both mainstream and alternative. While she did not work with Monstrous Regiment again after 1977, she has produced fifteen plays at the Royal Court and her association with Joint Stock lasted until its demise in 1989. She has continued to work with Max Stafford-Clark, director of *Light Shining*, through two decades (her most recent play, *Blue Heart*, was written for his company, Out of Joint). Her preferred collaborators seem to be men – Churchill has worked with Mark Wing Davies and Les Waters on multiple occasions, and she has co-written with David Lan and worked closely with choreographer Ian Spink. While her only productions at the Royal Shakespeare Company and the Royal National Theatre have been in their studio stages (the Barbican Pit and the National Cottesloe), those venues and the Royal Court are not exactly 'fringe' theatre, where 'fringe' used to imply severely limited resources, adverse material conditions, and rigorous touring schedules. To be sure, Churchill's work has toured regularly and has been staged at such medium-sized and small alternatives venues as the Soho Poly, the Almeida, the Half Moon, and the Traverse Theatre, Edinburgh. Still, one reason why she has become highly successful and influential is that she has worked at the edge of dominant theatre traditions and networks both inside and outside their primary structures.

Intellectual background

To further situate Churchill in the late seventies as part of a feminist-socialist trajectory which intercalated cultural products with theoretical preoccupations, I turn now to the link between her 'history' plays and the debates within the academic Left at that time about the methodology of historical research, domestic labour and the labour theory of value, and the relationship of ideology to culture. In the History Workshop Movement, centred at Ruskin College Oxford, a group of feminist historians moved the emphasis of the History Workshop on working-class struggle and labour history towards a feminist historiography which recognised women as discrete subjects, acknowledged the need for an analysis of gender and sexuality which did not simply reduce to class, and provided a theoretical ground for psychoanalytic explorations of sex and gender while retaining a concern for ordinary people and their socio-economic lives. In fact, in 1970, the first Women's Liberation Movement Conference was held at Ruskin College, sponsored by the History Workshop. By 1982, feminist ideas had sufficiently taken hold for their journal, the *History Workshop Journal*, to be subtitled *a journal of feminist and socialist history*. At the Birmingham Centre for Contemporary Cultural Studies (CCCS), women reacted against the dominance of men and men's topics of study, forming the Women's Studies Group which eventually published a critique of the Centre in the eleventh issue of *Working Papers* (1978).[8]

This and subsequent critiques focused on the excessive emphasis in the Centre's work on 'public' and class analysis to the neglect of the domestic sphere differentials, and also the limitations of notions of conceiving subjectivity and identity positions. Applied mainly to media studies and to the subcultures theory developed primarily by Dick Hebdige, women pointed out the exclusion of women's experience from the topics of typical CCCS analysis (pub life, soccer games, work), and also insisted on studying domestic and family life as the source of women's shared experiences of such cultural forms as soap operas, shopping for clothes and make-up, and listening to music. Seeing young women as a 'subculture', they suggested that 'when the dimension of sexuality is included in the study of youth subcultures, girls can be seen to be negotiating a different space, offering a different type of resistance to what can at least in part be viewed as their sexual subordination'.[9] By 1982, another important dimension of feminist and socialist cultural studies was brought to the table by Hazel Carby who, writing in *The Empire Strikes Back*, criticised white feminists for using the language of universal sisterhood which in fact erased and silenced the history and culture of black women.[10] Insisting on a theoretical model which accounted for a history of antagonistic relations of domination and subordination across and among class, gender, and race, Carby also insisted on representations which took account of these contradictions and struggles.

Churchill's plays from this period through the mid-eighties can be seen as a series of contributions to these discussions in theatrical terms. Some theatre scholars have suggested that the plays perform theory, or stage it on the bodies of the actors; I prefer to describe a kind of theatrical discourse which encodes its different sign systems to function as a unique representation of material and intellectual struggles of the times. Journalism, the media, politics and the courts each have a unique form of public discourse, and theatre should be seen as a similar yet different form of such discourse.

Churchill's ability to write short, tightly focused scenes linking personal experience to the deployment of ideology and state power made an argument in theatrical terms for the History Workshop's feminist insistence on incorporating women's domestic life into any comprehensive social analysis. This scene from *Vinegar Tom*, set at 'the landowner's house' begins with the image of a young woman tied to a chair:

> BETTY. Why am I tied? Tied to be bled. Why am I bled? Because I was screaming. Why was I screaming? Because I'm bad. Why was I bad? Because I was happy. Why was I happy? Because I ran out of myself and got away from them and –
> Why was I screaming? Because I'm bad. Why am I bad? Because I'm tied. Why am I tied? Because I was happy. Why was I happy? Because I was screaming.
>
> DOCTOR. Hysteria is a woman's weakness. Hystron, Greek, the womb. Excessive blood causes an imbalance in the humours. The noxious gases that form inwardly every month rise to the brain and cause behaviour quite contrary to the patient's real feelings. After bleeding you must be purged. Tonight you shall be blistered. You will soon be well enough to be married.
>
> (Churchill, *Vinegar Tom, Plays One*, p. 149)

Betty's subjective conflicts as she tries to understand her condition are represented in circular reasoning, resembling the vicious circle in which she is caught. The doctor uses the power and logic of medicine to label her rebellion (against forced marriage) hysteria, and prescribes torture and punishment masquerading as treatment. The goal of this treatment? Docile acceptance of marriage. When she flees to the 'cunning woman' to try to get some relief, she becomes evidence used against this woman's witchery. The contrast between the domestic situation in the landowner's house and other scenes in which unmarried women are poor and destitute (and also persecuted for witchery) etch the class distinctions between forms of control exercised over women at this time. Medicine and the Church team up as powerful and intertwined agents of oppression. Churchill dramatises these connections while also embodying the predicament of the female subject struggling to resist against the odds.

In *Light Shining in Buckinghamshire,* a poor woman is punished for vagrancy by judges who order her to be stripped to the waist and beaten from parish to parish, and an ecstatic Ranter is beaten by a church congregation after she tries to speak during the service. The staging of acts of violence on the bodies of women as forms of social control is a frequent aspect of Churchill's dramaturgy; however, these two plays were written before she had read Michel Foucault's *Discipline and Punish.* Jane Thomas has argued that Foucault is a key to Churchill's often grim endings and lack of prescriptive political closures: 'The characters in her plays can be seen to be constituted within a web of power relations which they unconsciously perpetuate. Although it is clear that, at particular moments in history, individuals, groups and institutions have been able to take economic, political or sexual advantage of various manifestations of power, they are neither its inventors nor its directors.'[11] Thus around the same time that the History Workshop was grappling with Foucault's philosophical history (articles start appearing in their journal in the early 1980s),[12] Churchill was staging aspects of his work through scenic pictures of social relations and dialogue which revealed the working of power through subjects and institutions. Churchill's reading of Foucault in 1978 makes a major contribution to her next period of writing, including *Softcops* (1984) which is a specific response to *Discipline and Punish.*

Feminist theatre in the Thatcher era

Three of Churchill's next plays form the heart of her specifically feminist writing. *Cloud 9, Top Girls,* and *Fen* were all produced between 1979 and 1983, in light of the feminist activism and feminist theory of the 1970s, but well within the period of Thatcherism which dominated Britain for a generation. With these plays, Churchill established herself as a major international playwright; in the United States, *Cloud 9* and *Top Girls* won Obie Awards, and *Fen* won the Susan Smith Blackburn Prize. Translations and productions appeared in many countries.

Cloud 9 took up the relationship between colonialism, sex and gender, and race while *Top Girls* specifically tackled a bourgeois interpretation of feminism which had become prevalent under Thatcher. Both plays used the historicising device of sharp contrasts between historical scenes and contemporary ones. *Fen,* on the other hand, used a more realistic dramaturgy (but not completely) based on oral histories of the lives of women living in the Fens where they are among the lowest-paid day labourers.

Top Girls made the most direct address to the contemporary moment of its production. In an often quoted remark, Churchill reported that, on a visit to the USA for a student production of *Vinegar Tom*, she was surprised to hear young women talking about how well the Women's Movement was doing since more women were getting high-paid and powerful jobs. Thatcher had just been elected Prime Minister, and Churchill felt impelled to a socialist correction of this mistaken emphasis on bourgeois individualism and personal achievement.[13] The resulting play took up the price of success for those 'high fliers' who embrace traditional male and capitalist values of competitiveness, achievement, and celebrity.

Beginning the play with a Judy Chicago-style luncheon party made up of famous women from the past, Churchill begins with an image of the transhistorical price of certain kinds of fame and distinction. Each culture and time exacted its own methods of control and punishment for unruly female behaviour. While nineteenth-century explorer Isabella Bird, Pope Joan, Japanese courtesan Lady Nijo, Breugel's Dull Gret, and Chaucer's Griselda had indeed lived extraordinary lives, they also suffered and compromised and finally *had not* been happy. They are also shown as self-centred and unable to communicate well with the others, something Churchill demonstrates through her often-used theatrical technique of overlapping speeches so that the women talk on top of each other. The contemporary Thatcher-like character, Marlene, has thrown this party to celebrate a promotion. It ends in drunken disorder.

This short scene is a curtain-raiser for the realistic and contemporary scenes which follow. They take place at Marlene's employment agency and at Marlene's sister Joyce's home, where Joyce takes care of Marlene's illegitimate daughter Angie. Angie adores 'Auntie Marlene' and dreams of living with her in London. In the final scene, a long argument between Marlene and Joyce, Churchill stages the class tensions and political differences between the sisters to mount her critique of a feminism without socialism:

> MARLENE: She's a tough lady, Maggie. I'd give her a job. / She just needs to hang in there. This country
> JOYCE: You voted for them, did you?
> MARLENE: needs to stop whining. / Monetarism is not stupid.
> JOYCE: Drink your tea and shut up pet.
> MARLENE: It takes time, determination. No more slop. / And
> JOYCE: Well I think they're filthy bastards.
> MARLENE: who's got to drive it on? First woman prime minister. Terrifico. Aces. Right on. / You must admit. Certainly gets my vote.
> JOYCE: What good's first woman if it's her? I suppose you'd have liked Hitler if he was a woman. Ms Hitler. Got a lot done, Hitlerina. / Great adventures.
> MARLENE: Bosses still walking on the workers' faces? Still Dadda's little parrot?

Haven't you learned to think for yourself? I believe in the individual. Look at me.
JOYCE: I am looking at you.[14]

This short excerpt shows the alignment of Joyce with their working-class father and the history of sisterly strife (Marlene identifies with the downtrodden and abused mother). The family argument at the kitchen table brings personal issues of success and happiness together with national political issues. Angie, the young fourteen-year-old who yearns for a better life, is the person whose future is caught in this squabble. Standing for a whole generation of young women who will inherit the future their mothers are making, Angie has the last word in the play. Waking up from a bad dream, and mistaking (correctly) her Aunt for her mother, she describes her dream as 'Frightening'. This was precisely the kind of focus on teenage girls' experiences which the CCCS women were insisting needed attention and study in the late seventies.

Perhaps the most interesting aspect of this play today is that in its attempt to redress the emerging political conservatism of its day, its own meanings were/are subject to change. Already by the time it was performed in San Francisco in 1985, audiences were arguing about its politics.[15] From a family-value frame of American conservatism, Marlene can be seen to stand for all feminists, bringing the play's point of view in the 1990s uncomfortably close to the recent calls for women to stay at home with their children, seeming to support the charges that feminism has failed women by promoting the workplace to the exclusion of marriage and motherhood. Theatrical art makes its meanings within and between the text, the production, and the moment of its reception – all three sides of this triangle contribute to signification.

Elaine Aston's recent study of Churchill emphasises the 'intense pleasures' *Top Girls* provided for women spectators (*Caryl Churchill*, p. 43). Although other feminist plays created an all-female representational site with all-female characters, few of them succeeded in mainstream venues, and few continue to find a place within the repertory of commercial stages. *Cloud 9* also provided intense pleasures for spectators along a range of sexual and gender identifications as it exploded onto the theatre scene in 1979. Here, the pleasure was a response to the inventiveness and outrageousness of then-unfamiliar techniques of cross-casting which Churchill used to theatricalise identity strain in the Victorian era and the then-present.

While there were several other uses of cross-casting in the early 1980s (the films *Tootsie* and *Victor Victoria* come to mind as does the television programme *Bosom Buddies*, which featured Tom Hanks, cross-dressed, in his first starring role), *Cloud 9* was the mainstream theatrical event that provoked great interest and a lot of experimentation with cross-casting effects in the theatre. Of course, gay drag had long been a venerable dramatic form, and cross-dressing was as old

9 *Cloud 9*, directed by Sarah Pia Anderson

as the Greeks, but it now quickly became highlighted as possessing a variety of possible forms and uses for resistance to the prescribed sex and gender regime of representation. A great deal of scholarship has subsequently been published on this subject; in theatre studies important debates on the subversive potential of cross-dressing, the historically changing meanings it has evoked, and the difference in appropriations of drag for gay, lesbian, and straight spectators has been one of the most lively areas of development in the field.[16]

Churchill developed the script out of a three-week workshop on sexual politics with cast members of Joint Stock which involved deliberate casting of people with a variety of sexual orientations. She writes:

> The starting point for our research was to talk about ourselves and share our very different attitudes and experiences. We also explored stereotypes and role reversals in games and improvisations, read books and talked to other people. Though the play's situations and characters were not developed in the workshop, it draws deeply on this material and I wouldn't have written the same play without it.
>
> (*Plays One*, p. 245)

The play's juxtaposition of Victorian times with the present (1979) came from the discovery in the workshop that the participants felt they had inherited Victorian traditions and ways of thinking about sexuality which they struggled to overcome or transform. Thus Churchill set the first act in Victorian Africa and the second in London in 1979. The characters had only aged twenty-five years, however, creating the sense that the characters of Act I had grown up into those in Act II, although, of course, this was impossible. Theatrically, however, Churchill could represent the presence of the past in the lives, minds, and bodies of living human beings.

The celebrated cross-casting in the first act set up the terms of identity struggle. Clive, the patriarch, was played by a man, but his wife Betty was played by a man as well. Edward, his son, was played by a woman and Joshua, his black servant, was played by a white man. Daughter Victoria was played by a rag doll. The exact meanings of these cross-cast roles have been subject to much discussion and, recently, significant revisions. For Churchill and the company, these were means of showing the internalisation of dominant power in the case of Betty and Joshua (both of whom want to be what Clive, the white man, wants them to be). Edward, on the other hand, is demonstrating sex and gender traits opposite to those he is being forced to emulate. Victoria, without voice or agency, might as well be a doll. In the second act, the doubling of the actors changed, and most actors in the present played their own sex, although Cathy, Victoria's daughter, is played by a man, underscoring her own gender struggles (see Churchill, Introduction to *Cloud 9* in, *Plays One*, pp. 245–7).

Beyond this most simple explanation, however, critics have seen many more implications in these stagings. Betty played in drag makes visible the impossibility of 'real women' taking a space on the stage of representation (Kristeva).[17] Joshua played by a white man refuses but also reinscribes racism through the allusion to minstrel blackface. Based on the biological bodies of the actors, it is difficult to avoid essentialising sex and gender. While the required Victorian/patriarchal behaviours are seen to be arbitrary and oppressive, the 'underneath' can be mistaken for the 'real thing'. Most recently, James Harding has pointed out that having a woman play Edward offers a visual image of the feminised male of stereotypical derision instead of offering a corrective to the imagination of identity linked to binary sex and gender categories.[18]

In intention, and I believe in its first wave of viewings, *Cloud 9* managed through these strategies to destabilise the normal, to make fun of, but also to critique, the disciplinary methods family and culture use to require compulsory heterosexuality and gender normativity. Anyone reading the reviews of the first production can see how this casting was received and interpreted.[19] However, as time moved on, both academic and popular thinking changed significantly as gay and lesbian studies have insisted on a more rigorous deconstruction of heteronormativity and as technology has repeatedly challenged what counts as 'normal' or even possible. Transgendered and transexual discourse has provided alternative and complex ways of reading the relationship between nature and culture, and representation has itself proliferated alternate sexual images and identities in the arts and media which go beyond the historical moment of *Cloud 9*'s conception.

James Harding looks at the stage images created by cross-casting, at the sexual acts actually performed on stage (only heterosexual), and at the liberal attitude of acceptance which he thinks left dominant assumptions intact: 'When it comes to alternative forms of sexual desire, *Cloud 9* makes acceptance easy because it represents homosexual and lesbian desire in terms that reinforce heterosexuality' ('Cloud Cover', p. 260). He notices, for instance, that the lesbian kiss of the first act is actually, visually, a woman kissing a man dressed as a woman, and so still heterosexual. Joshua and Harry decide to go to the barn to have sex, but instead of witnessing any physical contact between them, the scene takes place off-stage and is covered by a scene of cunnilingus between the heterosexual couple Clive and Mrs Saunders. While it is possible to answer some of Harding's arguments, especially within the transformative politics of the original production, this is undoubtedly a powerful and persuasive critique, one which critics will surely debate in print for some time. It is especially provocative to couple Harding's textual analysis with the question about the limits of representation on mainstream stages: that is, could *Cloud 9* only succeed as widely as it did on the stages where it played because it did not cross over some repressive boundary internal to the apparatus of theatre itself – at least that kind of theatre? Ideology is of course natural to those who live it, and may only become apparent in retrospect: what may have looked like a highly provocative and subversive play in 1979 may actually have been capable of being assimilated into a theatre apparatus which was able to contain its most radical contents (something which could be said of Peter Hall's 1997/8 revival, for example). Again, we find the excitement and provocation of witnessing what difference historical context can make to a play's reception.

Of course, a different historical context can make other elements of the play expressive for its production moment. British director Sarah Pia Anderson, who was working as a young woman in the London professional theatre in the 1980s, directed a production of *Cloud 9* at the University of California, Davis, in 1998. She found that the sex and gender contradictions of student life still carry a charge when directly expressed, but also that some profound dilemmas for middle-aged spectators emerge as the defining issues of the play:

> I think that when the play was performed initially it was partially perceived as a piece about utopia. The theme of sexual liberation, laid out in the second act became the focus for those people in the audience who were looking for a redemptive message. But in 1998, it is significant that the character of Betty, in the second act, is presented as more integrated and accepting of herself, yet simultaneously, she is also firmly into middle age, and facing life with a keen sense of aloneness. I think there is an emblematic poignancy about her situation (mirrored in the lives

of all the characters in the play) that speaks keenly and vibrantly to an audience today; there are no utopias and so how do we live together productively with that knowledge? It therefore opens itself to the current ambivalent and sometimes ambiguous attitudes toward 'sexual liberation' as a key (in and of itself) to personal and political salvation.[20]

Fen offered a different kind of response to Thatcherism – an attempt to stage the lives of those whose struggles were becoming invisible. Although based in historical research about the nature of life among working women of several generations, Elin Diamond is able to draw the connections between the play and its initial moment of production:

> *Fen* grows out of a particularly depressing moment in British politics. The Falklands war of 1982 brought unprecedented popularity to the Thatcher government, which in 1983 was returned to power with a landslide majority. In bitter homage to Thatcherite economic policies, *Fen* opened in January 1983 with a speech by a 'Japanese businessman' who praises the 'beautiful English countryside' and the fens' 'beautiful black earth' and all the multinationals (Esso, Equitable Life, Imperial Tobacco, etc.) that own a piece of them. With this unequivocal reference to global capital fresh in our minds, we meet the fen women '*working in a row, potato picking down a field*', an immemorial image of peasant labor.[21]

This production also grew out of a Joint Stock workshop, and, in this experience, the company was taking up one of the challenges of the History Workshop relative to the necessity to focus on the history of working women. The source for the play is Mary Chamberlain's *Fenwomen*.[22] This oral history documents the lives of agricultural labourers in a fen village, their personal and work experiences, their politics and their dreams. Churchill and director Les Waters read Chamberlain's book, and decided to hold two weeks of their workshop in Upwell, a village in the Fens, observing and talking to people, doing their own oral research.

The result is a taut, realistically specific play which represents the lives of multiple generations of Fen women, though it is set in the present. The original set design produced an actual dirt floor in which the characters picked potatoes but which also served as the floor in indoor scenes as well. Although, like *Light Shining in Buckinghamshire*, this play is about an entire community and the lives of its women (in the original production, one man played all the male parts strengthening the focus on the women's experiences), the central action is the love affair between Val and Frank, ending in the violent murder of Val when she begs Frank to kill her. Torn between her children and her lover, she is unable to imagine a way out of the Fens, or the possibility of a different life. Although this is a dominant through-line, the play also includes stories about union organising on the great-grandmother's ninetieth birthday, and manages to chart out a good deal of the village's past history of toil and struggle through various images and characters.

With such a desperately bleak ending, however, Churchill calls on her dramaturgical inventiveness in the final scenes: in an insistence on the different laws of theatrical illusion, the dead Val walks on stage alive again to start talking as a nineteenth-century ghost, or perhaps a medium, who now summons other voices and images – one of a woman walking on stilts, as ancient Fen people did before the Fens were drained – and provides an alternative space, almost a different play where the linearity of plot gives way to the desires and images of the Fen woman. Diamond has written that 'Churchill in effect moves the vanishing point. She decisively alters the logic of the illusion-apparatus in which women's desires cannot appear' (*Unmaking Mimesis*, p. 93). In the last moments, a character who was always unable to sing stands as if singing and 'we hear what she would have liked to sing'.[23] This alternative closing vision breaks open the closed dramaturgy of the preceding scenes. It is a gesture which links *Fen* to other moments in *Cloud 9* (the embracing of the two Bettys in the last scene), and the fanciful luncheon party in *Top Girls*. Thus Churchill refuses the finality and closure of stage realism by creating alternative theatrical fictions, parallel universes displaying a different logic and temporal scheme. These ruptures are one element of the politics of style, one of Churchill's means of refusing the closure of representation and the tyranny of the past.

New directions in Churchill's work

Beginning in 1986 with *A Mouthful of Birds*, Churchill began a series of formal experiments which seems to take her in new directions. This work, which includes her most recent plays *Blue Heart* and *Hotel* (1997), combines her longtime interest in the limits of sanity/madness with the limits of theatrical representation. Thematically, one might say that Churchill desired to dramatise how the past inhabits the bodies and identities of people living in the present, and to demonstrate that repressions released entail violent as well as ecstatic expressions. Brought to the limits of theatrical representation in previous plays, she pushed towards new stylistic means of treating these phenomena.

A Mouthful of Birds was her first collaboration with Ian Spink, the choreographer with whom she has since worked on *Lives of the Great Poisoners, The Skriker,* and *Hotel*. She co-wrote the play with David Lan, and Spink co-directed the play with Les Waters. Over the next decade, Churchill gradually moved more and more into using music and dance as alternative languages to dialogue, creating new forms of theatrical movement and an acoustical score of more varied registers. Besides Spink, composer Orlando Gough has also developed an ongoing relationship with Churchill. He created the musical scores for *Great Poisoners* and *Hotel*.

These experiments have produced a flexible dramaturgy which is not trapped in linguistic modes of textuality. As Churchill struggled to explore areas at the limits of what could be represented by conventional stage means, she has pushed on the boundaries of her theatrical lexicon. Unlike some of the younger writers who work directly with sources of creativity other than language (see chapter 14 for examples), Churchill seems to deepen her talent and experience as a wordsmith while fostering collaborations with specialists in other forms such as dance and music.

A *Mouthful of Birds* uses Euripides' *The Bacchae* as a source, and stages a group of seven people who let down their guards for 'one undefended day' and find they are possessed. They are identified by their occupations: a switchboard operator, a mother, a vicar, a secretary, an acupuncturist, a businessman, and an unemployed person. They are possessed in ways that make a certain sense and allow a certain critique: the businessman who makes his livelihood selling meat falls in love with a pig; the mother is urged to kill her baby; Derek, who compensates for his unemployment by weight training and emphasising his manliness, is seduced by the hermaphrodite figure of Herculine Barbin, whom Churchill read about through Foucault. These possessions, then, enable the persons either to experience the full weight of repressed desires or to find themselves in the grip of what they have most tried to avoid. Violence, of course, breaks out, and the enactment of Pentheus, dressed as a woman, torn to pieces by women, joins the play to its source material. In the last part of the play, the characters are no longer possessed and offer monologues about how they are coping (or not) after the experience of possession.

In this play, Churchill seems to be grappling with the desire to represent subjective experience which is often invisible (inner torment, fantasy, contradiction) and also to examine what happens when some of this desire is released. Politically, the play came from two impulses – Churchill's interest in portraying women as potentially violent, against the stereotype of peaceful women and violent men, and Lan's experiences in Zimbabwe where possession became a political act of resistance against the oppressive government.[24] Nevertheless, these more straightforward intentions do not do justice to the search in this play to confront 'irrational' aspects of ordinary life. It is as if Churchill is trying to stage what happens when a Foucauldian episteme breaks, when regimes of power shift. Jane Thomas, arguing for a Foucauldian reading of *Cloud 9*, writes: 'It . . . exposes as a fallacy the notion of liberation from power through the articulation of our repressed sexual "truths". The characters in *Cloud 9* do not escape the operation of power; they merely succeed in changing the strategic situations they are in' ('Plays of Caryl Churchill', p. 179).

While *Lives of the Great Poisoners* and *Hotel* seem to be technical exercises in developing Churchill's facility with the multiple stage languages of dance and music, it is *The Skriker* which best illustrates how these thematic and aesthetic concerns continue in her work. *The Skriker* is a representation of another realm, magic and fearsome, co-present with a recognisable world of everyday. Drawing on fairy stories and folklore in English literature, Churchill creates a shape-shifter figure – a woman described as old and 'damaged' – who haunts two young contemporary girls, Josie and Lily. Like Angie in *Top Girls*, they are representative of the underclass of abandoned and damaged children of recent years. In fact, the relationship between Angie and her friend Kit might almost be seen as the prototype for the friendship between Josie and Lily, proof that the CCCS call for attention to female teens' experiences needs to be constantly remembered and re-examined as time passes.

The Skriker is damaged because the world has damaged her. Her image is of ruined nature, ruined motherhood, ruined dreams. Fairy tales have turned night-marish and she is more than part witch. As representative of a context of danger and malice in which Josie and Lily live, she appears as an adversary from another world who embodies all the damaged goods of the girls' own world. At the beginning of the play, Josie has murdered her baby and is in a mental hospital, and Lily is pregnant. The two girls have their friendship and commitment to each other, but by the end the Skriker will succeed in separating them and pulling them each into her spells. In separate sequences, Churchill breaks time and logic to portray a parallel underworld existence. The Skriker takes Josie away to her Underworld where it seems that she has been gone for years and years, but, on returning, she seems mad to Lily because, of course, Josie never left the room. At the end of the play, the Skriker takes Lily to the Underworld too. This time, Lily thinks it will be like she is only gone a minute but she comes back to find it is actually generations later and her grotesque and damaged granddaughter rages at her. Writing in dance sequences and giving the Skriker a Joycean-like language, part fairy-like, part gibberish, this play transcends all Churchill's previous experiments, figuring the past as a haunting in the present, and making theatrically viable the interior landscape of schizophrenic subjectivity, which has its own logic and representational syntax.

Echoing the insistence that girls' culture deserves to be studied for its own resistances, Churchill writes scenes for children in many of her plays – scenes which allow both the mapping of ideology and the subject's attempt to resist to be graphically and convincingly staged. These scenes about children's subjectivity and its formation are a major through-line in Churchill's work. They exist embedded in the wide-ranging attempts to connect class, race, gender, sexuality to a network of power relations through writing plays about communities. In each case, one might say that the 'ethos' of a particular community is seen to shape the ground of experimentation and constraint available to the participants. Thus Victorian Africa juxtaposed to London in 1979, transnational politics in the local Fens, or unnatural nature embodied in the Skriker – all these sites represent certain possibilities and specific constraints. Churchill's gift as a dramatist was/is to make these sites palpable as theatre and, as images of contemporary struggles, to make sense of place and of self in a location of permeable boundaries.

Dissatisfied with language, Churchill nevertheless uses it to advantage. She has continually experimented with its power and its limits. Moving from overlapping speech to the clever 'nonsense' of the Skriker, her most recent production, *Blue Heart*, combines the limits of communication with free-flowing theatrical logic to create one play in which a family is stuck repeating one scene over and over with variations, and a companion play in which one phrase, 'blue kettle', is substituted for the actual words necessary to make sense of the sentences, while the characters' identities and tenuous connections to each other disintegrate. While imaginative and entertaining, and including an element of critique of the bourgeois family, these plays do not seem to achieve the break-through status of *The Skriker*. They do, however, form a promise of future work in multiple media that embraces impossible but compelling theatrical logics.

One way to understand Churchill's politics is through understanding her use of various theatrical styles. Plays like *Light Shining, Vinegar Tom,* and more recently *Serious Money* and *Mad Forest* show her mastery of epic dramaturgy to portray communities in the midst of epistemic change. Scenes of extreme realism are offset by theatrical breaks in *Top Girls, Cloud 9,* and *Fen* to prevent the fixity of traditional plot and characters. Since *A Mouthful of Birds,* while continuing to work in the styles she has developed, she has used dance and music to expand her theatrical means of breaking through the limits of representation. As she is a living writer, we can expect her work to keep changing along with the times.

In this period of 'post-feminism', it is not surprising that the most recognisable features of feminist theatre seem to be diminished – all women casts, women's history, overt identity politics. Socialism, too, sometimes seems to have dissolved under real historical events and also the pressure post-structuralism and post-modernism exerted on class analysis and on the challenge to the under-theorised idea of 'experience' which underlay the foundational texts of British Marxism and cultural analysis (I am thinking of E. P. Thompson and Raymond Williams). Yet the concerns of class have not vanished, and identity is still contested, if multiple. In the case of Churchill, *The Skriker* speaks to a time in the late 1990s when 'welfare mothers' like Lily and Josie are daily in the news, and *Mad Forest* (which I have not discussed here) combines a post-Marxist analysis of life in Romania after communism with the vampiric image of the past as a bourgeois visitor in a long topcoat.[25] Churchill's politics continue to be comitted, and to require a constantly evolving theatrical style adequate to the characteristics of life approaching the millennium.

[I know] quite well what kind of society I would like: decentralized, nonauthoritarian, communist, nonsexist – a society in which people can be in touch with their feelings, and in control of their lives. But it always sounds both ridiculous and unattainable when you put it in words.   Caryl Churchill 1982[26]

FIRST PRODUCTIONS OF MAJOR PLAYS BY CARYL CHURCHILL

Venues are in London unless stated.

1972   *Owners*, Royal Court Theatre
        Schreber's Nervous Illness, King's Head Theatre
1975   *Moving Clocks Go Slow*, Royal Court Theatre Upstairs
        Objections to Sex and Violence, Royal Court Theatre
        Perfect Happiness, Soho Poly
1976   *Light Shining in Buckinghamshire*, Traverse Theatre, Edinburgh
        Vinegar Tom, Humberside Theatre, Hull
1977   *Traps*, Royal Court Theatre Upstairs
1979   *Cloud 9*, Joint Stock, Dartington College of Arts, Devon
1980   *Three More Sleepless Nights*, Soho Poly
1982   *Top Girls*, Royal Court Theatre
1983   *Fen*, Joint Stock, University of Essex Theatre, Colchester
1984   *Softcops*, RSC, Barbican Pit
1986   *A Mouthful of Birds*, with David Lan, Birmingham Repertory Theatre, Birmingham
1987   *Serious Money*, Royal Court Theatre
1989   *Hot Fudge*, Royal Court Theatre Upstairs
        Icecream, Royal Court Theatre
1990   *Mad Forest*, Central School of Speech and Drama
1991   *Lives of the Great Poisoners*, with Ian Spink and Orlando Gough, Arnolfi, Bristol
1994   *The Skriker*, Cottesloe, Royal National Theatre
        Thyestes (translation), Royal Court Theatre Upstairs
1997   *Blue Heart*, Out of Joint, Theatre Royal, Bury St Edmund
        Hotel, Second Stride, The Place Theatres

NOTES

1 Ann McFerran, 'The Theatre's (Somewhat) Angry Young Women', *Time Out* 28 October – 3 November 1977, p. 13.
2 Elaine Aston, *Caryl Churchill* (London: Northcote House, 1997), p.25.
3 Churchill herself has characterised this period as a watershed, but she meant exclusively in terms of working with companies instead of working alone. I want to extend the range of this watershed to include the developing intellectual and political currents of that time. Caryl Churchill, 'Introduction', *Plays One* (London and New York: Methuen, 1985), p. xii.
4 See Rob Ritchie (ed.) *The Joint Stock Book; The Making of a Theatre Collective* (London: Methuen, 1987).
5 See for example, my *After Brecht* (Ann Arbor: University Of Michigan Press, 1994), pp. 81–107; and 'Rethinking Brecht: Deconstruction, Feminism, and the Politics of Form', *Brecht Yearbook,* 15, 1990, pp. 99–107; also Elin Diamond, 'Brechtian Theory

/ Feminist Theory: Toward a Gestic Feminist Criticism', *TDR,* 32:1, 1988, pp. 82–94; and 'Refusing the Romanticism of Identity: Narrative Interventions in Churchill, Benmussa, Duras', *Theater Journal,* 37:3, 1985, pp. 273–86; also Amelia Howe Kritzer, *The Plays of Caryl Churchill* (London: Macmillan, 1991); also Rhonda Blair, '"Not . . . but" "Not-Not-Me": Musings on Cross-Gender Performance', in Ellen Donkin and Susan Clement (eds.) *Upstaging Big Daddy* (Ann Arbor: University of Michigan Press, 1993), pp. 291–307.

6 Colin Chambers, interview, *Morning Star,* 27 September 1976.

7 Unattributed review, *Time Out,* 19 November 1976.

8 For accounts of some of these issues in British feminism, see Terry Lovell (ed.) *British Feminist Thought* (London: Blackwell, 1990); Joni Lovenduski and Vicky Randall, *Contemporary Feminist Politics* (London: Oxford University Press, 1993); and Michelene Wandor, *Once a Feminist; Interviews* (London: Virago, 1990).

9 Dennis Dworkin, *Cultural Marxism in Postwar Britain* (Durham, NC, and London: Duke University Press, 1997), p. 79.

10 Hazel V. Carby, 'White Woman Listen! Black Feminism and the Boundaries of Sisterhood', in *The Empire Strikes Back*, Centre for Contemporary Cultural Studies (London: Hutchinson, 1972), pp. 212–35.

11 Jane Thomas, 'The Plays of Caryl Churchill: Essays in Refusal', in Adrian Page (ed.) *The Death of the Playwright?* (London: Macmillan, 1992), p. 163.

12 Dworkin, *Cultural Marxism*, p. 248.

13 Amelia Howe Kritzer provides the most detailed account of the play's genesis in *The Plays of Caryl Churchill*, pp. 138–40.

14 Caryl Churchill, *Top Girls* in *Plays Two* (London and New York: Methuen, 1990), p. 138.

15 Writing about her 1987 production, Juli Burk explicitly tries to produce the play 'from the materialist-feminist perspective to question the price of Marlene's success rather than vilify her for her choices': '*Top Girls* and the Politics of Representation', in Donkin and Clement (eds.) *Upstaging Big Daddy*, p. 74.

16 See, for example, Sue-Ellen Case, 'Toward a Butch-Femme Aesthetic', in Lynda Hart (ed.) *Making a Spectacle* (Ann Arbor: University of Michigan Press, 1989), pp. 282–99; Jill Dolan, *Presence and Desire* (Ann Arbor: University of Michigan Press, 1993); Kate Davy, 'Reading Past the Heterosexual Imperative: *Dress Suits to Hire*', *TDR* 33:1, 1989, pp. 153–70; Moe Meyer (ed.) *The Politics and Poetics of Camp* (London: Routledge, 1994). Also, of course, Marjorie Garber, *Vested Interests* (New York: Harper Collins, 1993).

17 Julia Kristeva's early thinking had an impact on theatre scholars in the 1980s. For an account of her importance, see Reinelt 'Feminist Theory and the Problem of Performance', *Modern Drama,* 32:1, 1989, pp. 48–57.

18 James Harding, 'Cloud Cover: (Re) Dressing Desire and Comfortable Subversions in Caryl Churchill's *Cloud 9*', *PMLA,* 113:2, March, 1998, pp. 258–72.

19 See Linda Fitzsimmons, compiler, *File on Churchill* (London: Methuen, 1989), for review citations, pp. 40–54.

20 Personal interview with Sarah Pia Anderson, 2 September 1998.

21 Elin Diamond, *Unmaking Mimesis* (London and New York: Routledge, 1997), p. 92.

22 Mary Chamberlain, *Fenwomen: Portrait of Women in an English Village* (1975), revised (London: Routledge and Kegan Paul, 1983).

23 Caryl Churchill, *Fen, Plays Two*, p. 145.

24 See authors' introductions to *A Mouthful of Birds* (London: Methuen Theatrescript, 1986), pp. 5–6.
25 Churchill was one of a group of Left-wing playwrights who wrote quickly about the revolutions in Eastern Europe after 1989 (Howard Brenton and David Edgar also wrote major plays at this time). They can be seen as trying to keep a discourse of the Left alive by analysing through theatre both what happened and what the price for market capitalism will be.
26 Quoted in Aston, *Caryl Churchill* – in fact, at the beginning of her book, p. 3.

FURTHER READING

Primary sources: plays

Churchill's plays have appeared in many single editions published by Methuen and also by Nick Hern Books in addition to the ones listed below, which anthologise the main plays and a selection of early work.

Churchill, Caryl. *Plays One: Owners, Traps, Vinegar Tom, Light Shining in Buckinghamshire, Cloud 9.* London and New York: Methuen, 1985.
　　Plays Two: Softcops, Top Girls, Fen, Serious Money. London and New York: Methuen, 1990.
　　Shorts:Three More Sleepless Nights, Lovesick, The After-Dinner Joke, Abortive, Schreber's Nervous Illness, The Judge's Wife, The Hospital at the Time of the Revolution, Hot Fudge, Not Not Not Not Not Enough Oxygen, Seagulls. London: Nick Hern, 1990.
　　Plays Three: Icecream, Mad Forest, Thyestes, The Skriker, A Mouthful of Birds, Lives of the Great Poisoners. London: Nick Hern, 1997.

Secondary sources

Aston, Elaine. *Caryl Churchill.* London: Northcote House, 1997.
Blair, Rhonda. '"Not . . . but" "Not-Not-Me": Musings on Cross-Gender Performance'. In Ellen Donkin and Susan Clement (eds.) *Upstaging Big Daddy.* Ann Arbor: University of Michigan Press, 1993: 291–307.
Burk, Juli. '*Top Girls* and the Politics of Representation'. In Ellen Donkin and Susan Clement (eds.) *Upstaging Big Daddy.* Ann Arbor: University of Michigan Press, 1993: 67–78.
Carlson, Susan. *Women and Comedy.* Ann Arbor: University of Michigan Press, 1991.
Chamber, Colin, and Mike Prior. 'Caryl Churchill: Women and the Jigsaw of Time'. In Chamber and Prior (eds.) *Playwrights' Progress: Patterns of Postwar British Drama.* Oxford: Amber Lane Press, 1987: 198–9.
Cousin, Geraldine. *Churchill The Playwright.* London: Methuen, 1989.
Diamond, Elin. 'Refusing the Romanticism of Identity: Narrative Interventions in Churchill, Benmussa, Duras'. *Theater Journal* 37.3 (1985): 273–86.
　　'Brechtian Theory / Feminist Theory: Toward a Gestic Feminist Criticism'. *TDR* 32.1 (Spring 1988): 82–94.
　　'(In)Visible Bodies in Churchill's Theater'. In Lynda Hart (ed.) *Making a Spectacle.* Ann Arbor: University of Michigan Press, 1989: 259–81.

Unmaking Mimesis. London and New York: Routledge, 1997.

Dworkin, Dennis. *Cultural Marxism in Postwar Britain*. Durham, NC, and London: Duke University Press, 1997.

Fitzsimmons, Linda (compiler). *File on Churchill*. London: Methuen, 1989.

Harding, James. 'Cloud Cover: (Re) Dressing Desire and Comfortable Subversions in Caryl Churchill's *Cloud 9*'. *PMLA* 113.2 (March 1998): 258–72.

Innes, Christopher. 'Caryl Churchill: Theatre as a Model for Change'. In Innes (ed.), *Modern British Drama 1890–1990*. Cambridge: Cambridge University Press, 1992: 460–72.

Keyssar, Helene. 'The Dramas of Caryl Churchill: The Politics of Possibility'. In Keyssar (ed.) *Feminist Theatre*. Basingstoke: Macmillan, 1984: 77–101.

Kritzer, Amelia Howe. *The Plays of Caryl Churchill*. London: Macmillan, 1991.

Marohl, Joseph. 'De-realized Women: Performance and Identity in *Top Girls*'. *Modern Drama* 30.3 (September 1987): 376–88.

Quigley, Austin E. 'Stereotype and Prototype: Character in the Plays of Caryl Churchill'. In Quigley (ed.) *Feminine Focus*. Oxford: Oxford University Press, 1989: 25–52.

Reinelt, Janelle. 'Rethinking Brecht: Deconstruction, Feminism, and the Politics of Form'. *Brecht Yearbook* 15 (1990): 99–107.

After Brecht. Ann Arbor: University Of Michigan Press, 1994.

Thomas, Jane. 'The Plays of Caryl Churchill: Essays in Refusal.' In Adrian Page (ed.) *The Death of the Playwright?* London: Macmillan, 1992: 160–85.

12

GABRIELE GRIFFIN

Violence, abuse, and gender relations in the plays of Sarah Daniels

Introduction

Representations of the abuse of and violence against women are central to the plays of Sarah Daniels. This she shares with Andrea Dworkin, American radical feminist activist and campaigner against violence against women, whose work has informed Daniels's writings. In her introduction to *Plays 1* Daniels states that she wrote her perhaps best-known play, *Masterpieces*, in part as a consequence of having read Dworkin's *Pornography: Men Possessing Women*, and she also mentions Dworkin's *Letters from a War Zone*.[1] Both women have been attacked for their work which has been regarded as man-hating. Significantly, talking of her first play, *Ripen Our Darkness* (1981), Daniels wrote that 'nobody, except women, thought the men were drawn with any accuracy' (Introduction, *Plays 1*, p. x).

The notion of any form of 'extremism' on the part of women, 'extremism' here meaning simply a critique of women's domination by men, has always been a source of recrimination against women. This is demonstrated in Daniels's *Byrthrite* (1986), for example, which centres on women's persecution in the seventeenth century. Daniels herself has not escaped this fate. It is to her credit that this has not deterred her from addressing what remain abidingly serious issues: the oppression of women and their exploitation by men. Her most recent play, *Blow Your House Down* (1995), for instance, deals with the case of the Yorkshire Ripper, a figure of great terror for women in Northern England during the second half of the 1970s when he murdered and mutilated many women in a gruesome manner.[2] However, in this chapter I shall focus on Daniels's work published in *Plays 1* and *Plays 2*. There are two main reasons for this. One is that these collections of Daniels's plays are readily available to readers, a factor not unimportant in a context where the erasure of women's theatre work from theatre history has been a long-standing concern. Secondly, the period covered in Daniels's two volumes of plays, 1981 to 1994, has been one both of great productivity in women's theatre work and of great change.[3] Governed by the conservatism of Thatcherite politics in Britain in which women were simultaneously encouraged to participate in the economy and reviled for it, this period saw the rise of a number of British women playwrights. These include Pam Gems and Caryl Churchill who made a name for themselves as feminist playwrights in the 1970s and went on to successful careers in the 1980s. Gems and Churchill were followed by a second wave of women playwrights who came to prominence in the 1980s and include, for example, Timberlake Wertenbaker, Louise Page, and April de Angelis. More recently they have been joined by playwrights such as Phyllis Nagy who emerged as a new theatre voice in the 1990s.

The period 1981–94 also saw the move from issue-based theatre to a theatre preoccupied with formal innovation, a theatre of style and physical theatre. The shift is evident in Churchill's theatre, or, for example, in Page's move from her early issue-based play *Tissue* (Belgrade, Coventry, 1978), which deals with the subject of breast cancer, to her stylised treatment of death and old age in *Salonika* (Royal Court Theatre Upstairs, 1982).[4] The Cork Report of 1986 also noted that there had been a surge of explorations 'of new and experimental forms of physical and visual or non-literary theatre', that many companies had developed a 'vivid and varied new style of theatre based on design, sound and movement, often staged by performers with an art school background experimenting with new technology', and that 'this development ha[d] been reinforced by a growing interest in mime as a dramatic form'.[5] These changes effectively amounted to a gagging of issue-based theatre aided, in Britain, by changes in the funding policy of the Arts Council which actively promoted non-verbal arts.[6] It went together with an increasing preoccupation with individual psychology as opposed to the socio-economic context which shapes human relations (compare, for instance, Churchill's *Top Girls* with her later plays *The Skriker* or *Blue Heart*), and a diminution of both funding and platforms for women playwrights and women's theatre groups.[7] Reading Daniels's work against this backdrop provides some explanations for the particular status she has achieved in contemporary British theatre as a leading female playwright whose work has been persistently under attack from male critics (unlike that of Churchill, for instance).

In this chapter I shall deal with Daniels's plays in roughly chronological order. I intend to analyse the specificity of her *oeuvre* in relation both to work-internal issues and to the wider socio-historical context in which the plays were performed and published. The chapter will focus on four issues:

(1) that of the oppressed housewife, a key figure in Daniels's work;
(2) female bonding as a means of countering female oppression;
(3) the representation of violence against women;
(4) the problem of the endings of Daniels's plays.

House-wife[8]

Central to Daniels's plays has been the exploitation of women and their oppression by men. This has become an unfashionable topic in the 1990s when the talk is of girl power, women constituting 50 per cent of the work force, and men's virulent response against women's liberation. It has been at the centre of feminism, however, and in Daniels's work it found its first expression in the figure of the house-wife, a word deliberately hyphenated here to index the conflation of the figure of the house-maintainer, -cleaner, etc., with that of the wife trapped in an abusive heterosexual marriage. The middle-aged married woman without paid employment locked into an oppressive marriage makes her initial appearance in Daniels's very first play, *Ripen Our Darkness,* where she is the central figure in the shape of Mary, wife of a church warden, mother of three teenage sons living at home and of a lesbian daughter living with her lover. The appearance of this figure is in some ways not surprising, given that she was very much the initial object of the Second Wave of the Women's Liberation Movement as epitomised, for example, in Betty Friedan's *Feminine Mystique* (1963).[9] However, it is also the case that this figure, generally regarded as of no interest as she is no longer supposed to be the object of sexual desire, has been significantly under-represented in theatre[10] as in other art forms. In the housewife's previous incarnations in theatre, say as Nora in Ibsen's *A Doll's House,* her oppression was countermanded by the potential of further post-marital heterosexual relationships. Nora, for example, was not middle-aged or older; her transformation was from a still desirable woman into a tragic figure (one might argue that Diana, Princess of Wales, suffered a similar fate). Mary, in *Ripen Our Darkness,* on the other hand, represents a different kind of housewife, in a sense our mothers' generation of women: women now in their sixties and seventies who live(d) in a heterosexist world in which women were expected, and in consequence themselves expected, to marry (and for that marriage to last their lifetime), have children, keep a home, and not go out to work. We meet this kind of woman repeatedly in Daniels's plays: not only Mary but Daphne, too, in *Ripen Our Darkness,* conforms to this stereotype; in *The Devil's Gateway* there are Betty and Enid; in *Masterpieces,* we have Jennifer; in *Neaptide* Joyce, Claire's mother; in *Byrthrite* Helen, wife to the parson; in *The Gut Girls* the mother of Maggie, Eady; and in *Beside Herself* Evelyn and Lil. What these women share might be described as 'a long-term investment in heteropatriarchy, whereby economic dependence on their husbands, long-term marriage and conformity to the demands of men and the conventions of society have made it difficult for them to envisage change or a different life'.[11]

In Mary's case, in *Ripen Our Darkness,* matters come to a head as she finds it increasingly difficult to function within the symbolic order[12] with which her husband David identifies. This symbolic order regulates relations between women and men through the imposition of an androcentric linear structure in which women are the objects of male order. Although it supposedly decrees certain spaces as belonging to particular genders (i.e. the public sphere being 'male' and the private sphere 'female'), all space, as this play makes clear, is subjugated by the male. The opening scene of the play takes place in what the didascales ironically describe as '*Mary's kitchen*', ironically because the space is clearly not owned by Mary – she is relegated to the status of servant within this site which is invaded by her husband and her sons who behave like a colonial force come to brutalise an unknown country. David, Mary's husband, does not know where anything is. His feeble attempt at making breakfast, of taking over Mary's space, is undercut by his constant need to be helped by her. He is, in fact, incapable of owning her space despite his constant efforts to do so, indicated in the ways in which he keeps interrupting her and telling her what to do and say as if she were a child. David's reliance on Mary to know where everything is in fact resembles that of a child: he is the archetypal image of the man as the additional child in the (petit) bourgeois household who is unable, because unwilling, to take on any responsibilities for what are defined as domestic chores.

Mary finds it easy to keep order whereas David does not; he projects his disorderliness onto her, saying: 'And remember what we agreed, eh? What we worked out about being methodical, and getting things sorted out in a logical order so that it will give you more time to do things, to get important things fitted into the day' (sc. 1, p. 5). What is important here is what is important to *him*; his decision-making, such as inviting people to lunch without consulting her, registers no consideration for her. There is no expectation, either by him or by their sons, whose side against their mother David persistently takes, that Mary might have important things of her own to focus on. Mary's 'vagueness', as it is described by David, is in part projection, in part a recognition of a process which happens to Mary both prior to and during the play – she becomes vague, or withdraws, in response to the perpetual verbal bullying by her family to which she is subjected. Her suicide, at the end of the play, is her final refusal to engage further with the demands of the males who constitute her family and who have completely ignored her as a person in her own right. Significantly, she commits it in the kitchen, the site of the opening scene, symbol of women's space, but a space within which and from which Mary is constantly dislodged during the play. Just as her supposed space, the kitchen, has been violated by her male family members throughout the play so in the end Mary violates the only space left to her, her body, through killing herself. Although her suicide is humorously framed (she leaves a note for her husband saying, 'your dinner and my head are in the oven') and her death utopically redeemed through a re-awakening into an all-female paradise, it is hard to read this ending as a celebration of female liberation; rather, Mary's fate seems to mirror that of other women (Sylvia Plath and Anne Sexton spring immediately to mind) who found themselves unable, or no longer willing, to cope with the oppressions they as women faced.

However, all is not gloom for Daniels's housewives. In the course of her plays these figures become increasingly resistant to the pressures put upon them by their environment. Betty, Ivy, and Enid in *The Devil's Gateway*, for instance, end by doing what they want to do; Enid leaves her husband to go and live with her sister; she is joined by Betty's mother, Ivy. Betty sets off to Greenham Common. Jennifer in *Masterpieces* does not leave her pornography-consuming, violent husband but, fully aware of how she is and has been treated, she tells her daughter Rowena: 'I stopped bending over backwards, literally, for him, and instead unleashed the acrimonious recriminations which I'd kept bottled up for years . . . I don't want your pity. I've given as good as I've got, well, nearly' (*Plays 1*, sc. 11, p. 216). In *Neaptide* Joyce ends up using her savings and her understanding of the way in which women cannot win in a male-dominated society to enable her lesbian daughter Claire to flee the country with her daughter Poppy. As Joyce says to her daughter at one point: 'For me and my lifetime, I've had to adapt much more than you ever have' (*Plays 1*, pt 2, sc. 3, p. 317).

Women doing it for themselves and each other: cross-generational relations

The 'happier' endings for the housewives discussed above are predicated upon four stages of development in the female characters:

(1) women's recognition of their oppression;
(2) women's articulation of that recognition to other women;
(3) women's decision to fight this oppression;
(4) female bonding in the face of adversity.

In *Ripen Our Darkness* Mary is presented as mostly without female support. Although she discusses her situation with her lesbian daughter Anna, she has no sense of the possibility of change except by changing – i.e. killing – herself. Anna is unable to help her mother. In contrast, the all-female, lesbian household of Anna and her lover Julie, is based on mutual support and understanding – even though the women have differences of opinion. Whereas the class differences between Anna and Julie do not constitute an unresolvable problem for their relationship, the tensions between mother and daughter arising from their different life-styles prevent Anna from helping her mother effectively. Interestingly, this is not the case in *Neaptide* where Joyce, working-class and heterosexual, is capable of empathising with, and helping, her lesbian daughter Claire who has become middle-class through her education. Throughout this play Claire and Joyce are presented as at loggerheads; however, in her hour of need, Joyce comes to Claire's rescue with a plan for how she can keep her daughter Poppy. Mary and Anna are unable to do anything comparable for each other.[13]

Women's support of each other as a critical element in achieving change is one key to Daniels's representation of women's plight under patriarchy. In this respect Daniels's 'solution' to women's oppression resembles that advocated in Italian feminist thought[14] as epitomised by the work of the Milan Women's Bookstore Collective. Based on Virginia Woolf's notion of 'thinking back through our mothers' they postulate the need for a female social contract between women of differential power, one of whom functions as the symbolic mother, to enable women to overcome oppression. Before Mary kills herself she goes to see her daughter Anna because, one assumes, she is afraid that Anna might feel obliged to take on the looking after of her father and her brothers. To the last, Mary registers her concern for others:

> MARY. It's me that's supposed to worry about you. It's been lovely to see you. (*She turns to go, then says as an afterthought.*) I've often wondered, if anything happened to me, would you ever consider going home to look after them?
> ANNA. Let's not end on a sour note.
> MARY Good, I'm very glad of that. (sc. 7, p. 47)

Reassured that her daughter is safe from the fate of which she herself has been object, Mary returns home to kill herself.

In several of Daniels's plays it is the older, normally unobserved and usually put-down housewife or woman who acts as a support to the younger woman who has been able or is trying to live a life different from that of the previous generation of women. Not only does Claire's mother in *Neaptide* come to her daughter's rescue, together with Claire's sister Sybil; similarly, the headmistress in the school in which Claire teaches, herself a lesbian but utterly closeted,[15] attempts to support Claire by testifying on her behalf in court. Claire herself is driven to defend lesbian pupils in her school when they are caught kissing. She refuses to name the pupils in question and thus puts her job on the line. In *The Madness of Esme and Shaz* Esme rescues her niece Shaz, initially by taking her in on release from long-term stay in a psychiatric unit and subsequently, by freeing her from a second internment in a psychiatric hospital, and, significantly, by fleeing the country with her to begin a new life running a restaurant on a Greek island. In Daniels's plays it is thus always women who help women in their flight from violence and abuse, not men.

Violence against women

Violence against women can take many forms.[16] It is a persistent topic in Daniels's work, notoriously difficult to deal with since violence against women is such an unequivocally gendered phenomenon, indicting men. Women's violence against women manifests itself only in the form of denial and in physical violence as a response to victimisation. Women's violence against men is constructed as a final resort, and occurs very rarely in Daniels's plays: once when Rowena in *Masterpieces* kills a stranger, another time when Rose, disguised as a man, goes to war in *Byrthrite*, and again in the same play when the women persecuted as witches 'swim' the pricker, that is pretend to drown him. However, in all of Daniels's plays women are at the very least the objects of verbal bullying by men, the 'mildest' form of abuse. In most of the plays, however, the violation of women goes far beyond verbal bullying. Many of Daniels's female characters are the objects of domestic violence, from Carol in *The Devil's Gateway*, hit by her husband, to the sexual harassment, and indeed murder, of women which is the central topic of *Masterpieces* and is prominent in *Neaptide*.

The sexual abuse of women is one focus of all the plays in Daniels's second collection.[17] *The Gut Girls*, set at the turn of the century in Deptford, London, and 'about the young women who worked in the Cattle Market and were turned into domestic servants by the Duchess of Albany' (*Plays* 2, p. ix), represents sexual exploitation in class-based terms, with male members of the middle and upper classes especially being presented as exercising, or attempting to exercise, a version of the *droit de seigneur* in relation to young working-class women. Thus Annie, a sixteen-year-old new to the gutting sheds of the cattle market, works there because, having become pregnant following her rape by her employers' son when she was a domestic servant, she was turned out by her employers and needed to find other work. Not dissimilarly, one of the gut girls is assaulted with the intention of rape in the street by Edwin, an aristocrat, who visits the gutting sheds. However, her employment-related ability to wield a large knife saves her from sexual violation. Neither of these women is seen as having any course of redress – the possibility of sexual assault is constructed as part of the danger inherent in being a working-class woman.

This situation resembles that of the victims of incest who are central characters in Daniels's other plays, both in *Plays* 2 and in *Plays* 1. *Beside Herself* considers the impact of incest on women's sense of self and social relations. In it, Evelyn, a middle-class woman helping out in a Community Group House for people who are to be released into the community following long-term care in psychiatric institutions, has to come to terms with the fact that she was sexually abused by her father, a well-known, professionally much respected surgeon. Evelyn is constructed as having the equivalent of a split consciousness: a surface self, housewife Evelyn, who is unassuming, co-operative, caring and presents the philanthropic and nurturing side of a particular kind of conventionalised, middle-class, middle-aged, heterosexual femininity *and* an 'inner voice' or alter ego, Eve, who gives vent to Evelyn's 'true' feelings. The literal enactment of this split consciousness on stage through the use of two actresses playing Evelyn and Eve reinforces the notion of the separation of the compliant from the resistant aspects of Evelyn's self until Evelyn decides to confront her past at which point Eve 'turns and looks at Evelyn and slips away' (*Plays* 2, pt 2, sc. 10, p. 185). This suggests that Evelyn has incorporated the resistant aspects of herself and the process of healing can begin. Theatrically, the split of Evelyn into two figures works against the notion of the unified self of naturalist theatre to suggest the multiple and possibly conflicting positions that women may quite literally inhabit in patriarchy but which, conventionally, remain hidden.

Evelyn's long-term suppression of her sexual abuse at the hands of her father is brought to a crisis through her involvement with the Community Group House. There she encounters other victims of abuse such as Dave who was put into psychiatric care because he is a homosexual, and Dawn who was sexually abused as a child. Listening to their case histories forces Evelyn to make sense of her own life and confront her elderly father. The play contains multiple narratives of abuse which deny the notion that abuse is contained within specific frameworks. Evelyn's middle-class experience of incestuous abuse is mirrored by the story of the lower-middle-class character Lil, a care worker, and her daughter Nicola. Nicola was sexually abused by her stepfather and ran away from home. Lil, who had a suspicion of what was going on, nonetheless believed her partner Tony when he asserted his innocence. Only when confronted with her adult daughter who rejects her does Lil in turn begin to confront her husband about his abuse of her daughter. Both Tony and Evelyn's father deny the abuse, protesting their love for the female child in question and using that as a reason for validating their behaviour. *Beside Herself* thus focuses on how adult women come to terms with incestuous abuse, of themselves, of their daughters, of other women. The title, *Beside Herself*, points to

(1) the extent of incestuous abuse – beside any one of the women in the play there are others who have suffered similar fates;
(2) the notion of 'falling apart' or being beside oneself as a consequence of being violated;
(3) the idea of a 'split personality', a common phenomenon among women who have suffered sexual abuse as, in order to endure and survive the abuse, they shut off the violated part of themselves in the process of the abuse and afterwards.

The idea of the commonness of incest and sexual abuse of women is presented through the parallel narratives of the various female characters in the main part of the play and the ahistorical representation of the biblical women in the 'Prelude' which, akin to the opening scene of Churchill's *Top Girls* (1982) [see pp. 180–1], features women from another time in a contemporary setting, thus insisting on the continuity of the abuse women have suffered from men across time and cultures. The women who are or have been the victims of abuse are beside themselves or become so, either with anger or with pain or a mixture of emotions, in the course of the play. The lack of any ability to seek appropriate restitution leads them to shut down the part of their consciousness which understands their victimisation or leads them to self-harm or to other kinds of actions. None of this results in the punishment of the perpetrator but it all in various ways debilitates the women who are the victims themselves. The horror of the play lies in the assertion of the all-pervasiveness of incestuous abuse, its insistence that this abuse is not class-specific, that the abusers generally get away with it, that 'the system' as epitomised by psychiatric institutions supports the abuse by punishing the victims rather than the perpetrators and that, in this respect, sexual abuse in the late twentieth century operates in exactly the same ways as it has done in other times of history: women are the victims and are punished for it; men are the perpetrators and get away with it.

A not dissimilar story is told in *Head-Rot Holiday,* pessimistically set in a secure mental hospital from which the female patients, long-term inhabitants of the institution, appear to have no chance of escaping. As one of the characters says ironically: 'Is there anyone here who has been here less than eight years? And all most of them did was fart in front of their Social Worker' (*Plays* 2, pt 1, sc. 1, p. 196). The play is an indictment of the institutions and public services which constitute the so-called welfare state and are meant to support women. In contrast to *Beside Herself* in which the victimised women at most turn in on themselves in order to express their sense of worthlessness and degradation, several of the characters on whom this play centres have done more than 'fart in front of their Social Worker'. Ruth, one of the patients, stabbed her stepmother. As Ruth tellingly puts it: 'Someone's bad to you. You don't get a chance to be bad back but then you're bad to someone else because it has to come out. And they have to be bad and it goes on and on without hope' (pt 2, sc. 15, p. 240). Both Ruth and another patient Dee were the objects of incestuous abuse, and both turn to self-harm, attempting to kill themselves. As Dee says: 'It's keeping me alive. Every other fucker's done things to me. I'm going to do things to myself for a change' (pt 2, sc. 12, p. 231). *Beside Herself, Head-Rot Holiday,* and *The Madness of Esme and Shaz* all focus on the difference between women doing things *to* themselves and doing things *for* themselves, with the latter being constructed as empowering and the former as disempowering. In this context, it is worth noting that the first performance of *Head-Rot Holiday* was put on the all-female theatre group Clean Break [see main introduction, pp. 16–17], consisting of women who are ex-prisoners and thus have experience of the punitive institutionalisation Daniels so persistently attacks through her work. Clean Break, who have done things *for* themselves by becoming a theatre group and moving beyond the confinement of prison, form an ironic contrast as performers of *Head-Rot Holiday* which as a play denies the possibility of such a move. The audience is thus implicitly invited to consider the relative positions of the characters and the performers.

In *The Madness of Esme and Shaz*, Shaz, as well as Esme, now an older retired woman living alone, have been the objects of incestuous abuse. When Esme, Shaz's aunt, takes Shaz home from the psychiatric institution in which Shaz has been for thirteen years, she knows what Shaz's background is. As Elaine tells her: 'When . . . when we were children, your father and I, he [Esme's father] wouldn't leave us alone. You know to what I'm referring? . . . And I suspect, I expect that my brother repeated the same pattern of behaviour when you were a child' (*Plays* 2, pt 1, sc. 8, p. 301). Here, as in *Beside Herself* and in *Head-Rot Holiday*, the experience of incest is constructed as the result of a cycle of violence whereby the abused in turn become abusers, a pessimistic and conservative analysis which has much credence in socio-psychological contexts but which effectively denies the possibility of change and fails to account for those who, though abused, do not themselves become abusers. From a feminist perspective, this analysis is quite problematic, partly because of the denial of the possibility of change – and feminism has above all an investment in the change of women's situation – and partly because it does not account fully for the gendered nature of the abuse. After all, men abuse sexually but women, in their turn, on the whole do not do so if the gender-related statistics about sexual abuse are to be believed.[18] Like Dee in *Beside Herself*, Shaz in *The Madness of Esme and Shaz* self-harms – does unto herself what others have done to her by way of inflicting pain. One consequence for the women who are the victims of child sexual abuse is thus to turn on themselves. The other, also documented in the plays, is to be violent towards others. Shaz killed her baby half-sister which is why she was institutionalised. Both Ruth and Claudia in *Head-Rot Holiday* committed acts of violence. Significantly, in all three cases the women are violent against other women, not against those who abused them: men. Indeed, in *Head-Rot Holiday* the nurse in charge, Barbara, is violent towards the women patients.

Beside Herself, *Head-Rot Holiday*, and *The Madness of Esme and Shaz* reflect two major developments in the Britain of the 1980s: (1) the decline of the welfare state, signalled in *Beside Herself* and in *The Madness of Esme and Shaz* by the decanting of long-term psychiatric patients into the community, and (2) the 'discovery' or mainstreaming of child sexual abuse. The relationship between the two phenomena, as indexed in plays by women from the 1980s, is that women who have been sexually abused often end up in psychiatric institutions even though they are the victims of a crime rather than its perpetrators. In Valerie Windsor's play *Effie's Burning*, for example, first performed in 1987, the year in which the Cleveland case broke in the UK, an elderly woman reacts against the prospect of being made to leave the institution in which she has been for decades by setting fire to her bed. This character was institutionalised in response to an accusation of 'moral turpitude', an idea in this instance associated with the fact that she became pregnant with an illegitimate child following rape as a teenager. The 'discovery' in the 1980s of the long-term hospitalisation of such women in the early part of this century caused a furore in Britain, and only came to light when the then Conservative British government began the dismantling of the welfare state and the process of returning long-term patients of psychiatric hospitals into community care. It simply reinforces the line taken, however, throughout Daniels's plays that women are the victims of a patriarchal structure in which their abuse is condoned by institutions which judge *them* rather than the perpetrators.[19]

Endings and the problem of realism

Like Dworkin's, Daniels's plays thus argue that crimes against women do not count in this culture. None of Daniels's plays ends with the indictment of the male perpetrators of the crimes in any direct way. Instead, and as a consequence, the plays focus on what happens to the female characters. I want to relate these endings to the fact that Daniels's plays, though they contain a number of stylistic devices which undercut this effect,[20] are in the main realist. Such realism sits somewhat uneasily in a context in which *performance* has become the locus of theatrical innovation and in which the possibilities offered by realism to feminist playwrights have become the object of debate, with some viewing realism as a conservative form which is not helpful to feminists and others regarding it as offering possibilities for feminist representation [see pp. 26–27].[21] Sue-Ellen Case, for instance, asserts that 'realism, in its focus on the domestic sphere and the family unit, reifies the male as sexual subject and the female as the sexual "Other"'.[22] However, whilst Daniels's plays focus powerfully on the domestic sphere and the family unit, they can hardly be said to reify the male. Recent discussions of realism have stressed the idea that it both 'speaks to our desire for universality, coherence, unity, tradition, and . . . it unravels that unity through improvisations, embodied rhythm, powerful instantiation of subjectivity, and . . . impersonation'.[23] In 'Realism, Narrative, and the Feminist Playwright[24] – A Problem of Reception' Jeanie Forte discusses the dramatic and narrative strategies different women playwrights use as a response to the idea that realism 'supports the dominant ideology by constructing the reader as a subject . . . within that ideology'.[25] Forte asks 'whether a realist play could not also be a feminist play'. This is pertinent to Daniels's work and its reception since her plays are in the main realist in construction. By this I mean that they take place in recognisable times and places, feature 'plausible' characters, offer a predominantly linear narrative in which a problem is presented and 'resolved' within a hierarchy of, sometimes competing, discourses in which some positions are presented as more 'truthful' or desirable than others. However, as was made clear in the opening paragraph of this chapter, 'plausibility', for instance, is a matter of judgement – where women considered the male characters in Daniels's *Masterpieces* to be realistically drawn, male viewers did not. The endings of Daniels's plays are instructive in this context because the ways in which the dilemmas presented in the plays are resolved point to the problems women face within male-dominated society and to the position adopted by Daniels to these.

One might argue that most of the plays end with a defeat of the female characters. Most commonly, they exit from the male-dominated context in which they exist, aided by other women. Thus in *Ripen Our Darkness*, Mary kills herself and ends up in an all-female paradise; her daughter Anna has already exited from patriarchy through living in a lesbian relationship. In *The Devil's Gateway* Enid leaves her husband to live with her sister; Betty looks set to go to Greenham Common (a radical, all-female space); and Carol and Ivy set off to Bangor, together with Enid. In *Masterpieces* Rowena, having killed a man, is sentenced[26] which means that she will spend many years in an all-female prison, a segregated space for women who transgress. In *Neaptide* Claire, supported by her mother's money, flees to her sister in the USA, together with her daughter. In *Byrthrite* Rose saves Grace and Ursula in her disguise as a man and becomes a playwright at the same time that the Witchfinder General is formally instituted. In *The Gut Girls* virtually all the female characters end up in service or dependent on a man through marriage as the only other option, a situation few of them wanted at the start of the play. *Beside Herself* ends with the reunion of Nicola, the abused daughter, and her mother, and with Evelyn confronting her abusive father. However, as Evelyn says to her father: 'What could I possibly do to you that would undo what you've done to me?' (*Plays* 2, pt 2, sc. 10, p. 185). At the end of *Head-Rot Holiday* none of the patients have left as was predicted early in the play – the only person to get away, so to speak, is Barbara, the abused and abusing nurse, who leaves both husband and job, future unknown. The other women are still in the segregated space that they occupied at the opening of the play, with the more sympathetic female nurses having changed in their attitude to the patients as a result of what happened to Barbara, and two of the patients, Ruth and Dee, attempting suicide. *The Madness of Esme and Shaz* features another escape or evacuation: Esme and Shaz escape to live in Greece.

These endings, with the possible exception of those of *Ripen Our Darkness*, *Neaptide,* and *The Madness of Esme and Shaz*, are realistic in that they are plausible. One could argue that these endings consummately support the dominant ideology in that the women who are victims either continue to be punished and further subjected, indeed unto death in some instances, or they escape in slightly improbable scenarios of sudden, liberated funds and major changes of position on the part of older women. None of the female characters are constructed as 'making it' within the framework in which they are at the beginning of the play.

Against the notion that this constitutes a failing of the plays because it supports a dominant misogynistic ideology I would argue that this is representative of the unsupportability of these frameworks, that it reinforces the fact that women indeed *cannot* survive in such situations. To suggest that they could would be a way of supporting the status quo. One might argue, further, that the unchanging nature of the men in Daniels' plays is an indictment of men in patriarchal culture, that it makes a statement about the reality of how men are and have been, and, possibly more pessimistically, that the only change that women can hope for or aim at in this context is about and for themselves. Audre Lorde famously proclaimed that the master's tools will never dismantle the master's house[27] Daniels's plays consistently support this view. When Rowena kills a man in response to having seen a 'snuff' movie in which a woman gets killed, for instance, her violence does not result in change but in her being sentenced to life imprisonment.

Daniels's plays demonstrate unequivocally that men's domination of women, and specifically men's domination of women through sexual and physical abuse, is all-pervasive and not restricted by class, culture, or historical moment. Significantly, for instance, Grace, the older healing woman in *Byrthrite* who is persecuted as a witch, says that women were killed in the witch hunts 'because they were women not because they were special. When we have received foul attentions from lord and from farmhand alike, 'tis because we are women. It's a danger to claim it is because we are different in some way' (*Plays 1*, pt 2, sc. 8, p. 410). The danger lies in the fact that pointing to a specific group of women as persecuted for particular reasons denies the misogyny inherent in Western culture and thus fails to recognise that *all* women are the objects of oppression by men. The endings of Daniels's plays leave the viewer with the issue of how change might be achieved. One might argue that Daniels's theatre is intended to activate the audience into reviewing the problems and thinking about possible solutions *à la* Brecht.

To say that all women are oppressed became deeply unpopular within feminism during the 1980s because diverse groups of women such as black women and lesbian women increasingly claimed that not all women are oppressed in the same way and for the same reasons.[28] The resultant fragmentation among feminists was one factor in the decline of the popularity of feminism. Yet if one compares Daniels's plays with the essays and speeches in *Life and Death* by Andrea Dworkin, mentioned at the beginning of this chapter, it is clear that the reality depicted in Daniels's plays is one women from diverse classes, cultures, and races face every day, including in the 1990s. We need only consider two of the more famous cases of domestic and sexual violence Dworkin discusses – that of the murder of Nicole Brown Simpson, O. J. Simpson's estranged wife who left him after seventeen years of domestic torment, and of the sexual harassment of Anita Hill aired in the Hill / Clarence Thomas hearings (both cases ended with the men getting off) – to realise how commonplace the abuse of women remains. Or we might compare Dworkin's two chapters on pornography, 'Beaver Talks' and 'Israel: Whose Country Is It Anyway?' in which the author discusses Holocaust pornography, with *Masterpieces* to understand that the issues raised in Daniels's play are nowhere near resolution. In the late 1980s and 1990s, however, people no longer wanted to engage with this reality other than through the sensationalising press and voyeuristic documentary. This has had an impact on the kinds of plays women produce. Caryl Churchill's most recent plays, *The Skriker* (1994) and *Blue Heart* (1997) [see pp. 188–89] present the breaking of the sentence and the breaking of the sequence[29] propagated by Virginia Woolf in 1928 in *A Room of One's Own* as women's way of writing, to such an extent that the audience's focus is on the formal aspects of the plays, the stylistic innovations and devices rather than the issues. Yet the realism which Daniels favours is also found in other recent plays by women which, it seems to me, increasingly, focus on the family as well as social relations. Bryony Lavery's adaptation of Beatrix Campbell's *Goliath* (toured by Sphinx, 1997), April de Angelis's *The Positive Hour* (Hampstead Theatre, February 1997), and Cheryl L. West's *Jar the Floor* (West Yorkshire Playhouse, November 1997) are all examples of this. None are as radical in their indictment of men as Daniels's plays are. All, however, speak to the violence and abuse to which women continue to be subjected in this society. They are telling it like it is.

FIRST PRODUCTIONS OF MAJOR PLAYS BY SARAH DANIELS

Venues are in London unless stated.
Ma's Flesh is Grass, Crucible Studio Theatre, Sheffield (1981)
Ripen Our Darkness, Royal Court Theatre Upstairs (1981)
The Devil's Gateway, Royal Court Theatre Upstairs (1983)
Masterpieces, Manchester Royal Exchange, Manchester (1983)
Byrthrite, Royal Court Theatre (1986)
Neaptide, Cottesloe, Royal National Theatre (1986)
The Gut Girls, Albany Empire (1988)
Head-Rot Holiday, Clean Break Theatre Company, touring (1992)
The Madness of Esme and Shaz, Royal Theatre Upstairs (1994)
Blow Your House Down (based on the novel by Pat Barker) Live Theatre, Newcastle-upon-Tyne (1995)

NOTES

1 Sarah Daniels, Introduction, *Plays 1* (London: Methuen, 1991), pp. x–xi.
2 This was the topic of Pat Barker's novel *Blow Your House Down* (London: Virago, 1984) which addressed the issue of the Yorkshire Ripper from the viewpoint of poor,

working-class women driven into prostitution through economic necessity and the inadequacies of the British welfare system. Nicole Ward Jouve in *'The Street Cleaner': The Yorkshire Ripper Case on Trial* (London: Marion Boyars, 1986) and Deborah Cameron and Elizabeth Frazer in *The Lust to Kill: A Feminist Investigation of Sexual Murder* (New York: New York University Press, 1987) have also explored this issue.

3 This period saw the publication, increasingly slowed down, of the Methuen *Plays By Women* series, the last two volumes of which were edited by Annie Castledine, one of Britain's foremost women theatre directors, who has also directed Daniels's *The Devil's Gateway*.

4 *Tissue* was originally published in 1982 in the first volume of Methuen's *Plays by Women* series (see n. 3), and, subsequently, along with *Salonika, Real Estate,* and *Golden Girls* has been anthologised in *Louise Page: Plays One* (London: Methuen, 1990). Although a prominent dramatist in the 1980s, Page's writing career has since involved her more in radio and television.

5 Sir K. Cork *et al., Theatre is for All: The Report of the Enquiry into Professional Theatre in England* (London: Arts Council, 1986), p. 26, sections 83 and 84.

6 Cork (*ibid.*) detailed the decline in funding for theatre over fifteen years (to 1986), but noted steady increases for the National Theatre and the Royal Shakespeare Company, neither of whom have a history of promoting women's work, from 30% of the total Arts Council Drama allocation in 1970–1 to 47% in 1985–6 (p. 8). In contrast, touring drama, the arena in which most women's theatre functions, had seen a decrease in funding support of 46% (p. 9).

7 See *ibid.*, pp. 8–13, chapter 3, and p. 44.

8 *Housewife* was the title of Ann Oakley's pioneering book of qualitative research on the situation of housewives in Britain (Harmondsworth: Penguin, 1974). For a recent lesbian-feminist representation of the subject see Jo VanEvery's *Heterosexual Women Changing Families: Refusing to be a 'Wife'!* (London: Taylor and Francis, 1995).

9 Friedan was subsequently criticised by writers like bell hooks (*Feminist Theory,* Boston, MA: South End Press, 1984) and by lesbians for her focus on white, middle-class housewives as the norm of what constitutes the oppressed.

10 One exception here is the work of the British performer Bobby Baker whose shows have tended to focus on the daily experiences of housewives.

11 A good example of this occurs in sc. 7 in which Mary visits her daughter Anna and discusses her marriage with her. Mary makes the point that lesbianism is not the solution to patriarchy for all women and says, 'Some things you can't change' (*Plays 1,* p. 46). She has difficulty accepting that her thirty years of married life have been a waste and points out that Anna is one product of that marriage.

12 I use 'symbolic order' here in the way in which Julia Kristeva describes it in *Desire in Language* (Oxford: Basil Blackwell, 1980), pp. 124–47, and suggest that Kristeva's presentation of the relationship between the symbolic and the semiotic is a useful way of analysing *Ripen Our Darkness*. Briefly, the semiotic refers to a sense of non-differentiation from the maternal and the heterogeneity, non-linearity, and multiplicity of meaning which characterises infants' pre-verbal utterances. The symbolic refers to the effects of infants' entry into language which serves to impose the law of the father through separation from the mother, now no longer unproblematically available to the child, and an order which is sequential, progressive, and bordered by rules and regulations which drive the interpretation of utterances towards a single meaning.

13 This is, in a sense, a reverse story to Marsha Norman's 'Night Mother (London: Faber, 1984) in which the daughter kills herself, with the mother unable to prevent it.

14 Italian feminist thought is the only western feminist theoretical framework which has engaged significantly with power differentials between women and advocated the use of that differential as a source of empowerment for women. Importantly, this material makes very clear – as do Daniels's plays – that women will not overcome their oppression through help from men but through each other.

15 The issue of lesbianism in all-female school settings has been the object of plays such as Lillian Hellman's *The Children's Hour*, films like *The Killing of Sister George*, numerous novels, and many critical studies.

16 A useful introduction to the different forms of violence against women both across time and in diverse cultures is Jill Radford's and Diana E. H. Russell's *Femicide: The Politics of Woman Killing* (Buckingham: Open University Press, 1992).

17 Sarah Daniels, *Plays* 2 (London: Methuen, 1994).

18 See Christine Hallett, 'Child Abuse: An Academic Overview', in Paul Kingston and Bridget Penhale (eds.) *Family Violence and The Caring Professions* (London: Macmillan, 1995).

19 This fact is under-written by Sue Lees's *Ruling Passions: Sexual Violence, Regulation and the Law* (Buckingham: Open University Press, 1997) which shows that though the number of reported sexual assaults/rapes has gone up in the last ten years, the number of convictions has gone down.

20 For a more sustained exposition of Daniels's formal strategies such as her use of song, monologues, playing with time, etc., see Tracy C. Davis, '*Extremities* and *Masterpieces*: A Feminist Paradigm of Art and Politics', in Helene Keyssar (ed.) *Feminist Theatre and Theory* (Houndsmill: Macmillan, 1996), pp. 137–54, and Christine Dymkowski, 'Breaking the Rules: The Plays of Sarah Daniels', *Theatre Review*, 5:1, 1996, pp. 63–75. The notion of realism as effect is taken from Roland Barthes's 'The Reality Effect' in his *The Rustle of Language* (Oxford: Basil Blackwell, 1986), pp. 141–8.

21 For an overview of the realism debate see Patricia R. Schroeder, 'American Drama, Feminist Discourse, and Dramatic Form: In Defense of Critical Pluralism', *Journal of Dramatic Theory and Criticism*, 7:2, Spring 1993, pp. 103–18.

22 Sue-Ellen Case, *Feminism and Theatre* (Houndsmill: Macmillan, 1988), p.124.

23 Elin Diamond, *Unmaking Mimesis* (London: Routledge, 1997), p. v.

24 Daniels begins her introduction to *Plays 1* by stating that she 'didn't set out to be a "Feminist Playwright"' (p. ix) and ends it by writing: 'I didn't set out to further the cause of Feminism. However, I am proud if some of my plays have added to its influence' (p. xii).

25 In Helene Keyssar (ed.) *Feminist Theatre and Theory* (Houndsmill: Macmillan, 1996), pp.19–34, pp. 19–20.

26 This sentence is not made explicit, but Rowena's line in the final scene, 'I am going to have a long time to think about it [women's violation by men]' (*Plays 1*, sc. 17, p. 230), suggests it.

27 See *Sister Outsider* (New York: Crossing Press, 1984), pp. 110–13.

28 bell hooks's *Feminist Theory: From Margin to Center* (Boston, MA: South End Press, 1984) is one of the best-known feminist texts to take issue with the idea of a universally shared oppression among women.

29 *The Skriker* operates predominantly through word play; *Blue Heart* is built up through the repetition, with variation, of particular scenes.

FURTHER READING

Primary sources: plays

Daniels, Sarah. *Plays 1: Ripen Our Darkness – The Devil's Gateway – Masterpieces – Neaptide – Byrthrite*. London: Methuen, 1991.
Plays 2: The Gut Girls – Beside Herself – Head-Rot Holiday – The Madness of Esme and Shaz. London: Methuen, 1994.

Secondary sources

Aston, Elaine. 'Daniels in the Lion's Den: Sarah Daniels and the British Backlash'. *Theatre Journal* 47 (1995): 393–403.
Bono, Paola, and Sandra Kemp (eds.) *Italian Feminist Thought: A Reader*. Oxford:Basil Blackwell, 1991.
Case, Sue-Ellen. *Feminism and Theatre*. Houndsmill: Macmillan, 1988.
Cork, Sir K. *et al. Theatre is for All: The Report of the Enquiry into Professional Theatre in England*. London: Arts Council, 1986.
Daniels, Sarah. 'There are Fifty-Two Per Cent of Us'. *Drama* 152 (1984): 23–4.
Interview. In Heidi Stephenson and Natasha Langridge (eds.) *Rage and Reason*. London: Methuen, 1997: 1–8.
Davis, Tracy C. '*Extremities* and *Masterpieces*: A Feminist Paradigm of Art and Politics'. In Keyssar, *Feminist Theatre and Theory*, pp. 137–54.
Diamond, Elin. 'Brechtian Theory / Feminist Theory: Toward a Gestic Feminist Criticism'. *TDR* 32.1 (Spring 1988): 82–94.
Unmaking Mimesis. London and New York: Routledge, 1997.
Dworkin, Andrea. *Pornography: Men Possessing Women*. London: Women's Press, 1991.
Life and Death. London: Virago, 1997.
Dymkowski, Christine. 'Breaking the Rules: The Plays of Sarah Daniels'. *Theatre Review* 5.1 (1996): 63–75.
Faludi, Susan. *Backlash: The Undeclared War Against Women*. London: Chatto and Windus, 1992.
Forte, Jeanie. 'Realism, Narrative, and the Feminist Playwright – A Problem of Reception'. In Keyssar, *Feminist Theatre and Theory*, pp. 19–34.
French, Marilyn. *The War Against Women*. London: Hamish Hamilton, 1992.
Haedicke, Susan C. 'Doing the Dirty Work: Gendered Versions of Working-class Women in Sarah Daniels' *The Gut Girls* and Israel Horovitz's *North Shore Fish*'. *Journal of Dramatic Theory and Criticism* 8.2 (Spring 1994): 77–88.
Hart, Lynda, and Peggy Phelan (eds.) *Acting Out: Feminist Performances*. Ann Arbor: University of Michigan Press, 1993.
Keyssar, Helene (ed.) *Feminist Theatre and Theory*. Houndsmill: Macmillan, 1996.
Milan Women's Bookstore Collective. *Sexual Difference: A Theory of Social-Symbolic Practice*. Bloomington: Indiana University Press, 1990.
Minwalla, Framji. 'Sarah Daniels: A Woman in the Moon'. *Theater* 21.3 (1990): 26–9.
Reinelt, Janelle. 'Beyond Brecht: Britain's New Feminist Drama'. *Theatre Journal* 38.2 (May 1986): 154–63.
Remnant, Mary (ed.) *Plays by Women*. Vol. vi. London: Methuen, 1987.
Schroeder, Patricia, R. 'American Drama, Feminist Discourse, and Dramatic Form: In

Defense of Critical Pluralism'. *Journal of Dramatic Theory and Criticism* 7.2 (Spring 1993): 103–18.

Stowell, Sheila. 'Rehabilitating Realism'. *Journal of Dramatic Theory and Criticism* 6.2 (Spring 1992): 81–8.

Todd, Susan (ed.) *Women and Theatre: Calling the Shots.* London: Faber, 1984.

Wandor, Michelene. *Look Back in Gender: Sexuality and the Family in Post-War British Drama.* London: Methuen, 1987.

PART 4

THE SUBJECT OF IDENTITY

Editors' note

In this fourth and final section of the volume we bring together three chapters which indicate some of the multiple concerns and directions of women's writing for theatre at the close of the 1990s. For these contributions, 'The subject of identity' seems an appropriate title because it suggests the way questions of identity continue to dominate women's writing and further indexes the postmodern emphasis on the problematic of identity: its limitations as a concept, its fluctuating and elusive formations and re-formations, and its dispersal within contemporary hybrid, nomadic, cyber experience. While the second section on 'National tensions and intersections' explored the limitations of the concept of 'British' in the light of shifting notions of location and place, here we take up the limitations of the concepts of self, home, and political certainty in the situation of contemporary writers as subjects and as subject.

Much of women's writing as discussed in this volume has been anchored in what is called 'identity politics'. Although we have charted historical shifts from an all-inclusive definition of woman to a carefully parsed articulation of difference among categories of women organised by race, class, sexuality, nationality, and sometimes religion, these identifications have also been surpassed or, to be less reductive and linear, interwoven and complicated by the questioning of subjectivity itself, its formations, positions, and articulations with other simultaneous ones. One of the perplexing issues for late 1990s feminism is the relevance of a claim to a political and artistic voice based on gender in light of the instability and inadequacy of any formal content for such an identity. 'Woman' has become what Slavoj Žižek calls a 'rigid designator' – powerful as a structural performative, serving as an empty umbrella term for various constituencies which find their meaning in a negative relationship to the founding term.[1]

Two of the chapters in this section insist on retaining an important connection to identity politics. Meenakshi Ponnuswami and Sue-Ellen Case write about black women and lesbian women respectively, and set writing by black women and lesbians in the historical context of their reception. Ponnuswami describes the conditions under which black writing has emerged from obscurity since the early sixties, pointing to women's particular difficulty in being acknowledged and produced. She also focuses on the relationship of plays by black women writers to the question of memory and roots; the difficulty of evolving hybrid identities, forged from recent immigrations and torn with conflicting desires about belonging and definition. Case writes about the history of lesbian writing in relationship to gay writing on the one hand, but also in relationship to a newly evolving global space where the dissemination of 'lesbian' is both positively related to an expanding representational set of possibilities and yet negatively connected to global markets and multinational capitalism. Again, this points to an interrogation of the term 'British' in the title of the volume.

Claire MacDonald continues this trend by replacing 'playwright' with 'theatre writer' in an effort to find the most useful terms to describe the experimental, multi-form and -genre performance work undertaken by women who are directly addressing questions of self-dispersal and unstable identity through the formal composition of their performance pieces. Creating with dance, visual materials from the fine arts, video, and music as well as words, these theatre writers join cyber artists in pushing the limits of representational forms traditionally observed in theatres. While identity issues are central in this work – indeed Deborah Levy, one of MacDonald's central examples, writes from her personal connections to Judaism and to European Africa – the post-colonial condition of exile and dispersal are most prominent. Experiments with form become a contemporary means for approaching the inadequacy of any fixed identifications and for registering the urgency in discovering post-modern avenues of agency.

Case complements both Ponnuswami and MacDonald by moving sexual identities beyond fixed boundaries into cyberspace while insisting that economic, political, and gender relations must be present in any transnational analytic. Although one can choose to 'play out' any sex/gender on the Web, the Web itself is controlled by men. While Lois Weaver moves around the world as a queer performance broker, her identity as 'American' in both its imperial and colonial connotations seems to accompany her.

In fact, the dislodging of fixed identities and unified subjectivities has peculiar consequences for women's writing now. Phyllis Nagy, a lesbian writer who sometimes writes on lesbian or gay subjects, also writes plays in which there are no lesbian or gay characters (*Never Land*, 1998) or which, like *The Strip* (1995), may mix various sexualities, but still prompt lesbian critic Sarah Freeman to write, 'This is not lesbian theatre, nor is it a lesbian play.'[2] Sarah Kane, an important young writer who had a number of controversial plays produced at the Royal Court (see our main introduction to the volume), was another example of someone who did not easily fit categories. She was a woman, but the extreme violence and brutal representations of her plays *Blasted, Cleansed,* and, most recently, *Crave* aligned her more with the political writing of Edward Bond than with any of the established political women writers of the senior generation such as Caryl Churchill or Timberlake Wertenbaker.

When women said they did not want to be thought of as 'women writers' in the 1970s and 1980s, this usually bespoke a tendency towards conservatism or at the very least an unwillingness to be aligned with the political project of feminism. At the end of the 1990s, however, in a very different historical moment, it is sometimes difficult to know what a 'woman writer' might mean. If it does not signal any specific thematics or dramaturgy, or commitment to particular theatrical processes (e.g. collectivisation or women-controlled companies), then what exactly does it entail? If Jackie Kay is both a lesbian and a black writer, and, as here, we discuss her primarily in terms of colour, do we not reify one identity category while ignoring the other? If new young writers are beginning to create work which does not fit previous categories, how are we to engage that work with fresh categories and yet not lose sight of the fact that it comes from writers who are, in fact, women?

For this *Companion* volume, we have elected to call attention to the contemporary contradictions facing a critical enterprise such as ours, and to raise the possibility that, in the future, such grouping by nationalities, gender, sexualities, and race may become increasingly anachronistic or futile. At the same time, a deep conviction that the twentieth century can be and must be illuminated with reference to these same identity categories has also informed our purposes and goals. In any case, it does seem clear that talented, inspired women will continue to make performances in the new century, while their motivations, modes of delivery, and material practices may transform themselves beyond our current conceptual and linguistic imaginings.

NOTES

1 Slavoj Žižek, *The Sublime Object of Ideology* (London and New York: Verso, 1989), p. 99.
2 Sandra Freeman, *Putting Your Daughters On the Stage: Lesbian Theatre from the 1970s to the 1990s* (London and Washington: Cassell, 1997), p.154.

13

MEENAKSHI PONNUSWAMI

Small island people: black British women playwrights

> I've been puzzled by the fact that young black people in London today are marginalized, fragmented, unenfranchised, disadvantaged and dispersed. And yet, they look as if they own the territory. Somehow, they too, in spite of everything, are centred, in place: without much material support, it's true, but nevertheless they occupy a new kind of space at the centre.   Stuart Hall, 'Minimal Selves,' 1987[1]

Historians of post-war British theatre have typically taken as their starting-point the pivotal 1956, the year of the Suez Canal fiasco, the Soviet invasion of Hungary, the formation of the British New Left, and the first performance of John Osborne's *Look Back in Anger*. Black performers had been a presence on radio and television as early as the 1930s, but 1956 was likewise a critical moment for the emergence of a distinct black British theatre; it was in this year that John Elliott's television docu-drama about Caribbean immigrants, *A Man from the Sun*, was performed on BBC, that Errol John wrote *Moon on a Rainbow Shawl*,[2] and, critically, that Pearl and Edric Connor established the Edric Connor Agency to represent black artists in theatre, radio, and television. During the next thirty years, largely ignored by the rapidly expanding fringe movement and its sponsors and critics, black artists in the theatre sought to reflect the lives and aspirations of post-colonial immigrant communities whose populations in Britain had increased dramatically in the aftermath of the war and the dissolution of the British empire.[3] The years from 1956 through to 1963 witnessed a burgeoning of work for black actors, especially on the stage, and the performance of a series of plays by black writers, including Errol John, Wole Soyinka, and Barry Reckord. A number of amateur drama clubs such as the West Indian Students' Drama Group channelled the talents of younger artists.[4]

A good number of plays by black men were being produced by the end of the 1960s, mainly at lunchtime theatres and the Royal Court, establishing what may be said to constitute a 'first wave' of black and black British theatre in post-war Britain – Wole Soyinka, Mustapha Matura, Derek Walcott, Barry Reckord, and Caryl Phillips. Matura and such American playwrights as Ed Bullins and Amiri

Baraka, then known as LeRoi Jones, were staple features of Inter-Action's lunch-time theatres. By 1970, when the Institute for Contemporary Arts (ICA) conducted a Black Power season, there was enough momentum to produce the Black Theatre of Brixton.[5]

Although black women playwrights remained invisible until the 1970s, a number of women played crucial infrastructural roles in shaping black British performance arts during the earlier years. Pearl Connor, cited by many artists of the period as a pioneer and inspiration, ran the Edric Connor Agency (later the Afro Asian Caribbean Agency) from 1958 until 1974, and founded the Negro Theatre Workshop in 1963. Connor had studied law and was one of the first to professionalise the black British presence in the arts and to agitate against requirements for Equity membership, which discriminated against black artists (Pines, *Black and White*, pp. 35–7). Women typically worked as actors and singers on stage, radio, and television, but many also participated in early efforts to organise theatre companies. Pauline Henriques was instrumental in forming the *Anna Lucasta* understudies' company in 1947–8, and Carmen Munroe worked with the West Indian Students' Drama Group in the 1950s. Munroe later became one of the co-founders of Talawa, directed the 1987 British première of Derek Walcott's *Remembrance*, and played Shirley in the Channel 4 sitcom *Desmond's* (pp. 25–32 and pp. 56–64). Black theatre in the 1970s and 1980s continued to be buttressed by women: Yvonne Brewster collaborated with three other women – Carmen Munroe, Mona Hammond, and Inigo Espejel – to form Talawa in 1985;[6] Elizabeth Clarke was Associate Director and Dramaturge at the Temba Theatre Company. Talawa did not produce a play by a woman playwright until 1991 but worked 'from a female perspective' from its inception.[7]

Theatre of Black Women, 'Britain's first Black Women's Theatre Company', was founded in 1982 by Patricia Hilarie, Paulette Randall, and Bernadine Evaristo.[8] This was, interestingly, the same year that Yvonne Brewster became the first black woman drama officer in the Arts Council, a position she would hold for two years. The Theatre of Black Women was active for seven years, producing such plays as Jackie Kay's *Chiaroscuro* (1986) and Ruth Harris's *The Cripple* (1987), until funding was withdrawn by the Greater London Arts Council in 1989. The mid-1980s were especially active years: in 1983, Jacqueline Rudet founded Imani-Faith, another theatre group 'for and by black women'; the Black Mime Theatre was established in 1984; also in 1984, the Black Theatre Co-operative was awarded its first annual grant, of £62,000; and, in 1985, Talawa was founded with a GLC grant of 'eighty five or ninety thousand pounds'. Unsurprisingly, the first published collections of black British plays (which I discuss below) appeared in 1987 and 1989. The late 1980s and early 1990s saw the emergence of several Asian groups as well as another generation of black theatre companies. The Asian Co-operative Theatre was created in 1987;

Tamasha, a women's theatre group, in 1989; and Kali Theatre Company, also a women's group, in 1991. In the early 1990s, the Black Mime Theatre assembled a Women's Troop (Goodman' *Contemporary Feminist Theatres*, pp. 166–74), and a group of black women comedians was formed: BiBi Crew. Plays by black women began to be produced in significant numbers: Rudet's *Basin* and Maria Oshodi's *The 'S' Bend* in 1985; Kay's *Chiaroscuro* in 1986; Winsome Pinnock's *Leave Taking* and three plays by Theatre of Black Women in 1987 (the latter shortly before the company was denied funding); Oshodi's *Blood, Sweat and Fears* in 1988; Pinnock's *A Hero's Welcome* and *A Rock in Water* in 1989 (to name only a few of the best-known plays).[9]

A key lesson of this history is the importance of having a critical mass of performance texts. It does seem clear, for instance, that the survival of black theatre in the early 1970s was enabled by the presence of playwrights, even if they were often imported from the Caribbean and the United States. Joan Hooley, who abandoned theatre after the experience of the 'barren years' of the early 1960s and began writing for television, articulates the need for the playwright succinctly: 'I'm now writing, because we need to take hold of things', she stated in an early 1990s interview; 'I can make a statement and I'm able to suggest things to the media, and they have to do my work' (Pines, *Black and White*, p. 101). This strategy worked well for Hooley, who went on to write for the popular sitcom *Desmond's*, but, well into the 1980s, the Theatre of Black Women was one of very few groups to provide opportunities for aspiring women playwrights.

In 1987, Methuen published a volume of black British plays, followed two years later by a second volume. Edited by Yvonne Brewster, both volumes included scripts by women playwrights – Maria Oshodi, Winsome Pinnock, Jacqueline Rudet, all of whom, significantly, may now be described as leading figures among black women dramatists. These important collections seem to have exerted a persuasive influence on the editors of some collections of contemporary British drama, including publisher Nick Hern's *First Run* series and Methuen's 'identity politics' volumes of plays by women and gay and lesbian writers. In 1993, the London-based Aurora Metro Press published *Six Plays by Black and Asian Women Writers*, edited by Kadija George, and Brewster edited a third Methuen volume in 1995. Even as these volumes saw print, however, Joan-Ann Maynard of the Black Theatre Co-Op noted at the 1994 Black Theatre in Higher Education Conference that black British plays are unlikely to be published even when they 'have received critical acclaim'; 'unlike the American and Caribbean situation, . . . [t]here is no natural progression from production to text as is often the case with mainstream white playwrights'.[10]

Despite the scarcity of printed materials, recent scholarly discussions of theatre by black British women have been relatively conscientious and varied, if few in number.[11] The most comprehensive studies have been offered by Lizbeth

Goodman (*Contemporary Feminist Theatres*) and Elaine Aston (*Introduction*), each of whom includes a chapter on black theatre in a book-length study of feminism and theatre. Both scholars follow the now common practice of internationalising the study of feminist and women's theatre, surveying a trans-Atlantic continuum of performance art within a theoretical and contextual apparatus based in contemporary Anglo-American feminism. This apparatus compels them to engage in a more inclusive critical practice and at the same time to acknowledge the difficulties confronted by feminists who negotiate the boundaries between black art and white criticism (Aston, *Introduction*, pp. 79–80; Goodman, *Contemporary Feminist Theatres*, pp. 148–50).[12] Goodman is more interested in the tectonics of black and white feminisms than in racial and ethnic identity-formations, and therefore focuses broadly on the performance art of 'women of West Indian and South African descent whose work has been published in English and/or performed in England and North America' (case studies on Sistren, Djanet Sears, and Gcina Mhlophe alongside discussions of such British groups as Theatre of Black Women, Talawa, and Black Mime Theatre's Women's Troop). Aston's study is, as she puts it, 'rooted in a British context', and provides a particularly thoughtful review of the attempts by largely white women's theatre groups to pursue multi-racial policies, as well as an introduction to the work of Brewster, Rudet, Grace Nichols, and Theatre of Black Women.

A different approach is suggested by May Joseph's recent essay, 'Borders Outside the State: Black British Women and the Limits of Citizenship', which considers the staging of the immigrant body in relation to the dilemmas of national belonging, specifically the contradictions posed by the collision of common law and an authoritarian state. Joseph's widely interdisciplinary study includes the concerns raised in black British cultural studies (by Hazel Carby, Paul Gilroy, and Pratibha Parmar), as well as the work of trans-Atlantic feminism, race theory, and legal studies. A comparable approach is taken by the 1995 collection edited by Catherine Ugwu, *Let's Get It On: The Politics of Black Performance*, which I discuss below.[13]

The review above is a small and unfinished attempt to compensate for the lamentable silencing of black voices in discussions of post-war British theatre. The importance of record-keeping is clearly evident in the impact upon recent scholarship of such meticulous surveys of white British theatres as Catherine Itzin's *Stages in the Revolution*, John Bull's *Contemporary British Theatre*, and Michelene Wandor's *Carry On, Understudies* – works which had little to say about contemporary literary or performance theory but which nevertheless defined the field by the act of compilation. In spite of the presence of active theatre companies and, largely thanks to television and film, significant numbers of performers, the quantity of published information about black British theatre is still minimal, and critical attention has, as a consequence, been sporadic. Indeed, the absence of a critical infrastructure is in part responsible for the disappearance of groups which were active only a few years ago.[14] What also need further study at this point are the specific conditions of production of black British theatre and its complex historical contexts: the relationship of post-war British multiculturalism to the welfare state, to the emergence of state subsidies for the arts, and to the development of the vast fringe theatre movement. Such research would allow studies of theatre and performance the level of theorisation which has been possible in relation to film, music, and popular culture.[15] Although this chapter cannot fill the wide gaps, I will preface my analysis of a specific theme, retrieval and nostalgia, with a discussion of concerns which are generally relevant to the form and politics of the theatre of black British women: the political milieu of the mid-1980s, the racial politics of subsidy, and the generational shifts identified by younger artists of the period.

The political context: the mid-1980s

It was, undeniably, grass-roots activism which fuelled the activist goals and ideological imperatives of the post-Brixton generation of artists. This was particularly so of women, many of whom still define the political and community work of the 1970s and 1980s as the signal moment of their own politicisation. Long before the Brixton uprisings, women's groups which had been active in the Black Power movements of the 1970s began to organise themselves around gender-specific concerns; the first of many feminist organisations, the Black Women's Group, was formed as early as 1973. OWAAD, the important but short-lived Organisation of Women of Asian and African Descent, was formed in 1978 (and disbanded by 1983). In 1984, the inspirational volume 'Many Voices, One Chant' brought together black feminist theorists and activists in a resounding critique of white feminism and an affirmation of ten years of political activity; in 1985, the influential public history *The Heart of the Race* listed no fewer than twenty fixed women's groups, many with private addresses and newsletters.[16]

It has been argued that increased activity in black arts in the mid-to-late 1980s was related to increased state funding for 'ethnic' social programmes which followed the urban uprisings of 1980 and 1981 and the subsequent recommendations of the 1982–3 Scarman Report on Brixton. The relationship between the theatre, political activism, and the state is a particularly important issue for any analysis of post-war British theatre, black or white; indeed, the rapid expansion of *all* theatrical activity during the 1960s and 1970s can be directly linked to state funding, which in turn may be seen as one part of the state's more-or-less planned efforts in the post-war era to contain the radicalism threatened by the social restructuring experienced during the war. A central debate for many of the fringe groups of the period, especially those on the Left, was whether to accept subsidies and perform to larger audiences (thereby risking the possibility of complicity with the state and the arts elite) or to refuse subsidy and perform only among the true folk (risking permanent ghettoisation and the possibility of never finding an audience).

The state's cultivation of black arts in the aftermath of Brixton did pose some problems. Juliet Jarrett, for example, has argued that the effect of such programmes was to create a handful of poorly funded and marginalised spaces for black artists; she cites the example of Lubaina Himid, curator of 'The Thin Black Line', the ICA's mid-1980s exhibition of works by black women, who wrote: 'The Greater London Council threatened to withdraw its considerable funding to the ICA if something black did not appear that financial year.'[17] As early as 1987, Pratibha Parmar despaired that the 'assumption of shared subjectivities' which had fired black feminisms a few years earlier had somehow 'led to a political practice which employs a language of "authentic subjective experience"': 'many women have retreated into ghettoised lifestyle "politics" and find themselves unable to move beyond personal and individual experience'.[18] Sociologist Amina Mama suggested further that the 'state-funded projects' (which, as she puts it, 'gained ascendance under the contradictory conditions of Thatcherism and municipal socialism') dispersed the radical energies of the earlier grass-roots black British feminisms precisely because such projects were 'constituted along . . . ethnically specific lines': 'a growing focus on identity and a new competitive cultural politics', argues Mama, 'replaced the 1970s / early 1980s notions of black unity and wider anti-imperialist and black liberation struggles'.[19] In other words, subsidy was able to divide and rule by encouraging the development of inward-looking groups whose interests were obliged to centre on questions of selfhood and identity rather than political coalition.

Of course, dilemmas about whether to accept state funding can only vex those who have access to subsidy in the first place, and this was, as we have seen, rarely the case for black British theatres. In any case, although some groups do seem to have coalesced along specific ethnic axes, it is not at all clear that subsidy entailed political compromise or ethnocentric wrangling. Moreover, as May Joseph argues, the declaration of 'positionality' can be a means for black British women to contest the state's colonising of immigrant women's bodies, given the need for an 'emergent' and repressed citizenry – 'bodies "outside the state"' – to demand political participation within a state which at once controls and denies such participation. In such a context, writes Joseph, the announcement of one's location 'implies locating oneself as a subject already overdetermined by various contingent narratives' (p. 205). Implicit in this analysis is the suggestion that identity politics do not repudiate the anti-imperialist and global political imperatives of the mid-1980s; rather, the theatre produced by that political moment performs 'new kinds of multicultural citizenship' ('Borders', p. 199). The ideological legacy of the community activism of the mid-1980s, which drew attention to the need for new articulations of race, gender, and citizenship, is clearly discernible in this performance.

I would suggest that the most explicit manifestation of the kind of identity politics criticised by Parmar and Mama is in youth-oriented theatre initiatives, which appear to be the specific by-products of institutionalised multiculturalism in the educational sector.[20] Even here, however, in plays as varied as Jackie Kay's *Twice Over*, Zindika's *Paper and Stone*, Trish Cooke's *Running Dream*, and Winsome Pinnock's *A Rock in Water*, we find little evidence of what Mama calls the 'new competitive cultural politics'.[21] Rather, the youth plays quietly cross borders of age, class, language, ethnicity, and sexuality, moving insistently towards compromise and reconciliation.[22] Inevitably, some of the youth plays are cautionary tales directed at young women, warning of the dangers of sex and impertinence, but even such plays direct attention to the ways in which private and historical thresholds invariably merge for the new generation. A case in point is Zindika's *Paper and Stone*, a didactic play addressed to young women who try to break away from the stranglehold of their (stereotypically imagined) conservative immigrant parents. Offering grim glimpses into life beyond the nest – a nightmare of abandoned, exploited women – the play upholds a value-system in which a combination of hard work, higher education, and personal modesty are represented as safeguards against the depravity of the modern. However, Zindika's point is that even the most intimate or private moments of self-realisation are, for young black people, trapped in history: as a black girl eagerly takes her 'first step towards womanhood', the play suggests, she also steps towards the chaos of history, where she will eventually and inevitably 'have to pay the price of stolen power, stolen lands, stolen Nations' (*Paper and Stone*, p. 30).

New ethnicities

The youth plays also offer particularly interesting insights into the ways in which the political imperatives of the mid-1980s were translated by first-generation black Britons, and therefore into the whole dialectic of tradition and modernity which forms the basis for new articulations of ethnicity. For the most part, the theatre of black British women appeared to remain on the fringes of youth culture, choosing not to participate in the more anarchist subcultural strains of the late 1980s and 1990s. The same decade also witnessed an outpouring of creative work in black film and live arts. This boundary- and text-defying work has been admirably documented in Kobena Mercer's *Welcome to the Jungle* and Ugwu's path-breaking collection, *Let's Get It On*, which offer a historicised critical context for the discussion of contemporary black performance art. Both

Ugwu and Mercer identify the mid-1980s as a turning-point for a new generation of artists, not only the products of a moment of extraordinary cultural flux
but also the highly self-conscious agents of that change. 'This moment', writes
Mercer (himself a key voice of the generation which came of age in the 1980s),
'was registered as a "break" which widened aesthetic diversity within the expressive codes of diaspora culture' (*Welcome to the Jungle*, p. 19). Resisting any
notion of a 'homogenous essentialised black culture', and affirming a hybrid-
ised, post-modern, 'unruly polyvocality' as its transformational goal as much as
oppositional stance (Ugwu, *Let's Get it On*, p. 54), this self-proclaimed generation sought new artistic forms and conceptual topographies.

As Stuart Hall put it in his important 1988 essay 'New Ethnicities', it became
necessary 'to retheorize the concept of "difference"'.[23] At stake was, naturally,
the configuration of entrenched notions about authentic racial and national
affinities, but the newer voices sought also to rethink the liberal-pluralist politics
of institutionalised multiculturalism, and, at the same time and perhaps more
importantly, to examine the limits of post-modernism itself. Evelyn Reid, while
calling for a 'move to an ethnicity which enables syncretism', observes that such
a politics also 'presents a dilemma': 'how to maintain solidarity around a politics that is endlessly defining and redefining its position' (pp. 282–3). The resolution to that problem is, according to Mercer, Ugwu, Hall, and Reid, suggested
by the particular kind of politicised, diasporic post-modernism of the art of the
mid-1980s.

But, by contrast, the theatre of black British women has tended to develop
realist plots with clearly defined structures of conflict and resolution and an
emphasis on the private and domestic; even in such experimental pieces as Jackie
Kay's *Chiaroscuro* or Bonnie Greer's *Munda Negra*, non-mimetic segments are
invariably contextualised by realist scenes.[24] Such formal choices seem at first
sight to signal a repudiation of post-modernism generally as well as of the
expressive practices of youth sub-cultures, as it could be argued that realism
demands not only a narrower or more rigid conception of 'character' than is
enabled by the post-modern, but also a political affiliation with 'identity politics'
which analysts such as Parmar and Mama accused of having undermined a more
progressive feminist politics.

However, as my readings below seek to demonstrate, the cultural contexts
invoked by the plays are almost always diasporic and historicised, committed to
a politics of inclusivity across racial and national lines. This is particularly true
of history and memory plays, where realism does not always preclude a subversion of epistemological categories: when fractured and subjective memories are
placed in the wider context of immigrant and racial history, a deconstruction of
the processes of displacement, settlement, and cultural mutation seems inevitably to follow. In this respect, the performance of retrieval – and more specifically

the invocation of diasporic histories – allows otherwise private rites of passage to assume a wider significance in the political coming-of-age of new citizens.

Performing retrieval

watch her move
whom centuries have dealt with in
anecdotes

Angela McNish, in Bryan, Dadzie, and Scafe,
The Heart of the Race, p. 182.

My analysis of acts of retrieval and the performance of nostalgia centres on two history plays: Jackie Kay's *Chiaroscuro* and Winsome Pinnock's *A Hero's Welcome*. It is significant that few history plays by black British women set out to write biographies of famous persons.[25] Indeed, the plays do not overtly seem to intervene in received history, to correct the record, or reclaim the past, as 'alternative' histories on the British stage typically do; rather, they seem to begin with the recognition that histories are necessarily incomplete and incorrect, that traditions are always invented, and that black subjectivity has always evolved in conflict with the master-narratives of history. History plays by black women produce counter-narratives in which longings for the past become a means to express the inescapable crises which conflicting modernities impose upon black womanhood. The conflict between mutually exclusive configurations of modernity consumes the characters in these plays, who are compelled either to retreat into imagined histories (Leonora in Zindika's play *Leonora's Dance*), or to reinvent themselves as the agents of emerging worlds (Maeve and Evaki in Kay's *Twice Over*).[26]

It is unsurprising, then, that so many plays seek the apparent, relative safety of domestic spaces, the 'soft secret place' (Kay, *Twice Over*, p. 145) of enclosed communities and private memories, in order to examine circumstances which threaten isolation, exile, and insanity. It is precisely this kind of exploration that we find in many of the plays written from the mid-1980s onwards: the postcolonial retrieval of absolutist cultural affinities denied by slavery and colonialism; the performance of a different kind of black post-modernity which, ironically, denies such affinities; the act of remembrance as a specifically feminist performance; the relationship of immigrant nostalgia to the celebration of the creolised and trans-cultural.

Jackie Kay, Chiaroscuro *(1986)*

The evolution of the script of Jackie Kay's *Chiaroscuro* points to a recurring issue in the play: the difficulty of assigning definitive names and titles when one speaks from the borderlands of multicultural citizenship (the light-and-shadow interplay signified by the title). Originally commissioned by Theatre of Black Women as a short performance piece, the play received a reading at a Gay Sweatshop festival before being workshopped and produced by Theatre of Black Women. Kay revised the play significantly for publication, and the final version was published in *Lesbian Plays* in 1987. Unsurprisingly, the play is about placement, or as Kay puts it, about 'how . . . we assert our names'. Its four characters narrate their collective histories in the Brechtian epic sense of performing in the past tense, which Kay calls 'an elaborate déjà vu'. As each woman comes to terms with the mystery of her marking, she must not only 'tell the story of her own name' but also search for another name: 'She is in flux, reassessing her identity, travelling back into memory and forward into possibility' (p. 82).

The open, third space of *Chiaroscuro* thus embodies the new black Britain, which 'crept in from the margins of postimperial Britain', as Mercer (quoting Gramsci) puts it, to 'open up new ways of seeing, and understanding, the peculiarities of living in the twilight of an historic interregnum in which "the old is dying and the new cannot be born"'. Mercer identifies Kay as one of the new generation of black Britons 'who came to voice in the 1980s' and whose 'presence has critically transformed the culture', by 'seizing opportunities in the gaps and fissures arising from . . . the coincidence between the postcolonial and the postmodern' (*Welcome to the Jungle*, p. 2). What is particularly significant about this characterisation is the affirmation with which the past is negotiated; in Kay's play, the scars of the past can be retrieved without rancour and, with relatively little pain, can be reconsigned to memory. Although *Chiaroscuro* acknowledges that history has been responsible for imposing the fixity of names and for seeking to lock polymorphic and roaming subjectivities, the past is also seen to be an object of desire, a space which will allow an escape from the chaos of forgotten names and histories which marks the women's emergence into modernity.

However, the play insists that nostalgia be restrained: the act of retrieving the women's personal and racial histories is sentimentalised in the opening scene of the play, but the icons of this past are soon dropped 'reluctantly' into the memory chest, into which the women peer as if it were 'a wishing well' (Act I, p. 61). It is also significant that the desire to retrieve is focused on an imagined but fixed homeland. 'The country of origin', in Yomi's immigrant song, is represented as 'the place . . . where roots still grow', 'the place which might attach itself / to you / like a belonging' (Act I, p. 63). This, I would argue, is *not* the hybrid space which Mercer describes as constituting the 'common home' of the new generation. That common space is negotiated slowly and painfully in the later scenes of the play, as the young lesbian couple's fear of ostracism and solitude, and Aisha's fear of 'yearning for that other woman', confront Yomi's homophobia and latent cultural chauvinism. Although the common home is discovered in the here and now, albeit in a space which is not allowed to be England, the past is still cherished as a motherland, and the play concludes as it opens, with the radical feminist gesture of the women naming themselves in the images of their grandmothers.[27]

Kay's 1988 youth play *Twice Over* similarly investigates the difficulties of retrieval and the inevitable fears confronting those who are determined to unmask the past. Also a play about grandmothers, the play reverses the standard coming-out narrative when young Evaki discovers that her newly dead grandmother was a lesbian. *Twice Over*, however, is far more cheerful than *Chiaroscuro* about the promises of the new future – a festival of queer grannies and multi-racial families – and far less nostalgic about the memories which must be put away. The key difference lies in the plays' attitudes towards the need for authenticity: *Twice Over* is able to achieve its sense of the future as a carnival only by erasing racial and cultural specificity, whereas *Chiaroscuro* explores the extent to which the quest for authenticity (let alone the achievement) nurtures and protects, at the same time that the desire for such rootedness can disable communication altogether.

Winsome Pinnock, A Hero's Welcome (1989)

Like Kay, Pinnock belongs to the generation of black artists who were born and/or raised in Britain and came of age in the mid-1980s. However, *A Hero's Welcome*, Pinnock's first play, marks itself as a 'Caribbean' text: it is set 'somewhere in the West Indies' in 1947 and, as Brewster has noted, modelled after the 'traditional West Indian yard play'.[28] The play's meticulous realism is off-set by an intensely lyrical and melancholy subtext which is reminiscent of Errol John's *Moon on a Rainbow Shawl* – and indeed both plays retrieve the memories of the Caribbean, of the yard, of an irretrievable homeland, with the sharp poignancy of exile rather than immigrant discourse.

In Pinnock's play, this melancholy never quite develops into tragedy, although the play suggests that Len, the homecoming hero of its title – the true subaltern, returning after the war to cheering crowds – has been defeated by the very 'Home Country' for which he had gone to war. Len returns politicised and ready to 'fight for freedom', an emerging idealistic nationalism which is never allowed full expression in the play but which forms a moral core, juxtaposed against the materialism of the many who leave for England every day. As the play unfolds, so do the recruitment posters from the Home Country, luring young workers to the land of plenty, destroying Len's hopes for the future.

The play sentimentalises Len but remains neutral about the women's decision to emigrate. The options for young women are seen to be limited, given that marriage offers the only real opportunity for financial stability. The choice of partners is not promising: Len's bookish patriotism is marked by a degree of preachiness and asceticism, and the only alternatives are the irresponsible Stanley and a lecherous adulterer. At the same time, *A Hero's Welcome* enacts a longing for the abandoned homeland, in much the same way that *Chiaroscuro* had wistfully turned to an imagined, feminised community in search of a way to repudiate the crisis of post-modernity. Pinnock, like Kay, reminds us that the desire for homecoming is always contingent and the homeland itself incompletely remembered. We discover by the end of the play that Len had never actually committed the acts for which he was hailed as a hero: 'When I come back everybody was treating me like a hero', he explains; 'I couldn't disappoint them' (Act II, sc. 4, p. 54). His confession precipitates no crisis, because no national mythologies have been allowed to be founded upon the remembrance of his deed. The homeland thus remains intact, in spite of losing its young people to England and its heroes to ordinary life.

As an important consequence of the anti-climactic nature of Len's admission and his denial of heroism, the play suggests that nation-building and the search for heroes are masculinist fantasies. In both *Chiaroscuro* and *A Hero's Welcome*, the feminist retrieval of history is seen to contest the colonising of black women's bodies by patriarchy, capitalism, heterosexism, and the nation-state. The new history is indeed hybrid and decentred – post-modern, post-colonial, even post-national. As Hall argues, 'the process of *diasporization*' entailed by the new cultural politics means, on the one hand, that the art of the mid-1980s generation is energetically attentive to its 'rich cultural roots', but, on the other, that 'the relation of this cultural politics to the past' is elaborately intertextual:

> It is . . . complexly mediated and transformed by memory, fantasy, and desire . . . There can, therefore, be no simple 'return' or 'recovery' of the ancestral past which is not reexperienced through the categories of the present: no base for creative enunciation in a simple reproduction of traditional forms which are not transformed by the technologies and the identities of the present.
>
> (Hall, 'New Ethnicities', p. 170)

Because such a politics often finds expression in plays which depict post-colonial negotiations as they take place within families and small communities of women (a function, I would argue, of theatrical convention on the British fringe as much as a content-related choice of form), the material processes of that history seem to be buried even when historical questions of exile, belonging, or citizenship are at stake. Nevertheless, as my readings have tried to suggest, private experiences and memories filter an anxious desire for community; the search is always for an appropriate feminist way to encounter the terror of the public sphere. The closed spaces of rooms or houses are most often the setting for plays in which agoraphobia is a dominant character-note, as in Zindika's eccentric and lovely *Leonora's Dance*, Cooke's *Running Dream*, and Pinnock's *Leave Taking* and

Talking in Tongues.[29] These plays introduce a cautionary note, suggesting that the new black subjectivities are also tentative and hesitant in their reclaiming of the past, always alert to the rich irony of trading one small island home for another: 'lovesick with desire for the place you going to', as Len puts it, 'and heartbroken for the place you leave behind' (Pinnock, *A Hero's Welcome*, Act II, sc. 4, p.54).

CHRONOLOGY

1956 Pearl and Edric Connor establish the Edric Connor Agency, later the Afro Asian Caribbean Agency.

1957 Errol John's *Moon on a Rainbow Shawl* wins the *Observer* play award.

1963 Pearl Connor establishes the Negro Theatre Workshop.

1979 The Black Theatre Co-operative founded.

1981 *Coping*, by Patricia Hilarie, Paulette Randall, and Bernadine Evaristo, directed by Yvonne Brewster.

1982 Yvonne Brewster becomes the first black woman drama officer in the Arts Council. Holds position for two years.

1982 Theatre of Black Women, 'Britain's first black Women's Theatre Company', founded by Patricia Hilarie, Paulette Randall, and Bernadine Evaristo.

1983 Jacqueline Rudet founds Imani-Faith, a group 'for and by black women'.

1983 Theatre of Black Women, *Silhouette*.

1984 Theatre of Black Women, *Pyeyuca*.

1985 Yvonne Brewster, Carmen Munroe, Mona Hammond, and Inigo Espejel found the Talawa Theatre company.

1985 Jacqueline Rudet, *Basin*: Royal Court, Theatre Upstairs, London.

1986 Jackie Kay, *Chiaroscuro*: Theatre of Black Women, Soho Poly, London.

1987 Asian Co-operative Theatre's last production, *Jawaani* (by Asian women).

1987 The Theatre of Black Women, three productions: *Miss Quashi and The Tiger's Tail* by Gabriela and Jean Pearse; Ruth Harris, *The Cripple*; and *The Children*, also by Harris, the company's tenth production.

1987 Winsome Pinnock, *Leave Taking*: Liverpool Playhouse Studio.

1988 Jackie Kay, *Twice Over*: Gay Sweatshop, Drill Hall Arts Centre, London.

1988 Theatre of Black Women disbands when Arts Council funding is refused.

1988 Maria Oshodi, *Blood, Sweat and Fears*: Battersea Arts Centre, London.

1989 Tamasha Theatre Company, set up 'by a women's collective' 'to bring Indian contemporary drama to the British stage'.

1989 Winsome Pinnock, *A Hero's Welcome*: Royal Court, Theatre Upstairs, London.

1989 Winsome Pinnock, *A Rock in Water*: Royal Court, Theatre Upstairs, London.

1990s BiBi Crew: 'a comedy company highlighting Black women's experiences'.

1990 Black Mime Theatre's Women's Troop established. First play, *Mothers*.

1990 Zindika, *Paper and Stone*: Black Theatre Co-operative, Lyric Theatre, Hammersmith.

1991 Talawa moves to the Jeanetta Cochrane Theatre, which allows the company to begin producing three plays per year.

1991 Kali Theatre Company established.

1991 Winsome Pinnock, *Talking in Tongues*: Royal Court, Theatre Upstairs, London.

1992 Theatre Centre's *The Write Stuff*, 'a new writing initiative for Black writers'; 1992 programme for women writers.

1992 Zindika, *Leonora's Dance*. Public reading at 1992 Wordplay festival.

1993 Trish Cooke, *Running Dream*: Theatre Royal, Stratford East, London.

NOTES

My thanks to Sarah Morris and Linda Fitzsimmons at the University of Bristol's Women's Theatre Collection for helping me to locate several unpublished scripts. Warm thanks also to Catherine Ugwu and Lois Keidan for generously contributing information, insights, and lunch; to Yvonne Brewster for her thought-provoking correspondence; and to May Joseph, whose work first sparked my interest in this material and who has unsparingly shared her knowledge and time. The first version of this chapter was presented at the annual conference of the Association of Theatre in Higher Education (Chicago, 1997).

The phrase 'small island people' in the chapter title is from Winsome Pinnock's 1989 history play, *A Hero's Welcome*, in Kadija George (ed.) *Six Plays by Black and Asian Women Writers* (London: Aurora Metro Press, 1993), p. 47.

1 In *Identity: The Real Me*, ICA Document 6 (1987), p. 44. Quoted in Kobena Mercer's *Welcome to the Jungle: New Positions in Black Cultural Studies* (London: Routledge, 1994), p. 19.

2 Errol John, *Moon on a Rainbow Shawl*, 2nd edn (London: Faber and Faber, 1963).

3 I include all non-white racial and ethnic affiliations within the category 'black British', but my research and analysis privileges the work of the Caribbean diaspora in Britain – a choice dictated mainly by two factors, the need for focus in a chapter of this length, and the availability of material.

4 Little information is available about black British theatre before the 1960s. The materials in this chapter have been gathered from several sources, the most important of which is a collection of interviews: Jim Pines (ed.) *Black and White in Colour: Black People in British Television since 1936* (London: British Film Institute, 1992).

5 For information about Inter-Action lunchtime theatres in the early 1970s, see Roland Rees, *Fringe First: Pioneers of Fringe Theatre on Record* (London: Oberon, 1992), pp. 96–144, and Catherine Itzin's chronology in *Stages in the Revolution: Political Theatre in Britain since 1968* (London: Methuen, 1980). See also Malcolm Hay, 'The Black Theatre Co-operative', *Drama*, 149, Autumn 1983, pp. 11–12.

6 See Lizbeth Goodman, *Contemporary Feminist Theatres: To Each Her Own* (London and New York: Routledge, 1993), pp. 155–63; Elaine Aston, *An Introduction to Feminism and Theatre* (London and New York: Routledge, 1995), pp. 86–7; and Elizabeth Clarke, 'Black Theatre in England: A Perspective', *Banja*, 2, 1988, p. 64. Also see Yvonne Brewster's 1991 and 1993 interviews: 'Drawing the Black and White Line: Defining Black Women's Theatre: the Director of the Talawa Theatre in Interview', interview by Lizbeth Goodman, *New Theatre Quarterly*, 28, May 1991, pp. 361–8; 'An Interview with Yvonne Brewster, OBE', interview by Stella Oni, in George, *Six Plays by Black and Asian Women*, pp. 18–19.

7 See Brewster's 1991 interview with Goodman. Rather too much attention has been paid to Talawa's inability or unwillingness (during its first five or six years) to mount a play by a woman, and more generally on critical efforts to determine the group's relevance to studies of feminism and theatre. Recently, in an informal written exchange,

Brewster suggested that Talawa had always been concerned 'that the black men in this country get . . . enough of a really raw deal'. She added: 'Things have, however, changed quite a lot in the twelve years of our existence and we now are doing more black women's work than men's' (letter dated 11 May 1998).

8 Bernadine Evaristo, 'The Theatre of Black Women: Britain's First Black Women's Theatre Company', in George, *Six Plays by Black and Asian Women*, p. 16. The founders had been classmates at the Community Theatre Arts Course at the Rose Bruford College of Speech and Drama; there happened to be five black women there that year. In 1981, Hilarie, Randall, and Evaristo had devised *Coping*, which was directed by Yvonne Brewster.

9 This information has been compiled from several sources, including Brewster's 1991 and 1993 interviews, Aston, Evaristo, Goodman, Rees, and Hay (see nn.5, 6, and 8).

10 Joan-Ann Maynard, 'Trends in Black Writing for Theatre', in Ruth A. Tompsett (ed.) *Performing Arts International* Special Issue: 'Black Theatre in Britain', 1: 2, 1996, p. 54.

11 *Performing Arts International* recently published an entire special issue on black British theatre, edited by Ruth A. Tompsett, but the selections are conference proceedings and do not provide an adequately comprehensive picture of the field. Key discussions of the literature of the Afro-Caribbean and Asian diaspora either have ignored theatre altogether or have examined only the work of male playwrights (particularly Mustapha Matura, Edgar White, Caryl Phillips, Farrukh Dhondy, Hanif Kureishi, and Jatinder Verma). A notable exception is Mary Karen Dahl's essay, which includes discussions of work by Jackie Kay and Maria Oshodi: 'Postcolonial British Theatre: Black Voices at the Center', in J. Ellen Gainor (ed.) *Imperialism and Theatre: Essays on World Theatre, Drama and Performance* (London and New York: Routledge, 1995), pp. 38–55. The many studies of contemporary British theatre, when they have bothered to discuss black theatre at all, have likewise focused on plays by men.

12 See also Sue-Ellen Case, *Feminism and Theatre* (New York: Methuen, 1988), p. 95.

13 May Joseph, 'Borders Outside the State: Black British Women and the Limits of Citizenship', in Peggy Phelan and Jill Lane (eds.) *Ends of Performance* (New York: New York University Press, 1998), pp. 197–213; Catherine Ugwu (ed.) *Let's Get It On: The Politics of Black Performance* (London: Institute of Contemporary Arts, and Seattle: Bay Press, 1995).

14 As Yvonne Brewster recently lamented, 'Black Mime is no more, Carib Theatre Company is no more, The Black Theatre Forum is no more, Yaa Asantewa Centre is under terminal threat and so it goes on. There are so few black companies with regular grants left – Tara, Tamasha (Asian), Talawa and BTC (AfriCaribbean)' (letter, 25 May 1998).

15 See for example Ugwu's collection, *Let's Get It On*, Kobena Mercer's *Welcome to the Jungle*, and Angela McRobbie's *Postmodernism and Popular Culture* (London: Routledge, 1994).

16 Valerie Amos, Gail Lewis, Amina Mama, and Pratibha Parmar (eds.) 'Many Voices, One Chant: Black Feminist Perspectives', *Feminist Review* 17 Special Issue, July 1984, pp. 83–100; Beverley Bryan, Stella Dadzie, and Suzanne Scafe (eds.) *The Heart of the Race: Black Women's Lives in Britain* (London: Virago, 1985), pp. 140–51, 155–64, and 164–72. See also the introductory chapter of Amina Mama, *Beyond the Masks: Race, Gender and Subjectivity* (London and New York: Routledge, 1995), and Heidi Safia

Mirza (ed.) *Black British Feminism: A Reader* (London and New York: Routledge, 1997), pp. 6–8. Mirza's collection includes selections from several key texts which shaped black British feminist theory in the 1980s as well as an array of original feminist essays written in the 1990s.

17 Juliet Jarrett, 'Creative Space?: The Experience of British Women in British Art Schools', in Delia Jarrett-Macauley (ed.) *Reconstructing Womanhood, Reconstructing Feminism: Writings on Black Women* (London and New York: Routledge, 1996), pp. 121–3.

18 Pratibha Parmar, 'Other Kinds of Dreams', *Feminist Review,* 31, Spring 1989, pp. 55–65. Reprinted in Mirza, *Black British Feminism,* pp. 67–9.

19 Amina Mama, 'Black Women and the British State: Race, Class and Gender Analysis for the 1990s', in Peter Braham, Ali Rattansi, and Richard Skellington (eds.) *Racism and Anti-Racism: Inequalities, Opportunities and Policies* (London: Sage Publications, 1992), p. 97.

20 Such initiatives have played an absolutely crucial role in the discovery and nurturing of new playwrights. See for example Sita Brahmachari's account of Talawa's educational outreach efforts: 'Panel: Present Practice Bringing Students and Live Theatre Together', in Tompsett, 'Black Theatre in Britain', pp. 43–8.

21 Jackie Kay, *Twice Over,* in Philip Osment (ed.) *Gay Sweatshop: Four Plays and a Company* (London: Methuen, 1989) pp. 121–46; Trish Cooke, *Running Dream,* in George, *Six Plays by Black and Asian Women,* pp. 187–227; Winsome Pinnock, *A Rock in Water,* in Yvonne Brewster (ed.) *Black Plays: 2* (London: Methuen, 1989) pp. 45–91; Zindika, *Paper and Stone* (typescript, Bristol University's Women's Theatre Collection, 1990).

22 Maria Oshodi's 1984 play *The 'S' Bend* is the only exception I have encountered (British Library Playscript No. 2301). Exploring the cultural conflict between two young black women, one of African and the other of Caribbean descent, the play asserts an irreconcilable difference between the 'high educational value in the African' and the 'high material value in the other, coupled with a lack of cultural identity' (p. 29). In spite of this provocative thesis, the play was chosen for Royal Court's Young Writers' Festival in 1984, produced by the Cockpit Youth Theatre in 1985 and chosen for the first International Festival of Young Playwrights, Interplay '85, held in Sydney, Australia (Introduction to *Blood, Sweat and Fears,* in Yvonne Brewster (ed.) *Black Plays: 2* (London and Portsmouth, NH: Methuen, 1989), p. 93). However, Oshodi's other plays are politically progressive and feminist: *Blood, Sweat and Fears; Here Comes a Candle* (typescript, Bristol University Theatre Collection); another youth play, *Mag-zine* (in *Themescripts: New Plays for National Curriculum English* (London: John Murray Publishers, 1990), pp. 65–92). Even *The 'S' Bend* has interesting gender politics and shows a positive relationship between its Afro-British protagonist and a white girl.

23 Stuart Hall, 'New Ethnicities'. Originally published in Kobena Mercer (ed.) *Black Film / British Cinema,* ICA Document 7 (London: Institute of Contemporary Arts, 1988); reprinted in Houston A. Baker, Jr, Manthia Diawara, and Ruth Lindenborg (eds.) *Black Cultural Studies: A Reader* (Chicago and London: University of Chicago Press, 1996), pp. 168–9.

24 Jackie Kay, *Chiaroscuro,* in Jill Davis (ed.) *Lesbian Plays* (London: Methuen, 1987); Bonnie Greer, *Munda Negra,* in Yvonne Brewster (ed.) *Black Plays: 3* (London: Methuen, 1995).

25 Winsome Pinnock's biographical play about Claudia Jones, *A Rock in Water*, is an exception (first performed at the Royal Court, Theatre Upstairs, in 1989). Compare the vast array of biographical plays and monologues by white feminist theatres from the 1970s onwards.

26 Zindika, *Leonora's Dance*, in George, *Six Plays by Black and Asian Women*.

27 Ntozake Shange's work had an important influence upon *Chiaroscuro*, which is comparable to *For Colored Girls* in its politics and, more notably, its chorepoem form (Kay, *Chiaroscuro*, p. 83). Nevertheless, the play's originality has been remarked upon by British observers; see for example Joan-Ann Maynard's comment quoted in Dahl, 'Postcolonial British Theatre', p. 48; and Philip Osment (ed.) *Gay Sweatshop: Four Plays and a Company* (London: Methuen, 1989), p. lxv.

28 Yvonne Brewster (ed.) *Black Plays: 2* (London and Portsmouth, New Hampshire: Methuen, 1989), Introduction.

29 Pinnock, *Leave Taking*, in Kate Harwood (ed.) *First Run: New Plays by New Writers* (London: Nick Hern, 1989), pp. 139–189; Pinnock, *Talking in Tongues*, in Yvonne Brewster (ed.) *Black Plays: 3* (London: Methuen, 1995), pp. 171–227.

FURTHER READING

Primary sources: plays

Brewster, Yvonne (ed.) *Black Plays: 2*. London, and Portsmouth, NH: Methuen, 1989.

Cooke, Trish. *Running Dream*. In George (ed.) *Six Plays by Black and Asian Women*.

George, Kadija (ed.) *Six Plays by Black and Asian Women Writers*. London: Awora Metro Press, 1993.

Kay, Jackie. *Chiaroscuro*. In Jill Davis (ed.) *Lesbian Plays*. London: Methuen, 1987.

   Twice Over. In Philip Osment (ed.) *Gay Sweatshop: Four Plays and a Company*. London: Methuen, 1989.

Oshodi, Maria. *Blood Sweat and Fears*. In Brewster, *Black Plays: 2*.

Pinnock, Winsome. *Leave Taking*. In Kate Harwood (ed.) *First Run: New Plays by New Writers*. London, Nick Hern, 1989.

   A Rock in Water. In Brewster, *Black Plays: 2*.

   A Hero's Welcome. In George, *Six Plays by Black and Asian Women*.

   Talking in Tongues. In Yvonne Brewster (ed.), *Black Plays: 3*. London: Methuen, 1995.

Rudet, Jacqueline. *Basin*. In Yvonne Brewster (ed.) *Black Plays*. London: Methuen, 1987.

Zindika. *Paper and Stone*. Typescript, Women's Theatre Collection, Bristol University, 1990.

   Leonora's Dance. In George, *Six Plays by Black and Asian Women*.

Secondary sources

Amos, Valerie, Gail Lewis, Amina Mama, and Pratibha Parmar (eds.) 'Many Voices, One Chant: Black Feminist Perspectives'. *Feminist Review* 17 Special Issue (July 1984).

Aston, Elaine. *An Introduction to Feminism and Theatre*. London and New York: Routledge, 1995.

Brewster, Yvonne. 'Drawing the Black and White Line: Defining Black Women's Theatre: the Director of the Talawa Theatre in Interview'. Interview with Lizbeth Goodman. *New Theatre Quarterly* 28 (May 1991): 361–8.

Bryan, Beverley, Stella Dadzie, and Suzanne Scafe. *The Heart of the Race: Black Women's Lives in Britain*. London: Virago, 1985.

Dahl, Mary Karen. 'Postcolonial British Theatre: Black Voices at the Center'. In J. Ellen Gainor (ed.) *Imperialism and Theatre: Essays on World Theatre, Drama and Performance*. London and New York: Routledge, 1995: 38–55.

Goodman, Lizbeth. *Contemporary Feminist Theatres: To Each Her Own*. London and New York: Routledge, 1993.

Hall, Stuart. 'New Ethnicities'. In Houston A. Baker, Jr, Manthia Diawara, and Ruth Lindenborg (eds.) *Black Cultural Studies: A Reader*. Chicago and London: University of Chicago Press, 1996: 163–72.

Joseph, May. 'Borders Outside the State: Black British Women and the Limits of Citizenship'. In Peggy Phelan and Jill Lane (eds.) *Ends of Performance*. New York: New York University Press, 1998: 197–213.

Mama, Amina. *Beyond the Masks: Race, Gender and Subjectivity*. London and New York: Routledge, 1995.

Mercer, Kobena. *Welcome to the Jungle: New Positions in Black Cultural Studies*. London and New York: Routledge, 1994.

Mirza, Heidi Safia, (ed.) *Black British Feminism: A Reader*. London and New York: Routledge, 1997.

Tompsett, Ruth A. (ed.) 'Black Theatre in Britain'. *Performing Arts International* 1.2 Special Issue (1996).

Ugwu, Catherine (ed.) *Let's Get It On: The Politics of Black Performance*. London: Institute of Contemporary Arts, and Seattle: Bay Press, 1995.

14

CLAIRE MACDONALD

Writing outside the mainstream

Theatre outside the mainstream has tended to be a director's rather than a writer's theatre. This is not to say that experimental theatre has not offered new opportunities to writers, or that it has stifled the writer's voice. On the contrary, over the past two or three decades theatre has functioned as one of the most important cultural spaces for writers to experiment with form – and this has been especially important for women. The opportunity to collaborate with artists from other disciplines and to find new ways to explore the limits of stage language has generated a new kind of writing for the theatre, outside the confines of the well-made play; writing which is linked to developments in film and the novel and is conversant with the visual arts and dance as well as the language of television and film. Political theatre, physical and visual theatre, small-scale and fringe theatre, and collaborative work with the visual arts and dance have all created a contemporary theatre scene in Britain which is highly interdisciplinary, and which has functioned as an experimental arena in which the relationship between image, speech, and action has come under scrutiny.

It is outside the mainstream that women have been able to create new work informed by debates in feminism about the body, identity, and representation in particular. In the 1970s radical political and artistic feminist theatre companies helped to create the conditions for exploratory work by commissioning the work of women theatre-makers and writers [see pp. 60–1]. Of the many groups producing innovative work with writers were the visual and physical Blood Group, Scarlet Harlots (renamed Scarlet Theatre in the 1980s) and Monstrous Regiment. Certain key venues, often with women directors, also helped to create a climate open to experimentation. For instance, from the early 1970s The Oval House (London) supported many emerging writers and fostered feminist groups like Siren Theatre and Burnt Bridges. The all-women management company Arts Admin had, and still have, an important role in fostering the work of women artists amongst the largely radical and non-mainstream companies they have worked with since the mid-1970s. The early 1980s, however, saw the beginning of a different kind of radicalism in non-mainstream theatre which has continued into the 1990s. While fewer productions were funded, those that were had to be artistically and intellectually sharper. Theatre writer Deborah Levy has talked about the ways in which the leaner times of the 1980s restricted the opportunities for experiment, explaining that if writers wanted to work outside mainstream forms they had to be much clearer about what they wanted to do. For her this generated very disciplined work, which, as she says, 'had its own kind of energy and impetus, so in this way some very interesting, very polished, very articulate, very avant-garde work was made'.[1]

In the 1990s many of the women whose work was forged by feminism and experimental theatre have continued to make innovative and radical work informed by feminist artistic precedent and by more recent cultural debates around post-modernism and identity politics. Many theatre companies have not survived and there has been a general move towards smaller-scale and solo work. During the flowering of feminist theatre in the 1970s and early 1980s, 'alternative' and 'fringe' theatres and theatre groups fostered a diversity of theatrical forms and approaches, coalescing radical politics and aesthetic avant-gardism as part of a broad, counter-cultural movement. More recently, non-mainstream theatre has fractured and re-formed along very different lines – some of which seem to show new opportunities for women writers. The Women's Theatre Group, which had encouraged non-traditional, collaborative, and devised ways of working changed its name to Sphinx in the 1980s and has become more focused in its attention to promoting and nurturing women playwrights. In an article on the changing relationship of women theatre-makers and writers to theatrical methods, Alison Oddey cites Sphinx's Artistic Director Sue Parrish's view that the prevalence in the 1970s of writers working collaboratively or within briefs set by theatre companies was the result of lack of choice, rather than a clearly thought-out aesthetic.[2] Given the opportunity, many women writers in the 1990s have moved away from alternative forms and practices towards projects which offer them more autonomy as writers. Sphinx no longer includes, for instance, devised work – work which is produced largely collaboratively – within its remit. Other theatre companies have made a different choice. Scarlet Theatre (originally Scarlet Harlots), for example, continues to work with a diversity of writing approaches, nurturing the work of writers like Cindy Oswin and Jyll Bradley (see later), whose work cannot be easily categorised under playwriting, and may be collaboratively produced and highly visual.

One writer whose work was recognised early for its clarity and its theatrical and linguistic inventiveness is April de Angelis. Working from within the opportunities offered by feminist theatre in the early 1980s with *Playhouse Creatures* and *Iron Mistress*, her career has developed in interesting ways – both towards much more mainstream productions with a strong feminist edge, like her 1997 *The Positive Hour* (the only one of her plays currently in print as a solo edition),[3] and towards film and television projects, such as her 1995 film for British television, *Aristophanes the Gods are Laughing*, produced by radical film producer Tariq Ali. De Angelis has also moved into critical writing and adaptation,[4] and her current projects include fiction and film. Her work is interestingly positioned between a newer wave of 1990s playwrights – such as the late Sarah Kane and Phyllis Nagy – who may have benefited from the widening of conventional opportunities (as Sue Parrish argues), and the earlier generation of writer–makers from Bryony Lavery to Deborah Levy whose work was forged through the process of hands-on theatre-making within a radical theatre generation (or two).

Outside the mainstream, theatre continues to be influenced by visual art and dance and many writers still choose to work in collaboration with artists in cross-art-form projects. Very little of this appears in collections of printed plays. Finding and giving a context to the work of writers from the experimental tradition can be difficult: it demands that we rethink our ideas about what a text is, since the text may be a video, or a collection of notes, part of a score with visual images and music, or even an installation. It also demands that we rethink the role of the playwright. I prefer to use the term 'theatre writer' which seems to me to be a broader and less prescriptive working definition. She may or may not write complete plays, and when she does write plays her playwriting may not represent her full contribution to theatre. She may contribute a text to a collectively authored work; she may improvise a spoken text in her own performance, or she may create a work as author in which words are part of a visual and physical composition.

Conceptual playwriting: Bobby Baker, Rose English, and Jyll Bradley

Experiments with form have tended towards integration of the textual and the visual, creating performances which blur the distinctions between art forms. In such work the performance is a compositional whole in which the visual and physical 'score' is as significant as the written text. Much important solo work in which the theatre-maker combines the roles of writer, performer, designer, and director, has been produced in this way, as, for instance, in the work of Bobby Baker. Trained in fine art, Bobby Baker began her career making sculpture and installation, often focusing on the ironies of women's place in the art world by replacing traditional art materials with food. She began performing in the late 1980s, creating solo works in which she plays with ideas about the construction of the self through performances which combine verbal and visual metaphors. In *Drawing on a Mother's Experience* and *The Kitchen Show* she comments on the amusing, ironic, and sometimes painful relationship between the different sides of a woman artist's life: mirroring the domestic in the art practice and bringing her artist's eye into the domestic space. In *The Kitchen Show*, which originally took place in her own kitchen before an invited audience, she muses on colour and shape in the kitchen, on food and gadgets and the qualities of form. In *Drawing on a Mother's Experience* she creates a parodic homage to the great masculine abstract expressionist paintings created by Jackson Pollock. Her drawing is made on a double bed sheet and it is made from food. As she marks her sheet with the colours and textures of fish cakes and Guinness, blackcurrants and treacle she tells us a confidential story about her own journey into motherhood. In combining the verbal and the visual she is able to draw on multiple traditions of women's public and private lives: on gossip and confidences, jokes and burlesque. Her work is a comment on the complexity of women's sense of self and the way in which it is formed through language, objects, and narratives. Since the early 1980s this cross-disciplinary solo work has been an important forum for women to explore issues of identity and agency. Bobby Baker's work revolves around her own presence as performer. As writer and artist she is implicated in the text she speaks. She plays with the expectations of the viewer/listener about the public self she represents in performance and the private self of the writer/artist/mother. Baker's work is some of the best-documented in this field. She is articulate about the way in which her work is made and has re-made much of her work for video, taking into account the very different relationship of the spectator to the camera.[5]

The work of the theatre artist Rose English is less well known outside England, but her contribution to theatre as an artist and writer is widely appreciated by audiences, critics, and other theatre-makers. Like Bobby Baker, she appears in her own work. Her theatre works, however, are not performed solo. While they revolve around her own presence on stage they include large casts and often large-scale theatrical spectacle. Her texts are long, complex, and philosophical and have evolved out of a life-long interest in the female performer and her representation in public space. While she appears in her work as 'Rose' she dresses in a variety of costumes drawn from the history of popular entertainment: sometimes burlesque show-girl; once, in *My Mathematics,* as an equestrian performer with a horse; in blonde wig and evening dress in *The Double Wedding*; and, in *Tantamount Esperance* in beard and male costume. Only one of her plays has been published, as the title piece in the collection *Walks on Water*, but her work has been increasingly documented and written about by writers who have seen her perform over many years and know the work well.[6]

Rose English and Bobby Baker both came to theatre from a training in fine art. Their careers began during the 1970s and were influenced by feminist debates about the representation of women in art as well as by the Women's Movement itself. Art schools in Britain have often provided fertile ground for practitioners of experimental theatre. Despite the male dominance of art practice and art schools, during the 1970s the openness to experiment and to new concepts of performance proved fruitful for many women who later became performance artists, dancers, writers, and theatre-makers. Among the many possible examples of such women are the theatre-maker and designer Geraldine Pilgrim, whose company Hesitate and Demonstrate was one of the most exciting visual companies of the 1970s and 1980s, and the film-maker Sally Potter, who went from art school to train as a dancer and then to become a film-maker, integrating her visual, choreographic, and writing skills in films like *Orlando* (1991), or most recently *The Tango Lesson* (1997). For these and many other women the fine-art context not only provided a space for practical experiment, it also provided an intellectual environment in which ideas about agency, identity, and representation could be explored at a time when theatre was more concerned to represent the issues of women's lives within broadly naturalistic conventions.

One of the most interesting writers to emerge from this background in the 1990s is Jyll Bradley. Educated in the 1980s at Goldsmith's College and the Slade School of Art, London, Bradley began her career working with photographic installation. Like many other women artists in this field her interest has always been focused on issues of image and identity. Through working with self-portraiture and costume she began writing surreal theatre texts which mirror image, word, and action; the first of these, *Irene is Tied up with Concert Arrangements*, was shown in 1993 at the ICA, London. Her work now includes two commissions for BBC Radio 4 – an original play, *Filet de Sole Veronique* and an adaptation of Kate Chopin's novel *The Awakening* – and a play for Scarlet Theatre, *The Fruit has Turned to Jam in the Fields*.[7]

Bradley is the inheritor of several traditions favourable to women. Like Rose English and Bobby Baker she has been able to combine high art with the popular, subverting traditions of female comedy in order to deconstruct femininity. Her work has been described as 'a hybrid formed by grafting Joyce Grenfell with Sarah Bernhardt, Vita Sackville West with Enid Blyton'.[8] Politically, Bradley is a younger inheritor of a lesbian feminist practice which has now become much more interested in exploring transgressive aspects of sexuality, as well as recovering aspects of women's and lesbian history. Bradley considers herself a conceptual artist as well as a playwright, conceiving the design of her pieces – even to the point of asking audiences to come dressed in their gardening outfits! She does not appear in her pieces, but, like many women artists, she has developed long-term collaborative working relationships with directors – in particular Emma Bernard – who understand her approach to theatre.

All of these writers are interested in the possibilities of language alongside visual imagery. Each takes responsibility for aspects of the theatre-making process and production which are traditionally outside the province of the playwright: design, location, visual composition all come within their concept of 'writing' for theatre.

The act of writing: Deborah Levy

The writer I would like to consider most closely in this new writing context is Deborah Levy. Levy's work in the theatre crosses a number of different roles. She is not only a prolific writer, but is also an editor, critic, and director. She is articulate about the place of formal experiment in British theatre writing and its relationship to wider political and cultural issues, and her published work covers a range of genres, including theatre writing, novels, poetry, and cultural essays.

Trained at Dartington College of Arts in physical and visual theatre, Levy began by devising with visual artists and composers: 'my earliest beginnings were in performance – in collaborating with the particular languages of music, image and text and seeing how they work together' (Levy, interview in Charitou, 'Questions of Survival', p. 225). Her training emphasised the affinities between theatre writing and non-literary forms of composition in music and dance. From the beginning of her career her writing practice evolved in the theatre space through a process of dialogue with the other participants in the theatre-making process – directors, performers, designers, and composers.

Levy's work is consciously concerned with the way in which the territory of the imagination is shaped and constructed through culture and politics. For her, 'imagining' is itself political work rooted in material conditions. The way in which the writer herself engages in the act of writing is a significant aspect of that shaping. Imagining takes place when a woman in a room watches, listens, responds with her pen, and asks performers to extend that response into performance. The act of writing for performance is an act of engagement with the conditions of theatre – its institutional, physical and ideological conditions. It also, in Levy's terms, stands for the way we engage with the world. She explains that:

> Ideology is buried implicitly in the structure of our creative work: in our writing for the theatre, we place the audience by picturing it, and place our words on the page by visualising their presence in the mouths of performers, in the playing space, the space of address, where we assemble our attentions, direct them and let them be perceived by others.[9]

Within these terms Levy pays acute attention to the subjectivities of her character–performers and to the complex conditions which construct her own position as writer. Writing is an act of composition undertaken for a specific space, the stage, and in which the task of language is multi-faceted: it can generate questions which shape a process, it can give rise to dialogue, and it can create highly realised imagined worlds. Talking of the theatre-making process she says:

'The questions I ask myself when writing are: what is present on the stage? What do I want to be there? And I ask of my central characters: where is their power located? What is the difference between what they say and what they do?'[10]

It is the centrality of language to interdisciplinary cross-art-form theatre that Deborah Levy recognises in her anthology *Walks on Water*, which remains one of the few collections of texts from the intersection of performance art and theatre.[11] Her introduction to the collection bears witness to the plurality of writing practices within contemporary theatre, practices whose common assumption has been that new times demand new forms. Such work, Levy argues, is 'experimental, live, changeable and idiosyncratic', and draws more on 'popular culture, TV, film, fiction, avant-garde science, architecture, fine art and dance than mainstream theatre' (Levy, *Walks on Water*, pp. viii, ix).

Deborah Levy's theatre worlds are self-consciously fictional, since it is the artifice of theatre which interests her. Self-consciousness about role and character, using the artifice of theatre to explore the construction of the self, is one of the definitive elements of the experimental tradition. Influenced by post-modern theory on the one hand, and by structuralist experiments in the novel, film, and performance art on the other, it connects theatre to a wider tradition of avant-garde practice and cultural discourses.[12] For a writer like Deborah Levy it offers the opportunity to explore the representation of women through image and language and to find new ways to express female subjectivity and agency. Hers is a theatre of utterance – the world is spoken into being in the gap between the real world and the imagination. Regurgitated advertising jingles, myths of imaginary countries, other people's histories all rub up alongside each other. In the landscape of a Levy world Tampax might be a service station just outside Phoenix; the rural brutality of the American South might relocate to the border of Chechnya.

Levy's first play, *Clam*, was directed by Anna Furse for the visual theatre company Blood Group, and performed in April 1985 at the Oval House, London. Her first commissioned play, *Pax*, written for the Women's Theatre Group, was also staged at the Oval in August 1985.[13] Unlike Scarlet Harlots or Blood Group, the Women's Theatre Group did not have a tradition of working with experimental new writing. It had a strong commitment to working with writers and commissioning new work, but while that work was politically innovative it was largely naturalistic and issue-based. Levy was asked to write an anti-nuclear play. What she wrote was a play as epic in scope and as far away from domestic naturalism as possible.

In creating a play which was broadly anti-nuclear, Levy explored the relationship of the imagination and history; identity and selfhood. In *Pax* women have no home but they are at home in time, space, and history. The world of *Pax* is an artificial world in which four women meet on the edge of time and space in a place simply called 'the wilderness' or 'the retreat'. Their narratives variously explore the construction of femininity; relations between men and women; and issues of memory, place, and identity. Levy's characters are never fully drawn, but are symbolically named, are sometimes inconsistent and are often puzzling. In *Pax* the women appear as larger-than-life figures to explore the relationship of identity to history and to world events. They are representative of broad areas of personality and experience: the Keeper, the Mourner, Domesticated Woman, and the Hidden Daughter, or H.D. Together they conjure histories and possibilities. The Keeper tells history as the universal witness to the twentieth century: 'I was there in Barcelona and Catalonia . . . when the world was a blister waiting to be pricked' (Act I, sc. 3, p. 90). H.D. fills in the present and imagines her future. The Mourner searches for meaning in the present. As Levy explains, she is 'Me and you' (Afterword, *Pax*, p.112). The Domesticated Woman spouts (and thereby contradicts) platitudes of feminine satisfaction in the service of the family. The encounter between these figures is fast and vividly expressed: they meditate on past and present, on female desire and hope, love, and loss. The possibility of extinction is seen as the death of the imagination; the loss of a space to hope, to desire. It is not, as Levy explains, one of those 'last two minutes in a bunker' plays (Afterword, p. 112), but a large, richly textured piece which addresses what it has meant and means to live in twentieth-century Europe.

At a time when much work by women was concerned with expressing women's authentic feelings, Levy looked beyond the immediate issues to the construction of a sense of self in the images, ideas, and language through which we 'speak' the world. Language is used less to tell a story than to explore what stories are – especially how we use stories to construct ourselves and our world. As Levy herself explains: 'How we invent ourselves will always be a major theme in my work. I never really believed that there is one true authentic self or that there is an authentic homeland' (interview, in Charitou, 'Questions of Survival', p. 226). Many of the themes and ideas Levy uses in *Pax* appear in subsequent pieces – most significantly, perhaps, the idea that non-naturalistic or experimental work is inherently political since it allows for the disruption of the conventional relationships between character and story. It opens up a space in which Levy can explore self-invention, transient identities, and the relationship between who we are and what we tell ourselves.

The first production of *Pax* brought together an unusual and significant group of women. Levy states in her notes to the play that she wanted the production to be 'textually and visually articulate'; in other words, the density and poetry of her text needed equally strong artistic investment from other people. As I stated earlier, artistic collaboration has often been important to theatrical experiment. *Pax* brought together Lily Susan Todd and Anna Furse as the directing team; Camilla Saunders as the composer; and visual artist Wendy Freeman as the designer – all of whom Levy either had worked with before, or has collaborated with since. Conscious of the relationship between the process of making a piece of work and its final outcome, outside the mainstream Levy had always been able to work with artists who shared her artistic vision. However, in her production of *Heresies* for the RSC (1986), again directed by Lily Susan Todd, she came up against the problems of transferring a working process to mainstream theatre.

Her desire to write theatre texts which cross the boundaries between the visual arts and theatre and to work with directors interested in expanding the possibilities of performance in the theatre space, was frustrated by entering a more mainstream context – albeit one committed to new work. While it shares many of the same preoccupations as *Pax*, *Heresies* was a much less successful project. At the time of writing, Levy was emerging as an important writer of fiction, but her interests in performance were a challenge to conventional concepts of form and structure. *Heresies* proved a difficult and critically misunderstood project.

Heresies directly attempted to cross the boundaries of performance art and theatre, and to inject radical new form onto a mainstream stage. It received hostile critical reviews which implicated its collaborative process in the supposed failure of the piece. The opportunity to discuss the work in terms which referred to different theatre traditions and aspirations was entirely lost and the hostility and lack of seriousness in which critical response was couched underscores Levy's assertion, polemically expressed in her introduction to *Walks on Water*, that mainstream theatre is dogged by reductive and inappropriate forms of naturalism which leave it entirely outside any dialogue with contemporary fiction, film, dance, and music (pp. viii–ix).

Since *Heresies* Levy has largely returned to collaborative theatre work outside mainstream spaces. The fact that organisations such as The Magdalena Project and the Women's Playhouse Trust have commissioned her shows how important Levy's work is to breaking new ground for women in performance. She has adapted Lorca's *Blood Wedding* (1994) as a libretto for composer Nicola Le Fanu, worked on a performance piece, *New Text New Kingdom*, with dancer Laurie Booth, and has written and directed several pieces in collaboration with other artists. She worked with the two-man company Man Act on *Call Blue Jane* (1993), an exploration of masculinity and (objectified) femininity. In 1992 The Magdalena Project commissioned her to workshop, write, and direct *The B-File* – a project which subsequently travelled to Australia where Levy also directed her text *Honey Baby: 13 Studies in Exile* at LaMama, Melbourne (1994). To increasing critical acclaim, she has published two more novels: *The Unloved* (1994) and *Billy and Girl* (1996). In addition, Levy has also made artists' books and installations, and both wrote and directed *Shiny Nylon* (1994), a collaborative performance piece with artist Anya Galacio, dancers Kristine Page and Sean Tuan John, and composer Billy Cowie.

The development of Levy's writing across such a wide variety of media has sharpened and focused her theatre work. Her earlier interest in the construction of identity is much more clearly focused in pieces such as *The B-File* and *Shiny Nylon*. Stylistically the work is spare and minimal. Levy's attention is on the relationship between action, word, and image – between what the character–performers look like, what they say, and what they do.

In *The B-File*, five women performers wear the standard glamour outfit of the 'available' female: black dress and red lipstick. They are collectively and individually representations of one character – Beatrice – and speak as B1 to B5. No one performer ever fully occupies the character, instead they move from speaking as Beatrice to being interpreter for other Beatrices. 'Beatrice' is a subject in both senses of the word: she is the subject of investigation and she is the speaking subject: a subject position occupied at different times by different performers. The performers speak directly to the audience through microphones. They use Beatrice's persona to pose questions about identity. We learn that Beatrice is a kind of everywoman, a woman always on the edge, nomadic, displaced, and emblematic: 'Beatrice cleans offices at night with women in saris under orange strobe. She is eating dal and chapatis in a room full of small rugs from Calcutta. She is playing the pin ball machine with pimps and rough boys in arcades. Beatrice jangles her bracelets at borders' (*The B-File* in *Walks on Water*, p.154).

The on-stage identities of the performers move between the character they all, at times, embody and their persona as performers. As five women in black dresses they inhabit the dangerous border between objectification and empowerment by bringing glamour into play. In effect it is an exercise in empowerment: the work is made with the knowledge that the performance does not illustrate text but extends it into space. The women step into space as powerful actresses, they speak back. They are darkly ironic. They are never characters and therefore they never become identified with their role – they stand apart from it. Beatrice is a persona who moves between the five actresses, a floating figure, half-remembered, half-imagined.

The writer herself plays a part in *The B-File*. She is always present, speaking through the performers: 'I have put words in your mouth, Beatrice. Do my words fit you? If you are a persona I have revealed too much' (*The B-File*, p. 152). When, in the introduction to *Walks On Water*, Levy presents the Mexican performance artist and writer Guillermo Gomez-Peña as someone who 'articulates the experience of fragmented identity and plundered psyche . . . rearranges history, rearranges geography, rearranges language', she could be writing about her own work (p. viii).

The sense that character is not pre-formed but exists as the outcome of all that is said and done on stage, however contradictory, continues throughout her later work, as, for example, in *Shiny Nylon*.[14] *Shiny Nylon* is a site-specific piece, written for an empty warehouse in London, about the relationship between images, language, and action. The text is minimal. Levy's notes on objects and the use of space reveal a surreal aesthetic: 'a cobwebbed platform shoe', and 'a vast red curtain hung in the space – as if this might be in the last cinema in the world'. The characters are minimalist icons: Girl is 'paranoid and tearful' in blonde wig and leather shorts, and Boy 'wears a suit, red trainers and a false moustache'. A third figure, Bombay, is a faded movie queen in a blue gown carrying guns and microphones. Boy and Girl act; Bombay speaks. Boy slashes red velvet cinema seats; Bombay says, 'Yeah: that's the end of his broadcast to the British nation.' Girl cries; Bombay says 'That's the end of her broadcast to the European community.' Bombay speaks an English composed of brand names and television references, a kind of contemporary patois in the mouth of a faded movie star: 'This boy star tastes of Colgate,' 'He got vertigo', 'Girl got biceps and no one to write her obituary.' Language stakes out the boundaries in a world of fragmented identities. Theatre is cast as a public space in which unsettling and sometimes brutal things can be done and said. The performance involves sham and artifice; negotiates between what is real and what is illusion. Bombay carries pretend guns and real microphones. She speaks a language of the 'gaps': an English of the unstable space between a world vernacular and quotes from television. The work takes place on the borders of representation and on the borders of genre and discipline. Levy uses the performance space to explore the relationship between action, image, and spoken word: between what is said and what is done. Working with performers experienced in dance and theatre, and with a visual artist and a choreographer, Levy creates a complex visual, physical, and verbal text. The performance text is the totality of the writer's choices, including the decisions about space, movement, and objects which were made in conjunction with the other participating artists.

Textual evidence: fictional space

Deborah Levy's theatre work is sometimes difficult to appreciate fully on the page. The process of theatre-making to which she refers in notes and interviews is lost in publication and the texts themselves are pared away from the visual and physical context which is so important to her work. Each of her texts is both a pre-script, that is an indication of how to repeat the work, and a post-script, a description of an event which has happened. However, the printed play still often feels like an inadequate vehicle for the complexity of the work, which, as a compositional whole, can only be appreciated in the context of its production.

However, what is interesting about her as a writer who works across genres is that many of the ideas she works with in performance are also explored in her novels and poetry. The connections across the range of her work illuminate her contribution to theatre, at both a thematic and a formal level. The sense that all fictions are constructed worlds, and that each art form offers different kinds of opportunities to play with its formal qualities is central to her way of working. In part it explains her fascination with the possibilities of form. Making texts for bill boards, collaborating with a photographer on an artist's book, or making an installation with a visual artist are all ways of allowing form to come into contact with and to influence her strong, continuing themes and formal concerns.

At several times in her career as a writer, Levy has opted out of theatre for a while, but continued her explorations into performance through other media – especially in her novels. The full articulation of the dispersed and displaced identities enacted in her theatre work happens increasingly on the page, where she is in control of the discourse. This is not to relegate the theatre work to secondary status, but to propose that part of its function for her as a writer is to experiment with form in a way which allows her to translate performance ideas into the novel. Such an idea is far from new,[15] but for a writer as interested in form as Deborah Levy is, it offers a way for the formal qualities of the different media in which she works to connect with one another. The page can also be a performance site. At the same time the opportunity to create fictional experiments allows her to work more freely in performance, and to make work outside the form of the play. Her interests as a writer/artist change focus in relation to the cultural and formal space in which she shapes her work.

For the critic and for the student, reading a writer's work across genres can be a demanding task. Writers who work widely across form are often better known within one genre than in others and their work often suffers critically when it is difficult to embrace all of its aspects. A writer whose work shares many of Levy's thematic and formal concerns is the French writer and theorist Hélène Cixous. Like Levy, Cixous works across genres and is a writer whose work is best understood when its different aspects are allowed to come into relationship with one another.[16] Cixous and Levy use writing in some of the same ways: they investigate the ways in which female subjectivity is constructed within systems of representation and within cultural discourses. This means that they focus on the way in which the female subject is spoken within language and create fictions and theatre which explore the limits of representation. Within their writing practice, language is the material which helps to construct our world view and our imagination, the project of the writer is in part to struggle to open language up so that we are aware of its possibilities and the constraints of its gendered nature. In the practice of each of these writers, as with many others, the struggle with form is linked to and even driven by a profound sense of exile in the world. This sense of exile is expressed as a personal state, a political reality, and as a generative starting point for writing. Feminist art practice has often been a struggle to find an authentic voice, but for writers like Cixous and Levy the questions are much more to do with asking what kind of ethics and politics we have in a world where there is no authentic identity and no authentic homeland.

This counter-voice of feminism is very important in Levy's work and is informed by the conditions of her personal history. Personal circumstances can, of course, lead to very different conclusions in different writers but the conclusion to which Levy's background leads her, like Cixous and others, is that exile is emblematic of the post-modern condition. She has talked of the importance of writers such as Frantz Fanon, Homi Bhaba, Edward Said, Gayatri Spivak, and of course Cixous herself, all of whom have been informed by a sense of exile and have theorised that position in their critical work (Levy, interview, in Charitou, 'Questions of Survival', p. 227).

Like Cixous, Levy's personal history is connected both to Judaism and to European Africans whose identity is displaced in the modern world. Born in South Africa in the late 1950s, and having lived in Britain since her teens, Levy speaks in her work of the need to re-imagine a relationship to the world in a time of dispersal and complex, even contradictory, identities. Her project is the antithesis of the naturalistic theatre and fiction she rejects. The new work of mutual imagining which needs to happen between peoples in the post-modern world calls for above all new forms of expression.

I argued earlier in this chapter that Levy's work is concerned with the way in which the imagination is shaped through culture and politics and I have traced the way in which this concern is one which has developed throughout her work. The novel of Levy's which is most concerned with this, *The Unloved*, acknowledges a debt to Frantz Fanon, the psychiatrist and theorist of the post-colonial psyche, for his 'transforming challenging spirit'.[17] Levy's imagination is shaped by questions about identity and belonging which lead her not to definitive answers but to self-definition as a writer for whom these questions are an ongoing process; they inform and drive her work in all its manifestations.

Writerly identities are often much less simple than they may at first appear. If writers stage themselves in their work in complex and sometimes contradictory ways this is especially true when their work itself is staged on the borders of categories. Writers whose work embraces experimental traditions of practice and who also have strong political opinions and complex personal histories are interesting exemplars. The internationally acclaimed African-American playwright, novelist, essayist, and poet, Ntozake Shange, for instance, whose work acknowledges African-American vernacular speech patterns and performance forms, polemically stages her own presence on the page. By refusing to use upper-case letters, re-spelling her written texts to resemble the sounds of speech and creating rhythmic stops through slashes between phrases in her prose, she positions her written presence on the page in a way which forces the reader to confront her writerly identity: it asks us to 'read' her voice through visual cues. It uses the page as a place where political and artistic radicalism meet, creating new forms of text for new times.[18]

Some of the clues which Deborah Levy gives us as readers about her attitude towards her work and her relationship to it as a writer often take the form of fragmentary asides and introductory notes. In *The B-File* she explains that 'B is searching for home' (p.141); that the performers speak different languages, which 'of course can change in subsequent performances'; and that the choreographic possibilities of the piece are 'obvious to performers and director' (p. 142). Her notes indicate possibilities for production, but do not determine what that production might be. They imply that the project is always incomplete until taken up by other artists. They also refer to a feeling of nostalgia and longing for a place where one has never been. She stated in her opening remarks to *The B-File* that 'I was interested in yearning for a place and a person never met' (p. 141). There is no home, no authenticity, no closure, and no finality in Levy's works. Her characters are raw and unfinished because their hunger to 'be' is unassuageable, and there is nowhere for them to be present except in performance, or enclosed between pages. They are like the 'replicant' girl in the post-modern, 1970s cult film *Bladerunner*, who finds that even her childhood memories have been imported wholesale, assembled from fragments of someone else's life, not her own. Levy's texts are aphoristic and rhetorical. Her preferred stance is the question rather than the statement: the conversational opener rather than the definitive closure. At the end of *The B-File* Beatrice emerges as 'just an actress playing out what has been staged for her' (p.156). *The Unloved* ends with two girls turning a child's globe through Omsk, Stalino Bay, Baku, and finally 'the world stops at Alaska' (*The Unloved*, p. 234). The modern world is a continuous present of exile, longing for a place to call home, a place where maybe one has never even been. A desire with no object. An identity in flux. It is this dialogue with and about the self, which is dispersed across the genres in which she works, that Levy continually stages.

Levy is a daughter of the artistic and political avant-garde. Her work is part of a tradition of protest which pushes boundaries intellectually and artistically and in which the older terms which helped to define and fix a writer's public face – playwright, novelist, critic – are inadequate in the face of turbulent change. In these times an artist must go, like the migrant worker, or the itinerant story teller, or Beatrice who 'jangles her bracelets at borders', to the place where the action is. The cultural critic Paul Gilroy talks of the displacement of older theories of place and identity into newer conceptions of 'flow', stating, 'maybe the notion of the crossroads as a special location where unforeseen, magical things can happen might be an appropriate conceptual vehicle for rethinking the dialectical tensions between cultural roots and cultural routes'.[19]

As a critic and teacher – and as a writer engaged in theatre practice – I find these cross-border dialogues among the most dynamic in contemporary culture, because it is from the crossroads that new work emerges: work which is, in Levy's words, 'a kinetic fusion of eloquent language, some of which is spoken' (*Walks on Water*, p. ix).

I have tried to show here that, for women writers, one of the virtues of the experimental tradition in theatre has been the opportunity to explore the construction of selfhood in terms both of one's own artistic identity as a writer and of wider questions of female subjectivity and agency. Perhaps the most important aspect of theatrical experiment in the last several years has been the move towards the integration of the verbal and the visual so that, for the theatre-makers/writers I have discussed here, 'writing' is conceived as an exercise in composition which includes non-verbal material. They might all be described, as Jyll Bradley describes herself, as conceptual theatre artists.

It is not just ideas which are challenged in new interdisciplinary work but other cultural and material relations – for new work may circulate in unusual and often informal ways. What we have today in the theatre is really an 'expanded' notion of writing for performance which includes a variety of physical, visual, musical, and oral forms of composition within the category of 'writing'. We need now to look at writing as process rather than only as product and to relate that process to the development of a piece of theatre. We might look, for instance, at how the process of theatre-making is signified in the 'writing up' of performance for the page and at the relationship between the writer's presence in the theatre space and the form of the writing which emerges from it; or at the relationship between the space of theatre and the space of the page – at how performance is represented in 'mise-en-page'. A written text may be a point in a process, a suggestion for further work, a set of cues, a description of possibilities, or a record of what happened. It may include the acknowledgement of the input of performers, it may have alternative endings. We need to look at writing as part of a network of other visual and textual evidence about performance which the composer/writer/performer may be involved with as part of the compositional process.

That visual and textual evidence, essential to an understanding of works which cross the boundaries of performance art and theatre, is what is most often missing from the theatre text in print – if the work ever reaches the stage of being printed at all. An expanded definition of writing would allow both critics and theatre-makers to enlarge our conception of the practice of theatre writing to include a wider variety of compositional forms. It is these forms which we also need to be able to see in publication – a move which is politically important for women writers and artists if they are not to continue to suffer from the double marginalisation and invisibility of working as women within non-traditional areas.

FIRST PRODUCTIONS OF MAJOR PLAYS

Venues are in London unless stated.

Bobby Baker

Drawing on a Mother's Experience, ICA (1987)
The Kitchen Show, London International Festival of Theatre (1991)

Jyll Bradley

Irene is Tied up with Concert Arrangements, ICA (1993)
The Fruit has Turned to Jam in the Fields, Scarlet Theatre (1995)
On the Playing Fields on her Rejection, Drill Hall (1996)
Digging for Ladies, touring production, England (1998)
Filet de Sole Veronique, BBC Radio 4; touring production, England (1998/9)

Rose English

Walks on Water, Hackney Empire (1988)
The Double Wedding, The Royal Court (1991)
My Mathematics, Royal Festival Hall (1992)
Tantamount Esperance, Royal Court (1994)

Deborah Levy

Clam, Blood Group, Oval House (1985)
Pax, Women's Theatre Group, Oval House (1985)
Heresies, Royal Shakespeare Company, Barbican (1986)
The B-File, Chapter Arts Centre, Cardiff (1992)
Shiny Nylon, warehouse (1994)

NOTES

1 Levy, quoted in Irini Charitou, interview, 'Questions of Survival: toward a Postmodern Feminist Theatre', in *New Theatre Quarterly*, 35, August 1993, p. 229.
2 This comment is part of Oddey's interesting discussion about the politics of the theatrical method, in 'Devising (Women's) Theatre as Meeting the Needs of Changing Times', in Lizabeth Goodman (ed.) *The Routledge Reader in Gender and Performance* (London: Routledge, 1998), pp. 118–24, p. 120.
3 *The Positive Hour*, April de Angelis (London: Faber, 1997). Her anthologised work includes *Ironmistress* in Mary Remnant (ed.) *Plays by Women: Eight* (London: Methuen, 1990); *Crux* in Cheryl Robson (ed.) *Seven Plays by Women: Female Voices Fighting Lives* (London: Aurora Metro Press, 1991); and *Hush* in Pamela Edwardes (ed.) *Frontline Intelligence 1: New Plays for the Nineties* (London: Methuen, 1993).
4 De Angelis's adaptations include Charles Dickens's *Great Expectations*, in Michael Frayn (ed.) *Adapting Classics* (London: Methuen, 1996). With Susan Croft she has

contributed a critical article on collaboration in Trevor R. Griffiths and Maragaret Llewellyn Jones (eds.) *British and Irish Women Dramatists Since 1958: A Critical Handbook* (Buckingham: Open University Press, 1993).

5 Bobby Baker's *Drawing on a Mother's Experience* and *The Kitchen Show* are available on video from Arts Admin, Toynbee Studios, 28 Commercial Street, London, E1 6LS. Her work is also discussed in: Marina Warner, 'The Rebel at the Heart of the Joker', in Nicky Childs and Jeni Walwin (eds.) *A Split Second of Paradise* (London: Rivers Oram Press, 1998), pp. 68–87, and in Claire MacDonald, 'Assumed Identities: Feminism, Autobiography and Performance Art', in Julia Swindells (ed.) *The Uses of Autobiography* (London: Taylor and Francis, 1995), pp. 187–95.

6 Rose English's work is managed by Arts Admin and there is documentation on video in the National Sound Archive at The British Library. The sound archive is at 96 Euston Road, London, NW1 2DB (http://www.bl.uk). Her work is discussed in: Lynne MacRitchie, 'Rose English: A Perilous Profession', in *Performance Research*, 1:3, Autumn 1996, pp. 58–76, and Deborah Levy, 'The Eros of Rose', in Childs and Walwin, *A Split Second of Paradise*, pp. 41–53.

7 Jyll Bradley's texts are as yet unpublished, although the text of *Digging for Ladies*, a performance which recently toured gardens, is forthcoming in Lizbeth Goodman (ed.) *Mythic Women / Real Women* (London: Faber, 1999).

8 Quoted from *The Times* in Jyll Bradley's most recent press release (1998).

9 Levy quoted in Lizbeth Goodman, *Contemporary Feminist Theatres: To Each her Own* (London and New York: Routledge, 1993), p. 224.

10 Levy in Goodman, *Contemporary Feminist Theatres*, p. 42.

11 Deborah Levy (ed.) *Walks on Water* (London: Methuen, 1992). The collection contains *Walks on Water* by Rose English; *Slips* by David Gale, writer for the visual theatre company Lumière and Son; *1992* by the Mexican artist Guillermo Gomez-Peña; *The B-File* by Deborah Levy; and *Storm from Paradise* by Claire MacDonald.

12 See the discussion in Tim Etchells, 'Diverse Assembly: Some Trends in Recent Performance', in Theodore Shanks (ed.) *Contemporary British Theatre* (London and New York: MacMillan and St Martin's Press, 1996), pp.107–22.

13 Deborah Levy, *Pax*, in Mary Remnant (ed.) *Plays by Women: 5* (London: Methuen, 1987).

14 *Shiny Nylon* is an unpublished text. The piece was commissioned by the Women's Playhouse Trust and performed in 1994.

15 The Bauhaus artist Oskar Schlemmer talked about exactly this issue in relation to theatre and painting. As well as being interested in theatre for its own sake, Schlemmer used it as an experimental space which allowed him to play with form in three dimensions. For further detail, see RoseLee Goldberg, *Performance Art: From Futurism to the Present* (London: Thames and Hudson, 1988), chapter 5, 'Bauhaus'.

16 For an excellent discussion of the totality of Cixous's work see Morag Shiach, *Hélène Cixous: A Politics of Writing* (London and New York: Routledge, 1991).

17 Deborah Levy, *The Unloved* (London: Jonathan Cape, 1994).

18 For Shange's own analysis of her work, see her 1979 essay, 'unrecovered losses / black theatre traditions', in Richard Drain (ed.) *Twentieth Century Theatre: A Sourcebook* (London and New York: Routledge, 1995).

19 Paul Gilroy, 'It's a Family Affair', in *Small Acts* (London: Serpents Tail, 1993).

FURTHER READING

Primary Sources: works by Deborah levy

Levy, Deborah. *Ophelia and the Great Idea*. London: Jonathan Cape, 1985.

Beautiful Mutants. London: Jonathan Cape, 1987.

Heresies. London: Methuen, 1987.

Pax. In Mary Remnant (ed.) *Plays by Women: 5*. London: Methuen, 1987.

An Amorous Discourse in the Suburbs of Hell. London: Vintage, 1990.

Swallowing Geography. London: Jonathan Cape, 1992.

The Unloved. London: Jonathan Cape, 1994.

Billy and Girl. London: Bloomsbury, 1996.

Clam. In Stephen Lowe (ed.) *Six Peace Plays*. London: Methuen, 1996.

'The Eros of Rose'. In Nicky Childs and Jeni Walwin (eds.) *A Split Second of Paradise*. London: Rivers Oram Press, 1998.

(ed.) *Walks on Water*. London: Methuen, 1992.

Secondary sources

Charitou, Irini. 'Questions of Survival: toward a Postmodern Feminist Theatre'. Interview with Deborah Levy. *New Theatre Quarterly* 35 (August 1993): 225–30.

'Three Plays by Deborah Levy: a Brief Introduction'. *New Theatre Quarterly* 35 (August 1993): 230–2.

Childs, Nicky, and Jeni Walwin (eds.) *A Split Second of Paradise*. London: Rivers Oram Press, 1998.

Etchells, Tim. 'Diverse Assembly: Some Trends in Recent Performance'. In Theodore Shanks (ed.) *Contemporary British Theatre*. London and New York: MacMillan and St Martin's Press, 1996: 107–22.

Gilroy, Paul. *Small Acts*. London: Serpents Tail, 1993.

Goodman, Lizbeth. *Contemporary Feminist Theatres: To Each Her Own*. London and New York: Routledge, 1993.

MacDonald, Claire. 'Assumed Identities: Feminism, Autobiography and Performance Art'. In Julia Swindells (ed.) *The Uses of Autobiography*. London: Taylor and Francis, 1995.

MacRitchie, Lynne. 'Rose English: A Perilous Profession'. *Performance Research* 1.3 (Autumn 1996): 58–76.

Shange, Ntozake. 'unrecovered losses / black theatre traditions'. In Richard Drain (ed.) *Twentieth Century Theatre: A Sourcebook*. London and New York: Routledge, 1995.

Shiach, Morag. *Hélène Cixous: A Politics of Writing*. London and New York: Routledge, 1991.

15

SUE-ELLEN CASE

Lesbian performance in the transnational arena

'Lesbian' as an identificatory term has come under scrutiny from within a variety of debates. Each debate has offered a correction to the term, appropriate to the concerns of its critique. For example, sex radicals proffer the term 'dyke' to supersede the association between lesbian and the anti-pornography movement, and a younger generation has invented the term 'grrls' to mark a new form of sexual/gender identification. Yet nowhere is the term less stable in its referent, or more complex in its resonances, than when it circulates within the international context. This chapter seeks to formulate the question: 'Is it possible to frame a lesbian identification within and across national and cultural borders?' Specific to the concerns of this volume, the question might be: 'Is there a way to understand something called lesbian performance, which might apply across national and cultural differences?' These questions raise issues of forms of performance address and reception. Yet they also rest on a sense of how lesbian identities are structured within and through national and economic agendas. So, considerations of performance production and reception will intertwine with formulations of national identities to create a notion of how to recognise and respond to lesbian performance in the international arena.

Red love and homo solo performance

While there is, as yet, very little work done on understanding specifically lesbian practices within an international context, sexual politics which are located within a gender critique have long been considered as a politics that could be international. Feminism has developed a critique that attempts to understand gender oppression across the globe. Even before the feminist movement, however, we can find a critique of sexual practices tied to an international movement in the early communist writings of Emma Goldman and Alexandra Kollentai.[1]

As part of the international communist movement, Kollentai wrote *Sexual Relations and the Class Struggle* in 1918. In this manifesto, Kollentai forged a

pioneering call to extricate sexual practice from its bourgeois roots by disasso-
ciating desire from claims of possession, or ownership. At issue, for her, was the
organisation of emotional property known as 'the family', which secured private
ownership of desire through the practice of monogamy. Following Engels's critique in *The Origin of the Family, Private Property, and the State*, Kollentai
extended his idea of woman as property within the family to the idea of the
sexual practice of monogamy as buttressing the private ownership of desire.
Only when women could liberate themselves from such sexual ownership, which
lay at the base of the 'family', or monogamy itself, could they attain equality and
independence. While Kollentai could conceive only of heterosexual relations, she
nevertheless forged a tie between gender/sexual politics and an international
movement, for her notion of liberation was dependent upon an anti-nationalist
politic which called for political organisation in the global arena, along the lines
of class and gender. In the ensuing years, the international communist movement
continued to struggle against the formation of national identities, the most per-
nicious of which was the Nazi construction of 'German' identity, but the radical
notion of 'red love' was abandoned. Ironically, in the 1920s, the 'family' was
reconstituted as the proper sexual unit within Soviet politics.

However, if the Soviets abandoned the critique of monogamy as private ownership, lesbians might take it up as a way to imagine an identificatory process
within an international politic. Denied official access to marriage rights in many
countries and municipalities, lesbians could, effectively, represent the challenge
to the practice of sexual ownership as the basic unit of social organisation. They
could stand for a sexual practice that would not emulate the family unit, but
would challenge it as the basic unit used by many different national and religious
organisations to bolster up their own identificatory processes. Lesbians, denied
the right of marriage, could celebrate their outsider status, clearly demarcating
sexual ownership as a practice within capitalist patriarchal heteronormativity.
Moreover, as lesbians subvert the organisation of family, they also subvert conservative agendas which announce family as the central site for moral and social
organisation. As marriage and family seem to be normative practices that cross
national and cultural borders, forswearing sexual ownership could configure a
lesbian identificatory practice, which would answer Kollentai's call. The sexual
practices of lesbian non-monogamy could work effectively across national and
cultural differences where 'family' is the unit of sexual organisation tied to state
sanctions.

However, years of anti-communism across many nations, along with the AIDS
crisis, have led one prominent wing of the sexual movement to embrace quite the
opposite stance. Instead of following the communist model, one segment of the
sexual movement has focused its energy on the plea for marriage rights. It has
obtained success in several countries, such as Sweden and Norway, and captured

media attention in the USA. It would seem that lesbians seek to bolster up the family unit, even as it is used against them by different fundamentalist organisations. These lesbian politics make a plea for state-sanctioned marriage.

Yet there are those who would resist reconstituting bourgeois ownership within an alternative sexual movement. For example, The Dyke Action Machine performs a kind of cultural terrorism in New York. At the time of the 1997 Gay Pride celebration in Manhattan, they distributed 5,000 posters which illustrated one ecstatic bride dragging an unwilling one through what they call 'a landscape of matrimonial booty'. The poster illustrates two brides approaching a heap of china, silver, and other standard wedding presents as the links in their bond of love. The relation of sexual ownership to the ownership of commodities is literalised in the poster. From the perspective of the Dyke Action Machine, such public ceremonies as marriage secure lesbian desire as lawful and civil, fully prepared to accept all the basic premises of bourgeois convention and state law. They reject state and religious performances of 'belonging' – either to one another, or to dominant institutions.

In terms of performance, then, these two models suggest that we can either watch lesbian marriage spectacles, or look for another form of staging lesbian sexual relations. If lesbians would not perform 'coupledom' or the bliss of ownership, what form could read across cultures as lesbian in the tradition of Kollentai? I think the relatively new tradition of solo performance operates to suggest something similar to what Kollentai had in mind. I want to propose an example which begs an international reading of lesbian, or 'queer', performance, within this form.

In 1992, Lois Weaver, an American, was hired to become an Associate Director of Gay Sweatshop. Gay Sweatshop is the most prominent theatre in London for gay and lesbian performance.[2] During the years 1992–3, Weaver initiated a number of outreach projects to encourage independent lesbian and gay performers, called *One Night Stand*, *Club Deviance*, and *Queer School*. *One Night Stand* was a series which invited solo performers to produce their work in a cabaret format. The series enjoyed packed houses and enthusiastic audiences, especially in London and Manchester. *Club Deviance* was a similar project, bringing together the sense of lesbian and gay club life and an underground performance tradition. *Queer School* helped to prepare performers for a professional life, offering courses in technical and business skills along with acting and interpretation. Weaver was interested in reaching out to a younger generation of queers who did not go to the theatre, but who did frequent clubs. She was developing both new performers and new audiences. For Weaver, the form which suited this enterprise was the solo act.

Weaver had begun this work in the WOW Cafe in New York, which had housed solo performances (among other sorts) since the beginning of the 1980s.

The WOW Cafe, which still operates today, is a mixture of a club and a performance space, where parties as well as more formal scenarios take place. These one-person performances bear only a distant resemblance to the forms of traditional theatre. They replicate neither the interest in staging the words of an absent playwright, nor the hierarchy of power found in the constellation of playwright/director/actor. As a one-person show, the writer and the performer are one and the same; there is no dialogue, but only forms of the monologue; no 'fourth-wall' realism; and 'acting' in the traditional sense of developing a character is little used. Instead, the one-person 'queer' performance focuses on creating a gender-bending, or homo-sexualised *persona*, who performs a version of herself, combined with icons from popular culture, and familiar urban stereotypes. For example, Weaver performs her own such *persona* whom she calls Tammy Whynot – a take-off on the country singer Tammy Wynette. Weaver performs her own 'white trash', Southern, rural background, combined with a sexy, flirtatious, lesbian femme. As Tammy, she might sing, or recount experiences, dreams, or memories from her own life, or from the invented life of Tammy the *persona*. Over the years, Weaver has performed Tammy to MC shows, or to host other kinds of events. Most recently, Tammy's Christmas show played in London in 1996.

The *persona* fits easily into the revue format, where it can serve as an act, or, in Weaver's case, as the hostess/MC of the evening. The *persona* offers a pliable and adaptable form of performance. It is well suited to 'found' performance spaces, sometimes without a stage, or theatrical lighting. It can appear in the midst of a variety of occasions which might create something like an audience, from a party to a political rally. In one sense, the *persona* could be seen as a shell for improvisation. The *persona* can be improvised within and is open to interaction with the audience – particularly in the act of sexual flirtation. The club-type atmosphere of these performances encourages flirting, or the sense that a kind of available sexuality could promiscuously travel through the crowd. Everyone is performing, anyway, while dancing and talking. The *persona* is only a hyper version of what is already going on in the club, offering a staged fashioning of self and a kind of flirting that is a bit more generalised – more open to everyone who is watching. Flirting becomes part of the address of the performance itself. It is in this solo flirting that part of its subversive power lies.

The solo nature of this work ensures that the sexual affect of the *persona* would not be perceived as within the context of coupledom, or any reconstruction of the family-like unit. Instead, the sexual address of the 'solo homo' performance implies the opposite of sexual ownership: it signals a simulation of availability. The single performer is available for flirting with the audience, with no claim from any special quarter. As she circulates through the crowd, so does lesbian desire. Further, if the *persona* act is played within Weaver's series called

One Night Stand the title itself infers a short-term sexual liaison, which is generally understood to mean multiple one-night stands. This combination of availability with promiscuity locates queer solo performance within the mode of sexual circulation rather than within anything like the state-sanctioned rites of marriage. The circulation of desire and potential sexual practices works against the association of them with any kind of private ownership. Audience pleasure is not produced by watching a lesbian couple pledge exclusive rights of fidelity to one another, but in the enjoyment of the public availability of sex. Traditionally, the public and promiscuous practice of sex has constituted one kind of homosexual subculture. In the lesbian scene, clubs encourage public displays of foreplay. In the gay male lifestyle, the practice of public sex, in bathrooms, parks and other 'civic' spaces emphasises anonymous, multiple sexual contacts. So queer solo performance, with its potential to happen anywhere and with anyone, plays like public sex. It could represent the politics of the sexual movement as an anarchistic subversion of private ownership and state institutionalisation.

One Night Stand and *Queer School* launched the careers of several queer British solo performers. Laura Brigman, whose solo titles include *Junk*, and Leslie Hill both made work as a result of *Queer School*; Helena Goldwater, Stacy Makishi (*Tongue in Sheets*), and Parminder Sekhon developed solo performance pieces through participation in the *One Night Stand* series.

Clubbing the queer

Weaver's sense of the outreach mission of the Gay Sweatshop worked through a form that appears to be shared across national cultural differences. In the urban environments of New York and London, as well as other major cities in the industrialised West, queer clubs appear to share a common music, dress style, gestural mode, and other signs of what has been termed an underground, urban, sexual subculture. The identification of lesbian, then, in proximity to this subcultural style, is capable of international travel through its association with the club scene. The subcultural style works both independently from and in conjunction with agencies of multinational corporations. Many underground recording labels are small and local, while many of the fashions are put together from used, especially worn and ripped, clothing. Yet, how is it that the piercing styles on the Lower East Side of New York resemble so closely those found in parts of London?

From the small, local labels to raves sponsored by Coca Cola, much of the seemingly underground youth culture travels through means that rely on the success of richly capitalised businesses. For example, the underground scene is often accessed through high-end computer technologies (access to the internet), advertising, transatlantic plane flights, leisure time, university educations, etc. Perhaps here, the term 'international' serves best, not in the tradition the early communists found for it, but more in the sense of international trade routes, which import and export products composing the entertainment industry. While this trans-national movement of 'lesbian' performance might signal a more radical sexuality than the civil pleas for marriage rights, it also seems to have developed in consonance with multinational economic practices. Lesbian underground performance, while looking like poor theatre, actually travels in high style.

This sense of lesbian as cultural traveller would seem particularly troublesome if its relation to the forces of cultural imperialism were to go unquestioned. That is not to say that there is no resistant quality to be found within these queer solo performances, which are aimed at the club scene, but that they also help to support an uneven international trade balance. Take for instance the performance series Weaver helped to organise in 1993 at the ICA, called *Queer Bodies*. The series imported the US aesthetic into London, by bringing such highly visible queer solo performers as Holly Hughes and Tim Miller. Solo performance, in its US vestments, defined the 'queer'. A further series entitled *It's Not Unusual* followed in 1994, this time featuring local London queer performances. These, too, were solo performances which included the familiar mix of personal monologue, pop-cultural referents, and the creation of *personae*. How do we account for this appearance of the same form and style of performance in the USA and London? Certainly, it is not a simple case of influence: the American import was imitated by the English; nor is it the case that there is some 'essence' in homosexual life, which makes the performance of it similar across national and cultural differences. However, though imitation might be too over-stated, one cannot mistake the considerable influence American culture has on other nations, filtered out through the dominant entertainment industry, through television and movies, and through the multibillion-dollar advertising agency. MTV and Levi's, for example, have created the sense that 'lifestyle', which often means appropriately assembled commodities, can be constitutive of an identity. They bear the mark of the 'American' in their address. By their creation of international markets for their products, be they CDs or a pair of pants, they have also created the sense that lifestyle can travel across different cultures. Identificatory processes, such as 'youth' or 'queer' can be accessed through these commodities, or performance practices. In this context, hip hop and solo queer performances work similarly.

Underground performance practices are proximate to these forces, even if they insistently call attention to their resistance to them. 'Queer' *personae* reflect the construction of a 'lifestyle' identity, even as they ironise it in their send-ups of cultural icons. For example, Weaver's own *persona* of Tammy Whynot depends, in part, on the country music industry that has produced and distributed the songs of Tammy Wynette – even as Weaver ironises her 'poor theatre' relation to that image. Even as she 'queers' Tammy's image by making it into a flirtatious lesbian, she does so through imitating a kind of glamour the cosmetic and advertising agencies have produced for women. The American 'look' of queer culture, as of youth culture, does partially determine how it looks in London. Irony depends upon prior recognition.

Yet as queer performance participates in the forces of American cultural imperialism, it also reveals traditional stereotypes and historical practices which inhere in the national relationship between England and the USA. New York and London do share a common language of sorts, along with a strong political alliance nurtured, most recently, by the illustrious coupling of Reagan and Thatcher, along with the more homoerotic one of Blair and Clinton. While these conditions make a cultural trade in 'lesbian' rather convenient, they are also haunted by a historical, colonial relationship which reproduces the way in which the two cultures stereotypically differentiate themselves from one another. In other words, while American cultural imperialism seems to be 'occupying' many nations of the world, the old colonial relations between England and America also continue to haunt their cultural relations – even in dissident, underground, sexual subcultural practices. America might colonise the contemporary pop culture scene, but it also retains a colonised posture in regard to England. English culture still exerts considerable colonial power in the US imaginary, particularly in theatre, where the sun never sets on productions of Shakespeare.

We can see how this colonial haunting works, when we compare the reception of Weaver's work at Gay Sweatshop to that of her English, gay male co-director, James Neale-Kennerly. From a colonial perspective, Weaver's outreach project could be characterised as a 'friendly', 'folksy' one, reproducing a certain stereotype of American culture. The works were not 'serious' explorations of character and theme, but more pop-culture improvisations and camp renditions of 'queer' *personae* and their flirtations. They reflected a populist impulse to give everyone an equal chance to get on the stage, with less regard for training and talent than in the practices of the traditional theatre. In this way, they could never attain 'greatness', or the status of 'art'. Moreover, Weaver, in conversation, remarked that as a woman, even if lesbian, she quite conveniently fulfilled the image of the 'schoolmarm', who, even if working in a 'queer school', 'nurtured' younger artists. Now one might imagine a character out of a novel by Willa Cather. It also makes one wonder just how the character of Tammy Whynot might further confirm a class divide which the colonial subject must never cross.

In contrast, Neale-Kennerly worked more as a traditional director who developed new plays, reproducing the sense of the London stage as one of great plays – a stage of language and broad, political themes. As a man, he also better fit the traditional image of the director. Thus, in an overly simple way, the two directions of Gay Sweatshop were cast as English and male alongside American and female. Colonial biases fit neatly together with patriarchal ones in their reception. On the American side, a populist, friendly, aesthetic of solo queer performance, informally playing in clubs, with little regard for the requirements of traditional skills and training, could be perceived as Weaver's donation. On the English side, the continuation of the tradition of the great play, formally produced and cast, could be perceived as Neale-Kennerly's.

These stereotypes might have been at work in the funding decisions the Arts Council made in regard to Gay Sweatshop. In 1996, the Arts Council decided not to renew their grant to the company. This grant had provided the funding for Weaver's and Neale-Kennerly's salaries. While the reasons for the decision were complex, one admonition was the need for the theatre to develop new plays. The rumour among those working at the theatre was that the company lost its standing when it began to be perceived as 'amateurish'. The granting agency, composed, in part, of people who had worked in traditional theatres, felt that the important role a lesbian/gay theatre could play in London would be to reproduce the same forms and values as traditional theatres, but with lesbian and gay characters, or themes. Solo performances in club-type atmosphere were lowering the standards of the theatre. Thus, 'queer' as Gay Sweatshop might be, it was still entangled in national stereotypes and cultural practices which continue to carry a colonial legacy.

At this point in time, Weaver has left Gay Sweatshop to co-found an international booking agency for queer performance. Interestingly, it is called WhyNot International. Weaver's *persona* has become the logo for an international agency that will work to book queer performers into countries around the world. Tammy Whynot is now the MC international. What was once a connection essentially between the USA and England has now grown to include Australia, India, etc. What will the success of this organisation mean in each different country? How will its performers influence the construction of queer identities across cultures? How will queer identification processes be structured through this export/import arrangement? These are difficult questions, which require theoretical guidance to begin to formulate any answer, so let us review some of the contemporary ideas on this subject.

From *Three Guineas* to multinational capital

These examples, practices, rumours, may move us to ask: 'How may we come to better understand what the issues are in creating an international political performance movement?' 'What does it mean to identify people by gender or sexual preference across cultures?' Although there is still too little queer work done in this area, feminist theories have long struggled to come to terms with the role of gender politics across national and cultural differences. Insofar as homosexual politics are also a politics of gender, they may be informed by feminism's discoveries. It seems there have been at least two conflicting impulses toward the international in regard to feminism. One has been succinctly phrased by Virginia Woolf. She recorded this sentiment in 1938 in *Three Guineas*: 'As a woman I have no country. As a woman I want no country. As a woman my country is the whole world.'[3] State laws had exempted Woolf's status as woman from the rights of citizenship, such as voting and attending universities, and therefore she could imagine herself as outside the state. Once 'out there', she could reach across nations to other women in similar conditions because of their gender. In this way, Woolf's call to women resembles the sense that lesbians, outside marriage laws, might find a cross-cultural address.

In the tradition of Woolf, the African-American feminist theorist bell hooks expresses a sense of what she terms a 'yearning' for a 'common affective and political sensibility which cuts across the boundaries of race, class, gender, and sexual practice'. Hooks organises a 'fertile ground for the construction of empathy – ties that would promote recognition of common commitments and serve as a basis for solidarity and coalition'.[4] Likewise, Rosi Braidotti constructs those who wander that fertile ground as what she calls *Nomadic Subjects,* a 'political fiction', or a mythic nomadic subject who could practise 'emphatic proximit', or 'intensive interconnectedness'.[5] Hooks's notion of empathy could supply an important element in understanding audience relations to queer performances across cultures. As part of a 'yearning' for 'interconnectedness', we might empathise with lesbian performances that stage their desire to the audience – even if their *persona* seems 'foreign'.

In contradiction to these hopeful yearnings, Diana Taylor, in her book on state and theatrical spectacle in Argentina, entitled *Disappearing Acts*, describes an incident in which her own feminist reception of a performance caused the local audience to react against her. She recounts how, at a public forum in Argentina, she rose to critique a performance for its sexism, noting how it eroticised the state violence it depicted. Then, she reports: 'Someone from the audience called me a fascist for trying to restrict or censor what could be shown. [Another] refused to speak to me, except to point out that I wasn't Argentinean, hadn't lived in Argentina during the Dirty War, hadn't experienced torture and therefore knew nothing about it and should keep quiet. She dismissed me as a "Yanqui feminist".'[6] In other words, Taylor's intervention as a feminist was received, in part, as 'fascist' censoring and, in part, as another sign of American cultural imperialism, in which an American feminist imports her own issues into Argentina. Taylor notes that her words, which were meant as constative (a statement) were heard as performative – as an intervention in a local social process.

The dialectic between a 'yearning' for some sense of gender inequities across

nations and the need not to export First World Feminism has troubled the practice of feminist politics since the early 1980s. Recently, however, new concepts
within feminism are beginning to refine the critique. In particular, the new term
'transnational' has been adopted to replace the earlier sense of 'international'.
'Transnational', as it is defined by Inderpal Grewal and Caren Kaplan in their
book *Scattered Hegemonies,* seeks both to describe and to resist the current
accelerated mode of globalisation, in which the national permeates the local, but
in which the local mutates the global. In other words, it is particularly sensitive
to the way in which multinational corporations help to construct the local scene,
while, at the same time, noting how the local might resist those forces. Grewal
and Kaplan encourage us to consider a new way to situate peoples within the
feminist paradigm, critically noting that 'conventionally, "global feminism" has
stood for a kind of Western cultural imperialism that celebrates individuality
and modernity'.[7] In contrast, they hope to imagine a more collective nature to
the way people organise.

A further refinement of the transnational may be found in the anthology
Feminist Genealogies, Colonial Legacies, Democratic Futures. In the introduction, Jacqui Alexander and Chandra Mohanty also critique the earlier practice of international feminism as invoking a difference-as-pluralism model
that organises a strict division between the international and the domestic
without seeing their mutual interpenetration. They suggest that transnational
feminism corrects that earlier model by charting the movement of capital
among and within nations as a constitutive part of any gender analysis, rec-
ognising its local inventions as well as the kind of hyper-nationality created by
these 'scattered hegemonies'. Alexander and Mohanty also make a brilliant
connection in their work, which is not found in many of the other new transnational feminist concepts. Along with tracing the movement of capital, they
call for the study of the state enforcement of heterosexuality through its 'citizenship machinery, which makes lesbians into the disloyal citizen and thereby
suspect'.[8] The challenge, then, for 'queer' performance, is to pair sexual issues
with those of capitalism, colonialism, hyper-national, and transnational
forces. As international feminism has been oblivious to its heteronormative
bias, sexual politics have remained oblivious to transnational and neo-
colonial issues.

Now, with these strategies in hand, let us return to a consideration of international exchange, bearing in mind the movement of capital and gendering / sexual
identification processes. Thus far, we have concentrated on 'poor' live performance in underground venues, while attempting to link them to multinational
concerns. In so doing, we have mentioned air travel and e-mail access.
Continuing to follow the trail of capital, we find that the greatest outlay, in the
past decade, and the most dynamic exchange of capital have been in the area of

technology – particularly in new uses of the computer. So, as a final practice in transnational political thinking, let us consider the role computers play in relation to queer performance.

World as wide web

Weaver, travelling between London and New York, remains in touch with artists from a variety of cities and countries through e-mail. For itinerant workers, conventional addresses are inefficient. 'Snail mail', as it is called by those who use electronic mail, takes too long and often arrives at the wrong time. If Weaver is travelling, most of the performers with whom she works are likewise 'on the road'. With a small computer, a modem, and an account with something like CompuServe, which has local phone number connections in many major cities around the world, contact is only four seconds away. This convenience is somewhat costly, given the prices of laptop computers, modems, and services which give access to the World Wide Web, but in the long run, it is cheaper than, say, rent. If performers are staying with friends, with people in the theatres in various cities – living as they can, without the convenience of hotels, or even a projected annual itinerary – the computer serves as a surrogate for an address.

Beyond e-mail, there are many uses of sites on the web, which link users to information, interchange, and even something like performance. As Weaver's Whynot exchanges her wig and rhinestones for an electronic body, which will MC shows around the globe through electronic contact, many other performance-related enterprises are also uploading onto the web. For example, the American Theater for Higher Education (ATHE), the official 'body' of those who teach criticism and training in the theatre, organised a MOO. A MOO is an architecture on the net which allows several users to be simultaneously 'present' in 'real time'. The MOO has hosted a directors' forum, a playwrights' forum, and other scheduled events which bring together people from all over the world to interact about events in the theatre. Websites can offer sound, animated images, and even short video representations of actions. Many theatres and performance groups have websites now, posting their seasons, and offering samples of their work. Some groups even consider their web performances as part of their work. Likewise, gender groups and queer groups offer bulletin boards, where discussions occur around recent issues, animated fan pages, and links to information about legal matters, historical research, etc.

The internet is still primitive, in a way, and growing. New art forms are being created there, if only in their 'infant' state. It is possible, however, that it is training us to understand a future in what is called cyberspace – a virtual, electronic space where most business, personal communications, and entertainment will take place. Currently, the technology for producing this space is without sophistication. It requires gloves and helmet-like optical enhancers. However, imagine it someday as emulating a three-dimensional space, where the user will move and manipulate its components to accomplish tasks. Performances may take place there, in an interactive sense. Two people might choose an icon or avatar to represent them, and perform with each other in a constructed, imagined space. The illusion of what was once theatre will be complete, but without the passive audience position. Everyone will perform interactively, inhabiting a fictional space in *personae* of their choice.

If this occurs, and it seems likely that it will, what will be the role of the body? What will become the significance of the 'real' world? Along transnational considerations, who will own this space and design it? Who will have access to it? What will be inferred from its representations? From my perspective, the study and understanding of this new electronic phenomena is urgent for those of us in studies of performance and in studies of sexuality and gender. My book, *The Domain-Matrix: Performing Lesbian at the End of Print Culture*, makes an initial foray into the field. Likewise, a special issue of the journal *Women and Performance* focuses on sexuality and cyberspace.[9]

Anxieties and pleasures around the performance of sex and gender are the very signature of virtual systems. On the web, one may perform the role of either gender, without reference to one's own body or fleshly existence. Cybersex is a favourite pastime of many, who play as men or women, sharing fantasies with others who may or may not actually look like, live like, or behave like the scenarios they play out together on the web.

By necessity, one forms a virtual *persona* on this electronic stage, in order to compensate for the absence of actual bodies and material conditions. Known by a name, an icon, a complete website, or an avatar (a designated image used in navigating certain virtual 'worlds'), the user uploads an identity onto the web which must be constructed according to its capabilities. Many who have personal websites compose a space which conjoins images to texts to represent them there in that other space. Since, without some kind of research, one cannot determine the relation of the identity on the web to the 'actual' one, any chosen assignment of gender and sexual practice is queer in its very electronic construction.

The queer persona is thus the average identification on the web. Some praise this construction as liberating and pleasurable. They would contend that performing male one night, female the next, even transspecies identifications as a cat or bird, provide new, liberative forms of social and sexual interaction. Yet liberative as it might appear, the web is dependent upon a computer industry in which nearly all management functions, ownership and software creation are produced by men. In controlled economic zones in the Third World, women comprise the majority of the work force, using their smaller hands to make microchips for sixty hours a week and substandard pay. There is a frightening and oppressive gender bias operating in the industry. First World industrial nations have formed huge conglomerates during the 1990s, called 'synergies', to create pools of capital and labour for the invention, construction, and marketing of this new technology. Entertainment systems are merging with computer software giants to form new conglomerates of play and work. Corporations such as Sony are acquiring movie, music, publishing, news, software, hardware, and other companies to complete the full picture of the new virtual world.

Something larger than a nation is making its entrance, linking people across cultures and nations in seconds. At the same time, 'local' associations are forming through specific interests and with little investment. Hackers are disturbing the forces of ownership with their cry that 'Information must be free!' What will this new arena of performance be like? How will we protect women and minorities? What will be the outcome of cutting loose from the fleshly body, sometimes referred to as 'the meat'?

These are the questions of our future in performance, at work, at school, and at play, as the computer becomes our daily screen onto the world. We are only just now learning how to pose them and to begin to search for the answers.

GAY SWEATSHOP TOURING PRODUCTIONS AND OUTREACH PROJECTS: 1992–1995

One Night Stand (series), 1992
Queer School (series), 1992
Club Deviance (series), 1992
Queer Bodies (series), 1993
Threesome: three new plays: *Drag Act,* Claire Dowie; *Jack,* David Greenspan; and *Entering Queens,* Phyllis Nagy, 1993
Stupid Cupid, Phil Wilmot, 1993–4
In Your Face, Jan Maloney, 1993–4
It's Not Unusual (series), 1994
Fucking Martin, adaptation by Malcom Sutherland, 1994–5
Lust and Comfort (in association with Split Britches), Peggy Shaw, James Neale-Kennerley, and Lois Weaver, 1994–5
The Hand, Stella Duffy, 1995

Solo works arising from 1992 *One Night Stand* and *Queer School* series

Avatar, Michael. *Tiny Stars.*
Bradley, Jyll. *On the Playing Fields of Her Rejection; Digging for Ladies.*
Bridgeman, Laura. *Junk.*
Carr, Marissa. *Lady Much and her Burlesque Review; The Grotesque Burlesque Show.*
de Castro, Angela. *The Gift.*
Fischer, Ernst. *White Trash Love Machine.*
Makishi, Stacy. *Tongue in Sheets.*
Poem, Chloe. *Chloe Poems Healing Road Show.*

NOTES

1 Emma Goldman, *The Traffic in Women and Other Feminist Essays* (New York: Times Change Press, 1970); Alexandra Kollentai, *Sexual Relations and the Class Struggle and Love and the New Morality,* trans. Alix Holt (Bristol: Falling Wall Press, 1972).

2 For a survey of Gay Sweatshop's early and more recent lesbian history see Sandra Freeman, *Putting Your Daughters on the Stage: Lesbian Theatre from the 1970s to the 1990s* (London: Cassell, 1997), chapter 3, pp. 19–47.

3 Virginia Woolf, *Three Guineas* (Harmondsworth: Penguin, 1977), p.125.

4 Hooks, quoted in Rosi Braidotti, *Nomadic Subjects: Embodiment and Sexual Difference in Contemporary Feminist Theory* (New York: Columbia University Press, 1994), p. 2.

5 Braidotti, *Nomadic Subjects,* p. 5.

6 Diana Taylor, *Disappearing Acts: Spectacles of Gender and Nationalism in Argentina's 'Dirty War'* (Durham, NC, and London: Duke University Press, 1997), pp.17–18.

7 Inderpal Grewal and Caren Kaplan (eds.) *Scattered Hegemonies: Postmodernity and Transnational Feminist Practices* (Minneapolis and London: University of Minnesota Press, 1994), p. 17.

8 M. Jacqui Alexander and Chandra Talpede Mohanty (eds.) *Feminist Genealogies, Colonial Legacies, Democratic Futures* (London and New York: Routledge, 1997), p. xxii.

9 Sue-Ellen Case, *The Domain-Matrix: Performing Lesbian at the End of Print Culture* (Bloomington: Indiana University Press, 1996); *Women and Performance,* issue 1: 17, 1996.

FURTHER READING

Further critical reading on Lois Weaver

Case, Sue-Ellen (ed.) *Split Britches.* London: Routledge, 1996.

Davey, Kate. 'Peggy Shaw and Lois Weaver: Interviews (1985, 1992, 1993)'. In William Worthen (ed.) *Modern Drama.* New York: Harcourt Brace College Publishers, 1995: 1003–8.

Hart, Lynda. *Fatal Women: Lesbian Sexuality and the Mark of Aggression.* Princeton: Princeton University Press, 1994.

Weaver, Lois, and Peggy Shaw. 'May Interviews June'. *Movement Research* (Fall 1991): 4–5.

General

Alexander, M. Jacqui, and Chandra Talpede Mohanty (eds.). *Feminist Genealogies, Colonial Legacies, Democratic Futures.* London and New York: Routledge, 1997.

Braidotti, Rosi. *Nomadic Subjects: Embodiment and Sexual Difference in Contemporary Feminist Theory.* New York: Columbia University Press, 1994.

Case, Sue-Ellen. *The Domain-Matrix: Performing Lesbian at the End of Print Culture.* Bloomington: Indiana University Press, 1996.

Goldman, Emma. *The Traffic in Women and Other Feminist Essays.* New York: Times Change Press, 1970.

Grewal, Inderpal, and Caren Kaplan (eds.) *Scattered Hegemonies: Postmodernity and Transnational Feminist Practices.* Minneapolis and London: University of Minnesota Press, 1994.

Kollentai, Alexandra. *Sexual Relations and the Class Struggle and Love and the New Morality.* Trans. Alix Holt. Bristol: Falling Wall Press, 1972.

Taylor, Diana. *Disappearing Acts: Spectacles of Gender and Nationalism in Argentina's 'Dirty War'.* Durham, NC, and London: Duke University Press, 1997.

Women and Performance, special issue on sexuality and cyberspace, 1.17 (1996).

INDEX

Index